The Sociological Theory of Capital

Being A Complete Reprint Of The New
Principles Of Political Economy, 1834

John Rae

Alpha Editions

This Edition Published in 2020

ISBN: 9789354216947

Design and Setting By
Alpha Editions
www.alphaedis.com
Email – info@alphaedis.com

As per information held with us this book is in Public Domain.
This book is a reproduction of an important historical work. Alpha Editions uses the best technology to reproduce historical work in the same manner it was first published to preserve its original nature. Any marks or number seen are left intentionally to preserve its true form.

TABLE OF CONTENTS
AND SUMMARY OF PRINCIPLES

	PAGE
INTRODUCTION, ...	1

CHAPTER I.

[OF ECONOMIC AMBITION AND THE MEANS ESSENTIAL TO ITS REALIZATION], ... 7

> It is characteristic of man to provide for the wants of the future, by the formation of instruments; and his power to make this provision is measured by the extent and accuracy of his knowledge of the course of natural events.

CHAPTER II.

OF THE CIRCUMSTANCES COMMON TO ALL INSTRUMENTS AND OF THOSE PROPER TO SOME, ... 19

> There are three circumstances common to all instruments. (1) They are formed, or receive a capacity to produce certain events fitted to supply future wants, by labour [applied to materials,] either directly or indirectly. (2) Before their capacity is exhausted and they pass from the rank of instruments [back again] to that of materials, they yield a return, or produce certain events fitted to supply future wants, which may be estimated in labour. (3) Between the period of their formation and that of their exhaustion, a space of time intervenes. Some instruments can be easily moved from place to place, others cannot. The former are termed goods or commodities.

TABLE OF CONTENTS

CHAPTER III.

PAGE

OF CERTAIN CIRCUMSTANCES ARISING FROM THE INSTITUTION OF SOCIETY, ... 25

> Statement of some generally admitted principles concerning the nature of man and of society, which it is necessary to assume in the progress of the subsequent investigations.

CHAPTER IV.

[A METHOD FOR THE COMPARISON OF INSTRUMENTS], . 31

> Every instrument may be arranged in some part of a series, of which the orders are determined, by the proportions existing between the labour expended in the formation of instruments, the capacity given to them, and the time elapsing from the period of formation to that of exhaustion.

CHAPTER V.

[OF CERTAIN TECHNICAL] CIRCUMSTANCES GOVERNING THE AMOUNT OF INSTRUMENTS FORMED, ... 42

> In every society considerably advanced in art, that is, in every society the members of which have acquired an extensive knowledge of the trains of events supplying the wants of man, which the materials they possess [when formed into instruments] are capable of generating, there is no assignable limit to the capacity that may be given to these materials, or to the amount of [contrived] events which the instruments that may be formed out of them may bring to pass ; but that capacity cannot be indefinitely increased without carrying the stock of instruments owned by the society to an order of slower return—that is to say, without [either] extending the period between their formation and exhaustion, or diminishing their return [in proportion to the outlay on their construction]. It so happens, that, other circumstances being equal, [that is, principally, in the absence of increase of knowledge], the wider the circle of events embraced [or, of materials with which "natural events" are associated], the returns made by the instruments constructed take place in a more distant futurity. [In other words, with mere non-inventive expansion of instrumental production, the rate of return declines ; because the results are achieved either with greater outlay or more tardily.]

TABLE OF CONTENTS

CHAPTER VI.

OF THE CIRCUMSTANCES WHICH DETERMINE THE STRENGTH OF THE EFFECTIVE DESIRE OF ACCUMULATION, . 52

> The order to which the instruments formed by any society will be carried, is fixed by the relative estimation of its members of events taking place at present, and at a future period, which is denominated *the effective desire of accumulation*. This is chiefly determined (1) by the distinctness of the mind's conception of future events, which again depends on the strength of the intellectual powers; (2) on the desire felt for the production of practicable future events. The latter circumstance is regulated by the strength of the moral powers, or what in these investigations are termed the social and benevolent affections. As the existence of the individual is precarious, and his power of enjoyment continually diminishing, the more the state of feeling and action pervading any community separates individuals from one another, the more limited will be the range of events [or materials] which the effective desire of accumulation of the members of that community will embrace. On the contrary, as, though individuals perish the race remains, the more the interests of the individual are identified with those of others, the wider will be the circle of events which the accumulative principle will comprehend. Isolation of feeling and action weakens the accumulative principle by separating the interests of individuals, and so contracting its sphere of operation; community of feeling and action strengthens it, by connecting the interests of individuals, and exciting them to comprehend within the circle of their operations a more extended series of events.

CHAPTER VII.

OF SOME OF THE PHENOMENA ARISING FROM THE DIFFERENT DEGREES OF STRENGTH OF THE EFFECTIVE DESIRE OF ACCUMULATION IN DIFFERENT SOCIETIES, . . . 65

> The state of feeling and action, the consequent strength of the effective desire of accumulation, the orders of instruments and some of the circumstances thus produced, among hunting and pastoral nations, in the Chinese Empire, in modern Europe, and among the ancient Romans.

TABLE OF CONTENTS

CHAPTER VIII.

OF THE DIVISION OF EMPLOYMENTS, AND OF OTHER PHENO-
MENA PRODUCED BY EFFORTS TO ACCELERATE THE
EXHAUSTION OF INSTRUMENTS, ... 102

> When in consequence of the progress of art [invention] and the strength of the accumulative principle, there are many extended trains of [contrived] events, or arts, going on in any society, and when, consequently, there exist many sets of tools or instruments producing them, each individual betakes himself to the production [conduct] of some particular train, and to the formation of the instruments necessary for carrying it on. By this means, no instruments lie idle, which must be the case were every man to practise several arts; and, consequently, they are more speedily exhausted, and pass to orders of quicker return. This division of employments introduces the necessity of the exchange of commodities. The exchange of commodities is regulated by the labour respectively expended on them, in conjunction with the *time* at which it was expended, reckoning the effects of the latter by the orders at which instruments actually stand, [which last determines the prevailing rate of profit at any time]. The existence of exchange occasions a choice being made of some commodity, which is kept [uniquely made use of] for the purpose of being exchanged with all others, and so comes to name the rates at which they exchange, or to fix [express] their values. The commodity chosen for this purpose is termed money, and, among communities possessing the precious metals, consists of them. Exchanges are also effected by means of credit. . . . The general prevalence of credit, and of the use of money, has produced the [customary] mercantile mode of calculating the returns of instruments, by profits and interest. [This system of calculation, while exceedingly advantageous in the conduct of affairs, is a serious impediment to the philosophical understanding of capital.]

CHAPTER IX.

[OF INVENTION CONSIDERED AS A GENERAL SOCIOLOGICAL
PRINCIPLE], ... 132

> [It is necessary to investigate the causes of progress in any department of human affairs, and not to take them for granted, man being essentially imitative. Motives exciting to innovation and the opposing forces external to and within the inventor. Though in respect to the individual, manifestations of the inventive faculty imply a superiority in

some of the intellectual powers, in respect to a society they imply a preponderance of the social and benevolent affections. One of the final and contingent results, however, of intestine commotions, persecutions, wars, and the like, seems to be to advance the inventive faculty.]

CHAPTER X.

Of the Causes of the Progress of Invention and of the Effects arising from it, [as it Concerns itself with the Material World], . . . 151

Invention, the discovery of *new possible existences*, becomes an active principle by exerting a formative power on *old actual existences*. By reason of the nature of the world in which man lives, change exposes to his view new successions of events, which excite him to observe them, and weaken the retarding influence of the principle of servile imitation. The effects on instruments of the progress of invention, are to produce improvements in them, and to carry them on [back] to orders of quicker return, [and so for the time being to advance the rate of profit].

CHAPTER XI.

Of Exchanges between Different Communities [of Commodities other than Luxuries], . . . 204

Exchanges between societies, [that is, between the members of different societies,] are not directly regulated by the quantity of labor, [plus the time of its outlay], expended on the commodities exchanged. Increased facility in the exchange of utilities [articles which are not luxuries] operates in the same manner as the progress of invention and improvement, and carries instruments to the more quickly returning orders. [An interruption of the exchange of such articles may have, however, indirect effects precisely opposite to the direct effects.]

CHAPTER XII.

Of Waste, [or Pure Economic Loss], . . . 213

The loss which, in any society, the capacity of instruments sustains by the operation of fraud and violence [and other similar causes], seems to be nearly inversely as the strength of the accumulative principle; . . .

CHAPTER XIII.

OF THE EFFECTS RESULTING FROM DIVERSITIES OF STRENGTH IN THE ACCUMULATIVE PRINCIPLE, IN MEMBERS OF THE SAME SOCIETY, ... 218

> In the same society, instruments (excepting those that cannot be exchanged, forming a stock reserved for immediate consumption) are kept at nearly the same orders, because prodigals, or individuals in whom the accumulative principle is weaker than the average, can exchange the instruments they possess for more, according to their estimation of the future and the present, than they are worth, and therefore [do] transfer them; while frugal persons, or individuals in whom the accumulative principle is stronger than the average, find exercise for it in acquiring instruments transferred by prodigals. [It thus chiefly comes about that there is an economic stratification of the members of each society. This last leads to the consideration of some of the interrelations of the principles of accumulation and of population.]

CHAPTER XIV.

OF THE PRINCIPLE OF THE DIVISION OF LABOUR, . . 237

> The division of labour ought to be considered rather as a result than a cause. [That is, it comes into existence through the antecedent progress of invention. It is not, as Adam Smith supposed, a prime mover in the course of human affairs.]

APPENDIX.

ARTICLE I.

[OF THE NATURE AND EFFECTS] OF LUXURY, . . . 245

> There is a propensity among men to attain [a factitious] superiority over one another. This may be termed vanity, and is gratified by the evident possession of things which others have not the means of acquiring. It calls for the possession of commodities of which the consumption is conspicuous, and which cost much labor, though not better qualified, or but little better qualified, to supply real wants,

than other commodities costing little labor. The comparison
of the physical qualities of such commodities does not afford,
therefore, the means of measuring them by one another.
Hence the assumption, on which the preceding investigations have proceeded, that all commodities compare with one
another by their physical qualities [by the physical "events"
they produce], is incorrect. In so far as any commodity,
when compared with another, excels it only in the gratification it affords to vanity, it is to be considered a *luxury*; in
so far as it compares with others in the capacity which its
physical qualities give it to gratify real wants, it is to be
considered as a *utility*. The progress of invention and improvement have no effect in carrying instruments, directly or
indirectly producing luxuries, to more quickly returning
orders; on the contrary, they carry them to the most slowly
returning orders of which the strength of the accumulative
principle admits the existence. The labor expended in
the formation of luxuries, is so much direct loss to the
community, one man's superiority being here equivalent to
another's inferiority. The amount thus dissipated depends
on the force of the social and benevolent affections, and
intellectual powers, as compared with that of the selfish
feelings, and is therefore, inversely as the strength of the
accumulative principle.

ARTICLE II.

[OF EXCHANGE BETWEEN DIFFERENT COMMUNITIES OF COMMODITIES WHICH MINISTER TO LUXURY], . . 277

Increased facility in the exchange of luxuries has an immediate tendency (in contrast to what happens in the case of
utilities), to carry instruments to the more slowly returning
orders. [The first effects of restrictions upon trade in this
class of commodities, on the contrary, are beneficial, whereas
their ulterior effects may be injurious. The relative effects
of restriction and free competition, when opportunities for
observation present themselves, afford a means of ascertaining how far commodities are or are not luxuries.]

ARTICLE III.

OF THE OPERATIONS OF THE LEGISLATOR ON LUXURIES, . 286

The *art* of the legislator may apply to the purposes of the
state, funds *naturally* dissipated in luxuries.

ARTICLE IV.

[OF THE ART OF THE BANKER], ... 297

[PART I.—OF BANKING IN GENERAL.]

The modern art of banking consists in the generalization of all credit transactions [throughout a community], and an emission of paper money, or money of credit. Its introduction into any community by facilitating the exchange of instruments, quickens their exhaustion [and formation], and carries them to the more speedily returning orders.

[PART II.—OF PARTICULAR SYSTEMS OF BANKING.]

[The Scotch banking system described and contrasted with that of England. Further consideration of the utility of banks in increasing the efficiency of the money of a community, whether specie or banker's money. Strictures upon Adam Smith's views on monetary subjects.]

ARTICLE V.

OF THE *WEALTH OF NATIONS* AS A BRANCH OF THE PHILOSOPHY OF INDUCTION. [OF THE SPIRIT AND METHOD OF SCIENCE], ... 329

Adam Smith's great work is to be considered as a philosophical system, the object of which is to explain known phenomena, on popular principles, not as an inductive inquiry, leading to the discovery of the real laws determining the succession of those phenomena. [This last form of procedure alone can claim the rank of true science.]

ARTICLE VI.

[OF THE THEORY OF POPULATION], ... 354

[It is an error to assimilate man to the lower animals as regards the laws of his propagation. We have to take cognizance of things psychological and social as well as of things physiological and individual, and the former set of causes are of predominating influence both in advancing and declining states. The principle which increases and maintains the numbers of mankind may be termed *the effective desire of offspring*.]

ARTICLE VII.

[Of the Doctrine of *Laissez Faire* with Special Reference to] the Operations of the Legislator in Bringing the Arts of Foreign Countries to His Own, ... 359

> Instead of there being any grounds for a presumption against legislative interference, from the assumption that nature ought to be allowed to pursue her own plans; the presumption is, on the contrary, that nature gave man his peculiar faculties for the purpose that universally, and as well here as elsewhere, he might acquire the direction of events, by discovering the laws regulating their successions.

ARTICLE VIII.

[Of the Supposed Identity of the Causes Giving Rise to Individual and National Wealth], . . . 377

> [Part I.—When Assumed as a Self-Evident Truth.]
>
> The causes giving rise to individual and national wealth are not precisely the same. Individuals grow rich [generally and characteristically] by the acquisition of wealth previously existing; nations, by the creation of wealth that did not before exist, [which last comes about through invention.]
>
> [Part II.—When Deduced from an Ingenious Theory.]
>
> The legislator may stimulate invention by the introduction of new arts; [that is, by the encouragement of the transfer of old arts to a place where they are new, and where they make adaptations to the changed physical and social environment.]

Author's "Notes," 448

Residua, ... 466

Reader's Guide, ... 484

EDITOR'S PREFACE.

THE original work of which this volume is a reprint, was published in Boston in 1834 under the unfortunate title, *Statement of Some New Principles on the Subject of Political Economy, Exposing the Fallacies of the System of Free Trade, and of Some other Doctrines Maintained in the " Wealth of Nations."* [1] This title was a misnomer, for the chief part of the undertaking consisted not in strictures on the doctrines of Adam Smith, but in an independent, elaborate, and profound treatment of the general subject of capital. It is this last which has recently brought Rae into notice with the present generation of economists in connection with the world-wide discussion of capital, upon new and fruitful lines, inaugurated by Böhm-Bawerk.

I may add here that the first article by me upon Rae (" A Forerunner of Böhm-Bawerk," *Quarterly Journal of Economics*, January, 1897), had a title which was also in great measure a misnomer. Rae is not a mere " anticipator

---

[1] It was divided into three " Books " named respectively—" Individual and National Interests are not Identical" (two chapters, 77 pages); "Of the Nature of Stock and of the Laws governing its Increase and Diminution" (fifteen chapters and an "appendix," 280 pages); and " Of the Operations of the Legislator on National Stock" (three chapters, 29 pages). To this were added twenty-seven pages of " Notes " at the end of the volume.

Of the several defects in book-making which seriously handicapped the work, the most considerable was the putting first of all of two long-drawn-out chapters, highly controversial in their nature, and by far the most difficult in the whole. It must be that many a reader never got beyond or even through them.

of the discoverer" (to use one of Cannan's phrases), but the discoverer himself. By reason of the lack of a theory of invention, Böhm-Bawerk's doctrine of capital, although coming much later, is in essentials the less complete of the two. This contention I have attempted to substantiate in my second article ("Böhm-Bawerk on Rae," *Quarterly Journal of Economics*, May, 1902) reviewing Chapter XI. of the second edition of the *Geschichte und Critik der Capitalzins-Theorien*.

In view of the chief interest which now attaches to Rae's work, it has been deemed advisable, in response to numerous demands, to bring out this republication in an entirely new dress. That part of the second "Book" (the greater part) which possesses a unity of its own, and which deals predominantly with the subject of capital, is given precedence, under a more significant title, which attaches to the volume as a whole; and the remainder, considerably rearranged, is reproduced in an appendix. The original work in its entirety is thus made available and, it is thought, more readable.

It has not been considered advisable in all instances to distract the attention of the reader by indicating the minor editorial changes in the text; but care has been taken in every instance (with the exception of one passage on pages 8 and 9), to point out all alterations of consequence. Additions to the titles of chapters, and some wholly new titles supplied by the editor, are indicated by brackets in the Table of Contents which are not repeated in the body of the work. These new titles are occasioned by the appearance of new chapters in the editing, and by the fact that in some instances there were formerly no titles proper. As several publications have made extensive page references to the original volume, a Reader's Guide has been placed at the end of the present volume, by means of which the location in the reprint of any passage of the original can readily be traced.

A few words having a special bearing upon the biography are not out of place here.

When I first became interested in Rae's theory of capital, under Professor Taussig's direction in the economic seminary at Harvard University, there existed no printed information (except in his Preface) in respect to Rae himself; and for a long time nothing could be learned through inquiry in quarters which promised well in Canada and Great Britain. The late Professor Dunbar of Harvard, who always displayed a keen interest in the undertaking, urged me to persist, and at length a letter printed in the *Montreal Star* drew forth two replies, one from the Canadian antiquary Mr. H. J. Morgan, the other from the late Robert S. Knight of Lancaster, Ontario, a grand-nephew of Rae. This set me upon the right road to get into communication with several people who knew Rae personally. Of these the one who could tell me most was the late Sir Roderick W. Cameron of New York, a former pupil and life-long friend, at whose summer residence on Staten Island Rae died. Better still, I was able through the interest and kindness of this gentleman to come into possession of what few papers Rae left at his death. That is, I obtained all Rae's effects of a literary nature which seem now to be in existence. Apparently, from statements made by Sir Roderick, there was another set of papers which Rae had with him at the time, but which were destroyed or in some way lost. The papers I obtained were little more than odds and ends, mostly unfinished fragments on a great variety of subjects, unfortunately but little on economics. Their chief use has been to help me to a fair understanding of

Rae's life, which I have been able, however, only very imperfectly to set forth.

I have received much information and kind assistance in this part of my work from not a few people in Canada, the United States, Honolulu, and Great Britain. I trust they will accept this general acknowledgment of my sense of indebtedness to them.

To Mr. L. W. Zartman of Yale University my especial thanks are due for assistance in preparing the copy for the printer, and in reading the proofs.

I am also much indebted to Mr. Wilmot H. Thompson of the Graduate School of Yale, for revision of the classical quotations.

Finally, I wish here to express my obligations to Professor Irving Fisher of Yale University. His interest and encouragement have been of unfailing support. The proof sheets of the whole book have passed his able scrutiny, and his direct help in many other ways has been invaluable.

C. W. M.

BURLINGTON,
VERMONT, *July*, 1905.

BIOGRAPHICAL SKETCH.

THREE men of note have borne the name John Rae; and because of frequent misunderstanding it is worth while here once for all clearly to distinguish them. There is first, reversing the chronological order, the John Rae now living in England, born at Wick, Caithness, in 1845, educated at the University of Edinburgh (Hon. LL.D., 1897) journalist by profession, and author of several well-known works on economic subjects. Then there is John Rae, M.D., for some years surgeon in the employ of the Hudson Bay Company, author of a work on Arctic exploration, rewarded by the British government as the first discoverer of relics of the Sir John Franklin expedition. His education in medicine (completed in 1833) was obtained at the University of Edinburgh, but his degree, an honorary one, came from McGill University, Montreal, in 1853. He was born near Stromness, in the Orkneys, in 1813, and died in London in 1893. Finally, there is the subject of this sketch, who was born at Footdee, "then a small and detached suburb of Aberdeen," June 1st, 1796, and died at Clifton, Staten Island, New York, July 14th, 1872. So far as is known these three North of Scotland men were not kinsmen. The two last are often confounded, even by the best informed antiquaries, more especially because each was known as Dr. Rae, and each resided for a part of his life in Hamilton, Ontario.

Of Rae's antecedents and early life we know but little. His father's name was John, a merchant, "an entirely self-made man, the son of a peasant or small farmer." The mother was Margaret Cuthbert, whose family seems to have been rather well-to-do "large farmers, as farming went then." The son speaks of his father as fifteen years older than his mother, and of the two as markedly different "in character, disposition, habits, tastes, and education." There was one sister, Ann Cuthbert, and two brothers, James and Alexander. The elder brother, James, had remarkable inventive aptitudes, but was lost at sea in early life. The sister married James Innes Knight, and preceded Rae to Canada, at least as early as 1816, where Mr. Knight died not long after arrival. A son by this marriage, Robert Knight, has descendants now living in Canada; and descendants of a daughter, Jessie, who married a Mr. Thurburn, are living in Scotland. Later Mrs. Knight married James Fleming, a merchant of Montreal. There was a son by this marriage, Ramsay Fleming, Q.C., lately deceased. Rae himself had no children.[1]

While still a mere lad John Rae studied at the University of Aberdeen, being entered in Marischal College for the sessions of 1810-1811, 1811-1812, and 1814-1815. In 1815 he took the degree of M.A.[2] Later he studied medicine at the University of Edinburgh, but seems never to have taken a degree in medicine there or, indeed, anywhere else.[3] Beyond doubt a most precocious youth, and it must be admitted from what follows somewhat self-opinionated, he had apparently a quarrel with his instructors at the time

---

[1] Since writing the above, Miss Dorothy W. Knight, Rae's great-grand-niece, has forwarded to me the following information obtained from her cousins in Scotland:—

"The business of Rae's father was in connection with shipping, either as a ship builder or ship broker. He was in very comfortable circumstances—not great wealth, but more than the average amount of money. He was considered a very upright man, kind, and a lover of peace. Mrs. Rae was an exceedingly kind woman, and kept a comfortable home. She was a beauty; dignified in her manners, and paid great attention to the manners of her family. Mrs. Rae died a good many years previous to her husband—sometime between 1815 and 1820. Subsequent to her death Mr. Rae lost his money. Later, in his old age, he went a voyage with one of his sons [Alexander], and the ship was wrecked, and both father and son drowned."

[2] See *Fasti Academiae Mariscallanae*, ii. pp. 407 and 412.

[3] Considerable inquiry and incidental evidence in his papers make this statement practically certain.

BIOGRAPHICAL SKETCH

of his presentation. During the course of his studies he had "come to the conclusion that the physiological medical theories of the day were opposed to all true philosophy, and therefore fundamentally false"; he had also reached "a conclusion concerning the origin of man very different from the orthodox one." Writing to a friend late in life he said:

"I was preparing an inaugural dissertation, as was then the custom in Edinburgh, previous to taking my degree; its title was "De Vita," and I intended to propound in it my general views. I was prevented by leading men in Edinburgh who had taken an interest in me, among others Dr. Abercrombie, a physician in extensive practice, known to you perhaps as the author of some metaphysical works. They represented to me that the course I was preparing to take was highly presumptious and imprudent. I should at once have yielded to them with thanks, had they shown me that it was erroneous. But they would not listen to my reasons, they looked only at my conclusions. In this state of affairs I thought I would advise with my father. He knew nothing of philosophy and physiology, but he knew the world. His opinion was that if I was to fight I had better defer for a year or two till I gathered more strength, and then if, as I had proposed, I wished to go to Paris, where physiology was then more advanced than in England, he would consent. It was perhaps good advice, as I was then only twenty years of age. I had thus to pass a few years in gaining knowledge and experience. I turned myself to a subject kindred to my previous studies, and thus said to myself : If I am right, deep is the pit from which we men have opened to ourselves a passage. The deeper the pit the higher comparatively the height to which we have ascended, and therefore still greater the height we may hope to gain. Whence then are the forces which have so elevated us, and whence is it that humanity has been continually [lapsing] from the greatest heights to the most profound depths, and that its real substantial progress is to the philosophical eye so uncertain?"

In 1818 Rae made a tour through Norway, but in what capacity is not known. Apparently the event which was the great turning point in his life and which was to send him on the beginning of his wanderings had not yet occurred. Speaking of this time in later years, or of the year preceding, he says, "a small estate to which I was then reckoned heir would, I thought, furnish me with sufficient means to enable me to give all my energies for all the years I might have to live to these pursuits," that is, "to make at least a beginning" toward writing "a truly philosophical history of humanity." "But I was mistaken."

Soon after came the "change" in his "circumstances" to which he alludes in the Preface to his Political Economy, the exact nature of which we can only guess. Several things indicate, however, that it consisted both in financial disaster and an unfortunate marriage. A life-long intimate has written the present writer that Rae left Aberdeen "under a sort of bad luck, having married in haste." Still another acquaintance has said, speaking of the years 1844-1845, "He was then married, his wife in education far beneath him, she being the daughter of a Scotch shepherd."

As Rae was in his twenty-fifth year when he emigrated, the following shows that even years before the hand of adversity, which was never to leave him, had been already in some form or other heavy upon him. "Natural disposition, strange and very early misfortunes, had marked me for a student—not a barren book-worm—but a man eager for knowledge—knowledge as power—the power in my conception of being a lasting benefactor to man. Thoughts inspiring as these could alone have carried me over years of terrible suffering which I had endured before reaching my majority."

With this fragment casting a dark shadow on his early life we pass from the period of adolescence to that of middle manhood.

Rae landed in Quebec in the spring of 1821, where there is some evidence tending to show that he found employment for a time "in the lumber trade." At all events, he soon after set up a private school at Williamstown, Ontario, about fifty miles westward from Montreal, having been invited there to teach the children of some of the rich fur

BIOGRAPHICAL SKETCH xxiii

traders of the Hudson Bay Company. Not a few of his pupils came from a distance, and among them were his nephew Robert Knight and Roderick W. Cameron.

Two years before the publication of his *Political Economy* Rae gave up the school at Williamstown, and, residing in the vicinity of Quebec and at Montreal, devoted himself to preparing his work for the press. A considerable part of 1834 he spent in Boston, where he received (as reported by his sister) "great attention from some literary and distinguished characters." Not long after this he obtained the head-mastership of the Gore District Grammar School, an advanced public academy, at Hamilton.[1] Some excerpts from letters written by pupils of those days may not be out of place here.

"He was an accomplished scholar and taught the classics, having a Mr. Tassie as an English assistant. He was altogther a remarkable man. . . . He was quite different from ordinary men, or I think my youthful imagination would not have been so impressed as it was. He was undoubtedly a man of deep learning and research, and made a powerful impression on all who knew him. He was amiable and thoughtful of others." (George H. Mills, Esq., Hamilton, Ontario.)

"I have a very pleasant and grateful remembrance of dear Dr. Rae. He was very much respected and loved by all his pupils. I was with him at the then Grammar School from the spring of 1836 until December, 1837, when the Rebellion broke out, and our school broke up, the Doctor shouldering his musket and going to Toronto to fight the rebels.

"He was considered a fine scholar, well up in Latin, Greek and Mathematics, and specially qualified in Geology, and also understanding French. His mind was, in fact, a vast storehouse of knowledge, though he had not a happy faculty of dispensing it. But he had a very loving disposition that endeared him to us all." (Judge S. J. Jones, Grimsby Park, Ontario.)

[1] A recommendation for this position, signed by H. Urquhart, is dated November 6, 1834.

"Dr. John Rae was a man of great learning, and too little appreciated in his lifetime, like many others. . . . He was a great writer, sometimes writing night after night, and had a lot of manuscript. . . . His conversations with the boys that made his house their home was even more to them than their school studies. He entered into all their sports and amusements, often bringing his chemical knowledge into play." (J. R. Martin, Esq., Windsor.)

With this last especially may be joined the statement made by Sir Roderick W. Cameron that "Rae was a charming companion for young and old. He taught me rabbit, mink, and muskrat trapping, and other sports attractive to youth. . . . He was young in thoughts and acts to the end."

As already shown, Rae's quiet life as a teacher at Hamilton was broken at one period by military service. A letter among his effects, written by Allan N. MacNab, the commander of the Hamilton Volunteers, states, "He was among the first who accompanied me to Toronto on the breaking out of the Rebellion of 1837, and continued on duty at the Niagara frontier and elsewhere as long as his services were required." A letter of Rae to his sister shows that he was in action—quite a considerable skirmish.

As throwing a little further light on Rae's interests and activities during his residence in Canada, the following may be quoted from a scrap of manuscript:

"No paper formalities ever effectually resist the onward march of events. We had proof of that in Canada. One-eighth of the lands there were deeded with all the most binding formalities that the best lawyers could devise to the English Church. Yet all these lands have been taken from it. Thirty years since I ventured to predict to that Church that this and its other exorbitant pretensions would not stand. They were against the natural order of things, and they implied an injustice, viz., the putting Scotchmen in an inferior position to Englishmen. I was laughed at. Not a lawyer of any eminence but gave it hollow against us, insomuch that when we determined to make it a national question, and to lay a solemn protest against the whole thing before the British Parliament on constitutional grounds, I who am no lawyer was intrusted with the drawing

BIOGRAPHICAL SKETCH

up of that paper. It produced warm debates in both Houses, was on motion of the Duke of Wellington referred to the twelve English judges, who to their honor gave it in our favor."

At the end of 1847 and the beginning of 1848, there came to Rae, as far as we know without warning, what was almost a completely crushing blow—the loss of his school. A report was sent by the Trustees to the Governor-General, praying for the removal of the Head Master, on the ground of the "unsatisfactory condition of the school," and Rae's "inefficiency as a teacher." The school then numbered between sixty and seventy pupils.

The Governor-General declined to act by reason of lack of jurisdiction; and as the Trustees themselves could formally remove the incumbent only "for misdemeanours and impropriety of conduct," they apparently got rid of him by closing the school. The arguments put forward in the petition of the Trustees[1] lack the ring of sincerity, and Rae always felt that a cruel wrong was done him. Cherished among his effects is a considerable mass of letters of testimonial, written at the time by pupils and parents of pupils, all of a most flattering nature. A former acquaintance, writing recently, is of the opinion that undoubtedly the real reason for the action of the Trustees was Rae's religious views. He had become a good deal of a free thinker, and most of the Board were clergymen.

However this may be, Rae was turned adrift. He went first to Boston, and later to New York, where he obtained a position in some school. While thus employed he received the news of the death of his wife, who had remained at Hamilton. Her death took place August 17, 1849, under particularly distressing circumstances, into the details of which it is not necessary to enter. Letters written by friends and kindred at the time show that this must have been a sad bereavement to the already sorely oppressed man. Rae himself once alludes to it as "a great and soul-penetrating sorrow."

Already as early as January, 1849, Rae had been thinking

[1] This petition, now in my possession, is dated Dec. 30, 1847.

of going to California. Now that all ties binding him to old places and associations were severed, he prepared to carry his plan into execution. He took ship for the Isthmus late in the autumn. At Chagres he practised medicine for some time, and finally contracted as surgeon on the "Brutus," sailing from Panama. Of this part of his trip we have the following account: "Unfortunately she [the "Brutus"] did not sail as advertised, so that I waited at Panama five weeks, and not having given myself out for practice, spent every cent I had and more too. Worse than that, someone made the Captain, who was also mostly owner of the vessel, believe that I was no doctor, but only an old schoolmaster; and I believe if he could he would have shaken me off. Being moreover a mean, greedy fellow, he made my situation very uncomfortable. We had a great deal of sickness on board, and a passage of nine or ten weeks."[1]

In California Rae at first taught school at Colona, near Sutters Creek. Later he made cradles for washing and balances for weighing gold. There is no evidence that he turned gold miner himself. A large part of his stay in *El Dorado* was taken up by a severe illness which nearly ended his life.

Led on by scientific curiosity, as he explains, Rae went from California to the Sandwich Islands, arriving early in 1851. The twenty years of a restless and disappointed old age which he spent here were not without compensations. He was held in esteem by several men of importance, and had abundant material for the most absorbing physiographical and sociological studies. The fire of the ambitions of his

---

[1] This is taken from a letter, or series of letters written to Cameron, and published with the title "Dr. Rae in California" in the *Hamilton Gazette* for Dec. 19, 1850. It is not at all unlikely that there are other letters by Rae to be found in the files of that paper during the early fifties. Under date of Hamilton, Jan. 15, 1852, Cameron wrote Rae:—"I intend allowing Bull to publish extracts from your letter. I have written them out and will forward you a copy of the paper, as well as several copies to your acquaintances throughout the country." During that and the following year Rae wrote several long epistles to Cameron, which he plainly expected would be published in some journal. The present writer was not able to confer with Cameron in respect to this matter before his death.

BIOGRAPHICAL SKETCH xxvii

youth still burning strong within him, he went resolutely to work (after an interval of school keeping) on an agricultural enterprise, hoping that the money gained would some day take him to the literary centres of the old world. He worked with his own hands, and with such headlong zeal that his friends remonstrated. But all to no avail. Failure came here as in almost everything else to which he put his hand. He explains the exasperating details in a letter to Willson, but I pass them over.[1]

At least as early as July, 1853, while residing at Wailuku, Island of Maui, Rae was Medical Agent of the Board of Health, a position which he also held in 1869, and presumably during the interval. One of the most interesting of his papers is entitled, "Journal of a Tour around East Maui." This was a walking expedition, lasting a month or two, and made for the purpose of vaccinating the natives. It was evidently entered upon with the keenest zest. He saw everything; literally nothing of interest seems to have escaped him.

According to Commissions in my possession, Rae was appointed District Justice at Hana, East Maui, in 1859, and again in 1863. From all accounts he must have been given this office at other times as well, but there is no documentary proof at hand. The position was one of some importance. A correspondent in Honolulu mentions one particularly interesting case of sorcery that came before him. He lived, we learn from the same source, in a solitary place far back from the sea; and when he walked abroad his tall, spare form was seen always accompanied by two large dogs.

In April, 1871, Cameron wrote his old friend and teacher,

---

[1] The reference is to Hugh Bowlby Willson, son of the Hon. John Willson, "at one time Speaker of the Canadian Legislature." He was a barrister, engineer, promoter, general railway agent and commission merchant, author, and editor, during 1849, of the short-lived *Canadian Independent*, established in the interests of annexation. Rae was willing to be associated in this last enterprise, but was too much broken up at the time to take an active part. Willson's published works are on engineering and monetary subjects. Apparently he was a man of exceptional range of ability, but always unfortunate and poor. There is abundant evidence in Rae's papers that Willson was his best friend. Like cleaves to like.

to whom several times he had been of material assistance, "If you will come and spend your remaining years with me, I will defray all your expenses from Maui to my home." Rae accepted this invitation, and sailed on the steamer "Ajax" in July. The change of climate affected him seriously, so that he kept his room the following winter and spring, and finally passed away, as already stated, in midsummer. He was buried in Woodland Cemetery, Staten Island, in a lot purchased by Sir Roderick, "in which two others, one a faithful servant and the other a distant relative, are buried."

Thus far I have given in bare outline only the chief milestones, as it were, along the career of the man whose life is before us. It is necessary to fill in the gaps with some further account of what he did, and what he thought and felt. A scholar, not a man of action, what he did is of course to be found chiefly in his studies.

Some account of a speculation which interested him in early youth has already been given. Another one, of a different sort, at that period of his life, was a scheme "for determining the rate and setting of a current at sea." The device for this purpose (applicable to both surface and undercurrents) is described in some detail in one of his papers, but it is scarcely fitting to reproduce it here.[1]

Of the fate of this project Rae says writing to Willson:

"I was then under a very eminent professor of mathematics in the Marischal College, Aberdeen, the late Dr. Hamilton, and showed it him. He allowed it sound in theory and ingenious, but smiled it down as impracticable. Though not convinced I was obliged to yield and let it go, as I did not wish to irritate my father. . . . Dr. Hamilton's objection to my scheme was that it was very good on paper, but that in so boisterous an element as the ocean it was almost absurd to think it could be of any practical utility. He judged of the ocean from fanciful notions he had got sitting in his easy chair. I knew something of it then, and have

[1] The chief principle employed was that of the pressure of the water upon air in a cylinder to disengage at varying depths weights attached to bodies of different specific gravity.

lived on it many a long day since, and can see nothing absurd in the project. In fact, in weather in which a whale boat could live, there would be no difficulty in giving the globes their proper position in the water. In other weather, no attempt at deep sounding by the lead itself could be made with a prospect of success. Once a few feet beneath the surface all violent motion ceases.

"I cannot but think, however, that the temper of mind which led him to object was one with which all inventions are commonly, one might almost say reasonably, met. Nine out of ten of all mechanical schemes are abortive. In fact, they generally take their rise in this way. Some idea new, or conceived to be new, flits by chance across the brain of a man unaccustomed to new ideas. The novelty of the thing, and still more so the novelty of its occurring to himself, sets it on a point of view that puts all other conceptions out of sight and magnifies itself prodigiously. It becomes therefore his hobby, and he rides it, or more frequently it rides him. But the man who is consulted in such a case, especially if he has been in the habit of being so consulted, sees the thing in a very different light. He knows that these projects are almost all vanity, that some flaw in their conception makes them impracticable, or that a search would prove them not original. In short, that it is ten to one if this particular one succeed. Besides, if he be a man of reputation in science, he is annoyed at being obliged to give up time that is valuable to the task of finding out flaws, and accordingly takes hold of the first that presents itself. This shortens his labour, keeps his reputation safe, and is probably a charity to the inventor. In this way it perhaps is that the greater number of new inventions have not had the sanction of the learned, and that, if given at all, it has been in a mighty cautious manner. I know therefore that I should myself have great difficulty at present to get anyone to take hold of a single one of my schemes, and am aware that I am putting your friendship to a somewhat severe test in asking you to attempt it."

One of the "schemes" here alluded to was a device for a feathering paddle wheel for steam boats. There are diagrams and descriptions among his papers. The feathering was to take place in a vertical plane parallel with the keel, instead of at right angles with it, as is the case with feathering inventions now in use. The plan was probably therefore of little practical value, but it is of interest to note that Rae had the idea of the importance and possibility of feathering paddle wheels, probably before any one else. Among his papers, also, is considerable in the way of inventive speculation on the art of shipbuilding in general, and several essays on aeronautics.[1]

But what interests us most are Rae's sociological (in the broad sense of the term) rather than his mechanical studies.

In the Preface to the *Political Economy* he speaks of " a work on the present state of Canada, and on its relations with the rest of the British Empire," on which he had become engaged after taking up his residence in Canada. In 1832, while still at Williamstown, he addressed a petition to Sir John Colborne, the Lieutenant-Governor, praying for aid to publish a book " On the Present State and Resources of the Province " (title as given by H. J. Morgan). This petition was submitted to the House of Assembly and duly printed in its Journals, but there the matter seems to have been dropped. There is no record, so I am informed, to indicate that the composition was ever printed.

In all probability, this was the work mentioned in the Preface: one which Rae seems to have spent much labour upon, and to have valued in some respects above his *Political Economy*. In one of his letters to Willson he says:

" I had thoroughly studied Canada in both its natural and moral aspects, and could have told England what it really was and what it wanted. Had I had the least aid (£100 would have done it), I should have accomplished this; and looking soberly on the matter as a thing past, it is now my firm conviction that I should thus have averted all the disasters of the Rebellion and brought on a dozen years earlier that period of prosperity which the province now enjoys. I will not inflict you with my reasons for this

[1] In a letter (undated) written to Willson we read:—" After a little reflection I have decided on sending you a summary of that whole part of my century which relates to progression *through* water. I am partly led to this from having the chance of sending a heavy packet with safety by my friend J. W. Austin, Esq., of Boston, who has resided for some years in these islands in a position somewhat analogous to our Attorney-General, and who now is returning to his native soil. He will write you and receive your instructions as to transmitting this and the other papers he takes charge of."

conviction. Had this been so I could have brought out my ideas concerning some points on Political Economy with the prospect of a fair hearing."

And again in a letter to John Stuart Mill he writes apparently of this same literary undertaking as follows:

"I cannot go on with my account of the Sandwich Islands till I see and examine them all. . . . I have therefore thought of inditing a small work on Canada—Recollections of Canada. Many years ago I had formed the project of writing an extended work on the Province, had visited all parts of it, collected information of all sorts concerning it, and had written a large part. I had intended to publish this before my *Political Economy.* Unfortunately I was induced to put forth the latter in Boston, under the assurance from Mr. A. Everett[1] that it would be appreciated there. He was, however, I believe scared at it. Could not make up his mind, nor could any one there, if I was right or wrong, and so passed it by with praise of its style, etc. This damned it. My bad success here was a bar to my work on Canada, for as this was long and went to the bottom of things, my friends and the booksellers prognosticated that it would, like the former, be too heavy a work to be read. I kept the manuscript by me, adding to my stock of information as occasion offered, still thinking of one day bringing it forth. Among other mischances that have befallen, these manuscripts, sent to New York, seem to have been strangely lost. So there is an end of that.

"However, I think I could write a small book that would have a certain currency. I am more inclined to think this from the following circumstance. Some time before leaving Canada, a young friend came to reside with me, and having something of a turn for politics was very free in his inquiries as to my opinions and views of matters, which I gave him in full. On this foundation, for he knew nothing of these matters himself, he goes and writes an article for Blackwood. I just saw it before leaving America, and found it a reflection of my own thoughts, though sometimes dim or distorted. Since landing on these shores I have had letters from Canada asking if I were the author and stating that the article had had considerable success."

[1] This was Alexander H. Everett, brother of Edward Everett, diplomat, editor of the *North American Review*, writer to some extent on economic subjects. His review of Rae's *Political Economy* is in Vol. XL. of the *North American Review*.

Further than this, nothing is known of the nature or fate of this presumably profound treatise.[1]

The reception accorded his *Political Economy* was always a keen disappointment to Rae. He received practically nothing for it pecuniarily, as he informed Cameron; and it was not until nearly thirty years after it was published that he learned Mill had noticed it. Apparently he never knew that it was translated in 1856, in Volume XI., first series, of Ferrara's *Biblioteca dell' Economista*.

This is not the place to give any extended criticism of this work, pronounced by Professor Irving Fisher (*Yale Review*, Vol. V., p. 457) to be "truly a masterpiece, a book of a generation or a century."[2] I wish here merely to point out that its influence, even from the first, has been greater than is commonly supposed. A careful study of John Stuart Mill's *Principles* reveals many undoubted instances of indebtedness. Indeed, on the side of pure economics it may be said that it was Rae, more than any other, who modified the Ricardian basis of Mill's thought. To an equal extent, perhaps, is Hearn in his *Plutology* indebted to Rae. This is seen not so much in particular passages as in the method and spirit of this admirable treatise. The high commendation which Jevons, Marshall, and Edgeworth have bestowed upon Hearn's work, therefore, belongs in part to another. It may be also mentioned in passing that Professor Thomas Fowler in his *Principles of Morals* (Part II., Oxford, 1887, pp. 50-59) makes consider-

---

[1] According to one of Rae's old pupils, "J. S. Hogan made use of portions of Rae's history of Canada to get up an article for Blackwood for which he received £40 sterling." This same pupil "well recollects" Rae "often reading extracts from his History of Canada." Rae himself once makes bare mention of a "nearly completed physical history of Canada." There were two articles on Canada in *Blackwood's Magazine* during 1849, both unsigned, but dated Hamilton, Canada West, one or both of which must be that to which Rae and my correspondent refer. John Sheridan Hogan published in Montreal, in 1855, an essay on Canada which was awarded the first prize by "the Paris Exhibition Committee of Canada."

[2] Compare the opinion of Professor Edgeworth in Palgrave's *Dictionary of Political Economy*, and of Professor Sydney Sherwood in *Johns Hopkins University Studies in Historical and Political Science*, fifteenth series, pp. 582-584, and 590-591.

able use of Rae, drawing on him at second hand through the quotations given in Mill's *Principles*. An intellectual candle of real power, if it be not wholly placed under a bushel, shines far.

While at Hamilton, Rae had privately printed in 1843 an *Essay on the Question of Education, in as far as it concerns Canada*. The title page and a few detached leaves only of this monograph were found among his effects. Some effort has been made to obtain knowledge of the whereabouts of a complete copy, but without success. It is also known that in the last years of his life Rae had at least "nearly completed" another work "On Education," but what became of it has not been ascertained.

After his establishment in the Sandwich Islands, Rae's studies were most multitudinous, in fact too much so: little was brought to completion. Some essays on geology and on medical subjects were indeed written out and sent home either to Cameron or Willson, with the request that they be published in *Stillman's Journal*,[1] or in some other scientific periodical; but evidently nothing came of them.[2]

Among the manuscripts falling into my possession, by far the most extensive and orderly were those upon geology and kindred subjects, pertaining both to Canada and the Hawaiian Islands. These have been placed in proper hands, and may in part be printed.

But though much attention while in Maui was devoted to geology, to questions of the welfare of the native race, and to his mechanical inventions, Rae's chief study was upon the language. He had a theory that the Hawaiian race represented in great purity, by reason of its isolation, an exceedingly primitive culture; just as the old Norse culture is at present most purely represented in Iceland. He believed he was studying in the Hawaiian language a survival of a pre-Sanskrit language—the original tongue of a universal stone age. Apparently bold generalizations as to language-building, the relations between sounds and

[1] Later called *The American Journal of Science and Arts*.

[2] This was done, it appears, on two occasions, in 1852 and ten or twelve years later.

actions, were carrying him far into a most profound philological and anthropological speculation. I say apparently here, because of my ignorance of such matters, and because this part of his manuscript is the most fragmentary and chaotic of all.

Some of the results of his studies along these lines, and also on some other matters pertaining to the existing condition of the Hawaiians, we know to have been printed in a Honolulu newspaper, *The Polynesian*, during the early sixties.[1] A few excerpts from these articles being sent by an acquaintance, R. C. Wyllie,[2] to John Stuart Mill, led Mill to write Rae at least once; a communication which, however, was never received. A copy of a letter by Mill to Wyllie respecting Rae, found among the latter's effects, runs as follows:

BLACKHEATH PARK,
KENT, *Feb.* 3, 1863.

SIR,—I have had the honour of receiving your letter and the printed slips which you have been kind enough to send. These I have read with the attention due to any work of Dr. Rae, and they appear to me quite worthy of his intellect and acquirements. The picture which he draws of the dangers that menace the interesting community of which you are one of the rulers, is most formidable. Of the remedies which he proposes, I cannot be a competent judge, but, as far as my means of judgment extend, he seems to be right in much, perhaps even in all, that he proposes.

The other paper will, I think, place Dr. Rae very high among ethnologists and philologists. After having reached by independent investigation the highest generalization previously made, namely, that all languages have grown by development from a few hundred words, Dr. Rae seems to

---

[1] So far as the editor has been able to ascertain, the only copies of *The Polynesian* which are available for the period when Rae contributed to its columns, are in the British Museum—Vols. 15-19, covering from May, 1858, to April, 1863.

[2] Mr. Wyllie, as he states in one of his letters to Rae, was formerly "an East India merchant, railway director, and director (in fact, the starter) of the Pacific Steam Navigation Company." He was soon after deceased (about 1865 or 1866), holding at the time a high position under the Hawaiian Government.

have supplied the first probable explanation of the manner in which these primitive words may themselves have originated. If his hypothesis is made out, it is the keystone of the science of philology, it is *a priori* extremely probable, and the facts he brings forward establish a strong case of verification *a posteriori*. I hope that Dr. Max Müller has been put in possession of this important speculation.

It must be of great value to your country to have such a man as Dr. Rae settled among you.

It is very gratifying to me that you are disposed to carry the principle of minorities into practical operation. That such should be questions agitated in a country which three-quarters of a century ago was in the savage state is surely one of the most remarkable signs of the very hopeful times in which we live.—I am, Sir, your most obedient servant,

J. S. MILL.

His Excellency, R. C. Wyllie, Esquire.

After an interval Rae wrote Mill the following:

" SIR,—Permit me to render you my thanks for having taken the trouble some two or three years since to write my late friend Mr. Wyllie concerning some papers of mine that had appeared in the Polynesian newspaper of Honolulu, and of which he had sent you copies. You may well suppose I was much gratified by the favourable opinion of one whose judgment deservedly carries so much weight with it as yours in all philosophical questions. I address you at present to request a favour. I desire to dedicate to you a work on the Polynesian language and its connections with the history of speech, and consequently of humanity. You could have formed but a very imperfect idea of my views from my letter to Mr. Wyllie, which was not intended for publication, and in which, from its growing too voluminous on my hands, I often dropped the thread of my argument without pursuing statements I had made to their legitimate consequences. I cannot of course attempt to mend the matter here, or to give even a summary of my argument, but I may state the conclusions at which I have arrived, as well as those at which I might hope to arrive, and thus explain to you the reasons which urge me to make the request I have preferred.

" I believe it may be shown that the race from which the Polynesians spring was at the head of civilization of the age of stone, and were settled in Hindustan and along the southern and more fertile shores of Asia. It seems, too, that the facts on which my reasons rest are indisputable, the deduction perfectly logical, and the conclusion therefore irrefragable. This forms the first part of my book. The second pertains to the language. As to it, there have come into it two sounds, significant of themselves, which have a close analogy to the cries of the higher order of animals, and have somehow been modified by and incorporated into the articulate speech. The one is *a* (the broad Scotch or Italian a) and it may be translated action. The other is *o* which denotes distance and connection. This may seem a contradiction, but in reality if a thing be distant it must be distant from something else, and that something must therefore to the mind have some relation to it or connection with it. The articulate sounds or syllables of the Polynesian language are either simple vowels, or end in vowels. There are about forty of them, and the remarkable fact as to all of them is this: When the organs of speech with the aid of the breath shape an articulate syllable, they also themselves take a shape, form and movement, and in this language, this shape and movement have always an analogy to the thing or action which the sound of the syllable or conjoined syllable denotes.''

Here the letter breaks off.

Rae's manuscript in epistolary form addressed to Mill is rather voluminous.[1] Those parts which relate to political economy have been printed in the *Economic Journal* for March, 1902 (Vol. XII., No. 45) and in the *Quarterly Journal of Economics* for November, 1901 (Vol. XVI., No. 1). A small additional fragment appears as Article VI. in the Appendix to this volume.[2]

Among the friends of Rae's later life was Abraham Fornander, editor of *The Polynesian* at the time when Rae's articles appeared in that journal. In the years 1878-1885, Fornander published a three volume work, which attained some celebrity, entitled *An Account of the*

[1] It is not known whether a fair copy of any of this was ever sent to Mill, but it is not unlikely. Rae seems also to have corresponded with Dr. William Beattie in England.

[2] Some excerpts from Rae's miscellaneous manuscript are also introduced at different points indicated in the text.

BIOGRAPHICAL SKETCH xxxvii

Polynesian Race, its Origin and Migrations. In the Preface to the first volume, among other general acknowledgments of literary obligation, we read,—" The late Dr. John Rae of Hana, Maui, who, in a series of articles published in *The Polynesian* (Honolulu, 1862), first called attention to the extreme antiquity of the Polynesian language." This is the only reference Fornander makes to Rae. The present writer is of the opinion that Rae originated most of the ideas which were followed out in this work by his contemporary.

I may add in this connection that a transcription of one of the ancient legends of the Hawaiians with Rae's explanatory notes, found among his effects, has been printed in Volume XIII., No. 51. (1900), of the *Journal of American Folk-Lore*. It shows a vitality not found in Fornander's *Polynesian Race*.

Of Rae's inner life, especially on the intellectual side, we get occasional glimpses in his correspondence. Writing to Willson from Chagres, December 27th, 1849, he said :

" I have now for many years been an exile from the land which I had chosen as my home, and in which I had made up my mind to pass my remaining days, and within the present month, and in beginning old age, have become a wanderer and adventurer over the wide earth. You know the cruel injustice which has thus driven me forth. You partly know also the cruel sufferings thus entailed on me, and which have almost rent my heart. But this of good has resulted from all. Nature under a new face, humanity under an altered aspect; a sense of danger, and a necessity for action, have, as it were, renewed my soul, and enabled me to look calmly on what I have been and what I am. Thus I see myself as in times past destiny seemed to have stamped me, I can analyze, as it were, the elements of my then existence, and taking my stand on what new has broken in on it, can measure and look on it as a thing apart from the present.

" Fortune has not permitted me to be the student I would have desired. The study of such a one is in the spacious library where undisturbed and uncontrolled he can roam over the thoughts and read the souls of men of all times and countries ; or else the wide world itself, with all conveniences to explore it and examine the various aspects of nature and of man which it exhibits—or better still, each alternately. Only partially, only scantily have I enjoyed these advantages. But every man has a world of study within his own soul, and in the workings of the passions of those around him. This I have not neglected. . . .

"Alas for the student, ardent and feeling, and with hopes like mine, pursuing truth without dread as concerns self, and yet shrinking from it when at length grasped as a thing, though having within itself the energetic powers of a new and better order of things yet coming on the present world, if receiving it, like one of the phials of wrath of the apocalypse. I had determined that no important writing of mine should appear till after my death. Thus I could acquit myself to the Omnipotent for not hiding what He had allowed me to see of what at least appeared to me *light*, and avoid the suspicion of being actuated by personal motives. . . .

"What now I may do is uncertain. I know not even if my manuscripts are safe. Certainly a new spirit is awakened within me, and may lead to a new course of action, if I be not cut down by some of the chances which I see fall to so many around me. . . .

"Now as concerns Canadian independence, or annexation; that also as a thing interesting in itself, and more especially as one to be taken as a sign of other things of greater interest with which the present era seems pregnant, had occupied at least some little of my attention; but I had become accustomed to view it from a point and in a light different from that in which politicians of the hour necessarily regard it.

"Let me explain myself. When one commences the study of history, it is generally under the apprehension that this study will serve as a master key to the problems of the day, and will enable him not only to form just conclusions concerning them, but, if so prompted, to address his contemporaries with authority and power. But as he advances farther and farther in the pursuit, and if he has seized the philosophical spirit of investigating it which has begun to give its proper life to the inquiries of the age, he finds the eye of his mind conducted by it to a far higher elevation whence it takes in a great reach of the whole tide of humanity lying beneath, flowing on with unceasing current from the dim and cloudy mountains of the past in lengthened course to the immense and measureless future. Not only is his soul absorbed by the contemplation of the vast prospect, but he feels both the comparative insignificance of the immediate present and his own want of power to control it. What is a slight turning in the course or a little ripple on the surface of the huge stream which, under the guidance of energies so mighty is hurrying on so fast and so far? Not only do the questions of the day diminish before him to mere waves chafing the shore and serving little else but to mark the strength of the great feelings, sufferings, passions, or if you will, principles which, as it were blindly and confusedly, though doubtless under the real government of an Omnipotent hand whose workings pass his ken, impel the mighty mass along; but also he becomes sensible how insignificant individual efforts must be to control forces which he sees and feels bearing others and himself away with overwhelming energy.

"To one having learned to view things in this light, it must be difficult, and I found it impossible in New York, to write a popular article such as the interests of your Journal require on a question which if not in the temper in which it is agitated at least in the thing itself is profoundly significant."

In another letter addressed to Willson, undated, but apparently written from the Isthmus or California, we read,

"A change has come o'er the thread of my life. You have perhaps seen a horse of a sort of sluggish temper, not deficient in any of the externals that denote some degree of power, but yet who seemed incapable of anything but a stubborn, shambling gait which whip or spur made only more uncomfortable. Well, gather your reins, feel that you are well in your saddle, and spare not but dig the iron well into his sides. You will rouse him; and if you keep your seat through his first plungings and boundings it may be that you will be astonished how well and fast and far he will bear you. Such is the change that has come over the temper of my mind. The iron has pierced deep into me, it rankles in my very vitals, and for aught I see will do so till the grave cover me. I must be doing something, I have relief in action. . . . London, Paris, with a little capital in money and literary reputation have been my aim for years. There, with the assistance of libraries, museums, friends who could and might be induced to assist me, I have conceived I should have the fairest field for my literary and philosophical speculations, and for my mechanical schemes. The one would assist the other. Had it not been for those confounded Trustees, my plans were so laid that I feel pretty confident I should before this have been there, and it was this overthrow of my plans more than the mere ejection from the school that so nearly overset me, and but for you, I believe, would have given me my final quietus."

Writing still again to this faithful friend, from Hana under date of December, 1856, Rae says :

" If you would really help a man you must know how to help him. You must know in what his well-being and happiness consist, what therefore are his objects and aims. My earlier friends in Canada could not conceive or at least understand what were mine. They thought me foolish in burying the attainments and ability they were pleased to give me credit for in the subordinate position of a village surgeon, or still worse in that of a country schoolmaster. They could not conceive that my main need was quiet, to think out my thoughts. When after ten years of this sort of life I had sufficiently mastered my subjects and digested my problems and wished to put some of them before the world, they had changed their notion of me, and viewing me now as a mere schoolmaster stood aloof from me and my projects, and would give me neither effective countenance nor support. Some hinted that had I taken their advice I might have been in a very different position, while the prudent said, ' What are your chances of gaining by this? How much will it put in your pocket? Sit quiet.' Others again, looking on me as a mere adventurer, and measuring me from my humble place and comparing it with the magnitude of my enterprises, seemed to say, ' What, you a village teacher, think you can master such high themes? The man is mad : we will have nothing to do with him.' . . . I have found all men, even my most intimate friends, measuring the probable success of my schemes not from what they inherently were, but from the position of myself, the one bringing them forward. Thus I recollect well when I projected publishing my work on political economy, my friends were quite incredulous of my ability to controvert the doctrines of Adam Smith in any particular, and smiled part in pity, part in wonderment, at the presumption of one who had not been able to raise himself from the position of a country schoolmaster embarking on so hopeless an enterprise.

Now had they known my motives for contenting myself with what seemed to them so inferior a station, they might or at least they ought to have come to another conclusion. It was in truth because I was engaged in important speculations for which school life though a drudgery yet gave me many hours of quiet leisure, that I contented myself with it. I feared that if I then pushed really into the battle of life these speculations would be likely to dim before me, and probably at last fade in the distance. I now think I was wrong in this—events at least would seem to prove my having been so. At any rate, had I to run the same course over again, I would act differently. I think I ought to have studied law, for which through Judge Maclean the way would have been open to me, and secured to myself a certain social position that would have enabled me in no long time to have given myself to pursuits more congenial to my feelings. I do not believe that either great success or comparative failure in a legal career would have been able to turn me from the occasional contemplation and ultimate pursuit of the magnificent visions of my youth. Yet who knows?" . . .

There is evidence that at some time in his career Rae's friends, instead of being incredulous of his powers, had urged him to "push forward on some undertaking"; for in one fragment of epistolary manuscript we find the following:

" Now this was the way to make me sit still. Even the fancying to myself that personal advantage was in reality the end of my efforts was sure to confound me, and the holding this up to me as their true aim and object completely paralysed me. . . . It may seem incredible to you, but it is the real fact that these dinnings in my ears always brought a similar chaos over my thoughts, and if fool enough to try, I only floundered on from one instability to another. This may seem to you a strange, unnatural, almost mad humor of mine. So perhaps it was; it was at least what doctors call abnormal, the result probably in part of my peculiar organization, in part of cruel mental suffering in early youth, the fruits, the avengers perhaps, of a momentary yielding to violent passions. This gave to the world and all it holds a real air of mere vanity and vexation of spirit."

One more passage from a letter, or rather parts of different letters, may be quoted, written from Maui, but to whom it is impossible with certainty to say.

"From a very early period of my life I had turned my attention and, as occasion presented itself, bent all the powers of my mind to trace out the causes which have given shape and form to humanity, and from whence have come the laws which have hitherto governed and must in future govern its progress. . . . A train of singularly untoward and to me disastrous circumstances, and of such a character that for the honor of human nature I trust the history of few individuals can present a parallel [have impeded my endeavors]. . . . Nevertheless wherever I have been, and however situated, the idea of my youth has held possession of me, and has been the central point of all my researches and speculations. Now in my old age I am desirous of recording [as much as is possible of the results of my labours]. . . . I can scarcely hope to tell my fellow-men all that during my life I have gathered together from the recorded past and the actual present, of the paths we have travelled from our first appearance on earth to the present hour, and the ways we have to travel to the end. To me the sun is surely soon to set. Yet while daylight lasts I am desirous of adding what I can to those stores of knowledge and truth which are the only substantial inheritance which age can bequeath to age. I had thought of commencing by giving a sketchy outline of what I may call my system, and had in fact composed a great part of such outline. Certain circumstances, however, warn me that this plan is imprudent, and that it is better to put forth what I know and desire to tell in parts, mere fragments of the great whole which is spread out before my view. Each to other men will seem fragmentary; if I live long enough I may form them into a system, or rather the skeleton of a system, which perhaps others may fill up. One of these fragments is the relation which the Polynesian race and language bear to other races and languages, and to the origin of language itself. My investigations as to this last point have, I think, led me to some important discoveries. I am now preparing a work on these subjects which I hope to have published in London. I think it more likely than any other of my speculations to draw some share of public attention. I have not, however, confined myself to this alone, but have drawn out the plan and partly written some essays on subjects having a bearing on what is shadowed out in my mind as a real philosophic history of our race. It was thus that some months since I wrote the essay which I send. I had not, however, thought of publishing it for perhaps a year or two, nor even then until it had been submitted to the judgment of some scientific friend who might be competent to detect any mistake in the mechanical part, if any there were."[1]

And now to conclude this series of excerpts, we may set down the following: standing on a bit of paper by itself, and in so wavering a hand that it may well have been written during Rae's last illness.

" If we regard the generous impulses, the ennobling hopes, the lofty aspirations, that swell the breast of youth, we should say that the human heart was a soil in which the heaven-wafted seeds of every virtue might germinate and grow and flourish, and spread a paradise over the earth. But alas, when the time comes when each has to cast himself into the stream of actual life, the movements of whose impetuous current have come down from places and times far remote, the first plunge awakens him to the absorbing necessity of putting forth all his energies to maintain himself in the whirling tide. He loses sight of those landmarks which were to have guided his course. Progress, Progress, is his cry; and on he dashes, pushing aside and thrusting down."

But in all this one gets rather a distorted picture of the sort of man Rae really was. The reader must consider that these things were written late in life, and make allowances. He should, especially, group with them the impressions derived from the work put forth by Rae in his prime. Those who knew him in the flesh, not primarily as a man of science but as a teacher and friend, represent him as athletic in mind and in body; as cheerful, courageous, singularly devoid of all petty ambitions and meanness. He was built on a large plan.

One fault he had of an intellectual sort which stood seriously in his way as a successful writer, and that was a marked tendency to take in all the length and breadth of

[1] This may have been written to Dr. W. Beattie, for in a scrap of a letter addressed to him is discussed the same literary project.

any subject, and to sound its depths. Consequently he always went off into digressions, frequently of excessive length—a habit which grew upon him. But to take in the length and breadth of a subject and to sound its depths is the mark of genius. If Rae could have had suitable conditions for scientific work (such as seemed open to him in his early youth) he would undoubtedly have been steadied as well as stimulated—he would have shown proper concentration—and then with his powers of imagination and range of information, what results might the world not have had from him? Or if when he came to America he had settled in one of the larger cities, with access to libraries and contact with other well-trained minds, how different would his life have been? But nevertheless he did not altogether miss his mark. His work, not without influence when first published, though later neglected, did not die. The revival of interest came when others began to exploit the same field, and when the science as a whole had made a great advance. There now seems every prospect that this interest will widen, and intensify, and endure.

AUTHOR'S PREFACE.

(The work here presented to the American reader, was composed with the intention of being published in Great Britain; under this idea the following Preface was written. As it explains the design of the original undertaking, it has been thought proper that it should retain the place it was at first intended to occupy.)

To promote prosperity within, to guard against danger from without, have ever been esteemed the two great branches of the duty of the Statesman. But of all the sources of internal prosperity, or means of repelling external aggressions, no one, in modern times, is of greater efficacy than wealth. We have, therefore, no reason to be surprised, that statesmen should have endeavored to procure for their respective countries the greatest possible amount of it. If the laws they have enacted, and the regulations they have for this purpose established, have really answered the ends they were intended to promote, they are certainly praiseworthy.

Of the efficacy of such laws, for those purposes, politicians for a long time did not doubt; but a great revolution in public opinion has taken place, and almost all men who now pretend to understand the principles that should govern the policy of nations, agree in condemning them.

This revolution in the opinions of men, had its rise in France. It might have died there, however, with the sect from which it had birth, had not a man of surprising genius, placing himself at the head of the feeble party then supporting it, enabled them to give their principles currency throughout the nations of Europe. Adam Smith will be recorded among remote generations, as one having powerfully influenced the opinions and policy of the civilized world, during the eighteenth and nineteenth centuries. His great work no sooner appeared in Britain than it was read, and the opinions it maintained adopted, by every one who pretended to any knowledge of the important subjects of which it treated. It quickly, and with like success, spread through other lands. Never was the force which mere intellect possesses more strikingly manifested. To illustrate his speculations, to cast them into new forms suited to the varied tastes of various nations, became an employment by which men of undoubted genius thought themselves honored. His reasonings are the basis of numerous systems and innumerable essays. A voluminous library might be formed of the works of men who call him master. Nor were the dicta of a retired student acquiesced in, and embraced, only by theorists like himself. They have guided the councils, they have formed the text book of statesmen, and have had an important influence on the policy of nations.

Against doctrines supported by so great a weight of authority, what, it may be demanded, can possibly be urged? and how comes it, that so obscure an individual as the author of the following pages, places himself in opposition to them? Custom authorises me—in a measure calls on me—in answer to these questions, to state to the reader how I was led to form opinions opposed to this system, and why I bring those opinions before him.

Many years ago, I became engaged in a series of inquiries into the circumstances which have governed the history of man, or, to vary the expression, into the causes which have made him what he is in various countries, or has been in various times. It seemed to me, that, by gathering together all that consciousness makes known to us of what is within, and all that observation informs us of what lies without, the real agents in the production of the great events by which the fortunes of our race have been diversified, might be at least partially discovered, the laws regulating their procedure traced, and that thus the materials for a true *Natural History* of man might be reached. The pursuits in which I was then engaged led me to the subject on the side of physiology, and what is termed metaphysics, and imagining that I saw a ray of light struggling through the obscurity of the objects, amidst which these investigations placed me, I began to conceive hopes of being able to dispel some of the darkness, in which are involved causes that have produced, and are producing, results of the highest importance to us. To this pursuit I determined to devote myself. Such a resolution would scarcely have been taken by any one unless prompted by the enthusiasm natural to youth, and would not have been adopted by me, had I not had the prospect of enjoying every facility in following out the objects I had in view; but a sudden and unexpected change took place in my circumstances, and I exchanged the literary leisure of Europe for the solitude and labors of the Canadian backwoods. I found, notwithstanding, that this accident could not altogether put a stop to my inquiries, though it retarded them and altered their form.

I had early turned for assistance to the *Inquiry into the Nature and Causes of the Wealth of Nations*, and to the speculations of the political economists. But, I found their scope and design too confined, to advance the attainment of my purpose in the degree I had anticipated; and I had besides the mortification of perceiving, that the conclusions to which they led, were, in many points, opposed to those at which I had arrived. Encountering opposition where I had looked for support, I applied myself to ascertain, if possible, the cause, and, after having spent considerable time in the inquiry, conceived I had detected enough of fallacy in the speculations, even of Adam Smith himself, but more especially of his successors, to warrant the belief that my conclusions might be right, though the practical rules that might be deduced from them, would not coincide with those laid down in what is termed the science of political economy. But, though I became satisfied on this head, it was not my intention to have directly attacked any of the tenets of the school. Setting out from a new point, it seemed to me, that, however far I might advance, it would not be necessary for me directly to oppose, or to attempt to controvert, any received opinions.

During my residence in this country, the field of my

inquiries being much contracted, I again recurred to the disquisitions of Adam Smith, and of other European writers of the same school, in order to trace out more fully than I had hitherto done, the connexion between the phenomena attending the increase and diminution of wealth, and those general principles of the nature of man, and of the world, determining, as I conceive, the whole progress of human affairs. Though I was led to this study, simply from my desire to advance, as far as my situation permitted me, in a path of investigation which had, to me, a very lively interest, my prosecution of it had the effect of impressing me more deeply with a conviction of the unsoundness of the system maintained in the *Wealth of Nations*.

In this stage of my progress I became engaged in a work on the present state of Canada, and on its relations with the rest of the British Empire. These relations seem to me to spring from the mutual benefit arising to the colony and the empire from their connexion. The sect of politicians, to whom I allude, deny that any such benefit arises to either party. Were their reasonings correct, it would follow as a necessary consequence, that Canada is, in this respect, of no advantage to Great Britain, and would go far to prove, what, indeed, seems by many to be believed, that the sooner the connexion between them is dissolved the better.

Dissenting as I do, from the opinions of these theorists, it appeared to me, that the work I had undertaken required me to state some of the reasons on which I grounded this dissent, and that, without entering at length into any of the important questions involved in the discussion, I should be able at least to cast a shade of doubt over doctrines asserted with great dogmatism, and acted on with unhesitating confidence. In endeavoring, however, for this purpose, to arrange a series of arguments drawn from a modification of principles that originally suggested themselves to me when engaged in more enlarged inquiries, my work gradually assumed a far more extended and systematic form, than I had at first meditated; and I became engaged in the present attempt, to show that there exist great and radical errors in the whole system, sufficient to vitiate very many of the conclusions drawn from it, and from the fallacies introduced by which, the doctrines of free trade alone derive their plausibility.

In the prosecution of the argument, I have almost entirely confined myself to the consideration of the doctrines to which I am opposed, as they are developed in the *Wealth of Nations*. I could not have done otherwise, without becoming involved in the discussion of contradictory and conflicting opinions. Neither, as I conceive, is this limitation of essential importance to the determination of the points in debate. If Adam Smith be essentially wrong, none of his followers can be right. The system established by him stands, or falls, with him.

I am not ignorant of the dangers to which this attempt subjects me. Whoever ventures to attack a system received so generally, and supported by so great a weight of authority, is exposed to various evils. They who have embraced its principles are apt to slight and neglect, or, if that may not be, to conceive it their business to overthrow the heterodox doctrines. What of error they may contain is eagerly seized on, what of truth, is overlooked. " Who," asks Mr. Locke, " is there, hardy enough to contend with the reproach which is ever prepared for him, who dares venture to dissent from the received opinions of his country and party? And where is the man to be found, that can patiently prepare himself to bear the names, that he is sure to meet with, who doth in the least scruple any of the common opinions?" Though many things are altered since the days of Locke, mankind are but little changed. In his days, indeed, the prejudices of the times ran towards opinions, which, acquiesed in by many succeeding generations, were, therefore, conceived to have a real plurality of judgments in their favor. Now, on the contrary, to have been believed from of old, is deemed to indicate defect, and that alone is admitted as of approved strength, which has not been subjected to the test of time. In this, nevertheless, there is a perfect agreement, that men appeal not so much to truth itself, as to prevalent opinion, and are disposed to treat whatever stands opposed to it, as necessarily erroneous. It were, then, in vain for me, I am aware, in reply to the charge of presumption in challenging the opinions to which the celebrated author of the *Wealth of Nations* has given currency, to answer, that it is not so, and that, on the contrary, " he is the general challenger :" that his disciples form, in reality, but a sect, one setting itself in opposition to the belief of all preceding ages, and in its rise and progress presenting nothing dissimilar to the other numerous sects, which time, in its course, has seen appearing and disappearing : that, therefore, if we really appeal to authority, its decision is against, not for, the present political creed. Such arguments would certainly fall on deaf ears. The authority, in which men acquiesce, is that which is present, and to which they have been accustomed to yield assent. Whatever is opposed to this, and separated from it by distance of time or space, has no influence on their judgments.

But, although, instead of assistance, I have to look for opposition, from this quarter, I nevertheless believe, that I have an auxiliary of great power on my side. In political questions, before they see that they are wrong, it is common for men to feel that they are so. The progress of recent events seems to have excited a general sensation of this sort over Great Britain.

. . . .

It is natural that these circumstances should beget a sort of feeling of doubt. That, without pretending to question the general truth of the system established by Adam Smith, many should yet ask themselves, is the path which he has pointed out, truly that which always leads directly to the wealth of nations? In this temper of the public mind, I am inclined to hope that the application of new principles to a reconsideration of the whole subject, may be conceived to be an undertaking deserving, at least, of being examined, and that the defects of the following pages may not be thought sufficient to prevent what measure of truth they may contain, from being perceived and appreciated.

MONTREAL, 1833.

POSTSCRIPT.

In the preceding pages, the reader has an explanation of the original design of the work which I venture to place before him; but, in preparing it for publication in this country, I have made some alterations in it, the nature of which it is proper I should here state.

The doctrines which Adam Smith maintained with so much ability, never took so deep hold in this country as in England, and they have been more strongly opposed. There is hence, a very considerable difference between the state of public sentiment in Great Britain and America, concerning the most interesting practical questions of political economy. This is especially the case with regard to the policy of the protective system. The practical bearings of that system on the condition of things in this republic, have been discussed so often, and with so much ability, that probably few new arguments or facts concerning it can be brought forward by any one, least of all can they be expected from a foreigner. Although, therefore, I look on the effects of the policy pursued by the legislature of the United States, as affording the best practical illustration hitherto existing of the correctness of some of the principles I maintain, I have scarcely at all referred to them for that purpose, but have contented myself with showing how the benefits resulting from the operations of the legislature, in this and in other similar cases, are to be accounted for. I have thus omitted much matter that would have appeared, had the work been published in England, but which it seemed to me, would be at least superfluous here. These omissions occur in the third book, which is consequently much abridged.

To the second book I have made some additions, having given fuller development to the principles there explained, and traced their connexion with events at greater length, than is necessary for the mere purpose of exposing the fallacies of the theoretical views, the refutation of which was originally my sole design. As the additions were made in the progress of the work through the press, in one or two instances I have been led to refer to subjects to be afterwards treated of, which I found it impossible to comprise within such limits as would admit of their insertion. These omissions, however, do not occasion any break in the chain of reasoning. There are, also, some topics, which though I have introduced, I have but partially discussed, and merely so far as may serve to show some of their connexions with principles expounded. The most important of these is the subject of banking.

Boston, 1834.

INTRODUCTION.

OF all the circumstances connected with the "Inquiry into the Wealth of Nations," there is no one more remarkable than the fact, that its celebrated author leaves us in doubt what he himself understands by that "wealth," the nature and causes of which it is the object of his inquiry to investigate. His followers have scarce been more fortunate. They have sought, by definitions, to remedy the acknowledged defect, but have been unable to agree in the terms of them. The school is thus split into many little sects at variance with each other regarding the very elements of the science.[1]

It seems to me that this circumstance arises from, and very clearly marks the existence of, a great and fundamental defect in the principles of investigation on which Adam Smith and the school he founded proceeded;—an uniform tendency to hold that up as an explanation of other things, which, in reality, is the very thing itself to be explained.

It is the nature of wealth in the general, and the laws regulating its increase and diminution, that can alone, as I conceive, form the proper subject of philosophical investigation. These being determined, from them may be deduced the manner in which particular societies, or particular individuals, come to possess this or that amount of wealth. But, though such is the proper philosophical view of the subject, it is not that under which it appears to common observers.

Before men begin to speculate, they are obliged to act. They are therefore first led, in regard to any system with

[1] [Rae here refers to a quotation from Lauderdale which is reproduced as "Note A" in the Appendix.]

which they have to do, to fix their attention altogether on the phenomena exhibited by it, without attempting to reach the causes of those phenomena. It is usually long after the events themselves have thus been observed and noted, that to trace their causes becomes the employment of philosophers. The mere sailor, for example, regards the winds simply as connected with the different seasons, the various regions of the globe, and the particular aspect of the heavens at the time. This makes up the sum of his knowledge concerning them, which, notwithstanding, may be very extensive and of great practical utility. It is not his object to inquire into the general causes producing all these phenomena, nor into the laws regulating the general system of things, of which they make a part, and so of ascertaining the true nature of the different winds, the real manner of their existence, and the measure of their force and duration. He believes that while that system endures as it is, his knowledge will serve to direct his practice, and this is all about which he concerns himself. An extensive practical knowledge of this sort here long preceded a philosophical knowledge of the subject. It has been the business of the latter, as it has at last had place, to ascertain the nature of wind itself, and the causes producing all the different winds, and acting on them For this purpose the philosopher has turned himself to the investigation of whatever, in the general system of things, is connected with that concerning which he inquires;—to the constitution and properties of the atmosphere;—the effects of changes of temperature on aeriform fluids;—the motions induced by these, by the rotatory movement of the globe, and by other circumstances. From them he deduces the true theory of wind, and shows that it is in accordance with the observations and rules of him, who has been accustomed to view the subject in its practical bearings alone, and tends to elucidate and simplify them.

In a somewhat similar manner wealth was felt and noted in its effects long before, as a circumstance largely affecting societies, it was proposed philosophically to investigate its nature and causes. To mark those effects, " riches " and a series of other terms of the sort, were invented. Like all every-day words and phrases they apply to the obvious aspects of particular facts and occurrences, and have no necessary reference to the causes of those facts and occurrences. All such speculations are foreign to mere practice, and never even enter into the explanations and reasonings of the merely practical man. However complicated the social system of which any person engaged in the acquisition of wealth makes a part, he has no difficulty in tracing the manner in which that portion of it which he possesses has been acquired, nor in explaining how it forms to him a certain amount of what he calls capital. But in giving this explanation, it will be observed that for the elements of his statements, he has always recourse to the existence and continuance of certain circumstances and regular trains of events in the general system of human society. What the things may be which give origin and regular succession to these events is a speculation lying out of his road, and on which he probably never enters. Though, therefore, he can easily tell how he got that which constitutes his wealth, and how to him it comes to be wealth, he will yet probably confess that he is unable to say what constitutes wealth in general, from whence it is derived, or what are the exact laws regulating its increase or diminution. These are questions of which the solution is very clearly shown to be of great difficulty from the mass of discordant opinions concerning them.[1]

Adam Smith, in this and in other instances, by transferring without hesitation, terms made use of to mark and explain the affairs of common life, to denote the great phenomena which the affairs of societies present, falls, as it seems to me, into two errors. In the first place, he in a great measure misses that which is the real object at which his inquiry aims, the investigation of the true nature and causes of national wealth, and shows, by holding out sometimes one notion of it and sometimes another, according to the different lights in which at different times the subject presents itself to him, that he has no very definite ideas concerning it. In the second place, he naturally, and in very many instances, falls into the error of taking, what in truth are the results of general laws governing the course of this class of events for the laws them-

[1] [See " Note B " of the Appendix.]

selves, and so of elevating effects into causes. His procedure is not very dissimilar to what that of a philosopher would have been, who, desiring to investigate the nature of wind, should have assumed it as already known, not as an event, but as a thing, and should have conceived it his business merely to connect and arrange the various phenomena in relation to it, with which practice had previously made mankind familiar. Such a system could not have failed to have embodied great radical defects, for it would have been built on principles fundamentally erroneous.

His followers, by the use they make of definitions, appear to me rather to have introduced new evils, than to have applied a remedy to those already existing. Definitions give us the mastery of words, not of things,[1] and therefore by taking them as they have done, for principles of investigation, not auxiliaries to it, their labors have generally issued in adducing arguments instead of collecting and arranging facts, the former being the proper fruit of an attention to words, the latter of an inquiry into the nature of things.

I conceive that the fallacies of the particular doctrines I oppose, may be most effectually exposed by tracing out the true nature of that wealth, the manner of the augmentation and diminution of which forms the subject of controversy; that we can neither assume this as a thing already known, nor hope, by any mere intellectual effort, to comprehend it in an ingenious definition; that when it is really discovered, it must be, as has happened in other things, that disputes concerning its manner of existence, its increase and decrease, will terminate, or, instead of hinging on plausible arguments, may be settled by a reference to ascertainable facts. It is, therefore, such an investigation, that I propose partially to attempt; and it is chiefly on the results of it, that I mean

---

[1] A sailor would never think it necessary to explain what wind is. Were he asked to do so, it is very probable he would answer "that which blows," and this would be a correct enough marking out of the meaning attached to the word. Mr. Say, in like manner, defines value as what a thing is worth. "Valeur des choses. C'est ce qu'une chose vaut." Riches, again, he defines an amount of values. "Richesse, c'est la somme des valeurs." Capital, an accumulation of values. Vide *Epitome des principes fondamentaux de l'economie politique.*

to rest my demonstration of the reality of those errors, the conviction of the existence of which has been my motive for engaging in the present undertaking.

. . . .

Dugald Stewart prefaces the observations he makes on Adam Smith's great work, with the following remarks: "An historical review of the different forms under which human affairs have appeared in different ages and nations, naturally suggests the question, whether the experience of former times may not now furnish some general principles to enlighten and direct the policy of future legislators? The discussion, however, to which this question leads, is of singular difficulty; as it requires an accurate analysis of by far the most complicated class of phenomena that can possibly engage our attention, those which result from the intricate and often the imperceptible mechanism of political society;—a subject of observation which seems, at first view, so little commensurate to our faculties, that it has been generally regarded with the same passive emotions of wonder and submission with which, in the material world, we survey the effects produced by the mysterious and uncontrollable operation of physical causes."[1] The science of Political Economy he considers as a part of this great subject.

If the accuracy of these observations be admitted, as I think it must, the inquiries in which Political Economy engages, lead to the investigation of the general principles of human action, and it is to be considered but as a branch of a larger science, having for its object, to trace the laws to which man is subject as a moral and intellectual animal, acted on by the system of things existing in the world, and acting in turn on them; to explain from those laws the events which his past history, as far as known, exhibits; and to collect the means of ascertaining what will be the future course of it. While to be able clearly to unfold the laws regulating the events with which it deals would imply the capacity of tracing those regulating the whole system of phenomena of which man is the centre, just as to explain with accuracy the laws regulating the motions of one of the heavenly bodies,

[1] *Life of Smith.*

implies the knowledge of principles capable of disclosing the prescribed movements of them all.

I have already observed, that the subject first met me when engaged in the investigation of some principles which I conceived might in time assume a form capable of a general application of the sort. To attempt here an extensive generalization of this kind would be out of place, and is impracticable, because of necessity only a small portion of the phenomena are before us. Political Economy itself makes but a part of the subject to which such generalizations belong, and it is only one division of political economy of which we are to treat. It has usually been discussed under the heads of stock, wages of labor, and rent, and it is to the first of these that our investigations are to be altogether confined. It is only therefore in such parts of the subject as present a sufficient mass of phenomena, to warrant the procedure, that I shall attempt to introduce any very general principles. In other cases I will confine myself to the simple statement of facts admitted by all parties.

CHAPTER I.

OF ECONOMIC AMBITION AND THE MEANS ESSENTIAL TO ITS REALIZATION.

CICERO gives the following summary of the principles exciting man to action, and of the mode in which they lead him to act:——"inter hominem et beluam hoc maxime interest, quod haec tantum, quantum sensu movetur, ad id solum, quod adest, quodque præsens est, se accommodat, paullulum admodum sentiens præteritum, aut futurum. Homo autem, quod rationis est particeps, per quam consequentia cernit, causas rerum videt, earumque progressus, et quasi antecessiones non ignorat, similitudines comparat, et rebus præsentibus adjungit atque annectit futuras: facile totius vitæ cursum videt, ad eamque degendam præparet res necessarias. Eademque natura vi rationis hominem conciliat homini et ad orationis, et ad vitæ societatem: ingeneratque in primis præcipuum quendam amorem in eos, qui procreati sunt: impellitque ut hominum cœtus, et celebrationes, esse, et a se obiri velit: ob easque causas studeat parare ea, quæ suppeditent et ad cultum, et ad victum: nec sibi soli, sed conjugi, liberis, ceterisque, quos caros habeat, tuerique debeat."

"The chief distinction between man and the inferior animals consists in this. They are moved only by the immediate impressions of sense, and, as its impulses prompt, seek to gratify them from the objects before them, scarce regarding the future, or endeavoring from the experience of the past to provide against what is to come. Man again, as he is endowed with reason, by which he is able to connect effects with their causes, to perceive the principles which guide the progress of affairs, and to join together the present and the future, easily discerns the course of his whole life and prepares whatever may be necessary for passing it in comfort. The same intellectual powers also, which nature has bestowed on him, give scope to his affections, and join him to his fellows by the ties that spring from language and the connexions of social life. It is from this source that we must trace his peculiar provident love for his offspring, his concern for the interests of society, and his desire to mingle in its business and pleasures.

"From these principles it is that man is incited and enabled to provide beforehand whatever may be requisite both for utility and ornament, not only to himself but to his wife, his children, and all others who may be dear to him, or whom it may be his duty to protect."

It is unquestionably the capacity for perceiving, and retaining in his mind, the course of events and the connexion of one with another, that leads man to perceive what advancing futurity is to bring forth, and enables him to provide for its wants. This provident forethought distinguishes him from the inferior animals, and the degree in which he possesses it marks his rank in the scale of civilization.[1]

When he has gained any knowledge of the nature of things [the operations of nature] around him, he finds many that satisfy more or less perfectly his present wants. He knows, also, that if he live to see the future he will then have similar wants and desires. Some of the occurrences satisfying his desires and wants exist abundantly; others, sparingly or imperfectly. If he regard the future, he must wish that those occurrences of which he now can only obtain enough to satisfy his wants sparingly and imperfectly, should exist then, so as that he might be able to obtain them to satisfy those wants abundantly and perfectly.

His faculties of observation and reason generally give him

[1] [In contrast to the animals "man has thoughts far-reaching, he has concerted and long-extended plans." (Fragment of Rae's MS.) The animals, indeed (notably ants, bees, and the like), exhibit a certain degree of "provident forethought;" but it is non-progressive. Man is characterized specifically by ever-expanding wants, and hence by ever-expanding undertakings to satisfy them.]

the power of effecting this. For the objects affording satisfaction of his desire are mere arrangements of matter. His faculties of observation show him their nature, and the manner in which the train of events going on amongst them succeed each other. He perceives that the occurrences which are the means of satisfaction of his present wants, or which were of those he felt a little time since, and which will probably be of those he will feel in future, are either the immediate result of the nature and form of some things around him, or of the trains of events which, in consequence of that form and nature, are taking place among them. He cannot alter the nature of things, but in many cases, he is able to change their form, that is, the particular arrangement of the matter of which they are formed; and his reason instructs him, that if by doing this, he can so alter the trains of events proceeding from them or depending on them, that they may either form, or cause to be formed, or put in his possession, objects fitted to supply more perfectly or abundantly what probably will be his future wants, than any objects that would otherwise exist, he then is able to provide for the future. This in many cases he can do, and thus he acts.

A North American Indian in his canoe comes to an island in some lake or river, and finds near it a good station for fishing. He therefore determines to remain there for the fishing season. Towards evening he paddles his canoe to shore, lands, kindles a fire near a large tree, wraps his blanket about him, places his feet to the fire, his head to the trunk of the tree, and thus prepares for repose. In so doing, with the exception of kindling the fire, he takes advantage simply of his knowledge of the nature of the things around him, and seeks from them the best supply they can give him of what he wants, that is, of shelter from wind and weather.

It rains and blows during the night, the tree shelters him somewhat, but still he gets cold and wet. In the morning he spends some hours providing a better shelter against the inclemency of any such night in future. Of branches and bark he makes something like one half of the roof of a house, only much smaller, the open side being towards the south and the fire, the sloping side towards the north from whence comes cold and rain. Thus, though he cannot prevent the wind from blowing, or the rain from falling, his knowledge of the manner in which the trains of events forming these phenomena succeed each other, or if you will, his knowledge of the laws which regulate their motions, instruct him so to direct them, that the one shall not blow, or the other fall, on a particular spot, which he knows he may at some future time wish to remain calm and dry. This time may be distant, for it may not rain or blow so as to inconvenience him for a week or two, nevertheless to provide against it he gives a good many hours present labor.

Next evening, before going to repose, he finds the turf damp from the rain of the former night. He looks for an elm tree, cuts off a piece of its strong thick bark large enough for him to sleep on, covers it with the soft branches and leaves of the white pine, and forms a dry and soft bed for himself. Thus his knowledge of the materials around him enables him to form what he wants, a dry and soft place of repose.

In this island he discovers a small wild plumb tree, he relishes the fruit, but there is little of it. Resolving to return in succeeding seasons he lops the branches of the surrounding trees to give this room to spread, and expects thus to find next year a more abundant crop.[1] Here his knowledge of the manner in which trees and fruit grow and thrive, or his knowledge of the order of the trains of events which terminate in the full development of the tree and abundance of its fruit, enables him so to work on the matters around him, as to occasion them to produce more abundantly next season, than they have this, what then he will desire.

He thinks not of providing for any future want the means to supply which, will, without this, exist in sufficient abundance. Thus water, in such a situation, he knows he will always be surrounded with. Were the same Indian encamped in the woods, by a very scanty spring, he would dam it up,

---

[1] This is a possible supposition, but it is more probable he would neglect it, perhaps cut it down for the sake of reaching more easily the fruit it carried.

and cover it with branches so as to keep cool a quantity of water for his future occasions.

The proceedings of man are everywhere similar. He has always an end in view, he employs means to effect this end, and there is a manner through which he effects it. The end is a supply for future wants; the means, the bringing about of such events as may serve to supply them; the manner, a knowledge of the qualities with which nature has endowed the materials within his reach, of the series of events in consequence arising among them, and an application of this knowledge to produce, through his corporeal powers, such an arrangement of these materials, as may so change the issues of events that would otherwise have place, as to bring about those which he desires. It is true, that, in most instances, men simply copy the proceedings of others, and think not of the principles on which they conduct their operations, nor of the observations from which these must originally have been deduced. But, though the knowledge thus acquired from this storing of observations, and deduction of principles from them, is not the mode in which individual men operate, it is the mode in which the operations they carry on must have been first brought into practice, and on which they are all founded.

We may easily satisfy ourselves of this, by turning our attention to the manner in which any of the articles we use for the supply of our wants has been formed. Bread may be an example. A farmer, some two years ago, made choice of a particular field for the cultivation of wheat. Had he been asked why he did so, he could have stated the different circumstances in the soil, and the previous crops that it had carried, which had thus determined him. By ploughing and harrowing it a sufficient number of times, he thoroughly broke, and pulverized the land. This he did, because he knew, from observations he or others had made, that in this state the seed he intended to deposit there would when it came to germinate, more easily spread its roots around and draw nourishment from among the particles of earth amidst which it would grow. He allowed a considerable time to elapse between the several operations, that the weeds might have time to spring up and be destroyed. Thus he knew they would be prevented from afterwards injuring the growth of the crop. He also spread over the field, and covered in, a quantity of manure, because experience had taught that this substance gives vigor to vegetation. He then sowed the seed, in the mode, and quantity, and at the time, which observation had instructed him was the best, covered it with a harrow, and waited the harvest. When he perceived the grain sufficiently ripe, he cut it down with an iron hook having a form and edge which experience had ascertained to be best adapted for this purpose, made it into bundles, exposed them to the sun and air so that they might be dried, when this was effected, conveyed them to his barn and stored them there. Having lain there some time, the grain was separated from the straw by the process of threshing, it was then carried to the granary, where, having been kept for a longer or shorter period, it was thence taken to the mill, and, by a very ingenious process, reduced to small particles, and then separated by another process into three parts, of which the finest part, the interior of the grain called flour, being packed in sacks or barrels, was preserved for use. A certain portion of this, mixed with a particular ferment, wrought with the hand and exposed to the action of fire, became bread.

It is very evident, that all the steps of these various processes depend on a knowledge of the course of natural events, and are regulated by that knowledge. A long series of observations of this sort, and of reasonings deduced from them, could alone have enabled the farmer to prepare the ground properly for the seed, or, after the grain had come to maturity, to preserve it, to separate it from the straw, and fit it for being converted into flour. The observations on the trains of events connected with the production of this grain that have been committed to writing, fill many large volumes, and besides these, every farmer is obliged to have a great store of his own, to guide him in his proceedings. Thus, in the single process of cutting down and storing up this crop, his success in securing it uninjured depends on observing and noting well a great variety of particulars.

He observes the plant carefully, and discovers, from the appearance of every part, from the dryness of the stem, the drooping of the ears, the fulness of the grain, if it be in a proper state to cut down. If he make any error in this, he will either have unripe, and therefore shrivelled and light grain, or he will lose great part of it by its being shaken off the stem in harvesting it. Next, before he determine on commencing the operation, he regards the aspect of the sky, watches the rising and setting sun, notes the color of the air, the appearance of the clouds, the direction of the wind, the dew on the grass, and perhaps has recourse to that delicate instrument, the fruit of so many ingenious observations, the barometer. By means of all these, he is enabled to draw tolerably correct conclusions, in regard to the probable state of the weather for some succeeding days. This knowledge influences greatly his farther operations; for experience has taught him that the injury which severe rains, coming on the grain when newly reaped, would occasion, is very great. If, therefore, the weather promise to be fine, he will commence cutting it down a few days sooner than he otherwise would; if rain threaten he will wait a few days longer. When he has it reaped he gets it tied into bundles, which are put up in small parcels, and so disposed, that the wind may penetrate through them, and the rain be as much thrown off from them as possible, and thus the plant may have the best chance of being securely and quickly dried.

This drying is watched with care, and, when it is judged to be sufficiently advanced, the crop is transported to the barn, there to wait till the proper period of threshing it out arrives. All these processes are, it is evident, governed by rules drawn from assiduous and long continued observation, and their success depends on its extent and accuracy.

Were we to examine the manner in which all the articles that we provide for the supply of future wants are produced, we should find that they depend, in this way, on observations on the course of events, and on reasonings founded on these observations. Were proof wanting of this, we might turn at hazard to any complete treatise on any art. On examining it, we would invariably find it to contain a set of observations, the result of experience, and of reasonings, and rules, drawn from these observations.

Since then man provides a supply for his future wants by his reason directing his industry, through means of his knowledge of the course of events, to effect such changes in the form or arrangement of the parts of material objects, that these may produce articles fitted to afford this supply, it were desirable to have some common name to denote all the changes, which, for this purpose, he so makes. On this account I propose to give the denomination of instruments to all those changes that, for this purpose are made in the form or arrangement of the parts of material objects.[1]

The term instrument is, in general, properly enough employed, to denote any means for the attainment of some end. In common use, however, and as applied to material things, it seems to be restricted to such arrangements of matter as owe their chief efficacy to what are called the mechanic powers. Thus a lever or a wedge is an instrument, the manner in which each of them operate being chiefly explained on mathematical principles. A spade, which is a combination of the two, is also an instrument. The tools which carpenters use are instruments. We speak in the same way of instruments of husbandry, meaning by the phrase the articles used in that art, whose properties may be explained on mechanical principles.

In all these cases, however, other principles than those which are merely mathematical must enter into our calculations. In the simplest lever we have not only the properties of a mathematical line to consider, but also, the weight and strength of the substance used, and these make the difficulty in the proper application of such an instrument. A wedge operates in many ways, besides those that may be considered to be derived simply from mathematical principles; as for instance in the percussion, which it receives and communicates, and through

---

[1] [Our author does not express himself well here. Rae's idea is that he proposes to give the denomination of *instrumental production* to all those changes in materials which man makes in the pursuit of his economic ends. The instruments themselves are not the "changes," but the immediate result of them.]

means of which, if skilfully applied, the most solid rocks may be rent. The farther we recede from such simple instruments, the more extensive do we find the action of properties, which could only be ascertained by a long series of observations. It would be impossible, for instance, to give any *a priori* rules for the construction of that most useful instrument the plough. It is, no doubt, a wedge, but the particular form giving the greatest efficacy to it, is a point of very difficult determination, not yet, perhaps, fully ascertained. It is accurate observation that has guided the construction of it, to its present efficiency, and which may be expected to render it still more perfect.

Were we to enter into an examination of more complicated machines or instruments, such as the steam engine, or the cotton mill, the observation would apply with double force, these generally deriving their efficiency from principles, that have been the result of very extensive and accurate investigations of many series of events. In thus using the term, therefore, we shall rather deviate somewhat from common usage, than be opposed to it; and in doing so, our reasonings will only be subject to an inconvenience, to which all general reasonings must be subject, and which may be the more readily excused, as this use of the term may be defended from its derivation, its occasional acceptation, and the authority of authors of respectability.[1]

In general then, all those changes which man makes, in the form or arrangements of the parts of material objects, for the

---

[1] *Outils* ou *instrumens de métier*. Jamais mot n'a reçu une acception plus étendue que celle que je voudrais donner ici au terme d'outils, car je desirerais y comprendre depuis la fronde dont se sert le chasseur sauvage jusqu'à la machine la plus vaste, jusqu'au mécanisme le plus compliqué, jusqu'aux êtres animés mêmes qui facilitent le travail de l'homme. L'enclume du forgeron et le métier pour faire des bas, les aiguilles de la lingère et les pompes à feu, les navires et les bêtes de somme et de trait ; en un mot, tout produit matériel de la nature et du travail, tout objet vivant ou inanimé que l'homme emploie pour s'aider dans son travail industriel, voilà ce que j'appelle outils, instrumens de métier. Ce mot, dans son sens le plus étendu, n'exclut que les constructions."* *Storch*, Vol. I. p. 231.

* "Pourquoi les exclure? Les constructions sont des produits de l'industrie humaine consacrés à la reproduction ; partant ce sont des outils. Un champ lui-même est un outil qui ne diffère des autres qu'en ce qu'il n'est point un produit de l'industrie, mais un don de la nature." J.-B. Say.

purpose of supplying his future wants, and which derive their power of doing this from his knowledge of the course of events, and the changes which his labor, guided by his reason, is hence enabled to make in the issue of these events, may be termed instruments.[1]

In this sense a field [fitted for use] is an instrument. The changes effected in the matters of which it, [considered as mere land,] is composed, for the purpose of rendering it an instrument, are the levelling and if necessary making the surface dry by means of ditches and drains, the removing stones from it, the mixing and pulverizing the soil by the plough, the harrow, and the roller, and the incorporating with it various matters termed manures, which render it more fit for the support of vegetable life. The future wants, towards the supply of which it is an instrument, are food and clothing. The power which has made it an instrument, is the agriculturist's labor, directed by his knowledge of the nature of plants and soils. The change made in the consequent issue of events, is the abundant growth of species of plants different from those originally produced by it, and conducing to the supply of food and clothing; or, more generally, the conversion of various vegetable matters of the soil, and gaseous matters in the air, into the substance of particular plants. The wheat grown on this field is an instrument. The changes effected in it, are its having been separated from the straw by the process of threshing, and its having been made sufficiently dry by keeping and exposure to air, to be fit to manufacture into flour. The want it tends to supply is nourishment, by affording bran for the support of some of the inferior animals, as hogs or cattle, afterwards to be slaughtered, and flour for the use of man. The power is also the art and industry of the agriculturist. The change in the issue of events consists in the grain being ready for the manufacture of flour, instead of having been left to rot on the ground, to be consumed by vermin, or destroyed by the access of damp or by the want of air. Flour also is an instrument. The changes that have been effected in it are its having been separated from the wheat, and reduced to a fine powdery matter. The want it

[1] [More properly, may be termed the formation and use of instruments.]

tends to supply is food by the bread produced from it. The power, which has operated on it, is the art and industry of the miller. The change in the issue of events thereby produced is the existence of flour and bran, instead of wheat. Bread, until such time as it is in process of consumption, is an instrument. The change which it has undergone is that induced by the processes of kneading, fermenting, and baking. The want it supplies is food. The power which has operated on it is the art and industry of the baker. The change on the issue of events thereby produced is the existence of bread instead of flour.

Though it may seem strange to rank all these in one class, that of instruments, nevertheless, the doing so is rather unusual than improper. They are all means towards the attainment of an end, and, for the attainment of this end, that is, the production of bread, do they alone exist. The blade as it springs from the soil, and the [prepared] soil on which it grows, form together an instrument for this end; the plant when it has extracted all the nourishment from the soil which that can give, and is ripe on the ground, is an instrument; when it is cut and put up sheltered from the weather, it is still an instrument; so is the grain when separated from it; so it is when ground in the mill; so it is when in loaves, put apart for consumption, until the moment arrives when it is consumed. It is impossible, if we call it at first an instrument, to point out when it ceases to be so, until the moment when it is actually consuming.

All tools and machines are instruments. Thus a carpenter's saw is an instrument. The changes effected in the matters of which it is composed, for the purpose of rendering it an instrument, are, there having been given a fit form and temper to the steel plate of which it is made, and a handle having been adjusted to it. The wants which it tends to supply are multifarious, according to the uses to which it is put. The power that renders it an instrument is the art and industry of him who makes, and of him who uses it. The changes effected in the issue of events by its fabrication and use, are the dividing into regular parts suited to different purposes, a great number of pieces of timber.

In a similar manner it might be shown, that houses, ships, cattle, gardens, household furniture, manufactories, manufactured goods, and stores of all sorts are in this sense, instruments. But it is, I apprehend, unnecessary further to multiply instances; every thing that man, for the purpose of gaining an end, brings to exist, or alters in its form, its position, or in the arrangement of its parts, is an instrument.

As man is thus enabled to provide for the wants of futurity, by his knowledge of the course of events, it naturally follows, that in any particular situation, his power to provide for them, is measured by the extent and accuracy of his knowledge. If that knowledge be diminished, his power will be diminished. Thus a deficiency of skill in the art of agriculture, or of baking, will alike occasion a diminution of the quantity of food to be got from a field applied to the cultivation of wheat. Neither can his power be increased, but by an increase of his knowledge. It is impossible to point out any improvement in any art, which does not depend on some new observations, or reasonings, on the course of events connected with that art.

The generally admitted axiom, that knowledge is power, may not be strictly true. Many facts have been observed which have not yet been applied to any useful purpose, though it is probable they will, in time, be so applied. But, though it may not be strictly true, that all knowledge immediately gives power, it is so, that all power springs from knowledge, and is measured by its extent and accuracy. Neither can it be disputed, that it operates by enabling man's reasoning faculties, so to direct his industry, as to induce certain changes in the form and arrangement of the parts of material objects converting them into instruments. "Ad opera nil aliud potest homo, quam ut corpora naturalia admoveat et amoveat; reliqua natura intus transigit."

[Rae's language in the last few pages is not wholly consistent with his general teaching. The "want" which bread supplies is not properly speaking "food" (that is really only another name for bread), but the pleasure of eating and the sense of being nourished. These last are the artifically produced "events" which are the final goal of the long series of adaptations of means to ends. Not until bread has been eaten does it cease to be a part of that great and complicated mass of apparatus which Rae calls instruments, and which are usually known as economic goods.]

CHAPTER II.

OF THE CIRCUMSTANCES COMMON TO ALL INSTRUMENTS, AND OF THOSE PROPER TO SOME.

ALL instruments agree in the following three particulars;

1. They are all either *directly* formed by human labor, or *indirectly* through the aid of other instruments themselves formed by human labor.

Sometimes, though rarely, instruments are constructed by labor alone. Thus occasionally rough stone fences are put up, by the hand alone, without the intervention of even a single tool. But, in most instances, the aid of other instruments is employed. It is seldom, that even the most common laborer is not assisted in his operations by some implement or another. But, whatever instrument or instruments may have cooperated with labor in the formation of any other instrument, they themselves have been either altogether, or in part, formed by labor; and, by retracing the course of things farther and farther back, we inevitably come to the conclusion, that labor was, in this sense, "the first price, the original purchase money that was paid for all things," and thus that, directly or indirectly, it is to be looked on as the agent that gives form to every instrument.[1]

---

[1] [Rae is here dealing with a restricted aspect of the larger problem. He is perfectly aware, as the context indicates and as he shows more fully elsewhere that the universal cost of getting wants supplied is labor (mental and physical) together with waiting and the running of risk,—three elements which are present in every stage of the total process of production, in the formation of instruments as well as in the utilization of them. But here, where he deals

For the sake of simplifying the succeeding speculations, as much as may be, labor will be considered as the agent employed in the formation of all instruments. When the cooperation of other instruments is implied in the means by which any particular instrument is constructed, the degree in which they cooperate is understood to be measured by the quantity of labor for which their cooperation is, or might be, procured; and, in this sense, that cooperation is spoken of as an equivalent to labor. The rules, according to which the one thus measures the other, will be discussed subsequently.

2. All instruments bring to pass, or tend, or help, to bring to pass events supplying some of the wants of man, and are then exhausted.

Some instruments once formed, without the further intervention either of labor or of other instruments, produce events which directly supply our wants. Thus a peach tree yields its fruit to our hand. The operation of others only tends to the production of events supplying our wants. The growth of a crop of wheat is only a step towards the production of bread. Others require the help of either labor, or some other instrument. A row boat is useless without the labor of the man who plies the oar; a carriage, without the cooperation of the horses who draw it. All instruments, however, either produce, or contribute to the production, of events supplying some of our wants. Their power to produce such events, or the amount of them that they do produce, may be termed their *capacity*.[1]

It is necessary to have some common measure for the

only with the formation of instruments, for the sake of convenience, he leaves waiting and risk-taking out of account. He assumes for the purpose of getting the basis for a certain method of comparison of instruments in general, that instruments are all formed at one moment of time and that the technical and mercantile outcome of their formation is certain.]

[1] [The technical expression "capacity" of instruments is used by Rae here and elsewhere ambiguously. There is a decided difference between the "power to produce" or to further the production, of certain desirable events, that is, the initial capacity or yielding-power or productivity of a thing; and the whole "amount" of such events actually yielded during the life of an instrument, that is, its total output, its total capacity. Sometimes Rae means one, sometimes the other; but as a rule the latter. See Chapter V.]

GENERAL PROPERTIES OF INSTRUMENTS 21

purpose of comparing the capacity of instruments or the returns that are made by them, with the labor or its equivalents that went to form them. For this purpose, also, labor will be adopted, and the events brought to pass by any instrument will be estimated by the amount of labor to which they are esteemed equivalent by the owner of the instrument. As we proceed, it will appear, that this use of the term has no other effect than that of giving distinctness to our nomenclature. Besides, it often really happens, that the returns made by instruments directly compare with labor, because they directly save labor. For instance, wooden or metal pipes are occasionally used to conduct water from a spring to some dwelling-house. Were they not there, the water would have to be carried within the dwelling by some of the domestics, and therefore the instrument formed by the pipes may be said indifferently, either to supply a certain amount of water, or save a certain portion of labor.

With one considerable exception, afterwards to be noted, all instruments at length bring to pass, or aid in bringing to pass, all the events which they can bring, or can help to bring to pass. I shall use the term *exhaustion*, to denote this passage of things from the class of instruments, into things which are not instruments. When an instrument is said to be exhausted, it is meant that the matters of which it was composed have passed out of the class of instruments into that of materials.

Sometimes they pass from the one class to the other suddenly. Thus, articles used for food and fuel, bring to pass all the events for which they were formed, very shortly. The appetite of hunger is gratified, and heat is communicated to the frame, in a few minutes, and the faggot and the bread, having yielded all the nourishment and heat stored up in them, then cease to be instruments. Gunpowder brings certain events to an issue instantaneously. The bullet is discharged, and the rock split, in an instant. This sudden and complete exhaustion of the capacity of instruments is what is usually termed consumption. Sometimes the matters of which instruments are formed pass from the class of instruments to that of materials by degrees. Thus tools and articles of wearing apparel are in use for a long time before they cease to be instruments. A saw may be in employment for years; a hat defends the head for months. When the capacity of instruments is thus gradually exhausted, it is usually said that they are worn out, and this sort of exhaustion is termed wear.

Sometimes the capacity of instruments is accidentally done away with, and they consequently pass out of the class of instruments, without being exhausted. Thus a house may be burned, cloth may be eaten by vermin. They are then said to be destroyed. A partial degree of this is damage. In calculating the capacity of instruments, it is necessary to reckon the risk they run of destruction or damage. In any estimation of the capacity, for instance, of a crop of wheat, we have to make as accurate an allowance as may be, for the risk of its destruction or damage, by the inclemency of the weather or other accidents, before the harvesting of it be accomplished.[1]

3. Between the formation and exhaustion of instruments a space of time intervenes. This necessarily happens because all events take place in time. Sometimes that space extends to years, sometimes to months, occasionally to shorter periods, but it always exists.

The circumstances we have hitherto assumed as common to all instruments, and the events they generate, will, I believe, on examination, be found actually to be so. There is one circumstance, however, which it is necessary to assume as common to them all, and which in reality is not altogether so. In comparing the capacity of two or more instruments, which supply, or tend to supply, wants of the same sort, we may very often measure them by the relative physical effects, resulting from the action of the events brought to pass by

---

[1] [It is also necessary, especially in the case of machinery, to take into account the risk of an instrument being superseded through new inventions. In every progressive industry great masses of instruments are constantly being thrown on the junk heap long before they are worn out.

But this is taking the point of view of the individual rather than that of society. The community gains, as regards the capacity of its instruments, through a rapid advance of the arts; although individuals (particularly those with the least powers of adaptation) suffer pecuniary loss. Rae has in mind, obviously, losses which nobody gains.]

GENERAL PROPERTIES OF INSTRUMENTS   23

them. Thus, if the consumption of one cord of fire wood, of a particular sort, is capable of producing exactly double the heat which the consumption of another cord of another sort produces, a cord of the former, will have double the capacity of a cord of the latter, and, if the one be equivalent to four, the other will be equivalent to exactly two days labor. In the same way, a log of timber from Norway, about to be employed in the construction of a house, if of equal size, strength, and durability, with another from Prussia, may, with justice be considered as of equal capacity to it; and so of many other instruments. We shall see afterwards, however, that this mode of determining the capacity of similar instruments, is in many cases incorrect, and that the instances are very numerous, where the relative capacities of instruments of the same sort, depend on other causes than their mere physical properties. The assumption, therefore, that they may be so determined, is to be considered as hypothetical, and to be tolerated from the difficulty of otherwise treating the subject; in the same manner as the hypothetic existence of strictly mathematical lines, and the absence of friction and of the resistance of the air, is excused, in reasonings concerning the mechanical properties of matter. As in these reasonings, an attempt will be made to ascertain the extent, and mode of operation of those other causes; and, having traced what seem to be the great moving powers, and the laws governing them, we shall endeavor to discover the circumstances which retard or derange their motions.

It may be proper here to notice the acceptation, in which two other terms of frequent subsequent occurrence, are to be received. Some instruments are easily moved from place to place, and, on this account, there are peculiar facilities, in exchanging them with others. This seems to be the character distinguishing what are called goods, or commodities, from other instruments, and it is in this sense, that these terms will, in the subsequent pages, be employed.

[It is not through inadvertence that several times during this chapter Rae speaks of events which instruments "produce." His notion of production, made abundantly clear elsewhere, excludes the part man plays, and has reference only to the part played by the instrument—its functioning, its bringing things to pass as the last link in the chain of causation. His formula for the total process which we call production would be: man forms and directs instruments, which last produce events which constitute satisfactions of want, or, events leading toward satisfactions of want. It is desirable to make such a distinction, but without running counter to accepted terminology. For the part played by instruments, Rae himself, in this chapter and elsewhere, incidentally supplies us with an appropriate name,—generation. "The circumstances we have hitherto assumed as common to all instruments, and the events they generate. . . ."]

CHAPTER III.

OF CERTAIN CIRCUMSTANCES ARISING FROM THE INSTITUTION OF SOCIETY.

1. MAN hardly exists but in the social state. If separated from infancy from his fellows, his peculiar faculties scarcely at all develop themselves. His mental and bodily capacities and energies seem, also, to be moulded by the condition of the society of which he is a member. We may venture to predict, that three children born tomorrow, one in Caffraria, another in China, and a third in London, and remaining in their respective countries till the age of twenty, will be very different beings, and that each will possess the mental and bodily peculiarities, that characterize the particular community to which he belongs. The same things, though in a lesser degree, hold true concerning the men composing every nation. Whether these characteristics of different races, tribes, and peoples, proceed altogether from some peculiar hereditary conformation of the bodily organs, or from the effects of education, example, and habit, or from the combination of these, or from other causes, it is very certain that they exist, and that the moral and intellectual condition, as well as the bodily organization of men, vary, as they belong to this, or that society. Besides this, institutions, forms of government, and laws, influence somewhat the genius, and considerably affect the conduct, of every people, and these also are very various. It thus happens that every society has, what may be termed, a distinctive character of its own.

It is therefore assumed, in the succeeding investigations,

that the moral and intellectual powers, the knowledge, the habits and dispositions of the men composing every separate community, society, nation, state, or people (terms which, as far as our subject is concerned, may be considered synonymous), are such as to give it a peculiar character distinguishing it from other communities. It is also assumed, that the average character of the members of different portions of the same community is similar, so that, were a considerable number of the inhabitants of any particular state, taken from one part of its territories, they would closely resemble an equal number, taken from any other part. This latter assumption is not exactly accurate. There are great differences, especially in extensive states, between the characters of the inhabitants of different portions of the same territory. These diversities render it sometimes necessary to modify the conclusions that follow from considering the average character of the members of the same community as perfectly similar. Thus, the differerent characters of the inhabitants of England, Ireland, and Scotland, affect somewhat deductions in this subject, drawn from treating the characters of the population of different parts of Britain as uniform. In truth, every large society might be divided into several smaller societies, differing somewhat from each other. If they differ in some particulars, however, they agree in many more, and certain results follow from this agreement, which make it convenient to treat of them as one. If necessary too, the amount of the inaccuracy, arising from the assumption of a more perfect uniformity than exists, may be ascertained.

2. Man, as an organic being, is governed by laws similar to those which other organic beings obey. Our subject obliges us to advert to a consequence arising from one of them.

In the midst of the numerous revolutions and accidents to which the surface of the globe is subject, it is always abundantly replenished with animal and vegetable life, and the numbers of every race upon it are kept up to the quantity of materials fit for their subsistence which it affords them. The increase and decrease of the human species, follows the general law. This seems to be the foundation of what has been termed the doctrine of population. In the subsequent pages it is received, simply as a statement of the fact, that the numbers of every society increase, as what its members are inclined to esteem a sufficient subsistence, is provided for them.[1]

The great majority of the members of every community, procure their subsistence by labor, and, according to this principle, the number of laborers in every community must finally depend on the amount of those things esteemed by them sufficient for their subsistence, which is annually distributed among them. It has been supposed, however, that there is a constant oscillation above and below this limit, and that sometimes therefore the supply having to be divided among a greater number, the amount that each receives is less, sometimes, having to be divided among a smaller number, is greater, and thus that the wages of labor, though they always tend towards a fixed standard, never remain at it. Admitting that this continual vibration may take place, I conceive I may be permitted nevertheless to disregard it, and to assume that the remuneration awarded the laborer, is, in the same society, always a fixed quantity. As it is not intended to enter into any investigation of the principles determining the amount of the wages of labor in all societies, and at all times, nor to discuss the somewhat contradictory doctrines that have been maintained on this subject, the most simple assumption, and that, the errors arising from which may be supposed to balance each other, seems the best.

Even considering the subject however under the most simple conditions possible, there are still some difficulties attending it. The articles which the laborer uses, for food, clothing, etc., and which constitute his real wages, are continually varying. Thus, among the working classes in Great Britain, fabrics of cotton have, in a great measure, taken the place of those of linen, and wool for clothing; as coal has taken the place of wood for fuel. Seeing there is this change in what constitute the wages of labor, how then, it may

---

[1] [This is an uncritical following of the teaching of Malthus upon which Rae made a great advance in his later years. (Compare the last part of Chapters VI. and XIII., and the Article on Population in the Appendix.)]

be demanded, can wages at any two times be considered equal?

In answer to such a question, it may be observed in general, that all articles supplying the wants of the laborer, and forming his real wages, are fitted for this purpose by some physical qualities they possess, producing certain effects on his bodily organs, and through them, occasionally, on the perceptions and thoughts of his mind. One article, therefore, may be esteemed equal to another and different article, if the effects produced by both are equal. Thus a certain quantity of coal, may be considered equal to another of wood, if each gives out the same degree of heat. In many cases it is indeed very difficult to make this comparison with accuracy. This however is not absolutely necessary for our purpose, it being sufficient to conceive, that, what are termed the wages of labor, in the same society at different periods, are really equal quantities, whether we have, or have not, the means of measuring them, and ascertaining that they actually are so. This may evidently be assumed, if we suppose that the laborer is equally well nourished, clothed, lodged, and instructed, and has equal leisure, at the one period and at the other; whether he be fed, clothed, and lodged, in the same way or not.

As the vigor of mind and body, as well as the skill, of different individuals in the same society, are unequal, the rate of the wages of labor, even in the same society, is far from uniform. It is however difficult and in general reasonings unnecessary, continually to refer to this variety; and as it has, in consequence, been usually neglected, we shall not farther advert to it.

According to the preceding assumptions, labor, in the same society, is to be considered as an invariable quantity, and a day's labor as the unit, serving as the base for calculations, concerning the formation and exhaustion of the capacity of instruments. It is to be observed, however, that when so employed, it finally refers, not to the mental and corporeal effort exerted throughout the day by the laborer, but to the wages received by him. The laborer is, usually, merely the agent of some other person, and that other person is, in reality, the one forming the instrument constructed, as the wages of the laborers employed by him are the causes of its being constructed.[1] In cases, too, where the laborer works for himself, he rates his daily labor equal to a certain amount of some of the things he is in the habit of consuming, and this amount may be considered, as what he really gives to the construction of the instrument, in the formation of which he employs himself.

The rates of wages vary, very much, in different societies. A Chinese laborer, for example, subsists on very much less than an English laborer. On the principles of calculation which we have adopted, there is, therefore, a difference, in the quantity embraced by a day's labor in one country and in another, and we cannot immediately compare, by this means, instruments formed in one society, with those formed in another. Our system has, in this respect, an analogy to the different systems of numeration, with regard to weights, measures, and coins, adopted in different countries. It will, as we proceed, appear, that this diversity in the rate of wages, in different communities, has also other and more important effects.

3. Every society possesses a certain amount of materials capable of being converted into instruments. The surface of its territory, the various minerals lying below the surface, its natural forests, its waters, the command it may have of the ocean, and its consequent property in the minerals and animals contained in it, the rain that waters its soil, the elementary principles that may be extracted from the atmosphere, even, perhaps, the light and heat of the sun, are all to be regarded as materials, which, through the agency of the labor of its members, may be converted into instruments. The extent of the power, which the inhabitants of any state may possess, to convert into instruments the materials of which they have the command is however

[1] [This is one of the comparatively few places where Rae speaks specifically of "laborers" and touches upon the function of the *entrepeneur*. It is not "man" in general but the *entrepeneur*, in our state of civilization, who forms instruments from materials with the aid of hired "labor," which last thus becomes economically an analogue of "materials."]

variable; and increases, as we have seen, as their knowledge of the properties of these materials and of the events, which in consequence of them, they are capable of bringing to pass, increases. Thus the large extent of the knowledge of the civilized man, compared with that of the savage or barbarian, gives him the power of constructing a much greater number of instruments out of the same materials, and enables the European emigrant to convert the soil and forests of America or New Holland, into means of producing a great mass of desirable events, which it was beyond the technical capacity of the ignorant native to effect.

CHAPTER IV.

A METHOD FOR THE COMPARISON OF INSTRUMENTS.

As by the capacity of instruments is to be understood their power to produce, or bring to an issue, events equivalent to a certain amount of labor, and as they are also formed by labor, it is evident that the capacity given to any of them, and the labor expended in its formation, have determinable numerical relations to each other. The length of time likewise, elapsing between their formation and exhaustion, may be expressed in numbers. If a series then were devised, of such a nature, that any relation that can exist among these three quantities, in consequence of their varying proportions to each other, might be embraced in it, every possible instrument would find a place there.

It is to be observed that, in consequence of a principle soon to be explained, no instruments will be designedly formed, but such as have a greater capacity, or issue in events equivalent to more, than the labor expended in their construction. This circumstance renders the formation of such a series more easy, as it renders it unnecessary to take account of any other instruments than such as issue in events equivalent to more than the labor expended in their formation, or, what may be termed, the cost of their formation. To simplify the consideration of the matter, we may, for a little, proceed on the supposition, that every instrument is constructed at one precise point of time, and exhausted at another. In that case, every instrument would find a place, in some part of a series, of which the orders were determined by the period of time at which instruments placed in them, issue, or would issue, if not before exhausted, in events equivalent to double the labor expended in forming them. These orders may be represented by the letters A, B, C, * * Z a, b, c, etc. The relation to each other of the cost of formation, the capacity, and the time elapsing between the period of formation and that of exhaustion, of instruments in the order A, is such as may be expressed by saying, they in one year issue in events equivalent to double the labor expended on their formation, or would so issue, if not before exhausted. The relation between these, in instruments of the order B, is such, that in two years they issue in events equivalent to double the labor expended on them, and are then exhausted. Instruments in the order C, in three years issue in events equivalent to double the cost of formation; of the order D, in four years; of the order Z, in twenty-six years; of the order a, in twenty-seven years, etc. For the sake of facility of expression, instruments in the order A, or in the orders near it, will be said to belong to the more quickly returning orders; instruments in the order Z, or in the orders near it, or beyond it, will be said to belong to the more slowly returning orders.[1]

To imagine, in the first place, as simple a case as possible. An individual, say an Indian trader, is obliged to reside on a particular spot in the interior of North America, for somewhat more than a year. He arrives in autumn, and immediately sets about enclosing and digging up a piece of ground, for the purpose of having it planted with maize. He expends on this twenty days' labor. That labor he reckons equivalent to ten bushels of maize. He gets the maize planted, hoed and harvested next season, by Indian women, agreeing to give them part of the crop. After deducting their portion he has twenty bushels for himself, with which he leaves the place. The field he formed was then an instrument of the order A. The same individual has to reside a little more than two years

---

[1] [A more correct expression would be the "more quickly" or "more slowly" *doubling* "orders." The degree of speed with which an instrument yields returns, or the physical results of its functioning, is only one of the factors which determines the time in which it affords double the outlay on its formation, and which places it in a certain order.]

in another quarter of the interior. He clears, or has cleared on his arrival, another piece of ground, and also expends on this operation twenty days' labour. Owing however to the soil being overrun with small roots, and it being necessary to wait till they partially rot before a crop can be put on it, he is aware that it cannot be planted until the second year. It is then planted as before, and, as it happens, with the same event as in the former field, yielding him net twenty bushels of maize. This field then was an instrument of the order B. In the same way it is possible to conceive the formation and exhaustion of other instruments of this sort, answering to the orders C, D, E, etc., the capacity of them all being double the cost of formation, and the times intervening between the periods of formation and exhaustion, being respectively three, four, five, etc. years. Although, however, instruments exactly corresponding to the conditions assumed, may occasionally exist, and although it is possible at least to conceive their existence throughout a lengthened series, yet, in fact, they seldom do exist so as exactly to answer the suppositions. In by far the greater number of instances, neither are the times elapsing between the periods of formation and exhaustion, any exact number of years, nor are the capacities exactly double the cost of formation. But, in all variations of these three quantities from an exact correspondence with any of the orders, the proportions existing between them, will, nevertheless, always be such, as to make it possible to reduce the instruments in which they occur, to some order or another in our series, or to an order that may be interposed between two proximate orders.

Such variations may be reduced to three sorts. The first consists of instances where the capacity is double the cost of production, but the time, no exact number of years. In this case, the instrument does not exactly belong to any of the enumerated orders, but falls between two proximate orders: it may therefore be said to belong to an order, that may be supposed to be interposed between these two. Thus, an instrument being exhausted in between seven and eight years, and having a capacity equal to double the cost of production, might be said to belong to an order lying between G and H.

c

This designation would mark its character with sufficient accuracy for our purpose.

There are only two other cases. The capacity of the instrument may be exhausted before it arrive at an amount equal to double the cost of formation, or, it may not be exhausted until it has come to an amount greater than double the cost of formation. In the former case it is necessary to suppose the period of exhaustion prolonged, the excess of the capacity of the instrument over the cost of formation increasing at the same ratio, until the capacity double the cost. It will then be shown to belong to some particular order, or to lie between two proximate orders. Thus, let an individual have it in his power to make use of a small plot of ground for six months, and let him expend an equivalent to two days' labor in preparing it for receiving the seeds of some plant, sowing them, and cultivating the crop, and let it return him, at the end of six months, an amount, which, reduced to the value of days labor, would be 2·828. If then we suppose the period of exhaustion prolonged, the excess of the capacity over the cost increasing at the same ratio, in twelve months time the capacity will be 4; for, 2·828 is a mean proportional between 2 and 4. The instrument formed by the plants so cultivated, would therefore belong to the order A, that order doubling in one year.

In the case where the capacity comes to more than double the cost of formation, the order in which the instrument should be placed, is to be found, by retracing the progress of its capacity, under the supposition that it advanced at the same rate, until we arrive at a period when it was only double the cost. The interval between that and the period of formation, will then indicate the order to which it really belongs.

The bread fruit tree is perhaps twenty years old before it will bear; but ten of these trees, when in bearing, will, it is said, nearly supply a family of South Sea islanders with a sufficiency of this sort of food for eight months in the year. This sort of fruit tree requires, too, no other labor or attention than that bestowed in planting it. Suppose, then, that an inhabitant of one of those islands were to spend an hour in planting a few of these trees, and that, according to

THE COMPARISON OF INSTRUMENTS 35

the hypothesis of sudden exhaustion, on which we are proceeding, at the termination of the twenty-two years they are exhausted, yielding at that period an equivalent to two thousand and forty-eight hours' labor. If then we retrace the progress, at which the capacity of this instrument has advanced, we will find that it belongs to the order B. For instruments in that order doubling in two years, one hour's labor, if employed in forming an instrument of that order, ought to yield an equivalent to two hours, at the end of the second year; and being then employed in constructing other like instruments, at the end of the fourth year should yield an equivalent to four hours, at the end of the sixth to eight, and so the geometrical series, 2, 4, 8, 16, etc. would arise, which, carried out to the eleventh term, at the end of the twenty-second year, is 2048. It may perhaps serve somewhat to illustrate the matter, to suppose, that the individual who applied an hour's labor to planting the bread fruit tree, gave the same portion of time to the cultivation of another sort of plant, yielding its produce and perishing, at the termination of the second year from the time of its being placed in the soil, and the returns made from which are equal to double the labor expended on its culture. Instead of consuming the crop at the termination of the second year, he gives it to some other person or persons, on condition of their applying for his benefit two hours' labor, its equivalent, to the culture of a second crop; at the end of the fourth year, he proceeds in the same manner, and, continuing the process, at the termination of the twenty-second year, the produce of the labor of both hours, the one applied to the cultivation of the former plant, and the other to that of the latter, would be equal. The only difference in the cases would be, that the person in question would, in the latter case, have the trouble of making a bargain with one or more individuals every second year, and would then also have the power to apply, if he so chose, to the supply of his wants, the events, in this instance brought about by his previous expenditure; and that, in the latter case, he would have neither the power nor the trouble.

We have assumed, that all instruments are formed at one point of time, and exhausted at another. This is the case with but very few. The period of formation almost always spreads over a large space of time, and that of exhaustion, over another. It is evidently, however, possible to fix on a point, to be determined by a consideration of all the periods at which the labor going to the formation was expended, which shall represent the true period of formation; and on another point, determined from a consideration of similar circumstances regarding the times when the capacity was exhausted, which shall represent the true period of exhaustion.

Thus, suppose a small field in some new settlement in North America were formed by twelve days' labor, it would, were it of the order A, return in one year an equivalent to twenty-four days' labor, and then be completely exhausted and worthless. It might be, however, that it belonged to this order, although it neither yielded so much as twenty-four days' labor, nor was exhausted at the end of the year. Say, that the crop sown is wheat, and, that one bushel of wheat is equivalent to one day's labor. Were it at once exhausted, it ought to yield twenty-four bushels of wheat; it however only yields eighteen, and is not then exhausted. There is consequently a deficiency of six bushels. Now, six bushels at the end of the second year, at the same rate of doubling in a year, ought to produce twelve. Let us suppose that the next crop is hay, and that the net hay yielded the second year is one ton, equal to eight bushels wheat, then $(12 - 8 = 4)$, there is still a deficiency of four bushels, equivalent, at the end of the third year, to eight. If, therefore, the next crop of hay the third year, be equal to what it was the second, that is to eight bushels wheat, the deficiency will then be made up. Let us suppose that it is so, and that the field is at that time totally exhausted and useless. It is evident, that such a field, though not producing or being exhausted as by the supposition, yet producing and being exhausted, in a manner equivalent to the supposition, might, with propriety, be said to belong to the order A.

But, it is farther probable, that such a field might not produce quite so much grain, or hay, as we have even by the last hypothesis supposed, and would not even at the end of the third year, or for a much longer period, be exhausted; still, if the deficiency in the one were equivalent to the farther supply

THE COMPARISON OF INSTRUMENTS 37

in the other, it would evidently properly belong also to the same order.

Again, by the suppositions we have made, the labor, or its equivalent, was expended exactly at the commencement of the period of one year. It might however have been, that some part of the expenditure, going to the formation of this instrument, was made several months before the commencement of the year, and some several months after. But, had what was expended before, been proportionably less, and what was expended after, proportionably greater, the change would not make any alteration to the relation existing between the time and the expenditure, or, consequently, to the place of the instrument.

The spaces over which the several points of time, at which the formation of any instrument is effected, extend, and those over which the several points of time at which its capacity is exhausted also extend, frequently run into each other. Thus according to our system a riding-horse is an instrument. The space of time over which the whole period of his formation extends, commences when his dam is put apart for breeding, continues as long as any thing is laid out for the purpose of giving efficiency and durability to him as an instrument, and probably therefore only terminates a few days before the death of the animal. There would be a number of points all along that space, at each of which something had been expended on his account, and from the date of which, and the amount expended at each, data would be furnished, to ascertain the whole expense of his formation, and the precise point from whence it might be dated. The whole period of his exhaustion would also extend over a large space. It would commence when he was first ridden for pleasure, or business, and would terminate shortly after his death, when his hide went to the tanner, and his flesh to the dogs. An account of the several items expended, and the times when they were expended, and of the several items yielded, and the times at which they were yielded, would furnish data for determining the total cost of formation and capacity and the points to be fixed on as the periods of formation and exhaustion, and thus the place of the instrument could be determined.

Calculations of this sort would be intricate, and could not be well effected without having recourse to methods, not usually employed in investigations like the present. In point of fact, there is in practice, as we will afterwards see, a system of notation of instruments, which enables us pretty accurately, and very easily, to determine their place in such a series as we have supposed. It is sufficient for the end here aimed at, to perceive that when all particulars are known, concerning the formation and exhaustion of any instrument, and the periods intervening between these, data are then furnished for placing it in some part of such a series as we have described; and that it may consequently be assumed that every instrument does, in reality, belong to some one order in the series A, B, C, D, etc., or to an order that may be interposed between some two proximate orders of that series.

It may perhaps appear, that though, could instruments be considered apart, the foregoing explications might serve to show, that they might all be reduced to a place in our series, yet, as they very commonly act in combination, and as, in such instances, the events in which two or more of them issue are the same, it must be impossible to fix with accuracy the order to which each belongs. Thus, a horse and a cart form together an instrument for the transport of goods. The events, therefore, in which both issue, being the same, we cannot measure the part that may belong to each, in any other manner, than by appropriating to each the proportion indicated by their respective costs of formation, and hence they will both appear to belong to the same order, though perhaps they do in fact belong to different orders. But our subsequent inquiries will show, that the great mass of the instruments existing in the same society are, in reality, at about the same orders; and, that instruments acting in combination with other instruments, are almost always at the same orders. This objection is therefore removed, as all instruments acting in combination may thus be considered as one.

Instruments are frequently repaired. The labor or its equivalent, so expended, may be considered, either as a partial reformation of the old instrument, or as the addition of a new instrument to be combined in action with the old one. The

THE COMPARISON OF INSTRUMENTS 39

same rules therefore, apply to repairs effected on instruments, as to their original formation.

We have assumed, hitherto, that both formation and exhaustion are properties common to all instruments. There is however a class of instruments, that forms an exception to this general rule. An extensive and important class exists, of a nature so peculiar, that the instruments belonging to it are never exhausted, unless in consequence of some revolution in the circumstances of the society. That part of the surface of the earth devoted to agricultural purposes composes this class. The peculiarity arises from every portion of land so employed, forming two distinct instruments. A piece of land, that it may do its part in providing a supply for future wants, must first be rendered capable of culture, and then be cultivated. It is not necessary that he who renders it fit for culture, should also cultivate it, though it commonly happens that both operations are performed by the same individual. But by whomsoever the operation of converting waste land, into land bearing crops, be performed, two ends are always gained by it, the power of cultivation, and the actual culture. There is this great difference between them, that while the changes produced in a piece of land to fit it for cultivation are lasting (remaining unless some means be taken to do away with them), those that are effected on it by the actual process of cultivation are of short, or at all events, of limited duration. When an individual has converted a portion of morass or forest, into a field fit for the operations of tillage, it does not return again to the state of morass or forest. He has fitted it for being made an instrument of agriculture, or rather a succession of instruments of agriculture. The farmer, by manuring it, sowing certain seeds in it, and tilling it, forms it into such an instrument. The changes he thus effects, however, pass away. The seeds he sows, growing into plants of different kinds, are carried off; the manure yields part of its substance to them, and is in part dissipated; the soil that had been loosened and pulverized by the plough and harrow, is gradually again compacted and hardened, by the effects of the action of the sun and rain. As far, then, as it was actually an instrument of agriculture it is exhausted. But its power of being again formed into such an instrument remains, and the same operations, the same rotation of crops, may indefinitely succeed one another.

The individual who first forms a portion of land into these combined instruments, has probably in view, only the ends to be gained by one of them. His motive to expend labor on the formation of the field, is to fit it for immediate culture. But, he cannot effect this, without also rendering it capable of being cultivated to all succeeding times. The returns, which for this reason it makes in those succeeding times, form what is called rent; and this peculiarity in the nature of this sort of double instrument, is one of the chief causes of the existence of that particular species of revenue. Any portion of land, therefore, which bears a crop, considered as regards its fitness for being cultivated, is an instrument of indefinite exhaustion, and will not consequently coincide with the conditions by which the orders in our series are determined. We shall afterwards see, that in every instance it may, notwithstanding, be reduced to a determined place in that series. A portion of cultivated land, considered as an instrument actually subject to the operations of the husbandman, does not differ from any other instrument.[1]

In conclusion, it may be observed that the position in our series which any instrument will occupy, is determined by the following circumstances.

1. The shorter the space of time between the period of its formation, and that of its exhaustion, the nearer will any instrument be placed to the order A, that is, towards the more quickly returning orders.

---

[1] [Possibly the novel ideas set forth above will advantageously bear restatement.

Land made fit for cultivation, but not in process of cultivation, is an instrument toward the attainment of crops. It is formed from materials, that is, from mere land surface. The farmer, when he manures, plants and tills, makes an ephemeral superimposed instrument. Rent is paid, in Ricardian phrase, for the "indestructible powers of the soil"; but these powers are not "original," but were produced or rendered available by him who first brought a certain area of land surface into a state fit for cultivation.]

THE COMPARISON OF INSTRUMENTS 41

2. The greater the capacity, and the less the cost of its formation, the nearer will any instrument be to the order A; the less the capacity, and the greater the cost of formation, the farther will it be from A.

Generally, the proximity of instruments to A is inversely as the cost and the time, and directly as the capacity.

CHAPTER V.

OF CERTAIN TECHNICAL CIRCUMSTANCES GOVERNING THE AMOUNT OF INSTRUMENTS FORMED.

HAVING traced the general nature of instruments, and shown, that the relations existing among the circumstances by which they are affected, make it practicable to arrange them in a regular series, the object next claiming our attention, is, to ascertain the causes determining the amount of them which each society possesses, and to note the more remarkable phenomena which the operation of those causes produces.

The causes determining the amount of instruments formed by any society, will, I believe, be found to be four.
 1. The quantity and quality of the materials owned by it.
 2. The strength of the *effective desire of accumulation.*
 3. The rate of wages.
 4. The progress of the inventive faculty.

The nature of the second of these, and the circumstances on which its strength depends, will form the subject of the next chapter, but previously to entering on it, it is necessary to establish the following proposition.

The capacity which any people can communicate to the materials they possess, by forming them into instruments, cannot be indefinitely increased, while their knowledge of their powers and qualities remain stationary, without moving the instruments formed continually onward in the series A, B, C, etc.: but, there is no assignable limit to the extent of the capacity, which a people having attained considerable knowledge of the qualities and powers of the materials they possess, can communicate to them, without

OF TECHNICAL LIMITATIONS 43

carrying them [wholly] out of the series A, B, C, etc., even if that knowledge remain stationary.[1]

The capacity of instruments may be increased, by adding to their durability, or to their efficiency; that is, by prolonging the time during which they bring to pass the events, for the purpose of effecting which they are formed, or, by increasing the amount of them which they bring to pass within the same time.

A dwelling-house is an instrument, aiding to bring to an issue events of various classes. It more or less completely prevents rain, damp, and the extremes of cold and heat, from penetrating to the space included within its area. It preserves all other instruments contained within it, in comparative safety. It gives those who inhabit it the power of carrying on unmolested, various domestic occupations, and of enjoying, undisturbed by the gaze of strangers, any of the gratifications or amusements of life, of which they may be able and desirous to partake. Events of these sorts, it may bring to pass, for a longer or shorter time, or to a greater or less extent, within the same time. In the former case, the durability is increased, in the latter, the efficiency ; in both, the capacity is augmented. Dwelling-houses are built of different materials, and those materials are wrought up with more or less care. A dwelling might be slightly run up of wood, lath, mud, plaster, and paper, which would be habitable only for a few months or years, like the unsubstantial villages that Catherine of Russia saw in her progress through some parts of her dominions. Another of the same size, accommodation, and appearance, that might last for two or three centuries, might be constructed, by employing stone, iron, and the most durable woods, and joining and compacting them together, with great nicety and accuracy. Between these two extremes there are all imaginable varieties. According to that adopted, both the durability and the efficiency will be greater or less. These two may be separated from each other, at least in imagination, and therefore we may consider them apart.

[1] [In other words, in the absence of the advance of the arts, extension of industrial operations meets with a resistance, but that resistance is never absolute.]

If the increased durability that may be given an instrument be considered apart from the increased efficiency that will also probably be communicated to it, it must be regarded simply as an extension of its existence, and consequently as a like extension of its capacity. A dwelling-house lasts, we shall say, sixty years, but in other respects is perfectly similar to one lasting only thirty years. Considered as an instrument, the former is, therefore, exactly equal to two of the latter, the one formed thirty years after the other. A house lasting one hundred and twenty years would in like manner have the capacity of four houses, one formed now, a second thirty, a third sixty, and a fourth ninety years hence. The capacity thus increasing at the same rate as the duration, if the limits to the power of giving durability be indefinite, the limits to the power of communicating capacity are also indefinite.

But to give additional durability to the instrument there must be additional labor bestowed on its formation. An increase of the durability of an instrument may therefore be considered as a power communicated to it of giving existence to a new instrument at the end of a certain period, and purchased by a present expenditure. The effects [that is, the net economic result] produced by the change will be determined by the relations subsisting between the returns made by the addition, its cost, and the time elapsing between the expenditure and return. If we suppose the present expenditure necessary to produce the durability, to be always equal to the durability produced, then the compound instrument will be moved towards the more slowly returning orders, because the new instrument is in that case one of slower return. One dwelling-house lasts thirty years; another, the same as it in other respects, but costing double the expense of formation, lasts sixty years; the former house is an instrument of the order O, doubling in fifteen years. The part of the duration of the latter extending from the thirtieth to the sixtieth year, is to be considered, by our hypothesis, as a separate instrument. If we suppose, that during the time it is in use it returns as the other, at the end of the sixtieth year it will have returned only four, and, therefore, is an instrument of the order c doubling only in thirty years. The compound instrument will,

OF TECHNICAL LIMITATIONS 45

in consequence, be of an order between X and Y, doubling in between twenty-four and twenty-five years. The procedure of adding to the durability, by adding equally to the expense of formation, will have greater effect in placing an instrument further from A, the more it is subjected to its operation. Thus, were an instrument of this sort to have its duration prolonged to one hundred and twenty years, and at the same expense, the last thirty would return only four in one hundred and twenty years, whereas, had it formed an instrument of the order O, it ought to have yielded two hundred and fifty-six. Were the durability increased still farther, at the same cost, the divergence would be much greater, going on in a geometrical ratio. If, therefore, continual additions be made to the durability of an instrument, it cannot be preserved at an order of equally quick return, unless the several augmentations be communicated to it, by an expenditure diminishing in a geometrical ratio; that is, in a ratio becoming indefinitely less, as it is continued. This, however, cannot happen, for it would imply an absurdity. While instruments are in existence, they are either producing events, or giving a new direction to their course. But mere matter, unless in some very rare instances, is never acting, or acted upon, without undergoing a change. This we term wear, and the effects it indicates form consequently a definite power, to counteract which, a definite force must be found. It cannot then, be counteracted, by a force indefinitely small.

The same thing may be illustrated in another manner. When events are produced and governed by design, they in turn generate other events of greater powers than themselves, and these others, in a series rapidly increasing. Mere durability in instruments, may be considered as a capacity to generate future events, lying dormant in them, till the lapse of years exposes its existence, and gives it opportunity to act. The greater the time therefore, for the expiration of which it must wait, the less the chance of its being on an equality with rivals, whose powers are continually and rapidly multiplying either events, or enjoyments, whenever they have a field on which to exert their energies.

While the knowledge of the course of events which the

members of any society possess remains unaltered, and the materials they own are the same, the duration of the instruments they form cannot, consequently, be indefinitely increased, without their being moved, farther and farther, from the more quickly returning orders.

The durability of instruments refers only to those of gradual exhaustion; their efficiency, or the extent of their power to bring about events within a certain time, refers both to those of gradual, and of sudden exhaustion. If the knowledge of the course of events, and the amount of the materials remain the same, the efficiency of these materials when formed into instruments cannot be indefinitely increased, without that increase being at length made with additional difficulty, and through means of an amount of labor greater than was required in the earlier stages. The action of matter upon matter always depends on some cause. Those causes,—the inherent qualities and powers of the different matters around him,—are the means man employs to make one material to act so on another as to produce the events he desires, and he does so by applying his labor to give them such a form and position as may bring their powers into play. If we suppose any number of men to be fixed to one situation, and their knowledge of the qualities of the materials around them to remain stationary, they will naturally first make choice of those materials, whose powers are most easily brought into action, and which produce the desired events most abundantly and speedily. But as the stock of materials which any society possesses, is limited, its members, if we suppose them to acquire no additional knowledge of the powers of those materials, and yet to add continually to the amount of instruments they form out of them, must at length have recourse to such as are either operated on with greater difficulty, or bring about desired events more sparingly or tardily. The efficiency of the instruments produced must therefore be generated by greater cost; that is, they must pass to orders of slower return.[1]

---

[1][There is, in our present-day phraseology, a descent of industry in the society to a lower margin of productivity.]

OF TECHNICAL LIMITATIONS 47

This passage will be rapid, or slow, as the amount of knowledge possessed is small, or great. When art is in its infancy, and men know but a few of the properties fitting them for becoming instruments that are inherent in the materials in their possession, they cannot much vary their mode of proceeding on them, by combining, and giving new turns to their actions on each other. In more advanced stages of society, on the contrary, where the powers of a great number of materials are known, and where consequently their operations on each other may be combined, and multiplied to a great extent, the means by which the same end may be attained are very numerous. Some of them are more easy or expeditious than others but they differ by very slight degrees, and the instruments formed by successively adopting them, would occupy positions in our series not widely distant from one another.

If we then consider the capacity that may be given any amount of materials, by a society among whom the progress of art is stationary, as separated into the durability, and efficiency, of the instruments its members form, it would appear, that they are both subject to similar laws, and that neither can be indefinitely increased, without carrying the instruments constructed continually on, to orders of slower return. The same general conclusions must obviously hold good, concerning the capacity considered as combined of both. There is, however, a circumstance flowing from the consideration of this union, which is deserving of notice, as it has considerable effect in the relations between the cost and capacity of instruments, and, consequently, on the position to be assigned them. It often happens, that additional labor bestowed on an instrument, to give it greater efficiency, gives it also greater durability. Thus the same choice of materials, and the same careful and laborious formation of them, that render the walls of a dwelling-house effective in excluding the inclemency of the weather, give it also solidity and strength, and consequently prolong its duration. A tool, in the fabrication of which good steel has been employed, not only cuts better, but lasts longer, than one formed of inferior stuff. In such cases, and they are very numerous, the capacity being increased both as concerns durability and efficiency, by the same outlay, its proportion to the cost is greater, and a larger expenditure may be made on the formation of the instrument without moving it at all, or moving it but a short distance, towards the orders of slower return. Sometimes the same expenditure that gives efficiency to instruments, partly also increases their durability, and partly quickens their exhaustion. Thus, the majority of roads in North America, and in many other countries, are constructed altogether of the soil of which the surface happens to consist, arranged in a form adapted to the purpose. Such roads, unless in the best of weather, are very inefficient instruments in facilitating transport, and their durability is so small, that they are probably *reconstructed*, by repair, every four or five years. A road formed of small fragments of stone, in the manner that is termed *macadamization*, costs perhaps twenty times as much, but is both a far more efficient, and a far more durable instrument. Besides, however, being more durable, and efficient, the facility it gives to transport occasions an increase of transport, and its exhaustion is thus quickened. For example, the capacity of a road of this sort, may be adequate to the transport of two hundred thousand carriages; if this be spread over twenty years, it will be an instrument of much slower return, than if, in consequence of the annual transport being doubled, that number pass over it in ten years.

As efficiency and durability are frequently produced by the same means, so, it sometimes happens, that the means which would add to the one, cannot be employed, without diminishing the other. Thus there are many tools and utensils, that cannot be made very strong, and therefore durable, without being at the same time clumsy, and inefficient; and they cannot be made very light, and easy to work with, without being also of little durability. The difficulty in the combination of the qualities of durability and efficiency in the same materials, can only, however, be considered as absolutely limiting the capacity of those instruments, to support the weight of which, a corporeal exertion is required; and is consequently confined to wearing apparel, and to those tools, and utensils, which are altogether moved by the hand. When the weight rests on some firm basis, it can be poised; and, by the application of sufficient expenditure, friction can be removed. The circumstance of the qualities of durability and efficiency, depending on the same materials, has therefore, probably, on the whole, the effect of retarding somewhat, though not very greatly, the progress of instruments as greater capacity is given to them, towards the more slowly returning orders.

The various powers of the material world, seem to be connected at some common centre, and its several parts to exercise reciprocal influences on each other. Hence, a discovery of new properties in any one material, or more easy modes of bringing the old into play, generally extends the power of man over a great range of the other materials, which he had been in the habit of before applying to his purpose. When art, therefore, has made considerable progress, and comprehends within its dominion a multiplicity of materials, the variety of effects that may be generated, from the action, and reaction, on each other, of the numerous powers at its disposal, becomes illimitable. As in numbers, every addition multiplies amazingly the possible antecedent combinations, until at length the amount becomes too great to be ascertained. Hence it is, that, though among barbarous nations the ability of man to increase the amount of instruments he possesses may be [narrowly] bounded, among nations having made considerable advance in art, there seems no assigning any limit to it, other than that indicated in the second part of the proposition, the necessary gradual passage of the instruments constructed to orders of slower and slower return.

It is hence, that, if we turn to any community where art has advanced, we invariably see, that however much industry may have already exerted itself on the materials within its reach, the field for its possible future action seems rather increased than diminished, and that the farther we stretch our view over it, to the greater distance its extreme circumference recedes from us. The industry of the people of Great Britain, has probably been as largely applied to the materials which its limited territory possesses, as that of any other community presently existing; yet certainly there is no lack of matters on which it might be farther exercised. A large portion of its surface, and which wants not all the requisites for the

D

sustenance of vegetable life, lies, nevertheless, yet uncultivated. With the exception of the mountainous and rocky regions, heat, light, air and water, in sufficient abundance rest on every part of it, nor is the presence of many of the earths, the mixture of which forms a proper shelter for the tender radicle fibres, and a commodious storehouse for an important part of their nourishment, any where wanting. There is also in general a considerable supply diffused over the surface of the decomposing remains of former vegetables and animals, the material which constitutes nearly the whole solid food that the organic life of plants requires; and, even when this is deficient at one point, there are larger collections of it at some other. The outlay requisite, in many instances, to give such form to these materials, as to fit them for the purposes of the agriculturist, would, no doubt, be very great; still, whatever it might be, as the instrument formed would be of unlimited duration, the annual returns from it would, in time, exceed the cost of formation, and bring it within the limits of our series.

Were we to go over the various other instruments, the returns from which supply the wants of this community, we should perceive, that every where their capacities are capable of being greatly increased. One would not find it very easy to say, how much might be added to the durability and efficiency of dwelling-houses alone. The amount of the capacity for the facilitation of future transport, which might be embodied in railroads, returning ultimately much more than the cost of their formation, is incalculable; as is also, the degree to which mining operations might be extended. Even supposing all these, and many other instruments, to have acquired a vastly increased extent, both as concerns durability and efficiency; instead of limiting their farther increase, it would seem likely, rather to open up a still wider space, for the exertion of future industry in the formation of others. Were the soil universally cultivated, were railroads extended and ramified throughout the country, and were the riches of the mineral kingdom more fully brought out, the additional facility given to the formation of instruments, by the command afforded of the materials necessary for their construction, and

OF TECHNICAL LIMITATIONS 51

the ease with which they might be transported from point to point, would, it may well be supposed, be sufficient to give the means of a still greater increased construction of them, and a still farther advance of the amount of the capacities for the supply of futurity, embodied in the various instruments spread over the surface of the territory, or lying above, or beneath it. In short, the more we consider the subject, the more clearly shall we perceive the impossibility of fixing any [absolute] limit to the amount of the labor which may be expended in the formation of instruments, in this, or any other community, where art has made considerable advance.

This progress [that is, mere extension of industrial operations], while art itself remained stationary, would, however, undoubtedly, gradually carry instruments to more and more slowly returning orders, and would not therefore take place, unless the society were inclined to construct instruments of those orders. What the circumstances are, which determine individuals and societies to stop at this or that order of instruments [in any given state of the arts], will form the subject of the next chapter.

[Rae does not develop fully in this chapter, or indeed anywhere else, the bases for a generalized concept of diminishing returns. One additional aspect of the subject is brought out in the second paragraph of Chapter VII.]

CHAPTER VI.

OF THE CIRCUMSTANCES WHICH DETERMINE THE STRENGTH OF THE EFFECTIVE DESIRE OF ACCUMULATION.

IT has been shown, in the preceding chapter, that, in communities where an extensive knowledge of the materials within reach of the industry of their members has generated numerous arts, we can assign no limit, in the nature of the materials themselves, to the capacity for the supply of future wants that might be given to them: but, that the instruments so formed, pass, by a gradual and uninterrupted progress, to orders of slower and slower return. It is scarcely necessary to observe, that the increase to the capacity which may be given to instruments, cannot be restricted by inability to devote additional labor to their construction; for, as all instruments at the period of their exhaustion return more than the cost of their formation, they give the means of reconstructing others, returning also somewhat more largely than themselves. There are, nevertheless, in every society causes [not physical or technical] effectually bounding the advance of instruments to orders capable of embracing a larger and larger circle of materials, and the determination of those causes is the subject now claiming our attention.

Instruments are all formed by one amount of labor, or some equivalent to it, that is, by something either capable of yielding, or itself constituting some of the necessaries, conveniences, or amusements of life, and they return another greater amount of labor or its equivalents. The formation of every instrument therefore, implies the sacrifice of some smaller present good, for the production of some greater future good. If, then, the production of that future greater good, be conceived to deserve the sacrifice of this present smaller good, the instrument will be formed, if not, it will not be formed. According to the series in which we have arranged instruments, they double the cost of their formation in one, two, three, etc., years. Consequently, the order to which in any society the formation of instruments will advance, will be determined by the length of the period, to which the inclination of its members to yield up a present good, for the purpose of producing the double of it at the expiration of that period, will extend: according as it stretches to one, two, three, twenty, forty, etc., years will the formation of instruments be carried, to the orders, A, B, C, T, n, etc., and, at the point where the willingness to make the sacrifice ceases, there the formation of instruments must stop. The circumstances, therefore, on such occasions governing the decision of the members of all societies, must be the causes, fixing the point to which the formation of instruments may in any society be carried, and beyond which it cannot advance. The determination to sacrifice a certain amount of present good, to obtain another greater amount of good, at some future period, may be termed the *effective desire of accumulation*. All men may be said to have a desire of this sort, for all men prefer a greater to a less; but to be effective it must prompt to action.

Were life to endure for ever, were the capacity to enjoy in perfection all its goods, both mental and corporeal, to be prolonged with it, and were we guided solely by the dictates of reason, there could be no limit to the formation of means for future gratification, till our utmost wishes were supplied. A pleasure to be enjoyed, or a pain to be endured, fifty or a hundred years hence, would be considered deserving the same attention as if it were to befall us fifty or a hundred minutes hence, and the sacrifice of a smaller present good, for a greater future good, would be readily made, to whatever period that futurity might extend. But life, and the power to enjoy it, are the most uncertain of all things, and we are not guided altogether by reason. We know not the period when death may come upon us, but we know that it may come in a few

54 THE EFFECTIVE DESIRE OF ACCUMULATION

days, and must come in a few years. Why then be providing goods that cannot be enjoyed until times, which, though not very remote, may never come to us, or until times still more remote, and which we are convinced we shall never see? If life, too, is of uncertain duration and the time that death comes between us and all our possessions unknown, the approaches of old age are at least certain, and are dulling, day by day, the relish of every pleasure.

A mere reasonable regard to their own interest, would, therefore, place the present very far above the future, in the estimation of most men. But, it is besides to be remarked, that such pleasures as may now be enjoyed, generally awaken a passion strongly prompting to the partaking of them. The actual presence of the immediate object of desire in the mind, by exciting the attention, seems to rouse all the faculties, as it were, to fix their view on it, and leads them to a very lively conception of the enjoyments which it offers to their instant possession. The prospects of future good, which future years may hold out to us, seem at such a moment dull and dubious, and are apt to be slighted, for objects on which the daylight is falling strongly, and showing us in all their freshness just within our grasp. There is no man perhaps, to whom a good to be enjoyed to day, would not seem of very different importance, from one exactly similar to be enjoyed twelve years hence, even though the arrival of both were equally certain.

Nor, while we retain any taste for pleasures, is it easy to prescribe limits to the extent to which we may indulge in them, or to the amount of the funds they may absorb. Every where we see that to spend is easy, to spare, hard. Every one indeed looks upon those in the rank immediately above him, as rolling in superfluous extravagance. But, in every rank, from the prince to the peasant, there are very many individuals, who have difficulty in procuring funds to defray the cost of articles, the expenditure of which they look upon as necessary to their condition, and, for the remainder, in the different classes, who have more than their utmost real desires would call for, pleasure is so entwined with extravagance, in the forms in which she presents herself to each, that it is difficult fully to embrace the one, without coming within the circle of the other.

It would then appear, that merely personal considerations, can never give great strength to the effective desire of accumulation. A future good, as concerns the individual, when balanced against a present good, is both exceedingly uncertain in its arrival, and in the amount of enjoyment it may yield, is probably far inferior. Such considerations would undoubtedly represent it, as a great folly to deny youth or manhood pleasure, that old age might have riches not to be enjoyed by it, but which, like the fabled monster in the garden of the Hesperides, it must employ itself with restless care to guard for others,

>"Conservans aliis, quæ periere sibi
>Sicut in auricomis pendentia plurimus hortis
>Pervigil observat non sua poma draco."[1]

A prudent calculation of mere personal enjoyment, could prompt to nothing more than a provision for self, and would only lead to the making, as it is said, the day and the journey alike, and taking care that youth should not want pleasure, nor old age comfort. But, as passion is ever getting the better of mere prudence, this limit would every now and then be exceeded, and in numerous instances, the satiety of riot would be succeeded by the miseries of want. Wherever a large amount of means for the gratification of the present existed, they would be squandered, and no one, on the other hand, would be inclined to make any great sacrifice of the present, for the purpose of providing for the future. The strength of the effective desire of accumulation would be low, and only instruments would be formed as were of the quickly returning orders.

But man's pleasures are not altogether selfish. He receives pleasure from giving pleasure, and is far from the perfection of his existence when he does not draw his enjoyments, rather from the good he communicates, than from that which he

---

[1] C. C. Galli, *Eleg.* I. The whole elegy is illustrative of that isolation of feeling and action, and consequent individual misery and general weakness, that pervaded the Empire at the time.

reserves. Without the ties which bind him to others through the conjugal and parental relations, the claims of his kindred, his friends, his country, or his race, life would be to most men a burden. These are its great stimulants, and sweeteners, giving an aim to every possible exertion, and an interest to every moment. If, sometimes, they shadow our being with cares and fears, those passing shadows but prove there is a sunshine. The light of life only disappears, and its dreary night then commences, when we have none for whom to live. Then the whole creation is a void. Really to live is to live with, and through others, more than in ourselves. To do so we must do so truly.

"Love, and love only, is the loan for love."

If the mere pretence deceive others, it mocks and tantalizes ourselves, encircling us with a joy as unreal, as that which the looks and tones of affection shed round him, who receives them disguised in a borrowed garment. We cannot enjoy them, because we feel that they are not ours, but some other's whose dress we wear.

In so far as to procure good for others, gives a real pleasure to the individual, he is released from that narrow and imperfect sphere of action, to which his mere personal interests would confine him, and the future goods which the sacrifice of present ease or enjoyment may produce, lose the greater part of their uncertainty and worthlessness. Though life may pass from him, he reckons not that his toils, his cares, his privations, will be lost, if they serve as the means of enjoyment to some whom he may leave behind. These feelings, therefore, investing the concerns of futurity with a lively interest to the individual, and giving a continuity to the existence and projects of the race, must tend to strengthen very greatly the effective desire of accumulation. There would seem to be no limit to the possible extent of their operation. The more powerful and predominating they become, the greater must be their influence. It is true they are often feeble, and oppressed by other principles, and it is just as true that the world is full of deceit, hollowness, and unhappiness. As far as they exist, however, they form a real element of great power in the

THE EFFECTIVE DESIRE OF ACCUMULATION 57

determination of the course of human action, and one the nature of which would seem to indicate, and experience to prove, to be of great influence on the particular part of it that forms our present subject. In the succeeding pages, the terms, the *social and benevolent affections,* will be employed to denote them.

The strength of the intellectual powers, giving rise to reasoning and reflective habits, forms another important element in the determination of the course of human action. These habits in opposition to the passions of the present hour, bring before us the future, both as concerns ourselves, and others, in its legitimate force, and urge the propriety of providing for it. Although therefore, were our cares limited altogether to ourselves, the greatest strength of the reasoning faculty could prompt to but a very limited operation on the events of futurity, yet, the farther they extend to others, the wider is the circle of operations that we are led to embrace. These two principles of our nature, the social and benevolent affections, and the intellectual powers, serve indeed mutually to move each other to action, the affections exciting the intellect to discover the means of producing good, the intellect opening up a channel to the affections by giving the power to do good.

All circumstances increasing the probability of the provision we make for futurity being enjoyed by ourselves or others, also tend to give strength to the effective desire of accumulation. Thus a healthy climate, or occupation, by increasing the probability of life, has a tendency to add to this desire. When engaged in safe occupations, and living in healthy countries, men are much more apt to be frugal, than in unhealthy, or hazardous occupations, and in climates pernicious to human life. Sailors and soldiers are prodigals. In the West Indies, New Orleans, the East Indies, the expenditure of the inhabitants is profuse. The same people, coming to reside in the healthy parts of Europe, and not getting into the vortex of extravagant fashion, live economically. War, and pestilence, have always waste, and luxury, among the other evils that follow in their train.

For similar reasons, whatever gives security to the affairs of the community, is favorable to the strength of this principle.

58 THE EFFECTIVE DESIRE OF ACCUMULATION

In this respect the general prevalence of law and order, and the prospect of the continuance of peace and tranquility, have considerable influence.

These seem to be the chief circumstances, determining the relations between present and future good, in the minds of those in any society, who have a mind and a will, at the time they are forming habits. When habits are once formed, they regulate the tenor of the future life, and make slaves of their former masters. There are, however, in every society, very many who form habits, and pursue a certain line of conduct through life, not from any reasoning or choice of their own, but hurried on by the example of those around them, and the general direction in which the current of feeling and action sets throughout the whole body. It is evident, however, that the power that moves and directs the mass, lies not in them, but in those who govern their conduct in whole, or in part, by their own feelings and passions, and the reflections which the situation of circumstances around them suggests to them. These form the great moving principle, the others, like the balance-wheel in an engine, merely keep up, and give uniformity, to the motion they generate.

The desire to accumulate would then seem to derive strength, chiefly from three circumstances.

1. The prevalence throughout the society of the social and benevolent affections, or, of that principle, which, under whatever name it may be known, leads us to derive happiness from the [future] good we communicate to others.

2. The extent of the intellectual powers, and the consequent prevalence of habits of reflection, and prudence, in the minds of the members of the society.

3. The stability of the condition of the affairs of the society, and the reign of law and order throughout it.

It is weakened, and strength given to the desire of immediate enjoyment, by three opposing circumstances.

1. The deficiency of strength in the social and benevolent affections, and the prevalence of the opposite principle, a desire of mere selfish gratification.

2. A deficiency in the intellectual powers, and the consequent want of habits of reflection and forethought.

3. The instability of the affairs of the society, and the imperfect diffusion of law and order throughout it.

The reader may perhaps conceive, that, in enumerating these different circumstances, and deducing the strength of the effective desire of accumulation from the preponderance of the one class over the other, I am attempting an unnecessary refinement, and that the principle of a regard to self interest alone, though it may not, of itself, give great strength to this desire, yet, from its combination with other springs of action, must generally do so indirectly and ultimately and may, therefore, be assumed as a cause sufficient to account for the phenomena. If we confine our attention to the present times, and to particular parts of the globe, this may be readily admitted. Now, and in those places, a prudent regard to self interest would doubtless prompt many individuals to cooperate effectively in the increase of the general means of enjoyment. But there is nothing more apt to mislead us, when investigating the causes determining the motions of any great system, than to take our station at some particular point in it, and, examining the appearances there presented to us, to suppose that they must be precisely similar through the whole sphere of action. Because, in Great Britain, a regard to mere self interest, may now prompt to a course of action leading to making a large provision for the wants of others, we are, in reality, no more warranted to conclude that it will do so always, and in every place, than were the ancients warranted to conclude, because in their particular communities, the pursuit of wealth commonly generated evil, that it must therefore do so always and in every place.

There seem to be, in modern times, and in particular communities, two circumstances, that may lead an individual, from a mere regard to his personal interest, to pursue the paths of sober industry and frugality, and, consequently, to make an extended provision for the wants of others. These seem to be the desire of personal, and family aggrandizement, and a wish, conjoined with the pursuit of both, to rank high in the estimation of the world. The acquisition of fortune, is a road open to the ambition of all men, and, in the present days, is the only road open to that of most men. The mere desire to rise in the world, and envy of the superiority of other men, may excite many to enter on this path, and preserve them steadily in it. This sort of spirit, however, must be kept in strict check, by a large surrounding mass of genuine probity, and tenderness of the happiness of others, or it certainly breaks out into disorders.[1] There is none more easily tempted to evil, or more dangerous. It is the first to diminish the security of all compacts, and transactions of business, by fraud and exactions; it is the first to disturb the public tranquillity, by seditions and conspiracies. It is such a spirit, predominating over a character otherwise good, that Shakspeare paints in Cassius. Cæsar thinks him to be feared, because,

> "Such men as he be never at heart's ease,
> While they behold a greater than themselves;
> And therefore are they very dangerous."

It is this temper that spurs him on, "in envy of great Cæsar," to "humour, and win, the noble Brutus," to the assassination. It is the same spirit, that renders him unscrupulous,

> "To sell and mart his offices for gold,
> To undeservers;"

and, to wring

> "From the hard hand of peasants, their vile trash,
> By any indirection."

Whenever, therefore, the mere desire of distinction is the object for which wealth is generally pursued, there, the pursuit infallibly, at length, withdraws from the path of virtue, and excites those engaged in it, to a disregard of their own honor, and the suffering of others.

> "Magnum pauperies opprobrium jubet
> Quidvis et facere et pati,
> Virtutisque viam deserit arduæ."

When such is the character of only a small minority of those who pursue wealth, it is not injuriously felt. The

---

[1] [Are we not experiencing just such an outbreak of "disorders" in the phenomena of Trusts and get-rich-quick schemes, and "graft" of all sorts, at the present day?]

THE EFFECTIVE DESIRE OF ACCUMULATION 61

energy of their motion, rather quickens the progress of the whole, than retards it. It is very different, when such characters compose the majority of those engaged in such pursuits. A chaos of deceit, treachery, knavery, is then generated, in which truth, generosity, good faith, compassion, perish. Hence it was, that the pursuit of wealth, in ancient times, was held as absolutely incompatible with the lowest degree of liberal sentiment, virtuous spirit, or common honesty. Plato expressly says, that in commerce and traffic there is no such thing as an honest man, and numerous passages from the Greek and Roman writers might be cited in proof, that, in those days, it was admitted on all hands, that the character of the money-making man was uniformly vicious. The following is one of the most striking I can presently find.

"It is impossible for the same man to be given to sensual pleasures, and to the love of money, and to be religious. For he who is a lover of pleasure will be a lover of money, and he who loves money, must of necessity be unjust, and a violator of the laws of God and man."[1] It is here not thought necessary to give any proof of the assertion; on the contrary, it is taken as an admitted fact, from which a consequence may be deduced.

In those times, therefore, the pursuit of wealth was disreputable, and the self-love of no one could be gratified by the character it procured him. We are apt to conceive the observation of St. Paul, that "the love of money is the root of all evil, and infallibly leads to wickedness," as springing from the ascetic spirit in which he contemplated matters, whereas it is common to him with all the moralists of his time, even with the most liberal of them, and must be held as a mere statement of what was then an obvious fact. Thus Horace calls it the same thing, "summi materiam mali," and the voice of the whole age agrees with him. An assiduous care to the increase of fortune was then esteemed evil, and the source of evil, and was reprobated accordingly. It was evil, because generally

[1] Ὁ φιλήδονον καὶ φιλοσώματον καὶ φιλοχρήματον καὶ φιλόθεον τὸν αὐτὸν ἀδύνατον εἶναι· ὁ γὰρ φιλήδονος καὶ φιλοσώματος ὁ δὲ φιλοσώματος παντῶς καὶ φιλοχρήματος. Ὁ δὲ φιλοχρήματος ἐξ ἀνάγκης ἄδικος. Ὁ δὲ ἄδικος εἰς μὲν θεὸν ἀνόσιος εἰς δὲ ἀνθρώπους παράνομος. *Demophili Similitudines*.

proceeding from a grasping, sordid, selfish spirit. It was the source of evil, because the great exciter of fraud, knavery, and violence. It is in more moral communities alone, where the real springs of action are not selfish, and where a desire for the good of others is one of the chief movers, animating the exertions, and giving a tone to the feelings and actions of the whole body, that the virtuous and liberal mind, sympathizes with and approves the conduct of the man, who gives his days to labor, and his nights to engrossing care, for the purpose of increasing his gains. There, such a life is not deemed selfish, sordid, or unhappy, because there, it is known generally to proceed from a totally opposite spirit, and to have for its sustaining principle, the welfare of others, rather than of the individual; and there, it is esteemed praiseworthy, because there, its general tendency is good, not evil. There, too, ambition alone may, no doubt, lead those who want other motives into the paths of sober industry and frugality, because the desire of excelling in whatever is attempted, must impel individuals actuated by it, to every pursuit that other men gain credit by. It is not perhaps the object gained, so much as the gaining of it, which gives it value in their eyes. But, it is only where such conduct procures consideration, and respect, that we can expect it will be steadily pursued by such persons. Where patient and assiduous industry, and undeviating integrity, procure the highest name, and fame, they will be followed by many who value them not in themselves. But this observation only proves, that we have to seek for the general course of action of the individual, in the circumstances determining that of the society.

In modern times, again, and in particular communities, marriage and offspring, and the consequent desire of family aggrandizement, may often succeed in imposing on those, to whom the welfare of others is naturally of little moment, the necessity of providing for that welfare, and therefore may often generate and keep up a much stronger attention to the cares of futurity, than could be excited by a mere regard to self interest. But, it is to be observed, that the mode in which the passions prompting to marriage will operate, must depend on the feelings, and consequently, manners, pervading the

THE EFFECTIVE DESIRE OF ACCUMULATION 63

society. When the general feelings and morals become corrupt, marriage will never be sought after, by men in easy circumstances, for the mere pleasures of sense. Socrates remarks this to his son, when pointing out the obligations he owed him for giving him being [1] and every pure voluptuary is ready to curse, with Eloisa, " all human ties."

The indulgences to which these passions prompt, when the feelings become purely selfish, will, indeed, I suspect, be found to be the great weakeners of this very principle. Out of the heart are the issues of life, and the evils to which they give rise are the worst of any, because they contaminate the sources of all healthy energy and activity, at the very fountain head. It is to them, that Horace, in my opinion, truly traces, the load of mischief which in his time pressed on Rome, and which finally overwhelmed her;

> " Fæcunda culpæ secula nuptias
> Primum inquinavere et genus et domos:
> Hoc fonte derivata clades
> Inque patres populumque fluxit."

Even on the supposition of legitimate offspring, it is only in countries where the general sentiment applauds that course of action, that the man actuated by mere self interest, can be supposed to pride himself on rearing up and providing for a family, in preference to enjoying, without restraint, all the pleasures he may be able to procure. Cool, calculating, self interest, would thus speak. " Who knoweth whether his son shall be a wise man or a fool? Yet shall he have rule over all his labor, wherein he hath labored, and wherein he hath showed himself wise under the sun. This is also vanity. Whereof I perceive that there is nothing, better than that a man should rejoice in his own works: for that is his portion: for who shall bring him to see what shall be after him: it is good and comely for one to eat and to drink, and to enjoy the good of all his labor that he taketh under the sun, all the days of his life, which God giveth him, for it is his portion." We

---

[1] Καὶ μὲν οὐ τῶν γε ἀφροδισίων ἕνεκα παιδοποιεῖσθαι τοὺς ἀνθρώπους ὑπολαμβάνεις. ἐπεὶ τούτου γε τῶν ἀπολυσόντων μεσταὶ μὲν αἱ ὁδοὶ μεστὰ δὲ τὰ οἰκήματα. Xenoph. *Memorabilia*.

find accordingly that in states where mere selfish enjoyment is the chief principle of action, that the interests of posterity are neglected. Thus, among the Roman writers, the heir is always represented in an invidious light, and to save for him is represented as a folly. The writings of Horace, and the contemporary poets, throughout, exemplify the prevalence of this feeling.

" Parcus ob hæridis curam—
Assidet insano.—"

For a frightful picture of causes and effects, in this particular, the epigram of Martial to Titullus beginning,

" Rape, congere, aufer, etc."

might be quoted. But, it is time to conclude a digression, on which perhaps I have somewhat prematurely entered.

We shall then assume that there are motives, as above enumerated, derived from the principles of human nature, acting on all men, and exciting them to expend what they presently possess in providing for future wants, as there are others, derived from the same source, tempting them to lay it out in the gratification of their immediate wants. The strength of the effective desire of accumulation, in any man or society of men, or this desire manifested in action, is determined by the preponderance of the one class of motives, over the other. It is manifested, and may be measured, by the willingness of the individual, or individuals, to lay out a certain amount to-day, in order to produce the double of that amount at a period more or less remote, that is, at the expiration of one, two, three, etc. years.

[In this chapter Rae does not make sufficiently clear that it is a certain particular sort of regard for others—the desire " to endow the future " for them—which chiefly supports the accumulative principle. It is to be noted also that the phrase " social and benevolent affections " has no specific applicability as a technical term in this connection. This very form of words has been employed by one writer on economics to denote those traits of character which lead one to spend all in the present, entertaining one's friends, and the like. The poorest people in any community are as a rule good hearted and give freely to any one in need. This is one of the chief things which keep them poor. Individual selfishness enlightened by the reason plays a larger rôle in economic life than Rae gives it credit for. But his interest here being sociological rather than individualistic, he could hardly distribute his emphasis otherwise.]

CHAPTER VII.

OF SOME OF THE PHENOMENA ARISING FROM THE DIFFERENT DEGREES OF STRENGTH OF THE EFFECTIVE DESIRE OF ACCUMULATION IN DIFFERENT SOCIETIES.

The effective desire of accumulation is of different degrees of strength, not only in different societies, as compared with each other, but also in the several individuals composing the same society as compared together. Disregarding, however, for the present, the effects produced on the formation of instruments, from diversities in the strength of this principle among individuals in the same society, we are, in this chapter, to endeavor to trace solely some of those resulting from the operation of causes varying its strength in different societies. As has been already stated, there are three other causes operating in the formation of instruments; the quantity and quality of the materials owned by any particular society; the progress which the inventive faculty has made in it; and the rate of the wages paid the laborer. The first of these depending on the original constitution of the whole globe, and its different regions, and the correspondence between these and the corporeal system of man, is determined by circumstances, the consideration of which would be foreign to the present inquiry. With regard to our subject it is to be taken as an important but ultimate fact. The causes on which the progress of the inventive faculty seems chiefly to depend, will form the subject of a subsequent chapter. At present, the extent of that progress is to be received simply as a circumstance of admitted importance.

The rate of the wages of labor, the last of the causes affecting the formation of instruments, though a subject of investigation in itself highly interesting, and closely connected with this whole inquiry, is not, as has been already stated, to be otherwise considered in these investigations, than as an existing circumstance, the operation of which is also of importance in the determination of the extent to which the stock of materials, in possession of any society, will be wrought up by it, but the laws regulating which lie beyond our prescribed limits. So considered, a low rate of wages may be esteemed, in its direct effects, as producing the same results as an improvement in the quality of the materials operated on, or an extension of the power to operate on them, through an advance in the progress of invention. All these cause the same returns to be produced from a less expenditure, or greater returns from the same expenditure. They all, therefore, place a greater range of materials within compass of the accumulative principle, and occasion the construction of a larger amount of instruments. The advance of invention, however, differs from a lowering in the rate of wages, in being a quantity to the increase of which we can set no bounds, whereas, we soon arrive at a limit to the possible diminution of the rate of wages. In the principles on which they depend, and in their ulterior consequences they differ, I believe it will be found, still more widely.

The first example I shall take, of the effect of circumstances in moulding the characters of communities, and of these again, in determining the extent to which they carry the formation of instruments, will be that of the American Indian.

The life of the hunter seems unfavorable to the perfect developement of the accumulative principle. In this state man may be said to be necessarily improvident, and regardless of futurity, because in it, the future presents nothing, which can be with certainty either foreseen, or governed. The hunting grounds are the sources from which, among hunters, the means of subsistence are drawn. But these belong to the nation or the tribe, which alone therefore, can make more abundant provision for futurity by securing to itself a domain more extensive, or better supplied with wild animals; or meet poverty, by being restricted to one more narrow, or barren. As regards his future means of living, every member of such a community thinks of nothing but whether the supply of game will be plentiful or scanty; in the one case, he knows that he will enjoy abundance, in the other that he must endure want. In such societies therefore, the view can never be directed to any distant future good, which present exertion may secure to the individual, but is confined to what, by that exertion may be added to the power, or the territory of the tribe. What applies to the individual hunter, applies to his family. Their comfort depends less on his particular exertions, than on circumstances affecting the whole band, or little nation, to which he belongs. It is only in infancy that the wants of the young savage are, to any great extent, provided for by his parents. Afterwards he feasts, or fasts, like every other member of the community, as abundance, or scarcity reigns in the camp. That camp, indeed, may be said to form the family of the Indian. His whole thoughts, and affections centre there, nor has he any cares for a distant futurity, either for himself, or his offspring, separated from the common sufferings or enjoyments of his tribe.

Were the causes determining the future good or evil flowing to each of these great families, to be within reach of the energies of the individuals composing them, they would have a steady aim for their exertions, and having the means, might acquire the habit of purchasing future plenty and security, by present toil and privation, and of tracing out with certainty, remote consequences to immediate acts. But this is a mode of thought and action, to which the circumstances of their condition are opposed. As the utmost prudence, foresight and fortitude, can but little affect the future welfare of the individual, so, their power to promote the prosperity of the society, is limited and precarious.[1]

If a tribe of hunters occupy a healthy territory, and one plentifully supplied with game, they are pressed on by others,

---

[1] [The foregoing should be compared with Rae's position on individualism, "family aggrandizement," and "social and benevolent affections," in the preceding chapter.]

eager to seize on these advantages, and so are continually engaged in destructive wars. While the individuals composing such a tribe can slaughter their foes, that is, the surrounding tribes, or can drive them to a distance, they want for nothing. The defeat of their own tribe, is the only calamity they have to dread. This calamity is every now and then overtaking them.

War is always a game of hazard. In such a state of society it is peculiarly hazardous. There the art of war is surprise. The scanty population which the chase can alone maintain, is divided into small bands, living widely apart—mere points in a vast continuity of wilderness. In such situations warfare can never be open. The attacking party must advance with secrecy; were they to make their approach known, their enemies would only wait for them, if convinced of their own superiority; otherwise, they would retire, and, if acting prudently and skilfully, never suffer themselves to be seen, unless to strike their foes, themselves being safe, in some well-conducted ambush. But where success depends upon concealment, and surprise, it also depends on chance. No precautions can succeed in always guarding a small band, encamped in the midst of a great forest, from being unexpectedly assailed. No precautions can prevent the track of a party advancing through an enemy's country, from being occasionally discovered. Victory, or defeat, and all that follow them, depend on the slightest accident. Fortune is a goddess, on whose influence the schemes of the most skilful and greatest captains are always in some measure dependent, but here she reigns supreme.

The effects of these circumstances are increased by the character of the laws of war of the savage. His wars are wars of extermination. They cannot well be otherwise. Were he pressed to defend what he thinks requires no defence, but is prepared alike to execute on others or suffer himself, he might so do from the necessity of the case,—the plea which man always urges for every evil he inflicts on his fellows. He can neither safely let his enemies go, nor possibly retain them captive. In the former case they would be as much to be dreaded as ever, for in the woods half a dozen men may make war upon a nation, as wars are there conducted. That is, they may waylay, surprise, and slaughter detached parts. Nor can he retain captives, for they would both be useless, and also must escape. A plunge into the surrounding forest sets them free. Hence it is not conquest, as with other warriors, but destruction, that is his aim, and what he executes on others, when he has the power, he sees continually impending over him, from them, when fortune gives them the power.

Thus the whole existence of the hunter is chequered by quick changing extremes. Abundance, famine, the fierce joys of victory, the horrors of surprise and defeat, rapidly succeed each other, in an order which he can neither pretend to foresee, nor direct. Like all men in similar circumstances, he refers the events, of which his being is the sport, to the continual and capricious agency of supernatural powers. All the good that happens to him, is from their having been propitious to his designs, and from his having rightly interpreted their omens; all the evil that befalls him, arises, in his conception, from their hostility, or from his having mistaken, or neglected, some vision or token they sent him. The warrior turns back, in the middle of an expedition, if his sleep be disturbed by a dream betokening evil; the unsuccessful hunter accuses neither his unsteady hand, nor imperfect sight, but some magical influence hanging on his weapon, which only the priest or sorcerer can therefore remove. The direction of all events whose arrival is distant, seems thus to the hunter of the woods to lie entirely beyond his control; and, instead of endeavoring to make the ease, or abundance of the present, provide for the evils of the future, he prides himself in enjoying the good of to-day undisturbed by a single care, and in feeling and knowing, that he can bear the ill of tomorrow without a murmur.

Hence the Indian has a character altogether his own. Feeling himself hurried on by the course of events, not directing it, he thinks as little of refraining from the pleasures that course may offer him, as of shrinking from the pains to which it may expose him, and indulges, therefore, without restraint, in the enjoyments of the hour. His intellectual faculties, unaccustomed to deduce remote consequences from immediate causes, and still less accustomed to adopt as a ground for action, and to watch carefully, and anxiously, any concatenation of the sort, are feeble; either in themselves, or from inaction. His passions, on the contrary, are strong. Unaccustomed to reflection, the warm and generous feelings of affection and gratitude, as well as the darker ones of hatred and revenge, are often formed hastily, and on inadequate grounds, but while they last they are exceedingly vehement. His tribe forms the point in which all these feelings centre; it is in fact his family, with which all his joys and sorrows are in common.

An attention to the effects naturally flowing from this character, will explain many circumstances in the present condition, and past history of these tribes, which are in themselves interesting, and which are closely connected with our subject. Of all those circumstances, none is more remarkable, than their neglecting, or refusing, to adopt the arts of the new neighbors, which the discovery by Europeans of the country they inhabit brought, and has kept in contact with them. Surrounded as are the scattered wrecks of those once numerous tribes, by a great people, rapidly converting the soil, and almost whatever grows on it, or is hid beneath it, into instruments capable of plentifully supplying every variety of future want, they are yet unable to imitate them. This deficiency among them of the effective desire of accumulation, the principle leading to the formation of instruments, seems to arise both from a want of motives to exertion, and from a want of the principles and habits of action which would lead to effective exertion.

The settlement of their country by the European race, has in itself, gradually diminished, or entirely destroyed, the political importance of their tribes, and consequently, the ties binding together the members of each of these communities, and leading them to feel, and to act, in common. Nor have these been replaced by others. Those growing out of the family relations, in other states of society,—the anxious prospective care of the parent, and the exertions, the pleasures, and the duties thence arising,—have not had time to spring up. Hence the Indian continues to seek shelter in apathy, and to regard life and its enjoyments, both for himself and his children, as did his forefathers, gifts to be made the most of while they last, but which no care can secure, and which, therefore, it is his business not to provide for the continuance of, but to learn calmly to resign when called on. He thus sits, listless, in the midst of the incessant activity and industry that surround him, incapable of discovering an adequate cause for the never-ceasing care and toil. The motives that excite the white man, though possessed of means that would enable him with his more needy brethren abundantly to enjoy the present, to devote himself, instead, to labors to which no season brings a respite, in order to bring about events that may provide for the wants of some remote and uncertain futurity, are to him incomprehensible. Instead of applauding the conduct, in his secret soul he censures the mean, timorous, and, as it seems to him, selfish spirit, which prompts it.

But, besides a want of the motives exciting to provide for the needs of futurity, through means of the abilities of the present, there is a want of the habits of perception and action, leading to a constant connexion in the mind of those distant points, and of the series of events serving to unite them. Even therefore, if motives be awakened capable of producing the exertion necessary to effect this connexion, there remains the task of training the mind to think, and act, so as to establish it.

These deficiencies in the motives to exertion, and in the habits of action of the Indian, serve to account for the condition of the remnants of the tribes scattered over the North American continent, in situations where they are in contact with the white man. There is a general similarity throughout, that will, I believe, render an example taken from one part of the continent, sufficiently illustrative of the state of the whole.

Upon the banks of the St. Lawrence, there are several little Indian villages. They are surrounded, in general, by a good deal of land from which the wood seems to have been long extirpated, and have, besides, attached to them, extensive tracts of forest. The cleared land is rarely, I may almost say never, cultivated, nor are any inroads made in the forest for such a purpose. The soil is, nevertheless, fertile, and were it not, manure lies in heaps by their houses. Were every family to enclose half an acre of ground, till it, and plant in it potatoes and maize, it would yield a sufficiency to support them one half the year. They suffer too, every now and then, extreme want, insomuch that, joined to occasional intemperance, it is rapidly reducing their numbers. This, to us, so strange apathy proceeds not, in any great degree, from repugnance to labor; on the contrary, they apply very diligently to it, when its reward is immediate. Thus, besides their peculiar occupations of hunting and fishing, in which they are ever ready to engage, they are much employed in the navigation of the St. Lawrence, and may be seen laboring at the oar, or setting with the pole, in the large boats used for the purpose, and always furnish the greater part of the additional hands, necessary to conduct rafts through some of the rapids. Nor is the obstacle aversion to agricultural labor. This is no doubt a prejudice of theirs; but mere prejudices always yield, principles of action cannot be created. Where the returns from agricultural labor are speedy, and great, they are also agriculturists. Thus, some of the little islands on lake St. Francis, near the Indian village of St. Regis, are favorable to the growth of maize, a plant yielding a return of a hundred fold, and forming, even when half ripe, a pleasant and substantial repast. Patches of the best land on these islands are, therefore, every year, cultivated by them, for this purpose. As their situation renders them inaccessible to cattle, no fence is required; were this additional outlay necessary, I suspect they would be neglected, like the commons adjoining their village. These had apparently, at one time, been under crop. The cattle of the neighboring settlers would now, however, destroy any crop, not securely fenced, and this additional necessary outlay, consequently bars their culture. It removes them to an order of instruments of slower return, than that which corresponds to the strength of the effective desire of accumulation, in this little society.

It is here deserving of notice, that what instruments of this sort they do form, are completely formed. The small spots of corn they cultivate are thoroughly weeded and hoed. A little neglect in this part would, indeed, reduce the crop very much; of this experience has made them perfectly aware, and they act accordingly. It is evidently not the necessary labor, that is the obstacle to much more extended culture, but the distant return from that labor. I am assured, indeed, that, among some of the more remote tribes, the labor thus expended, much exceeds that given by the whites. The same portions of ground being cropped without remission, and manure not being used, they would scarce yield any return, were not the soil most carefully broken and pulverized, both with the hoe and the hand. In such a situation, a white man would clear a fresh piece of ground. It would perhaps scarce repay his labor the first year, and he would have to look for his reward in succeeding years. On the Indian again, succeeding years are too distant to make sufficient impression, though, to obtain what labor may bring about in the course of a few months, he toils even more assiduously than the white man. The wages of labor with him, are lower than with the white man, for his wants are fewer. But for this, the range of materials, coming within reach of his effective desire of accumulation, would be even more limited than it is, and the amount of instruments formed by him, less.

Similar observations will apply to all the remnants of the race, scattered through the parts of the North American continent, to which the industry and enterprise of the white man, have brought modern arts and civilization. They can no where be said to form an agricultural people. All the great tracts of land, reserved for their use, throughout the continent, retain their native forest character; and it is only at great intervals, where spots of soil appear offering peculiar facilities for cultivation, that the riches of the earth are even partially brought into action. When such materials are neglected, it is not to be supposed that others, requiring greater strength of the accumulative principle to form them into instruments, will be put to use. None, therefore, even of the most common handicrafts, which they see the white man continually exercising, are to be found among them. The axe and the knife, are almost their only tools. Their houses, their furniture, their clothing and utensils are all similar, and of a sort to serve only the needs of the moment. Nothing is either reserved or provided for a futurity in any ways distant. Their stock of instruments being thus confined to such as are of the most quickly returning orders, a vast mass of materials is neglected, which by another race, governed by other principles of action, are converted, or converting, into the means of abundantly supplying the necessities and enjoyments of a numerous population. They thus afford a striking instance, of the effects resulting from a great deficiency of strength in the accumulative principle. They have skill, adequate to the formation of instruments capable of ministering to the necessities and comforts of a numerous population, for with the powers of fire, the axe, and the hoe, the great agents in converting the forest to the field, they are well acquainted; they have industry, content with a very moderate, if immediate reward; yet, from inadequate strength in this principle, these all lie inert, and useless, in the midst of the greatest abundance of materials; and, the means for existence in the time to come not being provided, as what was future becomes present, want and misery arrive with it, and these tribes are disappearing before them. The white man robs their woods and waters of the stores with which nature had replenished them, and the arts, by the communication of which he would compensate for the spoliation, are despised.

Though the civilized man may be truly said to have been the greatest enemy of the Indian, yet he has not always been so wilfully, and, in many instances, he has endeavored to be his benefactor. But, though his endeavors may occasionally, for a time, have arrested the progress of the evil, they have never altogether removed it, or been of permanent advantage. Of all attempts of the kind, that of the Jesuits, in Paraguay, seems to have been productive of most good, and to have given the fairest promise of ultimate success. This partial success is evidently to be traced, to the usual talent of those fathers, in clearly perceiving the actual circumstances of the condition, and disposition of the men with whom they had to deal, and to their usual ability in converting these circumstances into means of accomplishing the ends they had in view.

Their plan presents two great features. They wrought upon the Indians through that which was alone in them capable of exciting to extended action, their love of their several nations, and devotion to their interests. They took every means to show them that they could, and would, promote these interests; and thus identifying themselves with the national existence and prosperity, transferred to their order a large portion of the strong feelings arising from benefits received from, and obligations and duties owing to his tribe, which are the great movers, and rulers, of the being of the Indian.

The efforts of the missionaries seem first to have been directed to convince the chiefs, and leaders, of the several tribes to which they penetrated, of the sincerity of their desire to be of service to them. As the messengers of a religion, promising peace on earth, and immortal happiness after death, they had claims on their attention which are foreign to our subject. Besides these however, as the possessors of the arts and powers of civilization, they had others, which were more palpable to the comprehension of the savage. Europeans were known by this unfortunate race, as possessors of powers so great, as to appear supernatural; but they had hitherto been known only as enemies and oppressors, the bearers of unspeakable calamities or utter ruin. Once then they were convinced, that the white men who now came to them, were really friends, and were desirous of exerting those powers for their preservation and happiness, which had hitherto been employed for their destruction, they were ready to welcome them as their best benefactors, and most powerful protectors. The usual intelligence, prudence, and fortitude of the fathers did not desert them on this occasion, and, though not without the expense of the martyrdom of several of the order, they succeeded in impressing the Indians with the belief, that they were really their friends. The rest of the task was comparatively easy. Convinced on this head, the savages willingly, and immediately, became docile disciples. Fully satisfied of the advantages which European arts give to a people, they set themselves with zeal to acquire and practise them, for the benefit of their several tribes. Though not for his individual advantage, or that of his family, would the Indian sacrifice present pleasure or embrace present toil; for the good of his nation he had been taught, and was ready, to bear or forbear any thing. The Jesuits had, therefore, only to teach what it was necessary to do, or endure. The details they have left us of their progress, are generally interesting, sometimes amusing, not unfrequently, to those unacquainted with the peculiarities of the Indian character, almost incredible.

They themselves, in the first instance, taught their proselytes how agricultural operations were to be performed, by taking the spade, and other instruments, in their own hands. But, when thus, by precept and example, they had brought them to be able to execute the several operations of ploughing, sowing, reaping, etc., the difficulty was but half over. Without the constant superintendency and vigilance of their instructors, they never would have practised them. Thus, at first, if these gave up to them the care of the oxen with which they ploughed, their indolent thoughtlessness would probably leave them at evening still yoked to the implement. Worse than this, instances occurred where they cut them up for supper, thinking, when reprehended, that they sufficiently excused themselves by saying, they were hungry.

By the indefatigable perseverance, and dexterous management of the missionaries, they were, however, at last, brought so to labor the earth, as, in that fertile soil and warm climate, to produce abundant returns. They were also at peace with one another, and feared by their enemies. The tranquillity, the security, and the plenty, they thus enjoyed, gave the Jesuits additional claims on their confidence and gratitude, which the good fathers seem to have taken care should be made sufficiently apparent to them. Hence it was, as Charlevoix tells us, that they thought they could never sufficiently testify their affection and gratitude for those, who had rescued them from barbarism and idolatry, and who, in spite of the most severe persecution, and the greatest toil, had procured them all the advantages they enjoyed. They continually recalled to mind the miserable state from which they had been brought: the parents instructed their children, and they saw with their own eyes, the condition of the neighboring nations, who had not participated in their happiness. It was by no means wonderful, as he continues, that these things produced an attachment for the missionaries, that was without bounds.

The additional authority and influence thus acquired, they employed in enforcing stricter obedience, and increased industry, and gradually leading on their disciples to the practice of the finer and more difficult arts. In this they perfectly succeeded, so that there were every where to be seen, says the same author, workshops of gilders, painters, sculptors, goldsmiths, watchmakers, carpenters, joiners, dyers, etc. In the exercise of these useful and ornamental arts, we must not suppose the artists were animated by the motives that excite similar labors elsewhere. They seem scarcely to have had an idea of personal property, or individual gain, but to have been as mere children, looking up to the Jesuits for every thing, and ready to do every thing for them, or submit to any thing from them.

"These fathers," says Ulloa, "have to visit the houses, to examine what is really wanted; for, without this care, the Indians would never look after any thing. They must be present too, when animals are slaughtered, not only that the meat may be equally divided, but that nothing may be lost." "It has been necessary," says Charlevoix, "to appoint superintendents, who inspect every thing accurately, and see if they are busy, if their cattle are in good condition, etc. The labors of the women are regulated, as well as those of the men. At the beginning of the week, there is distributed among them, a certain quantity of wool, and cotton, which they are obliged to return, on Saturday evening, ready for the loom. But, notwithstanding all this care and superintendence, and all the precautions which are taken to prevent any want of the necessaries of life, the missionaries are sometimes much embarrassed. This proceeds from three defects, of which the Indians have not yet been corrected, their improvidence, indolence,[1] and want of economy; so that, it often happens,

---

[1] Indolence and improvidence are, in our system, reduced to one defect. Indolence is, the not laying out present labor to secure future abundance. Improvidence, the squandering present abundance, in disregard of future coming want. They both proceed from the predominance of the present over the future, the low strength of the effective desire of accumulation.

that they do not reserve themselves a sufficiency of grain, even for seed. As for their other provisions, were they not well looked after, they would soon be without wherewithal to support life."

The mode of operation, which the Jesuits adopted, had undoubtedly the advantage of bringing out all the energies of the Indian. He was thus induced willingly, and therefore zealously and successfully, to apply his powers to the acquisition and practice of European arts, and, while the missionaries maintained their power, and formed a part of the polity which their sagacity and perseverance had established, it gave every token of prosperity and vigor. Their prudence and providence led into efficient action the desire, which every individual felt for the future prosperity of his tribe. The powers of the social and benevolent affections of the mass had free course, and what was wanting in intellectual energy being supplied by the fathers, the desire of accumulation of the whole body became sufficiently effective and strong, to form a larger stock of instruments. What, therefore, might, at first sight, strike us as the most difficult part of the project, the establishing a community of goods and interests, was, in reality, that which rendered it of easy execution. With all the advantages attending such a form of society,—the freedom from strife, jealousy, contention, and care, enjoyed by the great majority,—it had also the disadvantage of requiring, and therefore exciting, in the multitude, little or no exertion of the intellectual faculties. The converts had become, or were becoming, mere machines in the hands of the missionaries. The whole stock of instruments formed by the common labor, was in the possession of the fathers, and the share which the Indians received of the returns, depended on their pleasure. They were in fact regarded as beings of a superior order, whose actions were of necessity right, and whose slightest wishes were laws.

If we judge from what is known of the state of the American continent at its discovery, it would seem that this form of society, is that which the hunter, changing directly to the agriculturist, naturally assumes. His devotion to the interests of the tribe, passes there into affection for the person, and blind obedience to the will of the chief. The accounts we have of the condition of the kingdoms that the Spaniards found established in the most fertile regions of the continent, describe the power which the rulers possessed, and the reverence paid them, as excessive. The people seem to have, in general, approached the condition of slaves, and to have had a large share of the defects of that condition, a want of intelligence and energy.

Our own barbarian ancestors, such as they are described by Tacitus, have been often likened to the savage aborigines of North America. But, though there may be some points of resemblance, the parallel will be found to fail, in several important particulars, which, as they seem to have operated through the influence they have exerted on that principle, the effects of which we are at present considering, may be allowed to claim our attention for a little.

The race, whose occupation of the forests and wildernesses to the northward of the Roman Empire, made these, in the days of Rome's strength, to be regarded as the regions of mystery and wonder, in those of its weakness, of well-founded and increasing anxiety and dread, were properly shepherd warriors. Though the excitement of the chase frequently gave fit employment to their ardent spirits, and its toils to their hardy frames, and though its products ministered to many of their wants, their cattle were yet their main support, and to provide for the sustenance of these, their great business. But the possession of flocks and herds, implies a considerable degree of care and foresight, both in protecting and making provision for them, and in avoiding to consume too great a number of them. It also implies the existence of private property to a large amount, and, consequently, of strength in the ties binding families together. The parent, if he desires to see his offspring enjoy plenty, must exert himself to procure it for them. The performance of this duty gives him claims on their gratitude, and draws closer the connexion between them. The sort of life they lead too, demands less of severe exertion, and affords longer intervals of ease. It brings them together in larger bands and societies, of which each member has rights to defend and interests to provide for, and thus produces the rudiments of law, justice, and the policy of civilized society.

War may be said to be natural to them, as well as to hunters, but it is always open; concealment is out of the question; their greater numbers, and the necessity of having always with them a large train of domestic animals, render it impracticable. They have not therefore to fear being surprised and overcome, before they can have time to defend themselves. Hence, the members of a numerous and warlike pastoral nation, live in comparative security. They see that chance has less influence, prudence and resolution more. They perceive that they are not altogether the sport of destiny, but that their fate depends, in a great measure, on themselves. Their minds are less shaken, and their judgments less clouded, by superstitious fears and imaginings. The greater security they enjoy renders them also less relentlessly cruel. Utterly to exterminate their enemies is not necessary; to break, and drive them off, is sufficient. When, therefore, the fury of the fight is over, mercy has, with them, a place.

All these circumstances pertaining to the condition of pastoral nations tend strongly to excite the social and benevolent affections, and the powers of reason and reflection, and to give scope to their action among them. The pastoral ancestors of the present European race were fierce, cruel, and vindictive barbarians; yet, spite of these forbidding features of their character, we can as distinctly trace to them the sources of all the more generous and softer virtues, that give happiness to their descendants, as we can the free and independent spirit that bestows on them liberty and security. Such nations have, therefore, naturally a much higher effective desire of accumulation than nations of mere hunters. The strength of this principle, in fact, seems with them in general, so great, as to incline them to form instruments requiring a much superior degree of providence and self-denial, to that indicated by the breeding of cattle. They are prevented from doing so, by their wandering life, and by the wars in which they are necessarily constantly engaged. When, for instance, they are settled in a country suited to agriculture, and to which the knowledge of the art has penetrated, they have a tendency to become agriculturists; that is, to change the land, from which they draw their subsistence, from an instrument yielding a large return, in proportion to the labor bestowed on it, to one yielding a still larger return, though requiring proportionally more labor and time, and being, therefore, of a more slowly returning order.

But such a change, though increasing the whole population of the state, leaves fewer in it who can be spared from labor, and, consequently, fewer soldiers. In pastoral nations, almost all the men are warriors; in agricultural, only a few can be withdrawn from the labors of the field. The latter are therefore, naturally inferior to the former in military prowess, and are consequently subject to be conquered and destroyed by them. Such seems to have been the fate impending over Gaul, from the side of Germany, when the appearance of Cæsar gave another turn to affairs. The Gauls, we learn from him, though then inferior, had once been superior, in military renown, to the Germans. It appears likely, that the revolution had been occasioned, by their becoming an agricultural people, which they, in a great measure, were, in his time. The Germans, again, preserved themselves from the fatal effects of such a change, by the singular national custom, or constitution, that obliged them all, every year, to exchange the lands they respectively occupied. By this constant transfer of instruments, and of the materials of which they might be formed, they took away every inducement to work them up into orders of slow return, and confined the members of the community to the pastoral condition, which experience had doubtless instructed them, was most favorable to military prowess.

In the times of the Cæsars, Europe was thus divided, by an irregular line running east and west, into two great parts, the one occupied by the barbarians, the other by the Empire. To the northward of this line, were many rude nations, strong in the mental and corporeal energies of the individuals composing them, and in the willingness of each to devote his abilities to objects conducive to the good of all, but whose strength was largely expended in furious intestine wars. These contests, destructive as they were, did not, however, occasion any progressive diminution of the vigor of the whole body; it was only the surplus powers of the parts that thus ran to waste. The strength of the people of the empire was, on the contrary, derived from their union in one great body, and the power thence resulting of the energies of the whole being directed to any particular point. But this union, as it had been produced by compulsion, augured weakness in the several parts, and was the cause of weakness. What each contributed to the common good was not of will, but from necessity, and, in the strife thus arising, every man learned to consider his own good as separate from that of all others. Hence a continually increasing separation of interests, and consequent continual decrease of power and general decline. The gradually increasing weakness of the empire, while the strength of the nations to the northward, if not augmenting, remained at least unimpaired, rendered the arrival of a period when the former should be overpowered by the latter inevitable. These barbarians believed, that the riches of the earth belonged, of right, to the best; according to their creed, the bravest. Their most powerful and warlike tribes, therefore, possessing themselves of the more fertile regions, those bordering on the line dividing them from the empire, pressed violently against it, and, opposed by a force continually diminishing, at length burst through it.

Three great events, each leading on the other, would seem to have been the necessary consequence of this revolution. Of these, the first was the occupation of the whole continent by the barbarians, and the driving back the still onward-urging host of their brethren; the adoption by them of the arts which had previously flourished in the empire, and their becoming an agricultural people, was the second; and their running the chance of being in turn overpowered by the northern warriors, the third. Until the arrival of the first period, when, the continent having been completely overrun and ravaged by the barbarian multitude, had assumed a form closely approximating to that of the territories they had formerly occupied, there could be no approach to rest, but the tide must still advance. When the receptacle vacant for its reception was once completely filled, the mighty mass had to recoil on itself. The battle of Chalons fixes this period. Europe, with the exception of the corner occupied by the Eastern Empire, and which belonged rather to Asia than to it, seems then to have been reduced nearly to the state of one immense cattle-pasture. But the impetus that had been given still continued, and new hosts crowded on to share that, of which the last fragments had been divided. The reflux then of necessity took place. The hosts of the west and the south, under Theodoric and Elius, met those of the east and the north, under Attilla, on the plains of Champaigne. The vastness of the masses and the violence of the shock are shown by the destruction produced; the accounts of the period rating the slaughter variously at from one hundred and sixty-two thousand to three hundred thousand.

From this period the great body neither much advancing nor receding, was agitated chiefly by fierce internal commotions. The time when their violence terminated marks the second period, when the general prevalence of agriculture, lessening the number of warriors, diminished the extent and frequency of wars. The knowledge of the elements of it, and of the other arts, diffused throughout the various multitude that now peopled the continent, could not forever lie dormant. It has been already observed, that the strength of their effective desire of accumulation, had been such as to produce a tendency among them to give greater capacity even to the materials of which they had the command in the northern regions, though at the expense of changing them into instruments of somewhat slower return, by converting their lands from pasture to tillage. This tendency became inevitably stronger, as they advanced into more fertile soils and milder climates. The revolution itself took place gradually. The exact date of the preponderance of the one condition over the other, cannot, perhaps, be determined but by the effects produced by its arrival. It is only in the state of hunters, or shepherds, that nation can literally go to war with nation. In the agricultural state, it is not the men of the nation, but a small part of them, the soldiery, that fight. Taking this as the criterion, we might fix the reign of Charlemagne as that, in which war, as the business of European nations, properly ceased. The conclusion of that monarch's reign, has sometimes been reckoned the commencement of a period of weakness in the several states, and of want of ability in their monarchs. The historian, it is true, for centuries afterwards, finds no events that he esteems great to record. His art can call up no pictures of heroes leading armies to the field, conquering, or being conquered, overthrowing, or establishing kingdoms. Nevertheless, if the view we are taking is correct, it is from this era that we must date the commencement of strength, not of weakness. The people of Europe then began to rise in the scale of industry. They commenced a new era, to which no one can assign a positive termination, because it became their occupation to conquer nature, and not man, and, to the fruits of the one conquest, we can set no limit, whereas the utmost advantages of the other are very speedily exhausted.

It may here be observed, that the difference of the strength of the principle of accumulation in nations of hunters, and in pastoral nations, seems to mark out a very opposite destiny to a great country overrun by the one, to that which would await it from being subdued by the other. The naturally low degree of strength of the accumulative principle among nations of hunters, prevents them, as we have seen, from forming instruments of sufficiently slow return to embrace the materials to which the arts of civilized life might give capacity. While in their possession, therefore, they lie unemployed, and useless. The progress of civilization and art over the continent of North America, is now every day, bringing to light traces of their former presence, and evidence, consequently, of the existence there at some remote period, of a people far superior in these respects to the tribes that occupied all but the southern parts, when discovered by Europeans. The question has been asked, how did it happen that they, and the knowledge and power they possessed, utterly perished. In other instances, civilization has either protected its possessors, or, if they were overcome, has reacted on their conquerors, and spreading among them, has, so to say, subjugated and governed them in turn. The history of our barbarian ancestors has been quoted, as a circumstantial account of this seemingly natural progress. But, if the principles, the operation of which forms our present subject, be correct, they furnish a sufficient cause for the diversity of effects flowing from the two events, and show, that, instead of there being any reason for surprise at the hunter of the woods disdaining the labors and rewards of civilization, it is rather our business to inquire how he could ever have been led to adopt them. Had the nations whom the north poured forth on the south of Europe, been hunters, and, had no extraneous cause intervened, it is not improbable, that that continent would, even at the present day, have been one wide forest from side to side.

The third of the great events referred to, the evils and dangers arising to the ancestors of the present inhabitants of Europe, from their former brethren of the north and east, when the strength of their accumulative principle led them to put off the barbarian, and employ themselves in giving to the materials within their reach the capabilities for the supply of the wants of futurity which art showed that they possessed, were felt for many centuries. The change they were then undergoing, though it added very greatly to the total numbers of the several nations, lessened the numbers of the warriors. The instruments they formed being of the more slowly returning orders, though the whole income from them was much greater, the labor necessary to produce it was more than proportionally greater, and the portion of the population left free for the purposes of warfare was consequently less. It were foreign to our purpose farther to allude to this cause of commotion and revolution, than to observe, that the mischiefs and dangers arising from it, seem to have been moderated by the very gradual manner in which the change took place, and to have been counteracted, and finally overcome by the additional power acquired through the progress of invention in the arts of civilized life.

The next example I shall adduce, of the influence of the accumulation principle, will be that of the Chinese Empire. All accounts agree in ascribing to the people of this Empire, a peculiarity running through the whole structure of their social and domestic life, by which alone perhaps its mechanism can be well explained, and which seems to form its great governing and sustaining principle. Their moralists and legislators appear to have successfully endeavored to give to the feelings, naturally springing from the parental and family relations, an influence and authority, far superior to what these possess among other nations,—the power and unity of a regular system of duties and obligations. A father, as the immediate though secondary cause of existence, is regarded with much of the feelings that are elsewhere reserved for the infinite and eternal fountain of all existence, power, and perfection, and, consequently, claims, as a sacred right, a measure of love, reverence, and obedience, that to us seems perfectly unnatural. Both while alive, and after his death, he is reverenced, we might say adored. His descendants form a little distinct society bound together by the strongest ties, a system apart from all others, having a common centre of action of its own. What is conceived to be a reality in families, is metaphorically applied to the whole empire, and its several parts. The emperor is the father of his people, his affection for them as his children is held to be the animating principle of his actions, implicit obedience to him as their parent, who can only command what is good, is the first duty of his subjects. Each inferior magistrate is also regarded as the father of those over whom he rules.

The result has been so far happy, that the harshness of despotism is somewhat tempered by the mildness of the paternal character. We are so constituted, that no part can be assumed, and habitually acted, without in some degree moulding our nature to its form, and making that a reality, which may at first have been only a fiction. It has also been happy in the strength it has given to the connexions and affections of those belonging to the same family, or springing from the same stock. A man must be strongly excited to good, and deterred from evil, by being aware that his actions and fortunes are the objects of solicitude to every member of the little community to whom he is bound by the ties of blood and kindredship; that they rejoice at whatever he accomplishes that is honorable and happy; and are afflicted and disgraced by his imprudencies and errors.

But, viewing the system on another side we may perceive that evil has sprung out of it. The blending of the characters of parent and lord, and thus making of each head of a family an absolute master, the judge of right and wrong, places man in a situation dangerous to his weakness. It may encourage, at all events it enables him to gratify without fear, whatever vice or immorality is not necessarily open or declared, but may have a veil, however thin, of outward decorum thrown over it. Besides this, the absolute submission and unreflecting obedience which it inculcates, are much opposed to the expansion of the intellectual and moral powers. When all impulses are from without, it is impossible that the mental eye should turn steadily on the divinity within, or promptly and resolutely execute what it dictates.

We perceive a great attempt to organize a society, animated by the principles of love and affection, regulated by those of virtue. The form indeed exists, but under it there is little substance. Hence is generated a mass of apparent contradictions: viewed in one light, we see a great family, wisely and beneficently governed; in the other, a servile herd, crouching beneath the sharp lash of selfish despotism. On the one hand is presented to us a people, among whom doctrines of a very pure morality, of universal benevolence, of devotion to the public good, are inculcated both by reward and precept; among whom learning is held in such esteem as to be the sure, and, in theory at least, almost the only road to honour and authority; among whom the freedom of the press may be said to have been established a thousand years;[1] among whom outward decency and decorum prevail, and security and order are strictly maintained, not by military authority, but by their own good sense quietly submitting to the rule of the civil magistrate. On the other hand we see this same people, in private, abandoned to gross sensuality, to drunkenness and degrading licentiousness; in public, in affairs of trade and traffic, in the business and diplomacy of the state, making their individual advantage their sole practical rule of right and wrong.

[1] Where the press is merely a brush, and the types are blocks of wood, which a common workman carves out for a few pence, it must of necessity be essentially free. The best proof of this is, that books for which there is a demand, licentious publications for instance, are extensively circulated, notwithstanding all the efforts of the magistrate.

Such being the character of this singular people, our principles would give to them a less strength of the effective desire of accumulation than the generality of European nations, but a greater than that of other Asiatics. This desire is lessened by a propensity to sensual gratifications and selfish feelings, and by a state of society where there is any thing to endanger the security of future possession. All these produce a tendency to seek the enjoyments of to-day, at the risk of leaving the wants of to-morrow unprovided for. As compared with other than European nations, however, we might expect them to possess no inconsiderable portion of the virtues of prudence and of self-control. The general diffusion of a tincture of learning, and perception of something of the beauty and obligations of moral rectitude, the consequent subjection at all events of the more violent passions, and the great desire to provide for the wants of their families, which the strength of the connexion thus subsisting between parent and child engenders, raise them, in these respects, much above Asiatics in general. We should, therefore, a priori, suppose, that the instruments formed by them must be of orders of quicker return, and embracing a less compass of materials, than those constructed by European nations; but of slower return, and embracing a greater compass of materials, than those to which the strength of the accumulative principle carries the other nations of Asia. All who have written concerning this great empire agree in the statement, that the necessary cost of subsistence is there small, and the wages of labor low. To these two circumstances, determining their state, is to be added a third. The inventive faculty would appear to have been once very active among them; their knowledge of the arts suited to their country is very extended.

Durability is one of the chief qualities, marking a high degree of the effective strength of accumulation. The testimony of travellers ascribes to the instruments formed by the Chinese, a durability very inferior to similar instruments, constructed by Europeans. The walls of houses, we are told, unless of the higher ranks, are in general of unburnt bricks of clay, or of hurdles plastered with earth; the roofs, of reeds fastened to laths. We can scarcely conceive more unsubstantial, or temporary fabrics.¹ Their partitions are of paper, requiring to be renewed every year.

A similar observation may be made, concerning their implements of husbandry, and other utensils. They are almost entirely of wood, the metals entering but very sparingly into their construction; consequently they soon wear out, and require frequent renewals. A greater degree of strength in the effective desire of accumulation, would cause them to be constructed of materials requiring a greater present expenditure, but being far more durable. From the same cause, much land, that in other countries would be cultivated, lies waste. All travellers take notice of large tracts of land, chiefly swamps, which continue in a state of nature. To bring a swamp into tillage is generally a process, to complete which, requires several years. It must be previously drained, the surface long exposed to the sun, and many operations performed, before it can be made capable of bearing a crop. Though yielding, probably a very considerable return for the labor bestowed on it, that return is not made until a long time has elapsed. The cultivation of such land implies a greater strength of the effective desire of accumulation than exists in the empire.²

The produce of the harvest is, as we have remarked, always an instrument of some order or another, it is a provision for future want, and regulated by the same laws as those to which other means of attaining a similar end conform. It is there chiefly rice, of which there are two harvests, the one in June, the other in October. The period then of eight months, between October and June, is that, for which provision is made each year, and the different estimate they make of to-day and this day eight months, will appear in the self-denial they practise now, in order to guard against want then. The amount of this self-denial, would seem to be small. The father Parennin, indeed, asserts, that it is their great deficiency in forethought and frugality in this respect, which is the cause of

---

[1] La Harp, Vol. VIII. p. 289. *Lettres edifiantes*, Vol. X. p. 107.

[2] Staunton, *China*, Vol. II. p. 244. Ellis, *Embassy to China*, pp. 268 and 316. The best proof perhaps is in the premiums offered for their cultivation. See *Lettres edifiantes*, Vol. XI. p. 525.

the scarcities and famines that frequently occur. "I believe," he says, "that, notwithstanding its great number of inhabitants, China would furnish enough of grain for all, but that there is not sufficient economy observed in its consumption, and that they employ an astonishing quantity of it in the manufacture of the wine of the country, and of raque." As confirmative of his observations, he remarks the number of fires occasioned by the habit of drinking to excess before going to bed, and the prevalence, among the lower orders, of a malady called ye-che, produced by the same vice.[1]

A document given in the Jesuit's Letters, a translation from the Gazette of the empire in 1725, probably shows nearly what order instruments of this sort, and therefore of all sorts, really belong to: that is, the difference between a quantity of rice, or of any thing else, in possession at the end of harvest, and a quantity to be had in spring. It proceeds on the supposition that three bushels at the former period are equivalent, and, in ordinary years, when there is neither famine nor scarcity, will produce four at the latter. By purchasing at the former period, and selling at the latter, the writer therefore estimates, that thirty bushels will, at the end of five years, produce more than one hundred. The estimate is perhaps a little high, but from the nature of it, of the individual from whom it comes, and those to whom it is addressed, it is unreasonable to suppose that it is much too high. Taken in conjunction with a description of a scheme for raising funds, of which an account is subjoined,[2] it indicates that instruments in China are about the order D.

The deficiency of the strength of the effective desire of accumulation, is balanced by the smallness of the necessary cost of subsistence, and wages of labor, and by the great pro-

---

[1] *Lettres édifiantes*, Tom. XII. p. 199. The father Parennin seems to have been one of the most intelligent of the Jesuits, and had the very best opportunities for observation, having spent a long life among the Chinese of all classes. His testimony is much more to be depended on, concerning such a fact, than that of passing travellers, whose cursory observations extend only to what may be seen on the exterior of the habitations.

[2] [Here Rae refers to a long "note" appended to the original work, which is reproduced as "Note F" in the Appendix to this volume.]

gress which has been made in the knowledge of the arts suited to the nature of the country and the wants of its inhabitants. Where the returns are quick, where the instruments formed require but little time to bring the events for which they are formed to an issue, even the defective principle of accumulation of the Chinese is able to grasp a very large compass of materials.

The warmth of the climate, the natural fertility of the country, the knowledge which the inhabitants have acquired of the arts of agriculture, and the discovery and gradual adaptation to every soil of a variety of the most useful vegetable productions, enable them very speedily to draw from almost any part of the surface, what is there esteemed an equivalent to much more than the labor bestowed in tilling and cropping it. They have commonly double, sometimes, treble harvests. These, when they consist of a grain so productive as rice, the usual crop, can scarce fail to yield to their skill, from almost any portion of soil that can be at once brought into culture, very ample returns. Accordingly there is no spot that labor can immediately bring under cultivation, that is not made to yield to it. Hills, even mountains, are ascended and formed into terraces ; and water, in that country the great productive agent, is led to every part by drains, or carried up to it by the ingenious and simple hydraulic machines, which have been in use from time immemorial among this singular people. They effect this the more easily from the soil, even in these situations, being very deep and covered with much vegetable mould. But what yet more than this marks the readiness with which labor is found to form the most difficult materials into instruments, where these instruments soon bring to an issue the events for which they are formed, is the frequent occurrence on many of their lakes and waters of structures resembling the floating gardens of the Peruvians, rafts covered with vegetable soil and cultivated. Labor in this way draws from the materials on which it acts very speedy returns. Nothing can exceed the luxuriance of vegetation, when the quickening powers of a genial sun are ministered to by a rich soil, and abundant moisture. It is otherwise, as we have seen, in cases where the return, though copious, is distant. European travellers are surprised at meeting these little floating farms, by the side of swamps which only require draining to render them tillable. It seems to them strange that labor should not rather be bestowed on the solid earth, where its fruits might endure, than on structures that must decay and perish in a few years. The people they are among think not so much of future years as of the present time. The effective desire of accumulation is of very different strength in the one, from what it is in the other. The views of the European extend to a distant futurity, and he is surprised at the Chinese, condemned, through improvidence and want of sufficient prospective care, to incessant toil, and, as he thinks, insufferable wretchedness. The views of the Chinese are confined to narrower bounds, he is content, as we say, to live from day to day, and has learnt to conceive even a life of toil a blessing. The power which the singular skill and dexterity of this people, notwithstanding their deficiency in the strength of that principle that forms the subject of this chapter, gives them, to work up into instruments supplying a larger circle of wants, many materials that would otherwise lie dormant, is seen in various instances besides those referred to. It may be sufficient to mention the manufacture of silk, and the cultivation and manufacture of tea. They are both instances of the power of the inventive faculty to form instruments, soon bringing to an issue events, that repay, according to the rate at which labor is there repaid, considerably more than the cost of their formation.

However we explain it, it will I think be admitted as a fact, that Europeans in general far exceed Asiatics, both in vigor of intellect and in strength of moral feeling. The average duration of human life is also with them more extended, and property more secure. These circumstances give much superior power to the accumulative principle in the one continent, to what it has in the other, and occasion the instruments constructed in each to be of very different orders, and to form a strong contrast when compared together. The attention of an European, when he visits Asia, is arrested by the slightness and want of strength, solidity, finish, and consequently durability, of every instrument he sees. Were an

Asiatic city deserted, the place where it stands would, in half a century be scarcely discernible. The instruments constructed being of the more quickly returning orders, all materials which require much labor, and bring in only distant returns, are neglected. Mud takes the place of stone, wood of iron. In Europe, on the other hand, in proportion as the minds of the people are reflective and intelligent, and their habits moral, we find that the interests of futurity operate on them so largely as to occasion a great capacity to be given to materials, on which, in Asia, a very small capacity would be bestowed, or which would there be altogether neglected. The most stubborn morasses are drained, and converted into arable lands; roads, canals, bridges, fences, dwelling-houses, furniture, tools, utensils, in short all instruments whatever, indicate that the formers of them have regard to a distant futurity, and are willing to give up for its interests a large portion of the means of present enjoyment.

It is to be observed, however, that in Europe invention has in general made much greater progress than in Asia. Perhaps in their knowledge of agriculture and horticulture the Chinese equal most European nations, but in other arts they are far inferior, and, with the exception of them, no Asiatics, in the knowledge of these or of other arts, can compete with Europeans. On the other hand, the wages of labor in Europe, are far higher than in Asia. This circumstance, countervailing the other, would probably, in many cases, bring the durability and efficiency of the instruments constructed in both continents nearly to an equality, were it not for the existing difference in the strength of the accumulative principle.

The examples we have hitherto considered have been of societies, where the principle of accumulation has been either advancing, or, at least, not sensibly retrograding. It may be well to turn our attention to the effects produced by a sensible decrease in its strength. The history of the declining ages of the Roman empire furnishes us with such an one.

Rome may be said to have carried with her, from her earliest germs, the elements of decay. Her power was entirely that of force, a principle suppressing and subduing every thing, generating nothing; like flame spreading far and wide, investing whatever it catches with momentary splendor, but, like it, destroying that which feeds it, and going out at length leaving desolation behind it. The proper trade of the Romans was war. But when in agricultural countries war becomes the occupation of a community, and conquest the means by which it seeks to acquire wealth and greatness, evils arise which time, instead of mitigating, increases. When hunters go to war with hunters, or herdsmen with herdsmen, the object in view, besides overcoming their enemies, is to obtain possession of a portion of the surface of the earth, and the animals wild, or tame, nourished by it. Over such communities therefore, though war, passing like a destroying tempest, leaves ruin behind, yet time obliterates all traces of the devastation produced by it, and the same territory sees a new generation arise from the victors or vanquished, as free, happy, and prosperous, as their forefathers. But in states of society where the riches of the earth are not brought out by the wild or tame animals which its surface nourishes, but by the husbandman who tills it, there conquest can never be a permanent gain, unless through some permanent right acquired by it over the inhabitants of the territory subdued. Hence the fact of war being successfully pursued as a gainful trade by any community, seems to imply, that the conquered submit to slavery, either personal or political, probably partly to both. Gain was always the ultimate object aimed at by the Romans. It was not to chastise an insult, or to protect their citizens in the undisturbed prosecution of industry, that they fought or conquered. These might occasionally serve for pretexts, and were sometimes perhaps the exciting causes of war, but for the real fruits of victory they always looked to the spoliation of the vanquished, and tribute, in one shape or other, imposed on them. Every people with whom they came in contact was regarded by them first as an enemy to be subdued, afterwards as a province from which they were to be enriched. They were in truth a band of well disciplined robbers, whose virtue, law, religion, centered in their swords; courageous indeed, and keeping to their positive engagements with a fidelity common to brave men (and which, as it is for their interest, even scattered banditti observe), but whose course of rapine was still onward, relentless, merciless, unchecked by thoughts of the corporeal pains, or mental debasement it produced.

Such an empire could only have been formed by overpowering the finer and more generous and elevating feelings, and could not be maintained without having the effect of giving the preponderance to the debasing, selfish, and therefore destructive principles of our nature. It left but one great virtue, that of patriotism, with the Romans a sort of enlarged *esprit de corps*, and one great moral quality, that of courage, or the meeting danger undauntedly when the interest of the individual or the state required it,—a principle of action, it may be remarked, differing considerably from the more generous and self-devoting *gallantry* of the modern. These were strong in Italy while Italy was the governing power; but even they gradually disappeared as the provinces were amalgamated with it, and Italians ceased to be the conquering soldiery.

It were needless to enlarge on a subject so well known as that of the general corruption of Roman manners, from the time of the first Cæsar. Venality and licentiousness may be said to have been universal. I shall confine myself to one particular, as marking sufficiently the declension of those principles on which the strength of the effective desire of accumulation mainly depends. I allude to the decay of the family affections, of which evidence everywhere meets us. The men did not wish to be fathers, scarcely did the women wish to be mothers. The joys of the relation were to them too small, to be a compensation for the sacrifices it demanded. The bringing up of children cost the one parent too much money, and took from the other too much pleasure. If families were raised up, it was not from the natural influence of the parental affections, but in obedience to the laws, that the man might have the approbation of the magistrate, and that there might be citizens to the state. They lived, not in others, or for others, but for themselves, and sought their good in enjoyments altogether selfish. It was their aim to expend on their own personal pleasures whatever they possibly could. It would seem as if the majority, could they have foreknown the exact limits of their lives, would have made their fortunes and them terminate together. As they could not do so, the fortunes of many ended before their lives, as the fortunes of others held out beyond their lives. To reap, however, themselves, while alive, all possible benefit from what they might chance to leave others to enjoy after their death, they encouraged some of the members of a despicable class who seem to have constituted no inconsiderable part of Roman society. Parasites ready to minister to every pleasure, and to perform every possible service, waited on the man of wealth, in the hope and expectation of enjoying a portion of it after his death. They were more desirable than children, both because they were able to give something more than mere unsubstantial affection and esteem, and because they were willing to give it, while a son or daughter might imagine they had claims to receive what they could not be said to have labored for. The poets and satirists of the Augustine age, and of subsequent times, give sufficient evidence of the existence of a state, evil in itself, and the forerunner of many evils.[1] It gave occasion to the law compelling parents to leave their children a certain part, a fourth, of their property. Its prevalence may be judged of by the wording of the enactments increasing the children's share. It is stated, as a fact well known, that parents generally either disinherit, or omit their children in their wills, leaving the bulk of their property to distant relations, to strangers, or to slaves, to whom they give freedom;

---

[1] Horace, V. Satire, II. Book. It is worth while observing, that, according to this satire, to cheat these parasites into the service, by holding out a reward they were never to get, was reckoned a thing to be laughed at.— Probably the practice existed from a very early age, though I cannot give authority for it. Parasites are in Plautus' Plays, but these are in a great measure translations. The following quotation from that author, however, expresses a feeling, which I should suppose prevailed in Roman society at the time:

"Quando habeo multos cognatos, quid opus mihi sit liberis.
Nunc bene vivo et fortunate, atque animo ut lubet,
Mea bona meâ morte cognatis dicam interpartiant,
Illi apud me edunt, me curant, visunt quid agam, ecquid velim,
Qui mihi mittunt munera, ad prandium, ad cænam vocant."

and that thus, if their family is numerous, they, who during the lifetime of their father enjoyed affluence, find that his death leaves them in poverty.[1]

Nothing, surely, can more clearly show the extreme and pervading selfishness of the time, than its becoming necessary for the magistrate to compel the citizens to marry, and also to compel them to leave portions to their children. The existence of such a state of things implied a degree of isolation of feeling and action, so great, as necessarily to produce general weakness and decay. The general selfishness of the principles guiding the conduct of individuals, may be gathered from a prevailing proverb, "when I die let the world burn."[2] When such were the maxims ruling society, there could not fail to be a heedless sacrifice of the interests of futurity, an exhaustion of the means or instruments which the forethought of previous generations had employed industry to accumulate, without any correspondent reformation of them. Sallust, in a fragment quoted by Montesquieu, well describes the men of his day as a race who could neither themselves hold property, nor allow others to retain it.[3] Only such instruments could consequently be formed as were of very quickly returning orders, and, as the vigor of the accumulative principle decayed, the members of each succeeding generation saw a mass of materials fall from their grasp, which had afforded

---

[1] Quia plerumque parentes sine causa liberos suas exheredunt vel omittunt. *Inst.* Lib. II. Tit. 28. Capiunt quidem cognati omnia, et extranei, vel cum libertate servi; filii vero licet multi consistant; etiamsi nihil offenderint parentes, confunduntur, etc. Novel. XVIII. Pref.

[2] Ἐμοῦ θανόντος γαῖα μιχθήτω πυρί. Suet. A similar proverb "après nous le déluge," is said to have been often in the mouth of Madame Pompadour, one of the purest self-worshippers ever existing. It is perhaps worthy of remark, as showing the propensity of selfishness to grasp the present, that both the Romans and the lady were very prodigals even in what was entirely their own. The former it is well known rapidly exhausted their constitutions by every sort of debauchery and excess, the latter was as little economical of her personal charms. At twenty her lips are said to have been livid from the too constant application of her teeth to make them pout, at thirty she was haggard.

[3] "Merito dicatur genitos esse, qui nec ipsi habere possent res familiares, nec alios pati."

a plentiful supply to the wants of their more provident forefathers.[1]

The means of supporting human life diminished, and the numbers of mankind diminished with them. When vice itself did not sufficiently check the growth of the elements of life, it brought want and famine to its assistance. The history of the Roman world under the Cæsars, is a melancholy detail of the gradually decaying funds of the Empire, and the gradually decreasing numbers of its inhabitants. Italy, according to Pliny, and other writers, was in the old times crowded with people, thickly set with cities, and rich in all things ministering to the needs of its inhabitants. In his day, its diminished population depended for their sustenance on the productions of other territories. The change certainly was not owing to any alteration in the materials. "Non fatigata aut effœta humus," says Columella. The earth would have yielded the same returns, had they who possessed it been willing to expend what was necessary to give it the capacity of yielding them. As the materials were only wrought up to very quickly returning orders, they had necessarily a much smaller capacity, and the annual returns made by them were of consequence much less. Pasture took place of tillage; corn was brought from the provinces; and when the supply failed famine ensued. Even the construction of ships for the transport of this, and other merchandise, would seem to have been an effort to which the accumulative principle was scarcely equal. It was found necessary to encourage it by rewarding those

---

[1] [Several writers have ascribed the fall of Rome on its economic side, to the draining away of money to the East in payment for imported luxuries. This was not a separate and distinct cause of decline, but rather one of its concomitants. It is but one of the phases of the general and fundamental cause which Rae sets forth. The stock of metallic money of a community is a social instrument, the "instrument of association," as Henry C. Carey aptly called it, and it is secured in the first place and kept up afterwards in the same manner essentially as other instruments—by industry and the exercise of the accumulative principle. The present-day arguments as to the comparative unimportance of more or less money, do not apply to an age when extensive areas were lapsing from a money economy to a state of barter.]

who prosecuted that branch of industry.[1] Sometimes land formerly cultivated was allowed to lie entirely waste, and passed altogether out of the class of instruments. The forest and wilderness gained on the Romans, as they would now, for similar reasons, on an Indian population, were some of these tribes put in possession of the domains, anciently the property of their race, at present yielding abundantly to the provident industry of the whites. Had there been no irruption of the barbarians, the Empire must have perished, more slowly perhaps, but as certainly, from the operation alone of these internal causes of decay. They were occasioning a progressive diminution of the capacity which materials formerly possessed. Thus, it is to the Romans themselves as much as to the barbarians, that the destruction of the public edifices is to be ascribed. The stones were applied to private purposes. With the capacity for yielding a return, there necessarily perished the return yielded, and the power, consequently, of maintaining the same number of men, and contributing an equal amount to the wants of the state. Hence the population of the Empire, and the imperial revenue, diminished from age to age.

The diminution would have been much more rapid but for some counteracting causes. Rome, while she conquered and enslaved, gave peace, and peace enabled the arts to pass from country to country, and often, under her protection, carried them to regions before barbarous. Again, she herself, as she gradually proceeded to enslave the rest of the world, and encircle it in her empire, received into her bosom those who had been free, or were the immediate descendants of freemen, and retained something of their virtues. The ungovernable licentiousness, extravagance, and proneness to evil of the Italians, were tempered by the greater decency and frugality of the *new men* of many of the distant provinces,

---

[1] Nam et negotiatoribus certa lucra proposuit, suscepto in se damno si cui quid per tempestates accidisset ; et naves mercaturæ causa fabricantibus magna commoda constituit pro conditione cujusque : civibus vacationem legis Pappeæ : Latinis jus Quiritum : fœminis jus quatuor liberorum ; quæ constituta hodie servantur.
         Suet. in vita Claudii, XIX.

who flocked in to recruit the diminishing numbers of her citizens.[1]

These two circumstances, however, only retarded, they could not resist, the advancing degeneracy, poverty, and weakness, that were gradually sapping the foundations of the Empire, and exposing it to be overturned by external violence, or to fall to ruin by its own weight. While some of her provinces gave strength to Rome, she corrupted them; if she gave them her arts, she gave them also her manners. Like liquor, already begun to turn, mixed with what is yet fresh, the defects of the compound were not at first perceptible; by and by, the adulteration diffused through it wrought on the whole, and rendered it all alike worthless.

The propagation of Christianity over the Empire is to be reckoned as another of the causes retarding its decay. It is to be observed, however, that this took place too late for reaping the advantages, which the morality of the Gospel might have otherwise conferred; and that the corruptions of the times were so great as to lead its teachers rather to preach the duty of withdrawing from the world, than to inspire them with the hopes of remoulding the world to an accordance with a system of perfect purity of morals and benevolence of purpose. The effects of this cause were therefore comparatively small.

The reader will perceive that the subject we are upon might be stretched to an indefinite length. Circumstances have given to every community a peculiar character; the moral and intellectual powers of every people have received different degrees of developement, and the continuance of life is more or less probable, and the possession of property more or less assured, in one country than in another. All these particulars vary the relations between the present and the future, in the estimation of the members of different societies, and would therefore determine each community to stop short at some particular point in our series, towards which, the strength of the accumulative principle may be said to cause the instruments it forms continually to gravitate. Unlike the

[1] Tacit. *Ann.* C. 55, L. III.

operation of gravity, however, the force with which they tend to this point diminishes, as their distance from it decreases, and the farther they are removed from it, the greater the rapidity of their progress towards it.

The subject would not therefore be fairly exhausted until all the circumstances of the moral and intellectual state, and other particulars of the condition of every people, had been examined, and compared with the extent to which the formation of instruments among them is advanced. Enough, however, has perhaps been done to show, that this principle is of very extensive operation, and that in our subsequent inquiries, we are warranted in assuming the strength of the effective desire of accumulation to be a circumstance of primary importance, in the determination of the extent to which the formation of instruments will be carried in any society. We should now proceed to examine the more important effects resulting from variations in the strength of this principle in different members of the same community. It is however necessary first to consider some phenomena produced by the progress of it, and of the inventive faculty, and certain classifications of instruments and names applied to them, which have thence arisen. This will form the subject of the next chapter.

CHAPTER VIII.

OF THE DIVISION OF EMPLOYMENTS AND OTHER PHENOMENA PRODUCED BY EFFORTS TO ACCELERATE THE EXHAUSTION OF INSTRUMENTS.

EVERY individual endeavors to exhaust, as speedily as he can, the capacity of the instruments which he possesses. By rapidly exhausting the capacity of any instrument, the returns yielded by it are not lessened, but quickened. The powers it possesses to bestow enjoyment, or to aid in the formation of other instruments, are not diminished in quantity, but sooner brought into action, and it passes to an order of quicker return. When therefore the efforts of individuals, so directed, are successful, by placing the instruments operated on in more quickly returning orders, they stimulate the accumulative principle to give greater capacity to instruments of the sort, and proportionally increase the capacity of the whole stock of instruments owned by the society. It is to certain phenomena, in the production of which these two circumstances are the main agents, that we have in this chapter to direct our attention.

As the knowledge which mankind possess of the course of nature advances, and they discover a greater number of means to provide for their future wants, the instruments they employ for this purpose become very various. The exercise of the arts of the weaver, the blacksmith, the carpenter, the farmer, implies the existence of a great variety of tools with which they may be carried on. But, as a man can only do one thing at once, if any man had all the tools which these several occupations require, at least three-fourths of them would

OF SEPARATION OF EMPLOYMENTS

constantly lie idle and useless. It were clearly then better, were any society to exist where each man had all these tools, and alternately carried on each of these occupations, that the members of it should if possible divide them amongst them, each restricting himself to some particular employment. There would then be no superfluous implements, each set of tools would form an instrument much more speedily exhausted, and therefore of an order of quicker return than before. In cases where this could be done, common sense would point out the advantage of it. When, for instance, a man's loom came to be worn out, he would go to his neighbor and say, " I shall not make another loom if you will undertake to do what weaving I may require; in return I will give you some of the produce of my farm, or will do some blacksmith work for you." The offer would be accepted, and similar motives operating throughout the society, each individual in it would confine his industry, as far as possible, to the employment of some particular set of tools or instruments. It is not perhaps likely [obvious], that this was the manner in which that division of occupations with which we are now familiar was originally produced, but it must evidently have been produced in this way, had it not been otherwise brought to pass, as we see, in fact, that even now it is thus brought to pass in the progress of settlements in North America. In such situations, every man is at first probably obliged to be his own carpenter, glazier, tanner, cobbler, and perhaps to a great extent his own blacksmith. As the settlement fills up, and the population becomes sufficiently dense, he gives up this multifarious industry, and takes to some particular branch. The advantages of the change to the whole community, and therefore to every individual in it, are great. In the first place, the various implements being in constant employment yield a better return for what has been laid out in procuring them; being sooner exhausted they pass to a more quickly returning order. In consequence, their owners can afford to have them of better quality and more complete construction; the effective desire of accumulation carries them on to a class correspondent to its own strength. The result of both events is, that a larger provision is made for the future wants of the whole society.

Such a revolution can only have place, where the individuals exercising the different employments, have a ready communication with each other. In situations where they cannot easily communicate, either from distance, or difficulty of transit, such exchanges cannot take place.[1] If a man had to go twenty miles for every little piece of carpenter work that he wished executed, it were better for him to keep a few carpenter tools of his own. Neither is it likely to take place extensively unless where the accumulative principle has considerable strength, and where, consequently, a large amount of labor is wrought up in the several implements in use. Where, as in Hindostan, the loom is merely a few sticks, it would save one individual very little to employ another to weave for him. It is accordingly, in countries where the population is most dense, the facility of communication greatest, and instruments wrought up to the more slowly returning orders, that employments are most divided.

As a division of employments implies the existence of exchange or barter, so, as it extends, these exchanges become necessarily more frequent. Every man, to procure the supply of his various wants, has to employ the services of more individuals than he had before. The farmer, who used to manufacture his own cloth from his own fleeces, transfers these to some one else, and perhaps, after they have passed through the hands of the carder, the spinner, the weaver, the fuller, etc. part of them returns to him again in the shape of cloth for some garment that he is in need of. In an advanced state of society, very few wants are supplied but by articles or instruments which have passed through many hands. We can scarce then fitly pursue our subject, without some examination of the manner in which these exchanges take place, and of the rules by which they are regulated.

As all instruments exist solely to supply wants, so any man

---

[1][In Carey's terminology, separation of employments depends upon the "power of association." He believed that through an excessive scattering out of the people into the backwoods settlements in his day this power, and therefore its advantages, were in great measure lost. Compare Edward Gibbon Wakefield on the "barbarising tendency to dispersion" in all frontier communities.]

will consent to receive an instrument in exchange, or expect to give it in exchange, only as it is a means of supplying wants. It is the business of every man to adopt the readiest and easiest means he can devise to supply all coming needs, and it is solely because the medium of barter [exchange] presents the readiest means of effecting this end, that he adopts it.

But labor is the fund which all men have, out of which to supply their wants. Some have other funds besides, but every man has this, and strip a man of every thing adventitious, this alone remains to him. It is this, then, which a person may most fitly be said to expend, in provision for any future want. When one man exchanges this for that, he may be said to give the labor which he has expended on this, for the labor which has been expended on that, and labor for labor would seem to be the most simple of exchanges. It never, as we shall see, exactly takes place, but sometimes it is nearly approximated to, and, that we may set out from the most simple elements, we may suppose that it is actually arrived at.

Any man will be inclined to exchange one instrument for another, if, by so doing, he can save himself any part of the labor which he must otherwise expend in producing that other. A lives in some place where willows are to be had for cutting them; he employs himself in making willow baskets, one of which he finishes in two days; B offers him a straw hat for it. If he wants a straw hat, and thinks that, were he to set a making one, it would occupy him more than two days, and moreover, that neither D, E or F, who make straw hats, will give it for less: he will be inclined to make the exchange. In doing so, it is a matter of indifference to him what time B may have expended in making the hat, his only reason for entering into the transaction, is the saving of labor to himself he thereby effects. In reality, however, it is altogether likely that B has not expended more than two days in making it. For, supposing, as in this case we may, that both A and B have the same natural faculties, B, were he to set about making willow baskets, could make them as well and as easily as A, that is at the rate of one in two days. If then the straw hat cost him more than two days' labor, he would rather make a willow basket for himself than exchange his straw hat for it. Even if he had not the manual skill necessary, he would apply himself to acquire it, and take to the occupation of basket-making in preference to that of making hats; as we see, in employments where mere labor is concerned, that one is deserted for another according as it gives less or more wages.

It so comes to pass that in the same society, in all exchanges, as far as we can conceive mere labor to be concerned, one man, A, barters that which has cost him two, or twenty days' labor, with that which has cost another, B, two, or twenty days' labor. We must however bear in mind, that neither does A offer the article, nor does B receive it, simply because it has cost two, or twenty days' labor. A offers it, and B receives it, because it is an instrument to supply future wants, and under the supposition that it cannot be got for less than two or twenty days' labor. In such cases, the person desirous of making the exchange may indeed say to the individual with whom he wishes to exchange,—Sir, I assure you the article cost me two, or twenty days' labor, as the case may be; and being assured of this, the person so addressed may think it sufficient grounds to make the exchange, and may so conclude the bargain. But he does so, not because the other has expended two or twenty days' labor on it, but because, he having expended this, he concludes that it cannot be got for less; that if it has cost him two or twenty days' work, it would have cost any other, and would cost himself, the same labor. If he knows that the person desirous of exchanging is an unskilful or bungling workman, or if he sees that the labor has been injudiciously applied, he will not give what is demanded. He knows, in that case, that he can make it, or get it made, for less. Were one to employ himself in rolling a stone up hill and down hill for a month together, he would leave it as useless to him in the way of exchange as before he put his hand to it.

It may be laid down as a rule, then, that in as far as labor simply is concerned in all exchanges, one thing will be bartered for another, not in proportion to the labor that has been respectively bestowed on each, but in proportion to that which it is necessary to bestow on materials, similar to those of which each has been constructed, to make other articles equal to them in capacity to supply wants; that, if this basket exchanges for that hat, though each may have cost two days' labor, it is not exactly because each has cost it, but because neither a basket equally good as the one, nor a hat equally good as the other, can be made for less than two days' labor.

As a corollary from this, it follows that, whenever an article comes to be made with less labor than formerly, articles of the same sort which may have been previously manufactured, procure for their owners less of other articles in exchange than they did before. They exchange, not for what labor has been actually wrought up in them, but for what is now required to make others similar to them. Thus, supposing that a basket-maker, say in some settlement in North America, having to go on foot a considerable distance through woods and swamps for his willow twigs, requires one day to procure enough to make a basket, and that he takes another to work them up, he would then probably receive for each basket two days' labor, or articles having cost two days' labor. If now, however, a place where equally good willows grow is discovered near at hand, so that only half a day is required to get enough for a basket, and if this is generally known, he will no longer be able to exchange them at the same rate, because, as we have seen, other people would make baskets for less, that is, for one and a half days' labor, or for articles in the fabrication of which the labor of one and a half days had been expended. Any stock then he might have on hand of baskets made previously to this discovery, would only exchange for articles requiring for their fabrication the labor of a day and a half. The same rule that applies to this trivial instance, holds good in affairs of greater importance, and regulates a large amount of exchanges.

It can however never exactly happen, that labor will be exchanged, in this simple way, for labor. The formation of every instrument, besides labor, requires also the assistance of some other instrument. Even the basket-maker and the hat-maker, allowing them to get the twigs and straw they require, for the trouble of collecting them, would need, the one at least a knife, and the other a needle and thread. Auxiliaries so inconsiderable as these need scarce be noticed in the reckoning; but there are cases where these assisting instruments may be said to do a great part, others, in which they may be said to do nearly the whole of the work. In a steam-boat the engine may be considered as the great laboring power, though the services of the men who supply fuel, and regulate the motion of it and of the boat, enter also largely into the account. In a set of well-contrived, and well-finished pipes, for conducting water through a city to the different houses in it, the amount of human labor entering [directly] into the process is very trifling.

A weaver we shall suppose receives thread to weave into a piece of linen, and finishes the job in thirty days. Were he now, in return, to receive from his employer simply thirty days' labor, he would get too little; for, his loom being an instrument partially exhausted in fabricating the linen, this exhaustion ought to form an item in the account. Suppose that the effective desire of accumulation of the individual, is of strength sufficient to carry him to the order G, doubling in seven years, that the loom cost one hundred days' labor, and that it will be exhausted in seven years; it would then require to return two hundred days' labor, or an equivalent, at the end of that period. The return however is not delayed so long, but begins to come in daily, immediately after its construction. Calculating then what yearly return is equal to two hundred days at the end of seven years, in the estimation of a man who reckons one day now equal to two then, it will turn out to be nearly twenty days. We may allow that the loom is in employment three hundred days a year, it would therefore, on these principles, have to return two days' labor, for every thirty days during which it was in operation, and the weaver would consequently have to receive an equivalent to thirty-two days' labor; at least had he not a moral certainty of receiving this, he would not have formed the instrument, and were such return to cease he would not reconstruct it.

The transport of goods by sea is an event brought about as much by the agency of instruments, as by direct human labor. A vessel costs, we shall say, five thousand days' labor, is exhausted in seven years, and is navigated by three men. If she belongs to a person whose effective desire of accumulation carries him only to the class G, and supposing those who navigate her to be paid for three hundred days' labor, she must, on these principles, return about nineteen hundred days' labor annually. Say she is freighted to carry a cargo of timber, and that the voyage occupies three months. This transport being a part of the process of the formation of certain instruments, houses, furniture, etc., as necessary as any other part of it, the owner will therefore receive directly, or indirectly, from those engaged in their formation, an equivalent to not less than four hundred and seventy-five days' labor.

It is to be observed, too, that, even in cases where labor alone seems to be paid for, time generally also forms one of the items to be taken into account. Thus, an individual contracts, within three months, to fell the trees on a certain piece of forest land in a North American settlement. If then he be paid at the commencement of the three months, he will expect to receive less than if payment be deferred until the expiration of that time, and the difference between the two amounts will be regulated, as in other cases, by the particular orders to which instruments, in that particular situation, are generally wrought up. The same things hold good in all instances where labor is paid for by the work executed, or, as it is termed, by the piece.

The division of employments and consequent prevalence of the system of exchange, occasions a particular classification of instruments.

Before the division of employments takes place, the instruments which every man forms, or causes to be formed, are for his immediate use, and after it has taken place, the portion individuals reserve for this purpose makes still a considerable part of the whole of the instruments belonging to any community. Even the poorest beggar has some clothes to cover him; the opulent have houses, furniture, clothing, gardens, pleasure-grounds, &c. This part of the whole mass of instruments possessed by individuals or communities, is termed a *stock reserved for immediate consumption.*

The remainder of the general stock of instruments of individuals and of societies, with the exception of land, considered not as actually cultivated, but as having [been given] a capacity for being cultivated, is termed *capital*. The instruments to which this term applies supply the future wants of the individuals owning them, indirectly, either from being themselves commodities that may be exchanged for articles directly suited to their needs, or by their capacity of producing commodities which may be so exchanged.[1]

Capital itself is again subdivided into *fixed*, and *circulating* capital. Fixed capital consists of instruments which have a capacity for producing commodities to be exchanged, but are not themselves formed for the purpose of being exchanged. Circulating capital consists of commodities fitted for being exchanged, or of instruments in process of formation into such commodities.

It often happens that the division between fixed and circulating capital is drawn with difficulty, some instruments belonging partly to the one, and partly to the other. Thus a horse employed for agricultural purposes is a part of fixed capital, while an ox may belong partly to fixed, and partly to circulating capital, as he is reared and fed, in part for the services expected from him as an animal of draft, and in part for the price his carcase brings.

The total instruments owned by an individual, or a society, and comprehended under the terms a stock reserved for immediate consumption, fixed and circulating capital, have received the general appellation of stock.

All instruments, whether comprehended under the divisions capital fixed and circulating, or a stock reserved for immediate consumption, possess a capacity for supplying the wants, or saving the labor of man. But the wants which they supply

---

[1] [Apparently Rae excludes land, considered as the basal instrument of agriculture, from the category of capital, because it is an instrument of "indefinite period of exhaustion" and yields income in the form of rent instead of interest or profit. It is important to observe that Rae makes no use of the specific definition of capital here given, which follows closely the lead of Adam Smith. His working concept of capital coincides with all stock. The title of this second "Book," it will be remembered, was: "Of the Nature of Stock and of the Laws Governing its Increase and Diminution." This reprint would have been called the Sociological Theory of Stock, had that been a terminology which would speak to the present generation of readers.]

and the labor which they save, are in general not immediate, but future. Now we cannot estimate the same amount of labor saved, or wants supplied tomorrow, and five, or fifty years hence, as equivalent the one to the other. Thus if we compare together a hundred full grown trees, and as many saplings, it may be, that, estimated in the supply they yield the wants of futurity, they are alike. If the former be cut down tomorrow they may yield a hundred cords of fire wood, and if the latter be cut down fifty years hence they may yield the same. We should not nevertheless conceive, that they were equal the one to the other. What measure then are we to adopt for comparing them and other such instruments together, and thus finding an expression in a quantity of immediate labor for the whole capacity of instruments possessed by any community or for the whole stock of that community? The natural measure would seem to be the relative estimate, which the individuals concerned themselves form of the present and the future, that is, the strength of the effective desire of accumulation of the particular community. Thus in a community whose effective desire of accumulation is of strength sufficient to carry it to the formation of instruments of the order E, doubling in five years, an instrument, which at the expiration of five years yielded a return equivalent to two days' labor, might fairly be estimated as equivalent to one day's present labor; if at the expiration of ten years it yielded an equivalent to four days' labor, it might also now be rated at one day's labor, and so for other periods. This therefore is a mode of expressing in present days' labor the whole capacity of the instruments owned by any society which will be made use of in the following pages; and the terms, the *absolute* stock, and *absolute* capital of that society, will be employed to denote it.

The mode, however, in which the fixed and circulating capital and stock belonging to societies is usually estimated, is different. It is usual to estimate the instruments belonging to any society, by comparing them with one another as they actually exchange, some particular commodity being made choice of as the standard to which all other instruments are referred. To capital and stock estimated in this mode, the terms, *relative* capital and stock of societies, will be applied.

In cases where the effective desire of accumulation of a community has had opportunity to work up the materials possessed by it into instruments of an order correspondent to its own strength, the absolute and relative stock must, it is obvious, agree; but, in cases where the accumulative principle has not yet had time fully to operate, the former will exceed the latter. Thus, were we to suppose the returns made by the whole of the instruments belonging to a society, or their total capacity, to be suddenly doubled, without any addition to the labor employed in forming them, the total absolute stock of the society would also be doubled, while its relative stock would remain unaltered. The relations of the several instruments possessed by it remaining the same, whatever commodity had been adopted as the standard, when applied to measure the others it would give the same results as before. It never, indeed, can happen that any increase to the capacity of the instruments forming the stock of a society, so great and sudden as we have supposed, can take place; but however small such increase, it would have a real effect, and would occasion a difference in the amount of the whole stock as estimated in the one or the other manner. Every such increase is effected through the operation of the inventive faculty, and we shall therefore defer the consideration of the effects flowing from it, until we come to treat of the phenomena resulting from the progress of that faculty.

Though the division of employments consequent to the progress of science and art, and the operation of the accumulative principle, on the whole greatly accelerates the exhaustion of instruments, there are yet some particulars in which it tends somewhat to retard that exhaustion. In the most simple state of society, when art is so rude, and accumulation so little advanced, that each individual forms almost all the instruments he himself or his family exhaust, and when, consequently, the general stock of the community is nearly altogether a stock formed and reserved for immediate consumption, it can seldom happen that there will be either an over abundance, or a deficiency of instruments of any sort. As each individual can make an accurate estimate of his own wants and those of his family, prudent men, in such a state of things, provide only the instruments that may be of use to them, and do not form any but such as they foresee will come into employment as they are formed. But when individuals ceasing to form only instruments directly supplying their own wants, give the greater part of the industry they can command to manufacturing commodities for the purpose of exchange, as they have not the means of calculating with equal accuracy the wants of other men, it occasionally happens that some commodities are produced in excess, and that there is a deficiency of others.

When, again, the state of society is such, that each individual forms almost the whole instruments he requires, there is very little transport of commodities from place to place. The amount of transport necessarily increases with the separation of employments. This forms another drawback from the advantages arising from the extension of the division of occupations, and system of exchange. On account therefore both of many commodities being produced in excess, and of its being necessary to transport most from place to place, there are always, in such states of society, very many commodities lying idle, being neither under process of formation or exhaustion, but collected in masses at different points, waiting till some vacancy be found for them. The longer they continue in this state the farther they must pass towards the orders of slower return, and the more the operation of the accumulative principle must be retarded.

It seems to be chiefly from the desire of obviating somewhat these two disadvantages attending the general advance of art and industry, that, when the nature of the occupation permits it, individuals engaged in all the different divisions of industry place themselves as near each other as possible, and form villages and towns. Each can thus more easily adjust the amount of commodities he produces to the wants of other men, and thus also there arises a great saving of transport.

It is also in a great measure owing to the necessity of

transporting commodities from place to place, and to the difficulty of regulating the precise amount produced consequent on the division of occupations, that there arises an order of men, that of merchants, devoting themselves solely to the business of transport and exchange. Merchants are the great exchangers of society, regulating the production of commodities and collecting and distributing them to situations where the never-ceasing processes of formation and exhaustion are producing vacancies for them. It is their business to make these exchanges with the greatest possible rapidity, and least possible expense.

There is a general average time elapsing from the period of the formation of every commodity, until it pass from the individual having formed it, to the individuals who exhaust it in the supply of their wants, or employ it in the formation of other instruments. The merchant who effects the transfer of commodities between the other members of society is entitled to receive an amount exceeding that which he gave, by the return which the labor embodied in the commodity exchanged should yield for this average time, according to the general rate of return of capital in the community. If therefore the superior intelligence, penetration, and activity of any merchant—giving him the power of foreseeing with greater accuracy than his brethren where vacancies are about to exist, and what will be their extent, and of discovering where the commodities proper to fill them up may most readily be found, and most easily transported to the requisite places—enables him to effect these transfers with greater facility than usual, and within less than the average time, he will receive a proportionally greater return than other merchants. On the contrary, if, from a deficiency in these qualities, any merchant attempt the transfer of commodities for which there is no vacancy, or effect the transfer of commodities for which there is a vacancy, at more than the average expense, or in more than the average time, the returns his capital yields him will be less than those usually received by the other members of the community. Mercantile energy is thus stimulated to effect all practicable exchanges with the greatest possible celerity, and at the least possible expense.

The activity which is in consequence given to the process of exchange, is a circumstance exceedingly beneficial to the interests of the community. By lessening the distance between the periods of formation and exhaustion, and diminishing the expense of formation (for transport makes a part of that expense), the successful exertions of the mercantile portion of society have a powerful tendency to preserve instruments in the more quickly returning orders, and to excite the action of the accumulative principle. Our subject consequently requires us to examine somewhat more particularly the mechanism by which the business of merchants is conducted, and the mode of calculation by which it is practically regulated. Our attention too is more especially called to these, because it is from the former that the principles of the present science of political economy are derived, and on the latter that its nomenclature is founded.

The foundation of the mechanism of mercantile transactions is

Money.

Gold and silver, or, as they are called, the precious metals, are more properly entitled to the appellation of money than any other thing is, because they more generally pass for money than does any thing else. Their beauty, their incorruptibility, and some other of their qualities afterwards to be considered, have, in almost every country, rendered them the means of affording much enjoyment, that is, of supplying, to a large extent, certain of the wants of man. It seems likely that these qualities, joined to the facility with which they may be transported from place to place, first made them esteemed the most desirable of all commodities that one could possess. In the very frequent revolutions and commotions that occur in the earlier ages of society, articles that do not decay, can be hid, or carried off without difficulty, and are always estimable, would naturally of all others be most coveted. They thus probably were first chiefly sought after, for the purpose of being retained, not for that of being exchanged; even yet in many countries, partly from old habits, and partly from still prevailing insecurity, they are chiefly prized as of all things, those best fit to be hoarded. But, in whatever manner their use may have been introduced, or how much soever in some countries it may be dependent on a feeling of insecurity, at present or formerly prevailing, and prompting their possessors to keep not to part with them, they are now more generally sought for, for the purpose of being immediately passed away, forming, in the shape of money, the great medium of exchange; and it is solely in the part they thus act, that we have here very briefly to consider them.

When, in the progress of society, men divide into different occupations, and each ceasing to fabricate himself all the instruments his wants require, barters the instruments or commodities he forms for those formed by others, the system of exchange, as we have seen, commences. The introduction, to a greater or less extent, of some sort of money, seems naturally to follow. For when a man forms only one sort of instruments or commodities, it cannot at all times happen that he can exchange them with articles fabricated by other men, and necessary to supply his wants, because these other men, the formers and possessors of what he desires, may not at the moment have occasion for what he has formed. "The butcher has more meat in his shop than he himself can consume, and the brewer and the baker would each of them be willing to purchase a part of it. But they have nothing to offer in exchange, except the particular productions of their respective trades, and the butcher is already provided with all the bread and beer which he has immediate occasion for."[1] There are two modes by which the desired exchange may be effected. If the brewer and the baker have a commodity received by every one for all others, such as money is, they may each give the butcher a certain quantity of it for a quantity of meat, and when he requires their ale and bread, he may, in turn, send back to them also a quantity of money. Or, the butcher may be satisfied with the promise of the brewer and the baker, that, at some future time, when he has occasion for it, they will give him a quantity of ale and bread, or of something else. These two modes of effecting the object form the two systems of cash, or credit, by which

[1] *Wealth of Nations*, Book I. c. IV.

all the business of every country that consists not in barter, is carried on.

Pieces of gold and silver coined, that is stamped with a mark regulating and assuring by the authority of the magistrate the weight and fineness of each, enter largely into transactions of the former order; they make the bulk of the current coin of most countries. Supposing the whole of the exchanges of any country that are not simple barter, effected by money, and that gold and silver form the sole money, then the amount of them so employed [at any given level of prices] would seem to be regulated by two circumstances.

The first of these is the quantity of commodities that may exist to be exchanged. This again must depend on the quantity of materials wrought up into instruments, and on the progress of the division of labor [employments]. As the number of instruments increase, and as from their first commencing formation, until they are exhausted, they pass through more hands, the amount of exchanges must increase. As the number of instruments formed decrease, and as every man himself constructs a greater proportion of those necessary to supply his own wants, the amount of exchanges must diminish, and as the amount of exchanges increases, or diminishes, so must there be required [at any given level of prices] a greater or less quantity of the medium through which they are transacted.

In such a state of things as we suppose, could every man see exactly beforehand the whole series of the exchanges that would present themselves to him, every prudent man would so manage his exchanges, that is his purchases and his sales, as to provide himself with the exact amount of money necessary to effect every exchange that he might deem it advisable to execute. But no man can with accuracy foresee what transactions may present themselves to him, or when they may do so. The amount of possible future exchanges that may offer to any man, and the time they may occur, are exceedingly uncertain, depending on many things not to be foreknown—the operations of other individuals engaged in the formation of instruments immediately or remotely connected with those on which his means or industry is engaged, the course of the winds and seasons, the fortune of war, the progress of treaties, and numberless other events equally doubtful in their issues. Every man, therefore, would in such a state of things, suffer two inconveniences, he would occasionally have too much money, and occasionally too little. He would sometimes have a sum lying for a long time useless by him, and an advantageous purchase would sometimes present itself to him which he had not cash sufficient to effect. Between these two opposite evils, it would be his business to steer as safe a course as possible; he could not hope altogether to avoid them, but must be content to suffer occasionally from both. Which of the two it would be most prudent for him to run the risk of suffering from, would, I conceive, depend on another circumstance, forming the second of those that, under the suppositions we have made, regulate the amount of precious metals in circulation.

Every man must be more unwilling to run the risk of having a sum of money lying useless by him, by how much greater the amount of the returns he could have by turning it to the formation of instruments. If then, in the society of which any man is a member, instruments are not far removed from the first orders of our series, when they soonest double the expenditure of their formation, he will rather risk the inconvenience of having too little money by him, than the loss of having a sum in his coffers long unemployed, which might have been converted into instruments yielding large returns. But if, in the society of which he is a member, instruments are far removed from the first orders of our series, he will be disposed to reserve a greater amount in the hopes of making more by some advantageous bargain, than he could by expending it on the formation of any instrument. We should expect then to find, that, in countries where either the principle of accumulation is too weak to carry instruments on to the more slowly returning orders, or where it has not yet had time to do so, money would be scarce, and that, where this principle having had time to act, its strength has carried them to the farther orders, there money would be plenty. Such will be found to be the fact. In China, gold and silver are rarely seen, in the interior traffic of the country; in Holland, they have always abounded. In new settlements in America, where from the superabundance of materials, instruments are of very quickly returning orders, the amount of coin to be found is exceedingly small. When a man there has cash in his pocket, he finds so many things that he could with profit expend it on, that he can scarcely refrain from doing so.

An European visiting some parts of Upper Canada, is surprised when he comes to discover, that a few dollars is all the cash that even men comparatively rich may have lying by them. He is apt to conceive that they are poor men, and to describe the country as a poor country. In doing so, however, he does not make a correct use of words. He sees, for instance, a man who, ten years before, may have brought a sum of two hundred pounds to the place where he is now settled, without at present twenty dollars in his pocket, and who perhaps, were that sum suddenly demanded of him, might have difficulty to procure it. In one sense, then, the man is poor. But, were this man asked to sell his farm and his other property, he probably would not give it for less than a thousand pounds, and he might get this sum for it. If so, it is ten to one that he would lay out the greater part of it in the purchase of a larger quantity of land than he before possessed, and the remainder in improving that land, so that a year or two would see him just as bare of cash as before; and twelve years afterwards, if he went on prosperously, he would still have but a trifle of ready cash, though perhaps he might truly consider his property worth two or three thousand pounds, and might not be disposed to take less for it. He could hardly, therefore, be called a poor man. In this part of America, as formerly over the whole of it, " the scarcity of gold and silver money is not the effect of the poverty of that country, or of the inability of the people there to purchase those metals. The scarcity of these metals is the effect of choice and not of necessity. It is convenient for the Americans, who can always employ with profit, in the improvement of their lands, a greater stock than they can easily get, to save as much as possible the expense of so costly an instrument as gold and silver; and rather to employ that part of their surplus produce which would be necessary for purchasing those metals, in purchasing the instruments of trade, the materials of clothing, several parts of household furniture, and the iron work necessary for building and extending their settlements, in purchasing, not dead stock, but active and productive stock."[1]

But, though the loss of having more idle cash lying by one than can possibly be dispensed with, must be felt most sensibly where such cash can be most profitably expended, where instruments, that is, are not far from the first orders of our series, still it must always be felt. A man will never keep two hundred pounds in his chest, if he thinks it probable that one hundred will be sufficient, because he can always make something of the other hundred. Although however, men, in such cases, must be governed by what they think probably will happen, yet, as no man can foresee with certainty what may happen, every man will now and then be wrong in his calculations, and therefore, under the suppositions we have made, every man would occasionally suffer from having too little cash, as well as at other times from having too much.

The effect of both these sorts of losses must be, to place the instruments on which they operate in orders of slower return, than they would otherwise occupy. One wishes to purchase a pair of young horses of a particular sort; for this purpose he reserves a quantity of coin equivalent to four hundred days' labor; he happens, however, not to meet with a pair that suits him for the space of six months, when he purchases two, giving for them the amount he had anticipated. It is evident, in this case, that they have really cost him, not only the four hundred days' labor, but all that in the country in which he lives, that labor would have produced, besides paying for itself, during the six months he was looking out for the bargain. Now, as this additional outlay cannot add to the capacity of these instruments, to the strength, swiftness, beauty, and health, that is, of the animals, nor diminish their age, it must be esteemed as lessening the proportion between the return to be got from them, and the outlay expended on them, and must move them proportionally towards the orders of slower return. Again, it may have been that the person who at last sold the horses, may have been desirous of selling

[1] *Wealth of Nations*, Book V. c. III.

them for six months before he effected the sale, and that at the commencement of that period he may have met with an individual who would have purchased them, but not having anticipated the occurrence of so favorable an offer, happened not then to have the necessary cash. If we suppose them to have been merely useless to their owner during the period from thence elapsed, the service they rendered him being just sufficient to pay for their food and keep, still, this retardation in the return from the outlay in the formation of them as an instrument, also moves them for him so much towards the more slowly returning orders, and diminishes the activity of the accumulative principle. If the individual who raised them does not receive an additional price, proportionate to the delay, the occurrence will have a tendency to make him give up this branch of business.

Similar events taking place in the exchange of other instruments, would produce similar results, and therefore two evils would necessarily accompany the state of affairs we have supposed. There would be two drawbacks on the progress of the industry of the society, the one consisting in the expense of the circulating medium, the other in the loss arising from a deficiency in it. The two together would be in proportion to the amount of exchanges, which the progress of knowledge, the strength of the principle of accumulation, and the quality of the materials within reach of the society, caused to be transacted. The evil directly arising from them would be the consequent retardation of the returns from the industry of the society, an evil equivalent to a proportional diminution of these, and placing [the instruments producing] them in more slowly returning orders. The evil indirectly arising from them would be, the keeping a greater or less extent of materials without the reach of the strength of the accumulative principle of the society, and the consequent nonformation, to a greater or less extent, of instruments that would otherwise have been formed.

The proportion between the two would be determined by the order to which the strength of the effective desire of accumulation, and the time which it had had to operate, had carried the formation of instruments.

But the state of things we have supposed never exists. It scarcely happens, even to return to the sort of transactions we set out from, that a butcher, a brewer, a baker, dealing together, effect all their business either by direct barter, or by cash. The butcher would, in very many cases, be satisfied with the implied promise of the brewer and the baker, that, at some future time, they will give him a quantity of the commodities they respectively deal in, or of money, or some equivalent to it, equal to the price of the beef each received.

This mode of effecting the object, constitutes the system of credit, the second of the two systems by which exchanges are carried on. It has an existence in every country, and in most civilized countries, as is well known, the great bulk of transactions are carried on by the aid of it. Were the actual or implied promise, which the party receiving the commodity makes to him giving it, always fulfilled, it would in itself be unattended with any loss, and might possibly be so managed as almost entirely to supersede the use of coined money as a medium of exchange.

The whole amount of the purchases made by any individual within a limited time, is, in general, about equal to the sales he effects within the same time. If, therefore, in any community, all the exchanges, which are not direct barter, were to be transacted by credit, and were the obligations to pay granted by all persons engaged in business in it to expire at the same time, when that time came round, every individual would hold obligations to receive, to about as large an amount as he had granted to pay. If then each individual had granted obligations to pay, to the same persons as he had received others from, the business would be at once concluded by a reciprocal delivery of obligations. But this can scarcely ever happen; almost all the obligations to receive payment, which any individual holds, will be from other persons than those to whom he himself has granted obligations. The affair might however be managed, and the same end arrived at, by a transfer of obligations from hand to hand. A has bound himself to pay B fifty pounds, B to pay C fifty pounds, and C to pay A fifty pounds. If, then, A pay B, by giving him C's obligation, B can discharge his debt to C with it, and thus the debts and credits of the whole three be settled. By operations more complicated, but conducted on similar principles, nearly the whole system of exchanges of any community might be managed.

There are two obstacles to this mode of effecting exchanges by credit. The first arising from its inherent complexedness and difficulty, the second from the liability of the contracting parties to fail in fulfilling their engagements, from dishonesty, miscalculation, and accidents impossible to be foreseen. These restrict its application in general to transactions for large amounts, little doubtful in themselves, and which from their nature can be easily systematized and arranged. Such appears to have been the *viremens*, or transfers, at Lyons.[1] Such also are the transfers effected by the London bankers. In Russia, however, it would seem to be applied to transactions much more various, and complicated. Mr. Storch informs us that the creditors and debtors of the province of Kief, and several others adjoining—the proprietors, capitalists, merchants, those who want funds, and those who want to dispose of them,—meet in the month of January, in the town of Kief, to make such transfers, and that in 1804, the amount of their exchanges was upwards of twenty millions of rubles, or about three millions seven hundred thousand pounds sterling. Transfers similar to these are made, he adds, at Reval, and many other towns in the empire.[2]

There is another method by which the system of credits might be conducted, and which may be illustrated by an example taken from a country already referred to, where the causes exciting to its introduction, and giving prevalence to it, operate very powerfully. In many parts of North America, but more especially in new settlements in Upper Canada, the scarcity of cash, and perhaps other circumstances, often lead traders to adopt a peculiar plan of business. Every dealer provides himself with a general assortment of all sorts of commodities in demand in the settlement he inhabits, and reckons on being paid for them in the shape of grain, potash, pork, beef, and other commodities, in the formation of which

[1] Ganilh, *Des systèmes d'économie politique*, Tome II. p. 155.
[2] Storch, *Cours d'économie*, Tome II. p. 353.

his customers are engaged. But in this sort of barter, one article will generally fall short or exceed the value of the other, a pound of tea will not exchange for a hog, nor a quarter of wheat for a dozen pounds of sugar. To obviate the difficulty, the merchant opens an account with each of his customers, charging him with the goods furnished, and giving him credit for [crediting him with] the produce received, and in this way perhaps all the transactions between the two are managed, either by barter or credit, without the assistance of a dollar of cash. Nor is this all; a great variety of other transactions are also effected through his intervention. Any person who may have furnished him with an overplus of produce, or who has credit with him, can through his means settle most accounts or balances due on accounts. He may thus pay the laborers, and the artificers, and tradesmen, he may employ, by an order on the shop, or as it is called, store, of the country dealer. Besides these, the transactions of the storekeeper extend to the giving out of the raw produce of the country to individuals in the settlement, tradesmen, etc., who may not themselves have enough, and to the receipt in return of various articles, such as axes, shoes, boots, made-up clothes; and in this way through his books, a very large portion of the business of the settlement is transacted. It is not difficult to conceive, that the whole might be so transacted.

Were the country dealer always to have a supply of every article in demand in the settlement, at a reasonable rate, and were all contracts for the delivery of produce to him to be regularly executed, almost all the requisite exchanges might be conveniently effected through his books. But in this sort of traffic, as the merchant always has commodities to sell, and his customers have not always produce to return, it inevitably happens that they get into his debt. As his object is to sell as many goods as possible, he is very apt to allow many to run in his debt, who do not fulfil their engagements. He suffers from the dishonesty, or the imprudence and miscalculations of those who deal with him. Very many of his customers are much longer of paying him than they have promised, or they do not pay at all. Aware of the risk he runs, he is obliged to balance it by charging an additional sum, over and above what he would otherwise demand, on all commodities that pass through his hands. In some cases, this advance amounts to at least 30 per cent. In this way he makes, or endeavors to make, the prudent and honest persons who deal with him, pay for the imprudent and dishonest, who also deal with him. The former class, in consequence, keep out of the circle of all such transactions, as much as possible, and store-pay, as it is called, is depreciated.[1]

. . . .

Gold and silver would thus seem to have been considered, first, simply as themselves the most precious, and easily preserved of all articles; next, their capacity for being divided and re-united without injury, would seem to have led to their general employment in exchange for other things the acquisition of which their possessors found useful or necessary;[2] convenience then to have rendered it expedient to have them formed into pieces of a certain weight and fineness, when they began to constitute what is now called money; lastly, their general adoption as money would seem naturally to have rendered them proper measures to give fixedness to those obligations to future delivery of things in exchange, which the increased security and tranquillity of modern times, and the great amount of exchanges transacted, have in recent days introduced. In the two latter employments, as serving for real, or determining the rights which the possession of fictitious money conveys, they occasionally serve as media for exchanging all instruments, and, therefore, for determining and expressing their relation to each other, as things capable of being exchanged. In this way measuring all things exchanged, or capable of being exchanged, that is, all instruments, they come to denote the amount of instruments, or capital, or stock, which any man possesses. A person is said to be worth five hundred, or five thousand pounds, as he has instruments which, in exchange, would be measured by these sums respectively; and, as in common life all things are considered,

[1] [The omission at this point constitutes Part I. of the Article on Banking in the Appendix.]

[2] Thus the Knight parted with a link or two of his gold chain, when in need, and in more ancient times the traveller carried his bag of gold dust.

not as they are, but merely in their actions and relations, instruments come there, also, to be spoken about, and conceived of, altogether in the relation they have to certain pieces of gold and silver.[1]

These are not the only effects which the exchange of instruments for one another, and the consequent use of money as the medium of exchange, have produced in our conceptions of them. The system of exchanges, being attended by that of credit, implies the existence of some mode of ascertaining the amount to be rendered back, for instruments received in trust. It is sufficiently obvious that this must be determined by the order to which the principle of accumulation, and the time it has had to operate, has carried the formation of instruments in the society. If, in any society, instruments are at the order D, doubling in four years, then one receiving an instrument on trust, for four years, will, at the end of that period, have to return two of the same sort and quality. If they are at the order E, he will have to return two at the end of five years, etc. Thus it is a common practice in many parts of North America, especially in new settlements, to sell cattle and sheep on trust, the terms being that double the number thus transferred is to be returned in four or five years, as the agreement may be made. More generally, however, much shorter periods are adopted, for the settlement of accounts. The natural periods of a year, and a month, have in different times and places, been made choice of for this purpose. It is then necessary to calculate what is due by the one party to the other at these periods, and these calculations are naturally made in money.

Instead, for instance, of returning two cows at the end of five years, the bargain may be, that a proportional sum is to be paid at the end of the first, second, third, fourth, and fifth years. Were money paid for the cow immediately, the amount we shall say would be twenty dollars, the double of that, which would be the sum to be given were the time of payment deferred till the expiration of five years, is forty dollars. The annual payment can neither be a fifth part of the one sum,

---

[1] [That is to say, in Rae's peculiar terminology, we consider in common life only "relative stock" and disregard "absolute stock."]

AND THE SYSTEM OF EXCHANGE 127

four dollars, nor of the other, eight dollars, but one between the two, in this case about six dollars. Again, the bargain may be, that a cow be returned at the expiration of the fifth year, and that, for her use during that time, an annual remuneration be made; this would be a half of the former annual payment, nearly three dollars, and that sum accordingly, when such an arrangement takes place, is the usual yearly payment for what is called the rent of the cow. Whatever order instruments may be at, some similar calculation might determine, what should be the proportion annually paid for the use of any of them. The employment of money in these calculations has simplified them, by the introduction of general rules. The return which instruments make, is estimated at so much in the hundred, or per cent. that is, in the hundred pounds, dollars, or whatever may be the current coin. Reducing our orders to this phraseology, they would be respectively:—

A 100 per cent. per ann.   H 9 per cent. per ann.
B 41   „   „   I 8   „   „
C 26   „   „   J 7   „   „
D 19   „   „   K 6·5   „   „
E 15   „   „   L 5·9   „   „
F 12   „   „   M 5·5   „   „
G 10   „   „   N 5   „   „ etc.

It is on these principles, that all reckonings are made, not only of instruments given on credit, but of those retained. In the latter case, the annual return is termed profits of stock, in the former interest. There is, however, this difference between the two, that, in the profits of stock, is generally included the return that has to be made, for the mental exertion and anxiety, and bodily fatigue, of the owner of the stock. There is, also, a difference between them, in common language, arising from its being the practice to speak of the more favorable issues of instruments, as determining the rate, without reckoning those that have turned out less favorably, or unfortunately. Thus Adam Smith: "In a country where the ordinary rate of clear profit is eight or ten per cent. it may be reasonable that one half of it should go to interest, wherever business is carried on with borrowed money. The stock is at the risk of the borrower, who, as it were, insures it to the lender; and four or five per cent. may, in the greater part of trades, be both a sufficient profit upon the risk of this insurance, and a sufficient recompense for the trouble of employing the stock."[1] Here, ordinary profit evidently means, not the average profit, but the profit of favorable years. The average profit of a merchant, for example, is not properly the profit he makes upon his more favorable adventures, but what he makes on all those adventures that yield a profit, whether great or small, after deducting the actual loss he may sustain on others. The average profits of all the merchants of any country, also, include their very favorable, their less favorable, and their losing adventures. In this way, using the term profit for the return made from the outlay expended on the formation of the whole instruments spoken of, actual losses are also included in it, and, in speaking prospectively of future profit, the risk of future loss is included, and what Adam Smith calls the risk of insurance disappears. If in a country where the average profit is, in reality, only eight per cent., a particular merchant continue for some years to make ten per cent., he may indeed expect, and is perhaps apt to expect, the same return in future years; but, unless in so far as he can truly calculate on his mercantile sagacity and activity being above par, in so doing, he acts imprudently, and the chances are that he is undeceived by having to sustain actual losses in succeeding years.

We may then assume the rate of interest as a fair measure of the real average rate of profits in any country, and consequently of the order in our series, at which instruments are there arrived. So receiving it, we shall find that it agrees very closely with the preceding observations.

In China, we are told by Barrow, that the legal rate of interest is twelve per cent., but that, in reality, it varies from eighteen to thirty-six. The remarks of other authors agree pretty accurately with this statement, fixing the orders at C or D. The Dutch seem, of all European nations, hitherto to have been inclined to carry instruments to the most slowly returning orders. The durability given to all the instruments constructed

[1] *Wealth of Nations*, Book I. c. III.

by them, the care with which they are finished, and the attention paid to preserving and repairing them, have been often noticed by travellers. In the days when their industry and frugality were most remarkable, interest was very low, government borrowing at two per cent. and private people at three. The former indicated an order doubling in about thirty-three years, the latter, one doubling in twenty-three years. In ancient Rome, interest was in reality exceedingly high, from twelve to fifty per cent.[1] Were we farther to compare the orders in which instruments appear to stand in other countries, with the rate of interest in those countries, we should find the two everywhere correspondent. I apprehend, however, that this is needless, for, as the reader must on consideration perceive, it is impossible it can be otherwise. Loans, indeed, pass under the name of money, but money is only the means of effecting the loan, it is in reality instruments that are lent, and they must in return yield not much less [somewhat more] than what is paid for their use, otherwise they would not be borrowed, and [but] not much more, otherwise they would not be lent.

The system of calculation, the foundation of which we have been considering as connected with exchanges, is convenient for all engaged in the business of transfers, and answers their purposes very perfectly. When applied, however, to speculative purposes, it labors under the disadvantage to which all *practical general rules* are liable, when assumed as *speculative general principles*. According to it, stock is regarded altogether as measured by money, and an amount of stock is considered, simply, as an amount of money, or something that will bring money. The stocks, therefore, of different countries, are viewed as differing merely in amount, and every increase and diminution of the stock of the same country, as a simple addition, or subtraction, of an homogeneous quantity. These events being so viewed, have been assumed so to exist, and the general increase and diminution of stock have been treated of, as things as simple in their nature, as the rows of digits employed to mark the amount of money by which they are

[1] *Histoire de l'usure*, par Boucher, Paris, 1819, p. 25. The laws against usury, there, as elsewhere, increased, instead of diminishing the evil.

estimated. Some of the fallacies hence arising, will be presently noted; they will, I believe, be found to be the foundation of much of the contradictions, in which the reasonings on these subjects are involved.

[With respect to the particular subject touched upon in this last paragraph, see the Article on Method in the Appendix, the passage beginning: "Thus, if in any particular society, we were to be asked, what the capital of some other person were," etc. At the risk of anticipating somewhat, a passage from Chapter I. Book I. of the original is introduced here.]

The observation of Bacon is now trite, that men believe that the words they employ in the process of reasoning, serve the intellect as mere passive instruments, but that, in reality, they have often an active reflex power, through which, while the mind deems it governs them, they are enabled to usurp the command of it, and so misdirect its course.

Our author [Adam Smith] notices the errors, which, in this way, have arisen from the use of the term money.

"Money, in common language, as I have already observed, frequently signifies wealth; and this ambiguity of expression has rendered this popular notion so familiar to us, that even they who are convinced of its absurdity, are very apt to forget their own principles, and, in the course of their reasonings, to take it for granted as a certain and undeniable truth. Some of the best English writers upon commerce set out with observing, that the wealth of a country consists, not in its gold and silver only, but in its lands, houses, and consumable goods of all different kinds. In the course of their reasonings, however, the lands, houses, and consumable goods, seem to slip out of their memory; and the strain of their argument frequently supposes that all wealth consists in gold and silver, and that to multiply those metals, is the great object of national industry and commerce."[1]

It is remarkable that, in the use of the term capital, he himself leads his readers into a somewhat similar error. Capital means in common language a sum of money, or something for which a sum of money can be got; and, as

[1] *Wealth of Nations*, B. IV. c. I. [See "Note D" in the Appendix.]

the increase both of national and individual capital produces a sum of money, or something for which a sum of money can be got, the similar estimation of both by a row of figures is the thing that in this way naturally comes uppermost to the mind, and hence, the things themselves in both cases forming the increase not being immediately present to its thoughts, it heedlessly falls into the conclusion that they also are perfectly similar. In comparing, indeed, the national capital as it has existed at distant periods, the small national capital of remote periods with the large national capital of the present, we immediately perceive, that not only the sum at which the national wealth was formerly rated is increased, but that the things which constituted it are changed. The wealth of England is certainly ten times now what it was in the reign of Henry the VIII.; we do not conceive, however, that it is formed by multiplying tenfold such articles as constituted the sole riches of its inhabitants in that somewhat rude and barbarous age. We perceive here, that there is and must be, not only an increase but a change. When, however, we come to consider the smaller parts of which this increase is gradually made up, as the change here is not perhaps perceptible (and as all we see is the sum produced by it, the fact of the increase being more easily ascertained than the manner of it), the similarity of the terms naturally inclines us to conceive that it resembles the increase of individual capital, and consists of a mere increase *of* things, not of a change also *in* them.

CHAPTER IX.

OF INVENTION CONSIDERED AS A GENERAL SOCIOLOGICAL PRINCIPLE.

INVENTION is the most important of the secondary agents, to the influence of which man is subject. To us, it is the great immediate maker of almost all that is the subject of our thoughts, or ministers to our enjoyments, or necessities; nor is there any portion of our existence, which is not indebted to its antecedent forming power. Wherever it really is, it is recognised as one and the same, by this its formative capacity. It is always a maker, and, in a double sense, a maker. From the depths of the infinity lying within and without us, it brings visibly before us forms previously hidden. These are its first works. But neither does it intend to stop, nor does it, in fact, stop here. The forms which its eye thus catches, and its skill "bodies forth" into material shape, pass not away; they remain. Things of power, true workers, drawing to themselves, and fashioning to their semblance, the changeable and fleeting crowd that time hurries down its stream, they are, in truth, the only permanent dwellers in the world, and rulers of it. In this the double power of his works, the mathematician is as much a maker as the poet, and the poet as the mathematician; and genius in all its manifestations, may, in so far, be considered as the same power, and as excited to action by similar causes.

Our subject leads us to attend to invention, merely as it concerns itself with the material world. But, as the motives exciting the men in whom it is exhibited to give themselves up to its requirements, must be held among the chief of the causes of its manifestation, and as they who in this department have been most extensively inventors, have in general communicated little of the principles that animated and sustained them in their career, science and art being silent of themselves, we may be allowed to give wider compass to our view, and to cite, when our purpose requires it, those who have been real discoverers in any of the various regions over which the power of this principle extends.

The motives, exciting to this sphere of action, are not very apparent.

Man is essentially imitative; his instincts impel him to amalgamate with the mass. From the first moment of his existence, his faculties are on the stretch, drinking greedily in surrounding gestures, feelings, principles and modes of action, which he again communicates; he seems by turns a recipient of existing impressions, and a transmitter of them to others. Nor, unless he look far beyond himself, is there any evident motive for his endeavoring to extricate himself from the everwhirling circle of which he forms a part. Hundreds of millions have preceded him; to learn and practise what they have left, is the direct road to his goods, pleasure, and honor. Why then should the individual waste the sweets of momentary existence, in rashly and needlessly tasking his feeble powers to form a new path, when one already exists, along which so many have trodden, and which their footsteps have beaten smooth? One of the Jesuits having been asked, why the Chinese had made no progress in astronomy beyond the rude elements of the science that they had possessed from a very remote antiquity, answers, from the indolence, and want of application to these pursuits, of the men of succeeding ages, and from their preferring, like those of the present day, what they have esteemed their immediate and substantial interests, to the vain and barren reputation of having discovered something new. The reason, which the father Parennin assigns for the stationary state of their astronomy, may be transferred to all their other sciences, arts, and pursuits, which fifty generations have contented themselves with learning, practising, and teaching, as they received them from men of times more distant. A well weighed attention to what is for their present, and, as they say, substantial interests, has led them to do this, and forbid them to do more.

In that Empire, the door to wealth and honor is not absolutely barred to any one, and in this it would seem superior to other lands, that there, whoever possesses learning has a key that will infallibly open it. Let him who would raise himself superior to his fellows, give his youth to study, let him carefully make his own a due portion of the knowledge, the wit, the eloquence, or what passes for them, stored in the volumes his masters put in his hands. These acquirements will be the passports to the places round which riches and distinctions cluster. Making use of them industriously, prudently, perseveringly, he may certainly attain the rank of a skilful physician, a learned jurist, a practised and ready speaker, or, perhaps, a man versed in the constitution and policy of the empire, fit to take on him the office of a statesman, and share its rewards and honors. He may be attended by obsequious crowds ready to flatter his vanity, minister to his pleasures, conceal his weaknesses; alive he may be honored, dead lamented,—why then abandon these sure and substantial advantages, to pursue what there is but a chance of gaining, and which, even if at length attained, is but empty fame,—a breath,—the filling at the best,

"A certain portion of uncertain paper."

The practical wisdom of the Chinese answers at once, it were folly.

Is that which is sound, practical wisdom among those Asiatics, the reverse of it among us Europeans? The reader may determine, by casting his eyes about him, to discover who are the men, who have been most successful in attaining wealth, comfort, respectability; in avoiding dependence, misfortune, calumny. Whoever, or wherever, he may be, certainly he will not find it is they who have sought to be, or have really been, men of genius.

We in vain search for any sufficient motive exciting to this course of action, unless the good arising from communicating good, and the consequent desire to be a benefactor in the most extended possible manner.¹ This desire is the proper aliment of genius. " Leave me not," the lay [has] it,

> ——————" In its loneliness,
> Its own still world, amid th' o'er peopled world,
> Hath ever breathed to love."

When very strongly felt, it irresistibly impels those who are conscious of capacities equal to the attempt, spite of every obstacle to be overcome, or pain to be endured, to task themselves to the performance of works of permanent and diffusive utility. To reflective minds, and large and generous natures, the creations of genius must present themselves as of all works, those most extensively conferring enjoyment and power,² and their successful execution as of every enterprise the noblest; nor need we wonder that to such it should have a voice of magical, and almost resistless attraction.

When the peasant poet of Scotland seeks to recall an image of his earliest self, he finds there uppermost this master passion, this " boundless love " of his fellows and his native land, urging him to make it appear by something worthy of it, and marking its strength. This was the wish,

> " Ev'n then a wish (I mind its power,)
> A wish that, to my latest hour,
> Shall strongly heave my breast,"

that led him to the realms of song. This was in truth the genius,

> " Sua cuique deus fit dira cupido,"

who " threw her inspiring mantle over him," and awakening powers else torpid, enabled him to draw from out the vulgarity before hiding them, images not idly falling, and to fall, on many a heart: patriotism ardent and self-devoting; passion

---

¹ This is to be received as concerns our existence, limited to the earth and to time, the only light in which it can with propriety be considered in these speculations. Were we to view it as belonging to the universe and to eternity, action directed to the purposes referred to, would not be impeded from the considerations thus presented, but would, on the contrary, derive from them freedom and energy.

² Videtur inventorum nobilium introductio inter actiones humanas longe primas partes tenere. LORD BACON.

manly yet tender; love without the coarseness of the one class of society, or the affectation or epicurism of the other.

Who can estimate all the effects of these hasty fragments of the poet's art? If we consider the subject well, and weigh it fairly, we shall confess, that their author has exercised an influence already greater, and far more abiding than any of the men of his country and age. It is thus that genius manifests the potency of the principle that inspires it, and that the simplest lays of the simplest bard, may have a power passing far, that of the triumphs of the statesman, or the warrior. The one wakens energy, otherwise dead, into action, the other merely directs that action.

"But," it may be said, and not without a show of reason, "why, if genius is roused and moved by principles so pure, does it happen, that the undoubted possessors of it, are themselves so often defaced by faults, and that we speak of them, and their aberrations, as if naturally conjoined? Ambition, the desire of excelling, a much more questionable motive, would rather seem its proper stimulant."

As we are not attempting to investigate the governing principles of classes [or individuals], but of societies, it were, perhaps, enough in answer to observe, that the existence of genius among a people, implies at least the diffusion of a tincture of generous feelings, somewhere throughout the mass. If we were to see an individual periling his own life to rescue another from impending danger, it might be doubtful to us whether the action proceeded from a desire of saving the person in danger, or of the applause and praises following the doing of it; but that applause, and those praises, would themselves evince a general perception of the moral worth of such an action, supposing it to proceed from the purest motives, and correspondent sympathy in the pleasure likely to be experienced from it. Vanity could receive no gratification from a deed of this sort, where the spectators only regarded it as an incomprehensible piece of rashness. In like manner, though it seem to us, that many who have eminently succeeded in the pursuits of which we speak, have been actuated merely by the desire of gratifying a selfish vanity, still, that the attainment of these objects should be followed by the warm and sincere applause, that alone constitutes genuine fame, is a proof at least, of the existence somewhere, of a due appreciation of the motives from which these pursuits are supposed to proceed, and of sympathy with the pure gratifications their success is presumed to yield. But it enters into my design to show, that, without supposing the two classes actuated by different principles, there are sufficient causes for those wanderings, as they are called, of genius from the common path, for that contrariety of course, [and for] that seldom intermitting opposition and strife, which have almost everywhere been maintained, between the society in which they existed, and the individuals, who have been ultimately the great instruments of ameliorating and elevating its condition. Such an exposition, removing part of the obstructions to our view, will make it appear, that it is not so much from the diversity of the moving powers, as from the imperfections of the bodies impelled, that this jarring and contrariety of action arises.

It is necessary to premise, that for the present purpose, two classes occasionally confounded together, must be kept apart. Real inventors, the men whom we have alone to consider, differ from mere transmitters of things already known. The latter are an acknowledged, and very useful class, in all societies, but they neither encounter similar difficulties, nor produce similar effects to the former. They neither oppose, nor direct the current.

In the gradual progress of things, the media for communicating ideas have been changed; types have come to do, in a great measure, the office of the voice. What in ages past would have formed a discourse, or harangue, is now a book, or part of a book. Among the many vast consequences of the revolution, we overlook the small one of its occasioning the classing under one name, of those who are enlargers of the stock of knowledge, and those who are merely efficient communicators of portions of it. They are all successful authors, authors, that is, of books which are read. Just so, the bard or bards of the elder ages of ancient Greece, who first embodied in song the deeds of the besiegers of Troy, and they who, in after times, repeated the verses they had learned, were all chanters of heroic lays. Many, too, of the latter may have been more successful chanters than the former, for they sang to ears prepared; but there was between them, notwithstanding, an essential difference. There is also a line distinguishing the mere framers of books, from the original makers of their materials; it may not be very easily drawn indeed; but this is unnecessary for our purpose, it is sufficient to have pointed out its existence. It may be observed, too, that as of bards, so of authors, they who are mere compilers and repeaters, may be more successful than they who are real inventors, they may better suit their productions to particular times, tastes, and exigencies, and, besides, they can always find an audience prepared, by previous training, to applaud.

The tendency of these pursuits is to withdraw those occupied in them from the daily business of society. They fill not the places open for them, and which they are expected to fill; even when necessity pushes them for a time into them, and compels them to mingle with the crowd, they are marked as not belonging to it. Abstract and scientific truth can only be discovered by deep and absorbing meditation; imperfectly at first discerned, through the medium of its dull capacities, the intellect slowly, and cautiously, not without much of doubt, and many unsuccessful essays, succeeds in lifting the veil that hides it. The procedure is altogether unlike the prompt determination, and ready confidence, of the man of action, and generally unfits, to a greater or less degree, for performing well the part. He, again, who dwells in the world of possible moral beauty and perfection, moves awkwardly, rashly, and painfully, through this of everyday life, he is ever mistaking his own way, and jostling others in theirs. To the possessors of fortune, these habits only give eccentricity; they affect those of scanty fortune, or without fortune, with more serious ills. Unable to fight their way ably, cautiously, and perseveringly through the bustle of life, poverty, dependence, and all their attendant evils, are most commonly their lot.

"Toil, envy, want, the patron, and the jail,"

are calamities, from the actual endurance of some of which, or the dread of it, they are seldom free. These, however, they share with other men; there are some peculiarly their own.

Pursuing objects not to be perceived by others, or if perceived, whose importance is beyond the reach of their conceptions, the motives of their conduct are necessarily misapprehended. They are esteemed either idlers, culpably negligent in turning to account the talents they have got, dullards deficient in the common parts necessary to discharge the common offices of life, or madmen unfit to be trusted with their performance; shut out from the esteem or fellowship of those whose regard they might prize, they are brought into contact with those with whom they can have nothing in common, knaves who laugh at them as their prey, fools who pity them as their fellows. Their characters misunderstood, debarred from all sympathy, uncheered by any approbation, the "eternal war" they have to wage with fortune, is doubly trying, because they are aware, that, if they succumb, they will be borne off the field, not only unknown, but misconceived. To have merely to pass without his fame, the poet paints as a fate capable of adding double gloom to the shades below,

"Sed frons læta parum, et dejecto lumina vultu,
. . . .
——Nox atra caput tristi circumvolat umbra."

What must it be to those, then, who feel that, ere final oblivion hides them, calumny must for a time prolong the memory of their existence?

Imperfect man is ever prompt, without any consideration of the motives of the agents, to conceive of the evils he endures as of wrongs received, and to be avenged, on the doers of them. We need not wonder, then, that the manifold sufferings of genius should sometimes place it in opposition to humanity itself, and that, in the inconsistency and recklessness of passion, it should turn in anger and in scorn, as its bitterest enemy, on that of which it is, in heart, the truest lover.

These are circumstances, largely affecting the possessors of this faculty, even before they have succeeded in making it manifest, before they have been able to give outward shape to their inward conceptions. There are others, operating similarly, after they have succeeded in producing them. What is really new, has to encounter obstacles of two sorts. It is the nature of men to be copiers, and, with exceedingly few exceptions, they are nothing more. Mere followers they are of rules, walkers in well-beaten paths. Whatever, therefore, is in any degree really new, being probably beyond these rules, is also beyond their judgment. Nor is this the worst; it is also very frequently in opposition to it; it disagreeably disturbs and jars the existing systems, by which men guide their feelings and reasonings. Hence the works of almost all men of really inventive powers, have, at first, been either slighted or decried. Cervantes, one of the most powerful and original geniuses of modern times, and who ultimately operated as largely on affairs as any man whom they have witnessed, was placed by his contemporaries far below the subservient taste of Lope de Vego, and, in his last days, had to turn from Don Quixote to a theme correspondent to the bombast of his age.[1] It is needless to multiply examples,—in a similar walk Tasso, and Shakspeare; in another, Hume and Montesquieu; in another, Bacon and Galileo, experienced at first either comparative neglect, or partial, or general opposition. Few names that now pass current, but rose with difficulty, and were nearly again submerged in their earlier progress, by the shock of opposing prejudices.

The practice of printing, has gradually, as it has extended the circle of readers, produced effects on the productions of genius, not here to be passed unnoticed. The author looks to what he calls the public, to those, that is, who read—or rather to his own talents for producing works that will find readers— for the pecuniary rewards of his productions. This circumstance has had much effect, both in turning the powers of men of talents to subjects that may generally interest, and in obliging them to treat them in a manner, suited to the tastes and notions of the crowd.

Odi profanum vulgus et arceo,

is a sentiment that they neither avouch, nor act upon. That

---

[1] We cannot read the romance of Peresiles and Sigesmundi, published after his death; it had more success than any of his works. "Jamais cet homme célèbre," says one of his biographers, "ne fut à sa véritable place: on dédaigna ses talens, on méconnut ses vertus, on fut insensible à sa misère."

their work may be popular, men of the highest original genius bring it out cautiously, and in a diffused form. Their experiments are timid. Being, in their way, manufacturers, they cannot afford to make such as might deteriorate the value of their goods. They must not venture on a dish altogether new, they confine their powers to the discovery of something that may give piquancy to the old. If the practice be not prejudicial to the progress of invention itself, it is fatal to the lasting fame of the inventors. The mass keeps swelling, from generation to generation, but how, cannot well be noted. This result has, however, little to do with our subject; there is another which has much.

It being conceived to be within the compass of talent, to procure, in this way, its own reward, genius of the highest order, if its productions are not of a sort to bring a price from a bookseller, receives now less recompense than even in ages not so able [generally] to appreciate the benefits conferred by it; and, from the same causes, the propensity to neglect it is greatest where the reading public is the most numerous. The promoters of the abstract sciences, and the arts, are no where less efficiently aided, than in Great Britain. There, the observations of Lord Bacon apply nearly as forcibly as ever. "It is enough to restrain the increase of science, that energy and industry so bestowed, want recompense. The ability to cultivate science, and to reward it, lies not in the same hands. Science is advanced by men of great genius alone, while it can only be rewarded by the crowd, or by men high in fortune or authority, who have very rarely themselves any pretensions to it. Besides, success in these pursuits is not only unattended by reward or favor, but is destitute of popular praise. They are, for the most part, above the conceptions of the commonalty, and are easily overthrown, and swept away, by the wind of popular opinion.[1]

---

[1] "Satis est ad cohebendum augmentum scientiarum, quod hujusmodi conatus et industriæ præmiis careant. Non enim penes eosdem est cultura scientiarum, et præmium. Scientiarum enim augmenta a magnis utique ingeniis proveniunt; et pretia et præmia scientiarum sunt penes vulgus aut principes viros, qui (nisi raro admodum) vix mediocriter docti sunt. Quinetiam hujusmodi progressus, non solum præmiis et beneficentia hominum, verum

Without speaking of the sciences, and, in the arts, confining our attention to those exertions of the inventive faculty the benefits of which, obstructed by no unforeseen obstacle, have been very largely felt, how many, even of the most successful of these, have been adequately rewarded ? How many of them have left their authors in poverty, or brought them to it ! The personal history of most men, who, in modern times, have brought into being those arts by which human power has been so largely advanced, is little else than a narration of misfortunes, and ingratitude.

Nor are the sweets of success itself, in any department of invention, even if tasted, uncontaminated by much of bitterness. It is chiefly felt at the time, as superiority, on which wait envy and flattery. Malice, and insincerity, the great separators of man from man, and poisoners of the pleasures of existence, follow close after. He who gains it, attains an elevation commanding, but joyless, and unsafe.

> "Though high above the sun of glory glow,
> And far beneath the earth and ocean spread,
> 'Round him are icy rocks, and loudly blow,
> Contending tempests on his naked head,
> And thus reward the toils, which to those summits led." [1]

It is death alone that can give him the full sympathies of his fellows. When the earth wraps her noblest, none any longer envy him; all lament the benefactor, no one sees the rival or the master.

These are circumstances disturbing the course of genius, coming mainly from misapprehensions from without; there are others flowing from weaknesses, and imperfections, within.

There are, in every society, rules of conduct, and practices of life, which the progress of events has gradually marked out, and general observance hallowed. Of these, some are founded on the principles of morality and religion, some on caprice, some on prejudice. The breaking of any of them is always

etiam ipsa populari laude destituti sunt. Sunt enim illi supra captum maximæ partis hominum, et ab opinionum vulgarium ventis facile obruuntur et extinguuntur."

[1] *Childe Harold.*

esteemed a crime against society, and in reality is so ; the observance of them constitutes a character, in public estimation, perfect. The mere man of society, that is, the man of merely imitative action, learns them uninquiringly, and diligently : they make up indeed, almost all he knows, and all the interests of himself and family requires he should know, of right and wrong. If he transgress them, it is secretly and cautiously. He makes amends by unscrupulously and unsparingly gratifying, whatever is not forbid by the letter of his code, or by his own convenience. The inquirer into principles, again, takes a wider range, it is not the morality or religion of Italy, of France, of Britain, of North America, after which he seeks, but religion and morality in general. He attempts to learn, not what is delivered, but what is. The consequence is, that, while the mere man of the world is never at a loss, but proceeds securely in the direct path to general approbation, the man of speculation very frequently wanders from it. To say nevertheless, either that he knows not what is good or fit, or that he is not desirous of observing it were untrue. The eye of the rider glances over hill and dale, marks the streams, the woods, the hamlets that diversify the prospect, and the whole configuration of the country he traverses, and so he knows the road. The animal he rides knows it too ; he knows it as giving exercise to his limbs, and bringing him by every step he makes, forward, or right, or left, nearer to some stable-door. Ten to one that, practically, the latter has a more accurate knowledge of it than the former, and that, while the irrational shall sagaciously and unhesitatingly follow it out, without missing a single turning, or making one blunder, the rational, especially if the fancy take him to preserve something of a straight line, shall have to pass from track to track, to leap many a hedge and many a ditch, and having been obliged after all to make detours in abundance, come out at last weary, jaded, and bemired.

The ills which men of genius thus occasion and endure, from seeking for their rules of action, altogether in the relations which they perceive they have to the general system of human society, without sufficiently regarding those which necessarily connect them to the little system of some particular society, are merely errors in the actual course pursued, not in the motives from which that course was adopted. There are others more fatal, coming, not from mistakes in action, but from errors in the motives to action, and from the imagination that it may be allowable willingly to do a small evil, if a large amount of good follow it. This is unquestionably a moral error, to which men of high powers must, from the consciousness of these powers, be peculiarly liable. It were painful to bring forward instances of their succumbing to the temptation.[1]

It is thus that a power, which seems to be at first wakened to life, and to draw its earliest aliment, from the promptings of strong desires in man, to unite himself extensively with his fellow men, to exist with them, and for them, rather than in himself, as it gathers strength, and predominates in any individual, generally renders him so dissimilar to other men, in his feelings, habits, motives, and modes of action, that it in a

---

[1] It is strange that Cicero, as in the following passage, should seem to countenance this most common and dangerous of moral sophisms. "Quid? si Phalarim, crudelem tyrannum et immanem, vir bonus, ne ipse frigore conficiatur, vestitu spoliare possit; nonne faciat? Hæc ad judicandum sunt facillima. Nam, si quid ab homine ad nullam partem utili, tuæ utilitatis causa detraxeris: inhumane feceris, contraque naturæ legem: sin autem is tu sis, qui multam utilitatem reipublicæ atque hominum societati, si in vita remaneas, afferre possis, si quid ob eam causam alteri detraxeris, non sit reprehendendum.—Communis utilitatis derelictio contra naturam est, est enim injusta. itaque lex ipsa naturæ, quæ utilitatem hominum conservat et continet, decernit profecto, ut ab homine inerti atque inutili, ad sapientem, bonum, fortemque virum transferantur res ad vivendum necessariæ: qui si occiderit, multum de communi utilitate detraxerit."—*De Officiis*, L. III.

Such reasoning, followed fairly out, would not stop until it assumed the form which Sir Walter Scott has given it, in the speech of Anselmo.

"You are to distinguish, my son," replied the alchymist, "betwixt that which is necessarily evil in its progress and in its end also, and that which being evil, is, nevertheless, capable of working forth good. If, by the death of one person, the happy period shall be brought nearer us, in which all that is good shall be attained, by wishing its presence,—all that is evil escaped, by desiring its absence, etc. If this blessed consummation of all things can be hastened by the slight circumstance, that a frail earthly body, which must needs partake of corruption, shall be consigned to the grave a short space earlier than in the course of nature, what is such a sacrifice to the advancement of the holy millenium."—*Kenilworth*, c. XXII.

A living author, in the character of Eugene Aram, gives also a striking picture of the dangerous tendency of the same sophistry.

great measure separates him from them. Whatever he may be, or may hope to be as an inventor, or author, as a man he is misconceived and misapprehended. Among the men with whom he lives, he lives as not of them, a magic circle is drawn round him which neither he can pass without, nor they, within. Like the attractive and repulsive powers, which one magnetic influence communicates to matter of the same sort, the different direction in which the great moving and cementing principle of society has been made to flow in him, and in them, incessantly repels, and keeps him at a distance from them.

This disjunction and isolation affect various natures variously. Some cannot endure it; they cannot live but in the constant and intimate sympathy and communion of their fellows. They feel all the loneliness, and little of the grandeur of the desert. They pant for the land of life, and either turning to it, are lost in it, their former existence being remembered but as the wanderings of a dream; or they perish, from their incapacity to mingle with it. Their finer and gentler natures fed, but not strengthened by contemplation, recoil from the coarse and boisterous spirits, with whom they are brought into contact. They sink in the conflict and pass from life itself,

> " A precious odour cast
> On a wild stream, that recklessly sweeps by;
> A voice of music uttered to the blast,
> And winning no reply."

To others of firmer mould, the action of these alternately attracting and repelling powers, the passing from one state of being to another completely opposite, from the turmoil of spirit excited by braving and bearing back a world opposed, to the concentration of contemplative solitude, though wasting, is invigorating. Like steel which is first made to glow in fire, and then plunged in water, the fineness of their temper is brought out by the play of opposing elements. It is observed by Mr. Moore, in his life of Lord Byron, that but for the opposition he encountered, the noble poet had never stood forth in might; that persecution found him, as Rousseau, weak, left him strong.

Some, again, the world without affording no resting place, entrench themselves in the world within. Their excursions outwards, are carried on as into a country permanently hostile. To insult, to attack, to overthrow, not to subdue, or establish, is their aim. These are the skeptics, men seemingly abandoning every other hope but that of making manifest their power, a power that has often been greater than they themselves have conceived, and which, doubtless, would many times have been more happily exerted, had they found themselves in happier circumstances. When we read, for instance, the speculations of Hume, we do not always recollect that he had been a needy dependent brother of a Scotch land-holder, had failed in the only attempt he had ever made to establish himself in the world, by entering on business, and had come to middle life, known only as a bookish recluse, unable to do good, and only to be tolerated, because he was too inoffensive to do harm to any one. Such an existence may well account for much of that shrinking within himself, that absence of all heart, that habitual distrust, rather rejoicing to overthrow, than hoping to establish, which characterize his philosophy. Who can tell how great has been the influence of that philosophy, in producing what has been, what is, and what is to be, in Britain and in Europe? Of this we may be assured, that they are least aware of it, who are most affected by it.

There are yet others of higher minds, who, through hopes disappointed, and errors committed, over the waste of the world, and the ruins of their own hearts, can look confidently and courageously forward, to a brighter, though far distant prospect. It is in this spirit that Lord Bacon bequeaths his fame to posterity, and it is through it, that he, who has been to us so notable a benefactor, yet holds converse with us. The manly and generous confidence with which he relies on the better parts of human nature, and, in the midst of so many discouraging circumstances looks forward to the ultimate reign of truth and happiness, constitutes indeed, I may be allowed to remark, no small part of the charm, and perhaps of the utility of his speculations.

But, however the opposition between men of practice, and men of speculation and invention may operate, it certainly exists, and there are perhaps few of the latter, who have been gifted with dispositions so happy, or fallen in times so fortunate, as not to have experienced some of its evils. Nevertheless, if the view which has been presented be correct, this opposition between the two classes, the one engaged in the application of what is already known to the production of the means of supplying future necessities or pleasures, the other, in the discovery of something yet unknown and which may serve the same purposes, arises, not so much from a difference in the motives to action, as from a diversity in the modes of action: and the principles of our nature exciting to the advance of invention, would seem to be nearly identical with those giving activity to the effective desire of accumulation.

The difference between the two is rather in degree than in kind. He who labors to provide the means of enjoyment to wife, children, relations, friends, pursues an end in some degree selfish. It is his own wife, his own children, his own relations, whom he desires to benefit. The fruits of the labors of genius, on the contrary, are the property of the whole human race. On this account, though, in the individual, manifestations of the inventive faculty imply a superiority in some of the intellectual powers, they rather imply, in the society, a preponderance of the social and benevolent affections. It is this general acuteness of moral sensation, and lively sympathy consequently with the pleasures arising to the individual, from the success of exertions for purposes of general good, that can alone excite, and nourish, the enthusiasm of genius.[1]

[1] [In these last two paragraphs Rae seems to run sociological and economic considerations together, with a result which is not altogether correct. The difference between the two sets of motives under consideration is, apparently, one not of degree but of kind. We must certainly admit that those who in our society, especially during the last two centuries, have made the most wonderful and useful "application of what is already known to the production of the means of supplying future necessities or pleasures"—those who have in our own day given us not the knowledge of the properties of electricity, but the incandescent light and the trolley—are as a rule men of a certain "practical" type of character, who have done this work undoubtedly for money and the things money

But, though there are two of the circumstances giving strength to the principle of accumulation, on which the progress of the inventive faculty is equally dependent, there are yet a set of causes, the effects of which, while they paralyze the exertions of the one, rouse the other to activity. Whatever disturbs, or threatens to disturb, the established order of things, by exposing the property of the members of the society to danger, and diminishing the certainty of its future possession, diminishes also the desire to accumulate it. Intestine commotions, persecutions, wars, internal oppression, or outward violence, either, therefore, altogether destroy, or at least very much impair, the strength of the effective desire of accumulation. On the contrary, they excite the inventive faculty to activity. The excessive propensity to imitation, which is natural to man, seems the only means by which we can account for this diversity of effects. Men are so much given to learning, that they do not readily become discoverers. They have received so much, that they do not easily perceive the need of making additions to it, or readily turn the vigor of their thoughts in that direction. "They seem neither to know well their possesions, nor their powers; but to believe the former to be greater, the latter less, than they really are."[1] Whatever, therefore, breaks the wonted order of events, and exposes the necessity, or the possibility, of connecting them by some other means, strongly stimulates invention. The slumbering faculties rouse themselves to meet the unexpected exigence, and the possibility of giving a new and more perfect order to elements not yet fixed, animates to a boldness of enterprise, which were rashness, had they assumed their determined places. Hence, as has often been remarked, periods of great changes in kingdoms or governments, are the seasons when genius breaks forth in brighest

will bring. To make money, it must be remembered, is with us the conventional standard of success in the realm of affairs.

But when all is said, Rae's teaching holds without a flaw in one respect, and that is, that every institution and individual activity, economic and otherwise, is carried on, and has its being, in the environment of the general moral order.]

[1] *Novum Organum.*

lustre. The beneficial effects of what are termed revolutions, are, perhaps, chiefly to be traced, to their thus wakening the torpid powers; the troubling of the waters they bring about, undoes the palsy of the mind.[1]

On this account courage distinguishing well between things difficult and things impossible, and calmly estimating them not as they appear to vulgar prejudices, but as they are, seems to be a necessary element in the composition of genius of a high order. Without the possession of such a faculty, it is impossible clearly to discern the things which changes have brought to light or produced, or to make free use of them. The comparison which Lord Bacon makes between Alexander the Great and himself, is far from being forced. Neither could have accomplished what he did, had he not been able to despise what had only a vain show, and to discover and trust to real though underrated powers.[2]

[It may be worth while to add to this chapter a fragment of Rae's unpublished manuscript which runs as follows:—]

"It is through his intellectual and reasoning powers that man has the capacity to call into existence what are called the advances of the arts. But these, his intellectual and reasoning energies, do not rouse themselves to such enterprises, but seem to be dormant within him unless excited by his feelings, emotions, passions. In the absolute solitude of the wilderness, where his soul is stirred by none of these, he degenerates nearly to the level of the brute, seeking only food

---

[1] [See "Note L" in the Appendix.]

[2] "Atque hac in parte nobis spondemus fortunam Alexandri Magni: neque quis nos vanitatis arguat, antequam exitum rei audiat, quæ ad exuendam omnem vanitatem spectat.

"Etenim de Alexandro et ejus rebus gestis Æschines ita loquutus est: Nos certe vitam mortalem non vivimus; sed in hoc nati sumus, ut posteritas de nobis portenta narret et prædicet: perinde ac si Alexandri res gestas pro miraculo habuisset.

"At ævis sequentibus Titus Livius melius rem advertit et introspexit, atque de Alexandro hujusmodi quippiam dixit: Eum non aliud quam bene ausum vana contemnere. Atque simile etiam de nobis judicium futuris temporibus factum iri existimamus: Nos nil magni fecisse, sed tantum ea quæ pro magnis habentur, minoris fecisse."

and protection from the inclemencies of the weather. It is in society alone that he finds those influences that move and feed his moral and intellectual nature, and give him his proper life. He is in fact the creature of society, and all his passions, emotions, feelings, may in one sense be considered as so many social instincts binding him to it. Now in herding animals, and in this regard man is a herding animal, it is not the individual but the herd that moves. If the individual attempt a separate and independent movement [beyond a certain point], he is sure to find that it is ineffectual as to the herd, and dangerous to himself. If one blessed or cursed with keener eyes and a more sagacious nose than his fellows discover in the distance fresher and greener pastures, and direct his course to them, he becomes a wanderer from the flock, a stray one, a lost one. It is the same among men. One whose powers transcends those of his fellows and who, trusting to them, advances far beyond them, is so bedimmed to their eyes by the mists of distance that they think he has gotten out of this real, living, and tangible world, and is walking in the clouds, is wandering in the unreal splendors of fairy land. It is only when by chance the course of subsequent events brings them to the spot where they discern the marks of his footsteps, that they say one to another,—why, such a one was not in the clouds at all: he was walking on solid ground. How blind was man in those days! Such a one is said to have come before his time, or, which is much the same thing, to have been out of place."

CHAPTER X.

OF THE CAUSES OF THE PROGRESS OF INVENTION AND OF THE EFFECTS ARISING FROM IT, AS IT CONCERNS ITSELF WITH THE MATERIAL WORLD.

INVENTION is the only power on earth that can be said to create.[1] It enters as an essential element into the process of the increase of national wealth, because that process is a creation, not an acquisition. It does not necessarily enter into the process of the increase of individual wealth, because that may be simply an acquisition, not a creation.

. . . .

Would we take time to consider of it, we must perceive that such an increase of national capital as individuals [usually] make of individual capital,[2] is at least, unlikely, seeing there is no apparent cause for it. Considering capital in general, the only use we can discover for it is its enabling the community to draw from the resources the country affords, the necessaries, conveniences, and amusements of life, its supply of which, according to our author, constitutes its real wealth. It is only so far as it is instrumental to this end that we can see a use, and therefore find a reason, for its existence. Now,

---

[1] I make use of the term creation, because that of production, which otherwise I should have preferred, has been employed in another sense. I trust my motives will not be misconceived. "Etiam inventa quasi novæ *creationes* sunt, et divinorum operum imitamenta, ut bene cecinit ille :

"Primum frugiferos fœtus mortalibus agris
Dididerant quondam præstanti nomine Athenæ :
Et *recreaverunt* vitam, legesque rogarunt."

Novum Organum, CXXIX.

[2] [That is, a mere "accumulation," or "multiplication of items."]

as one individual is more provident and prudent than another, we can easily conceive how one may come to procure for himself a greater share than another of the national funds, the means, or instruments, serving to unlock the stores which the nation [already] possesses; but it is not so easy to conceive how, or for what purpose, a general increase of these means or instruments should take place, without some accompanying discovery of an improvement in their construction by which they may put additional stores within reach of the nation.

We may easily perceive this, by attending to any of the numerous small items of which the national capital is composed. I shall take an example of a very small one. The only instrument used for threshing out grain in Great Britain, until of recent years, was the flail. Hence one or more flails formed a part, though a small part, of every farmer's capital, and therefore all the flails that all the farmers had, a part, though an exceedingly inconsiderable part, of the national capital. So simple an instrument and one so easily formed, was made, I believe, generally, by the farmer or his servants, though sometimes by professed mechanics. In whatever way fabricated, it is evident, however, that the number of flails made, though from the convenience of having a supply provided beforehand they would exceed, could never much exceed, the number of persons employed in the operation of threshing. A professed flail-maker, indeed, if diligent and intelligent, might, by the aid of these qualities, have been able to make them cheaper than his neighbors, and, if economical, to extend his business and come to have some amount of capital in this shape. But, though thus, by his industry and frugality, an individual might have accumulated capital under this form to an extent to which we can set no precise limits, the national capital never could have been so increased, because, if one person by greater diligence and activity made more flails, another, from a deficiency of these qualities, would make fewer; or, if we suppose all the makers of the instrument to be alike industrious, and thus the stock of it to accumulate so as to do more than supply the wants of the threshers, the article would remain on their hands, and they would naturally cease to produce the superabundant supply.

While, therefore, the instrument retained this less perfect form, it is, I think, pretty evident, that, though individuals might accumulate capital by making flails, neither the national capital, nor the national revenue, would be much increased by their efforts so directed.

About forty years ago, the easier and more perfect method of executing this process, by what is called the threshing machine, was invented. This new instrument, though far more expensive than the former, yet, performing the operation more effectually, and with much less labor, became naturally things which farmers were desirous of having. A farmer could have had no motive to accumulate but a very trifling capital in the shape of flails, because half a dozen were as useful to him as half a thousand; but he had a great motive to accumulate a considerable capital in the shape of a threshing machine, because it would save him much annual expenditure of labor, and the operation so performed, separating the grain more effectually, would give him a small addition to the corn yielded by his subsequent crops. Accordingly its invention was followed by the accumulation in this form of a large amount of capital, and so by an increase of the whole agricultural capital of the nation. But, besides this direct effect, the saving it produced in one of the main processes of agriculture augmented the profits of the farmers, and tended, therefore, to make all farmers cultivate their farms more perfectly, and some to engage in improving land not before cultivated. Both the direct and the indirect effects of this invention, therefore, must have helped, in no inconsiderable degree, to augment the agricultural capital, and so the whole capital of the nation.[1]

"It readily occurs to every individual that the quantity of hardware, the number of pots and pans, is in every country limited by the use which there is for them; that it would be absurd to have more of such utensils than are necessary for cooking the victuals usually consumed there; and that, if the quantity of victuals were to increase, the number of pots and pans would readily increase along with it, a part of the increased quantity of victuals being employed in purchasing them, or in maintaining an additional number of workmen

[1] [In this paragraph Rae closely follows Lauderdale.]

whose business it was to make them."¹ But, though the national capital cannot thus be supposed to accumulate in the shape of an additional number of pots and pans [of any fixed type], individuals who deal in hardware frequently accumulate capitals in this shape, to a large amount. We can easily conceive, that the national capital also might accumulate in this shape, were some discovery, producing an improvement in the manufacture, to occur. Were a method discovered of procuring and manufacturing platina, or some metal similar to it, at only four or five times the cost of brass, it would, without doubt, be employed in the fabrication of kitchen utensils of all sorts. Not being acted on by fire, and other destroying agents, it would save a great deal of the drudgery of the kitchen, and, though more costly at first, would probably, on the whole, be preferred by good economists. Thus, pots and pans becoming more expensive articles, the amount of national capital, or stock, accumulated in them, would be much greater, and, through this improvement, the whole national capital would, with advantage to the society, be somewhat augmented.²

If any one will, in a similar manner, consider any of the other articles which help to make up the national capital, I think he will have difficulty in assigning a sufficient reason, from any of the views presented in the *Wealth of Nations*, for its increase, unless he connect this increase, somehow or another, with some improvement in the particular department of industry of which its production makes a part, or in some other department dependent on it. He will perceive, that, though there is no difficulty in conceiving that an individual may accumulate a very large capital in the form of any of those articles or commodities, the total of which make up the national capital; with the exception, perhaps, of money itself, there is difficulty in discovering a reason for the accumulation of any of them, throughout the whole community, so as to form any sensible addition to the national capital.

It may perhaps appear, that, in whatever shape the individual members of the community may accumulate capital,

---

¹ *Wealth of Nations*, B. IV. c. I.
²[For use of terms, see the end of the chapter.]

yet, that the efforts of the greater number being thus directed, they might accumulate it under some shape or another. We are not, however, it will be recollected, here discussing a possibility, but a self-evident principle; not what might be, but what must be. Now, there is no necessity for imagining that this must be the case, for, without entering at all into the minutiæ of the subject, it is not difficult to perceive that the action of the principle which prompts to save, itself brings about a state of things, which diminishes the desire to save. A person must be most desirous of getting money when he perceives, that by the acquisition of it, he could make a great deal out of it; when it is manifest to him, that, if he had a sufficient capital, he could enter on some branch of business that would be very profitable. When an opening of this sort presents itself to a prudent and enterprising, though poor man, the exertions he makes to gather together a small sum are sometimes almost incredible. But, if the principle were to prevail so generally as to fill up every branch of business within the society, the desire to acquire capital so as to enter on some of the particular businesses carried on in the society would naturally be diminished throughout the whole country; and this general diminution of the motives to accumulate, might be sufficient to preserve the national capital within the bounds it had acquired, and prevent it, for a time, from gaining farther increase.

Nor is there any thing in the appearance of human affairs, which should induce us to conclude that the increase of national capital ever does, in fact, proceed, unless in conjunction with some successful effort of the inventive faculty, some improvement of some of the employments formerly practised in the community, or some discovery of new arts. If we cast our eyes over the results which either reading or observation presents to us, concerning the condition of different nations, we gather from our review, that many of them, in regard to the acquisition of wealth, have apparently remained stationary for ages, although undisturbed by external violence, and unmolested by internal tumults. During all the time, however, the process of individual accumulation was going on; men were continually rising from poverty to affluence, founding families, and leaving wealth to their descendants: but this wealth passed away from them; what the father gathered was not able to maintain his race, and they gradually sank to the rank from which he had emerged. The proportion, meantime, between rich and poor, and the total wealth of the community, remained but little changed.

At length, in some quarter or another, an improvement began to be perceived. What do we find to have been the most prominent accompaniment of this change? Is it a diminished expenditure—an increased parsimony—a frugality before unknown? I believe not. Any great diminution of the expenditure of a whole community, it will be found difficult to trace, but we shall always discover that invention has somehow or another been busy, either in improving agriculture and the other old arts, or in discovering new ones.

It is only when some great and striking improvement issues from the exertions of the inventive power, that we in general attend to its effects. Every one readily grants, that, but for the invention of the steam engine, the capital of Great Britain would want much of its present vast amount. We perceive not so readily the numerous small improvements, which have been gradually, from year to year, spreading themselves through every department of the national industry. But, though not so palpably forced on our observation, we pass them by, they nevertheless exist, and sufficiently account for the manner in which the national capital has been augmenting, by being gradually accumulating in them, without the necessity of supposing that it ever has augmented precisely as that of individuals generally does, by a simple multiplication, under the same form, of any or all the items of which its amount was before made up.[1]

Adam Smith himself admits, that a country may come to be fully stocked in proportion to all the business it has to

[1] [Rae goes too far here and gives improperly a collectivist bias to the whole discussion. Because individuals may increase their capital merely by a process of simple multiplication (or, as he calls it elsewhere, by a process of "acquisition" in contrast to one of "creation"), it does not follow that "generally" they do so accumulate. The antithesis should not be between the individual and society, but between the principles of invention and mere acquisitive accumulation (which Rae himself brings out later), working in different individuals. After all, it is the individual who invents, not society.]

transact, and have as great a quantity of stock employed, in every particular branch, as the nature and extent of the territory will admit. He speaks of Holland also, as a country which had then nearly acquired its full complement of riches; where, in every particular branch of business, there was the greatest quantity of stock that could be employed in it.¹ It would then appear that, even according to him, the principle of individual accumulation, as a means of advancing the national capital, has limits beyond which it cannot pass. The same cannot be said of that increase which is derived from the attainment of those objects at which the inventive faculty aims. Had Holland, sixty years ago, been put in possession of the astonishing improvements in mechanical and manufacturing industry, which, since that period, have sprung up in Great Britain, who can suppose that she would have wanted ability to continue in the successful pursuit of wealth; or, that she would not have started forward with fresh vigor in the career, and advanced in it with greater rapidity than in any former period of her history?

There is no avoiding the admission, that, to every great advance which nations make in the acquisition of wealth, it is necessary that invention leading to improvement should lend its aid; and, granting this, it necessarily follows (as when one cause is discovered sufficient to account for the phenomena, we should confine ourselves to it), that we are not warranted to assume that they make even the smallest sensible progress without the aid of the same faculty.

To this general observation there are only two apparent exceptions. The progress of commerce by the increase of some particular branch of it, or by the opening of fresh branches; and the settlement of new countries.

If these, however, should be esteemed exceptions to the observation with regard to any particular nation or nations, they are extensions of it with regard to all the nations of the earth; implying that the increase of general wealth is connected with the general spread of invention, or inventions, over the world.²

¹ *Wealth of Nations*, B. I., c. IX.
² [The two foregoing interpolations are from Bk. I., Chap. I., of the original; the first from p. 15, the second from pp. 19-24.]

Besides the circumstances determining the progress of invention arising from the nature of man, the inventor, there are others depending on the modes in which the principles of that nature are excited to exert themselves in this sphere of action, and gradually to discern and develope the qualities and powers of the various divisions of the material world.

The surface of the earth presents a vast variety of materials. Soils, climates, minerals, vegetables, the fish of the waters, the birds of the air, and the beasts of the field, are endlessly diversified, and, could we bring back the surface of the globe to the state in which it existed when man first made his appearance on it, we should probably scarcely find any two points in all respects alike.

This diversity of materials seems to have been [originally] the great exciting cause to the progress of art and science, men having been every now and then compelled or induced to adopt new materials, and, as they changed from the one to the other, to have been gradually led from the knowledge of the most simple and obvious qualities and powers, to a perception of those which are more complex, and difficult to discern.

Tracing any invention upwards to its first beginnings, we shall discover that these have been exceedingly rude and imperfect, proceeding from the simplest, and what would seem to us, the most obvious observations; and that it has advanced towards perfection, by having been led to change the materials with which it originally operated, and passing from one to another, has at each step of its progress discovered new qualities and acquired new powers.

I believe a lengthened inquiry into the history of inventions would lead to the following conclusions:—

1st. Arts change materials. It having become difficult or impossible for men to obtain the materials with which they had been accustomed to operate [in any branch of industry], they have been led to adopt others, and, retaining the knowledge of the qualities and powers of the old, have added to them those of the new.

2d. Different arts adopt the same materials. Men have been encouraged to operate with new materials, from materials being presented to them evidently better suited to their purposes than the old, could they be made submissive to their art.

3d. The operation of these circumstances has slowly diminished the propensity of mankind to servile imitation, and given a beginning to science, by bringing to light the qualities and powers common to many materials—the general principles of things.

The limited objects of the present inquiry, however, forbid our entering into the lengthened train of speculation, that would be necessary fully to establish these conclusions by an adequate investigation of the progress of inventions. I shall content myself with adducing a sufficient number of instances to show, that this continual change has been a circumstance operating very beneficially and efficiently, in enlarging the bounds of human knowledge and power.

When men are deprived of the materials with which they used to operate in the production of necessaries, and between them and want have only such as are similar, but not the same, one of two things must happen. They must either conquer the difficulties of the new matter, or must perish. In the earlier ages of the world, it is scarce to be doubted, that the latter event was of not infrequent occurrence. Tribes forced from their homes by more powerful tribes, must have been often led by hope, or driven by despair, into regions that had not before yielded to the dominion of man. But the materials which different regions present to human industry, are very seldom precisely alike. The new would differ from the old, in being in some respects worse, in others better adapted to its purposes, than they. The difficulties are much more apparent than the benefits, the former having generally to be overcome, before the latter be apprehended, or distinctly perceived. The attempt, then, would probably never be made, but for the promptings of necessity. Its success has two advantages. The subjection of the obstacles carries the inventive faculty a step farther forward; the larger returns made, owing to the circumstances in which the new material is superior, increase the rewards of industry. As the success of the attempt would advance the skill and the power of those who made it, so its failure would abandon them to famine. In the former case, the individuals whose intelligence and courage overcame the obstacles, would be exalted by posterity into gods and demi-gods; in the latter, the field would remain open to more successful essays, in other times, and by other races. An inquiry, however, into the progress of the arts essential to the existence of man in any form of society, would carry us back to ages too remote, and involved in an obscurity too deep to penetrate.

None of the arts which are not necessary to the preservation of human existence itself, has probably had greater influence on the modes which that existence has assumed, than metallurgy. Without the metals, it would be impossible for the series of instruments to be continued from which the wants of civilized society are supplied, and without them, consequently, mankind could never have emerged from barbarism. There are few arts, either, in which the processes have probably at first been more rude, in which they have ultimately attained greater perfection of skill, or in which the progress has been more gradual, and more dependent for its advance on the variety of the materials operated upon. Some metals are found in quantity pure; the ores of some are easily reduced, of others, with great difficulty. Of all the substances he attempts to classify, none, from their number and variety, give greater trouble to the mineralogist. The discovery of the qualities of such portions of these metals as were found pure, would soon make them be considered as the most useful of substances, and occasion their being sought after with avidity. The supply of them in this state being exhausted, or they who had employed them moving into regions where they could no longer be found, recourse would gradually be had to the less pure and less easily reduced ores, and from thence to metals and ores wrought with still greater difficulty. Thus we find that gold, silver, and copper, the metals that most frequently occur native, were those first in use; iron came last, and was probably then esteemed the most precious. Weapons of gold and silver were edged with it, in the same manner as were wooden implements, such as the old English spade, in more recent days. But for the gentleness of the ascent, it is altogether likely, that the art would never have attained the eminence it has gained. Had the earth, for instance, possessed no metallic stores but the more abundant ores of iron, by far the most useful in the present days, it seems not unlikely, that no metal would ever have been wrought. The steps by which it rose, were, however, too numerous, and the vestiges left of them are too indistinct, for me to attempt here to trace them, were I even prepared so to do. I prefer rather, in illustration of the subject, to refer to an art which has been in practice for thousands of years, and to an implement in daily use.

The plough, in its most simple form, is an instrument the invention of which would naturally follow the domestication of the ox species. Men accustomed to loosen and stir the earth, with the inefficient implements of that ancient period, could scarce in time fail to remark, that the sluggish strength of this animal might aid them in the operation. They seem to have turned it to this purpose, by a very simple contrivance. A long crooked sapling, similar to the clubs used by boys in some of their games, but larger, had its thick, curved end sharpened to a point, and its other extremity attached to something like what is now called a yoke, coupling two oxen by the neck. The long straight part of the implement passed between the animals, the part turned downwards rested on the earth behind them, and when they moved forward, along soil very easily impressed, would mark it with a furrow, which might be deepened by a man walking close after, and pressing it downwards. He was assisted in this operation by the addition of a handle projecting upwards, the point was hardened by the action of the fire, and another person guided the oxen. Such was probably the earliest plough, and those that are used in many parts of the east, to this day, differ not much from it, with the exception of the point being defended by a sort of iron tooth, and the wood not having a natural, but an artificial curvature. In Java, a man when he has done his day's work, carries home his plough on his shoulder, as a woodman does his axe. The defects of such an implement are to us very plain. It only scratches the soil, it cannot make what we call a furrow, and it is only very light, sandy soil, or the sort of mud in which rice is cultivated, on which it is at all capable of acting. As the quantity of this sort of soil is in all parts of the world limited, men were gradually forced to attempt the tillage of land more difficult to subdue. Over the greater part of Asia, they have done so, by a simple enlargement and strengthening of the first rude implement. The model immediately before their eyes seems to have so confined their powers of invention, that they attempted no change but this. In that part of the world, if we except China, and the countries bordering on Europe, the earth is consequently scratched, or at best stirred, it is not in our sense of the word ploughed. The improvements which we have made in the operation are twofold; the first concerns the effect produced on the soil, and the second, the ease with which it is produced. The furrow we form makes each portion of soil operated upon, describe about one third of a circle, thus blending all the parts of the surface together, leaving it very open, and placing the vegetable fibres in the position best suited to induce decay. The turn, too, thus given to each portion, puts it out of the way of the next, which is therefore, with comparative ease, moved into its proper position.

It seems not to have been until the instrument got to Europe, that it assumed a form capable of executing such an operation. Such was probably the Roman plough, the woodwork of which is thus described by Virgil:

> "Continuo in sylvis magna vi flexa domatur
> In burim, et curvi formam accipit ulmus aratri,
> Huic a stirpe pedes temo protentus in octo,
> Binae aures, duplici aptantur dentalia dorso.
> Caeditur et tilia ante jugo levis, altaque fagus,
> Stivaque, quae currus a tergo torqueat imos;
> Et suspensa focis explorat robora fumus.

An elm bent with great strength in the woods, is forced into a *buris* and receives the form of the crooked plough. To it are fitted the *temo* stretched out eight feet from the lower end, the two *aures*, the *dentalia* with the double back, and the *stiva* which bends the lower part of the plough behind. The light lime tree is felled beforehand, for the yoke, and the lofty beech for the other parts, and the smoke seasons the wood hung up above the fire."[1]

I see not that this *buris*, which has given some of the

[1] Georgic I. 170. Translated by Adam Dickson, *Husbandry of the Ancients*.

commentators a little trouble, can be any thing else than the original crooked sapling, here swollen to a large elm knee, forming the body of the plough, *inflexi grave robur aratri*, and to which all the other parts are appended. From it, instead of the longer straight part of the sapling, stretched forward a separate piece, termed the *temo* or pole, and the *stiva*, or handle, was retained. So far there was very little difference from the original instrument, but in the *aures*, the ears, we have the beginnings of the mould board, and there is a place for the reception of the *vomer*, the large cutting iron share. These appendages, the more difficult soil of some parts of Italy probably introduced; and when adopted in one part, they could scarce fail to spread over it all.

The plough thus changed into an instrument for turning over, not merely stirring the soil, was carried by the Romans into other, and more northern regions, and transmitted to other races. These and subsequent revolutions, obliterated the imitation of the original curved sapling. The curve became an angle formed by a short downright beam or pillar, the *sheath* or *forehead*, fitted into the shortened pole or *temo*, and bearing, as before, the chief stress of the draft. Greater symmetry and lightness were thus given to it. The mould board gradually attained its present form, the coulter and another handle were added. In recent days, it has been made nearly altogether of iron. In Britain, where this revolution in the material was introduced, it is deserving of notice that the metal implement, only that its parts are slenderer, is an exact copy of the wooden one. There is yet too the *sheath*. In some, at least, of the American iron ploughs, the sole connexion between the upper and lower parts, unless that given by the mould boards themselves, is a strong bolt screwing tight. For a plough of such materials, this last metamorphosis of the original sapling or *buris*, would seem the better construction.

Thus, the moving of this implement from one region and people to another, the consequent adaptation of it to different and more difficult soils, and the change of the materials of which it is formed, seem to have been the occasions of its successive improvement. They have stimulated the faculty of invention, and weakened the propensity to servile imitation.

The instrument, so changed, it may be remarked, is on its return to countries in which, perhaps, it first assumed form. English ploughs are to be seen in India, and some modification of them must, in time, become the general plough of the country.

Our next example of the effects of these circumstances on the development of the inventive faculty, will be taken from the progress of sacred architecture. It conspicuously exhibits the strength of the principle itself, and the trammels by which its energies are sometimes confined.

When men worship the deity, they find their devotional dispositions assisted by the presence of external objects, partaking of his attributes. Thus, whatever brings sensibly before us the ideas of very great power, and unlimited duration, fills the mind with thoughts that are very near akin to devotion. Hence, men in almost all ages and countries, have either made choice of particular natural objects, inspiring such ideas, as concomitants of their devotions,—they have worshipped turning to the sun, or in groves, or on the tops of mountains; or they have formed things, having in their conceptions a sort of unison, in this way, with the object of their worship.

Of all the people who have employed themselves in formations of this sort, and devoted a portion of their industry to the construction of instruments serving, in some degree, to satisfy those natural longings of the human mind after something bringing before it the perfections of the deity, none have been more eminently successful than the Egyptians. The suddenness with which the art there attained an excellence, that even now commands our fullest admiration, is a phenomenon well deserving the attention of speculators on the extent of the human powers when roused to free and active exertion.

Several circumstances seem to have contributed to determine the form which architecture there assumed, and to carry it at once from infancy to maturity.

One of the manifestations of power most apt to attract the notice of men in the early stages of society, as very great, is the moving of large blocks of stone. To men altogether ignorant of the mechanic powers, however strong and numerous, to move a cubic stone of the weight of only two tons would be impossible; for, enough of them could not get hold of it. To men again, having made a certain degree of progress in art, and aware of the advantage, for instance, of the lever, though it might then be practicable to move into an upright position pillars of even a few tons weight, such objects would still seem very striking displays of power. They would also impress them with the ideas of extended duration, which the indestructible nature of the material, is calculated to produce. Accordingly we find that the erection of such columnar masses, has been a very common act of men, in rude states of society, in their efforts to draw themselves near to some conception they have had of the great first cause.

But it is not mere blind power, and eternal duration, that is attributed to the deity; besides this, all men ascribe to him unerring wisdom, and most men, boundless benevolence. Regularity of design, then, especially if combined with visible utility, renders any object of great and changeless power, more fitting to inspire religious sentiments. On this account the sun, of all objects continually before our eyes, is that most generally turned to with religious feelings.

Symmetry of design may be given to collections of columns, by preserving them at regular distances, and forming them into circular, or straight lines. The circles of the Druids in Scotland, and in other parts of Europe, are examples of this sort of form. Greater unity would be given to an erection of this sort, by the addition of horizontal pieces, stretching from the top of the one pillar to that of the other, and partially roofing in the fabric. Such an addition would also heighten the notion of power embodied in the work. The poising large masses of stone on the summits of elevated columns, must have appeared a stupendous exertion of power, to those who first contemplated it. Such seems to have been the character of the famous druidical temple of Stonehenge. A form similar to this, would therefore seem likely to be that, which the ancient Egyptians must have been inclined to give the religious edifices they constructed, when leaving the higher grounds, they began to descend and occupy the plains; and such is, in fact, the general outline which the ruins of their edifices yet present. But they possessed arts which enabled them to give their edifices a degree of grandeur, far superior to the rude structures of the ancient Britons.

They were probably either themselves workers of stone, or had the means of knowing how stone may be wrought. The more ancient Troglodytes were perfect in the art of cutting stone. Their labors were confined, however, to forming excavations in rock, they do not seem to have ever thought of dividing these rocks into fragments, and again reuniting them into some required form. Indeed, this is an idea, that could not very readily occur as a means of facilitating the formation of structures of the sort. Here, as in other instances, the beginnings of art are simple, but laborious. It is invention that abridges the amount of labor necessary for attaining the end, and substitutes skill and contrivance, for toil and perseverance. A sort of necessity, brought about by the occupation of a new region, and the desire to have rocky edifices on the alluvial plane, probably led the Egyptians to effect this revolution.

The possession of another art, made it of less difficult execution. Egypt, a long level valley periodically overflowed, afforded peculiar facilities for the transport by water, of even the heaviest articles. The largest masses separated from the rocks that bordered the great canal, into which it was transformed during the time of the inundation, had only to be moved to rafts stationed close by, when they could be transported to any required situation. The riches also of that celebrated valley, then probably recently exposed to human industry by the retiring waters, and which the efforts of fifty centuries have not yet exhausted, gave the inventive faculty as its instrument, an almost unlimited command of labor. Genius was not wanting to reach lofty conceptions, or to apply the means put in its hands so as to give them an adequate form. The works it produced were the admiration of antiquity, and are the astonishment of modern times.

Architecture, with the other arts of Egypt, was carried to Greece. It retained, nevertheless, the same essential character, the effects it produced arising from the magnitude and proportions of massive blocks, arranged in columns and transverse pieces. A comparison of the two does not give the one much superiority over the other. Both possess sublimity and unity of design, and beauty of execution, and if the Grecian has greater elegance, the Egyptian has greater grandeur. But if the colony did not much excel the parent country in architecture, there is no comparison between them in the sister art of sculpture. Architecture and statuary were combined by the ancient Egyptians. The earliest human figures cut in stone, that have come down to us, are those executed by them, on their columnar fabrics. They represent the human body in one position. The arms close to the trunk, the legs close to each other, the back applied to the block, of which the statue is a part. This position of the body forms evidently the most easy design which a novice in the art, when first attempting to shape in stone some representation of the human figure, could conceive. That the Egyptian artists should have commenced with such figures, seems natural enough, but that, after having learned to execute the prodigious and highly finished works in statuary, which they have left, they should still have adhered to this position, can only, I apprehend, be explained from the influence of the spirit of imitation. The achievements of the ancient Egyptians, in the whole art of shaping stone into forms giving the ideas of sublimity and beauty, may well be supposed to have filled the minds of their descendants with awe and admiration, since their remains so powerfully affect even men of the present day with these sentiments. It is scarcely in human nature greatly to admire any productions of genius, and to form others much surpassing them. Under the influence of such a sentiment, men are rather inclined to confine their efforts to making additions, than to exert them in attempting alterations, prudence whispering, that the former will be received as sufficient proof of their capacity, while the latter might be censured as proceeding from their arrogance. When a certain point has once been gained, future artists seek the principles of their operations, not in the powers of nature and of man, but in what they term the rules of art. These rules seem to have effectually confined the art of statuary, as far as the human figure was concerned, to the limits marked out by the first essays. Even figures in porcelain had the same character, an appendix being put to the back, indicative of the original stone block. The restraining influence of the spirit of imitation is rendered more remarkable, from the figures of the inferior animals being executed with considerable spirit.

When the art was transferred to Greece, the change of country undid its trammels, and its productions assumed all the life, grace, and beauty, which varying and natural attitudes bestow.

The mechanical part of architecture underwent a revolution among the nations that were finally consolidated into the Roman Empire, by the adoption of the arch, and the employment of cement. The Egyptians and Grecians were stonecutters; the Romans, masons. The spirit of imitation prevented this change in the material part, from producing, immediately, a corresponding change in the ideal. Under the Romans, the arch and the column were combined. It was not until after the ruin of the Empire, when architecture recommenced among other races, that it assumed a new form, correspondent to the change in the mechanical part, and suited to the purposes and times.

When arts, other than those of their native wilds, first began to be any thing to our rude ancestors, the art of the mason, received by them from the Romans, was properly the capacity of shaping a stony mass into a form, realizing some of their imaginations, from materials, which could be easily transported to the point required. While the Egyptians and Grecians had had to apply their powers to changing the figures and positions of masses of rocks, they possessed the art of constructing a rocky mass. The instrument of the former was the chisel, to carve into shape, of the latter, lime, to work out to shape. The beginnings of the former art in Africa, and of the latter in Europe, are marked by the same lavish expenditure of human labor, though in different modes. In the former, the human hand, slowly, by dint of strokes intermitted not for generations, dug out caves, or carved pillars. In the latter, also, the human hand cemented small fragments of rock to small fragments, till in the lapse of years, the mass gradually swelled out into some desired form. The extent of the operations of the one was limited, by the powers of industry, to put large blocks and columns of stone into the requisite positions, and by the strength and durability of these materials. The operations of the other again, were limited, solely, by the cohesive qualities of the mass it formed. The effect at which both aimed, grandeur, the union of power, durability, and useful design, was mainly produced in the former, by the vastness and symmetry of the several parts, in the latter, by the same qualities combined in a whole.

The art was probably at first applied in modern Europe, to the construction of places of strength. Solidity to resist the battering engines, height to prevent the fortress being scaled, and the advantage of having scope to annoy the besiegers, produced the massive battlemented towers and castles of the ancient barons. As its materials were the most durable, principles to which we have already adverted, soon led to its application to structures devoted to the purposes of religion.

A plain wall of small stones and lime may convey the idea of durability, but only in a slight degree, that of power or design. A circular or angular column of the same materials, if very elevated, is better fitted for these ends, but still, is far inferior to one composed of a solid block. A lofty stone arch, again, is one of the most striking displays of power that human art exhibits. The aspect of a mass so ponderous, hanging thus securely in high air, fixes the attention, and fills the mind with awe. It is, accordingly, by a skilful management of the arch, that the grandeur of effect of what we term the Gothic architecture, is chiefly produced. All the other parts are subordinate to it, and confined within the smallest limits sufficient to bring out its powers. In the more perfect specimens, there is no dead wall; a congeries of lofty arches, supported on short, or slender pillars, is wrought into a magnificent and beautiful whole. The feeling of admiration here springs from the consideration of the power manifested, in maintaining in its place the whole high and hanging fabric; whereas, in the Grecian architecture, it rather arises from a perception of that displayed in the formation and elevation of each separate member.

The progress towards perfection, of this order of architecture, was much more slow, considering that it scarcely ever remained wholly stationary, than was that of the Grecian, for it is, in reality, far more difficult. Several causes contributed to its advance. The great extent of country over which its elements were diffused, occasioned the use of various sorts of stone, and produced the advantageous effects arising from a continual change of materials. The art of the mason improved, strength was obtained by joining stones into one another, rather than by cementing them together. The use of freestone, a rock easily wrought into shape, probably had considerable effect in producing this improvement. The architect was thus enabled to bring out, in greater fineness, all the parts of his fabric. The feelings of men, also, set towards the pursuit. Kings, nobles, a proud and powerful priesthood, stood ready to reward and applaud its successful creations, and assembled multitudes gazed on them in silent and delighted admiration. It has been truly said, that it formed much of the poetry of the age. In the want of other species of intellectual excitement, men were needs very strongly moved by an art, that thus wrought on stone and lime, they knew not how, to pourtray some of the deepest feelings of their hearts. It seems to have been only slightly retarded, by a propensity to servile imitation. The various kingdoms into which Europe was split, and the difficulty of intercourse amongst them, gave courage to the artists, who were themselves the greatest travellers, to attempt works from which they would have shrunk, had those who were to judge of them had easy access to established models. Nevertheless, there is a fact, which shows that the oppressive influence of this principle was far from inert. The epochs of the most rapid advances of the Gothic architecture, were the periods succeeding the conquest of kingdoms by new races. This circumstance has given occasion to several, to conjecture that it stands indebted to the knowledge of its principles which some of these conquerors brought with them. The supposition is improbable; we have no reason to believe that they brought any thing else, than what necessarily belonged to such men, a bold and untrammeled spirit. This, indeed, is an essential element, and one, as we have seen, of great power in the composition of genius.

It was thus that the prominent defects of the art under the Anglo-Saxons, an exuberance of dead wall, and want of elevation, were remedied by the Normans. The Saracens in Spain, wrought also a similar change.

At no preceding period, did there exist men, so much given to the erection of permanent structures as modern Europeans, and their American descendants. Their command of materials, their resources of power, are by much superior to those possessed by any antecedent people. It is certainly, then, surprising, that they should be servile copyists of the arts of those whom they fitly look on, compared with themselves, as barbarians. I apprehend we can only explain the phenomenon, from the influence of the instinct of imitation. The extended intercourse between all parts of the world, the diffusion of the products of book-making, and of picture-making, render us familiar with existing models of all sorts. An artist, therefore, who has to construct any great edifice, finds it safest to copy from some one whose merits have been acknowledged, and takes the measure of a Grecian temple, or Gothic church. Thus, at least, he covers himself from censure. Hence it is, that we so often see, in the cold foggy climate of Britain, or in the boisterous one of North America, an imitation of some structure that had been admired in Greece. The claims to admiration which the copy possesses, fall, however, far short of the original. In the first place, it wants that evidence of perfect design, which arises from the complete and easy accomplishment of a purpose. What answered the mild climate, and serene skies of Greece, is felt to be inconvenient, and therefore defective, elsewhere. Next, it is most probably a very deficient copy. The effect of the Grecian structures, depends, as we have seen, in their consisting of large masses of stone. Our imitations are probably the work of the mason, or possibly the plasterer, and convey, therefore, no idea of power, the very essence which it is desired to embody. There is hence, also, generally, a failure in the execution. When the mind is full of any great idea, it knows when it has got an adequate expression for it, and rests not satisfied until it has fitly and accurately embodied it. But, if this great presiding idea be wanting, there is nothing within, distinguishing the right from the wrong, or preventing the commission of the greatest errors. Our mason-work and plastered fabrics, are consequently, often masses of incongruities.

Our choice of Gothic models, for similar reasons, generally fails as completely. A large cathedral, indeed, must be admired anywhere, but this is too great a work to be attempted. A copy is probably taken, from some chapel. We forget, that what was admirable for its purpose in some small ancient rustic hamlet, is out of place in our cities; that the arches, which, to simple peasants living in huts, seemed magnificent, to the chieftain, issuing for a time from his naked fortalice, elegant, must appear mean and insignificant, to those whose halls are nearly as lofty; and, that the whole pinnacled and buttressed structure, crowded on and perhaps overtopped by square unseemly buildings, devoted to meaner uses, shows among them, trifling, and fantastic, like a toy erected to please children.

The examples we have hitherto considered, are of the same arts changing materials. Those which we have now to attend to, are of different arts adopting the same, or similar materials. When arts are brought together, they borrow from each other. Men perceive that some materials, or instruments, or processes, employed in the one, could they be transferred to the other, would be the cause of its yielding larger returns. They are encouraged, therefore, to attempt the change, and experience shows that such attempts perseveringly pursued, are generally successful.

Efforts of the inventive faculty, succeeding in effecting such transfers, are more important than those in which it accomplishes simply a change of materials, for they tend more than they to weaken the powers of the propensity to imitation, and establish general principles, applicable to all arts. Hence we observe, that, in countries where many arts flourish, there are most general principles, least servile imitations, and very often, a continual onward progress. Barren apart, they show generative virtues when brought together. I take it, that it is chiefly from this circumstance, that the seats of commerce have been so generally the points from whence improvements in the arts have emanated. Thus, also, countries where various different races, or nations, have mingled together, are to be noted as coming eminently forward in the career of industry. Great Britain is a remarkable instance of this; so are the United States of America. When individuals meet from different countries, they reciprocally communicate and receive the arts of each, adopt such as are suited to their new circumstances, and probably improve several. Servile imitation can there have no place, for there is no common standard to imitate. Countries again, where only one art is practised, and where the population is composed of one unmingled race, are generally servilely imitative. Such are some purely agricultural countries. Experience shows, that, from the influence of this propensity, improvements, in these, always introduce themselves very slowly. Leaving, however, these general reflections, we should now turn to particular instances of passages in this way, of processes and inventions from art to art, and consequent improvement of old, and generation of new arts. But, as these will be chiefly recent, and European, there are one or two circumstances, affecting generally their progress in this part of the globe, to which it may be as well previously to advert.

The rough and variable climate of Europe, compared with the regions that have given origin to most of the arts now prevailing in it, renders the necessary cost of subsistence much greater. To live at all, in most parts of Europe, men must consume a greater quantity and better quality of food, or they must be more warmly clothed and comfortably lodged, than in regions nearer the equator. The influence of this circumstance has probably been somewhat increased by another. Along the Mediterranean, civilization seems to have gained great part of its advance by colonization, and it is to be observed that this movement of men from one region to another, proceeds from different motives than others impelling them to a change of seat. Men are often compelled by necessity to migrate in tribes and nations, but emigration in small parties, proceeds from choice.

They cannot well be induced to leave, not only their homes, but their kindred and nation, unless from the hope of bettering their condition, and, if their project miscarries not, they do in fact better their condition, and are indemnified for the pains of emigration, by a greater command of the necessaries and comforts of life. Thus habits of larger consumption are introduced, than absolute necessity might demand. Both circumstances would have the effect of augmenting the expense, or the wages of labor, and of creating an additional difficulty, to the passage of the arts of warmer climates into these more northern regions. It is very evident, for example, that an European workman could never have sat down to a Hindoo loom, for the purpose of fabricating a garment to himself; it would have been much better for him to keep to his sheepskin jacket. Before the transfer of any art could be effected, invention had to supply it with additional facilities. Stimulated by its wants, by the new scenes in which it found itself, and by the new materials submitted to it, it accordingly seems always to have succeeded in doing so. There is, perhaps, scarcely an implement in general use in Africa, or in Asia, excepting from it China, that has not passed with improvement into Europe.

In modern Europe, too, the strength of the effective desire of accumulation, seems to have been always greater than in any other part of the old world. This circumstance has much facilitated the passage into it, of the several arts, and balancing the higher rates of wages, and more stubborn materials, has rendered the formation of very many instruments there practicable, which the weaker accumulative principle of the Asiatics, or Africans, would have left unattempted.

It is worth while to remark, that there is a considerable analogy in this particular, between the different conditions of society in that continent and Asia then, and what exists between them now, in Europe and North America. The general wages of labor seem always to have been higher in Europe, than in Asia, in the same way as the wages of labor in North America, are now higher than in Europe. The same process, too, that carried the arts to Europe, seems now aiding their passage across the Atlantic. As flame often sets against the wind, for that it is fed by it, so invention seems to hold its course against opposing obstacles, for these obstacles excite its powers and minister materials to their action.

The progress of the knowledge of the natures and qualities

of particular substances, gradually introduced a knowledge of the properties and natures of substances in general. Men first see in the concrete, afterwards in the abstract. Thus, the discovery of the several mechanical powers, and the knowledge acquired of the nature of each, led in time to the general principles of mechanics. A knowledge of the mathematical properties of substances, as in land-measuring, and in the regular figures of architecture, led to a perception of the general properties of figure, or of space as an affection of matter, and, at last, to the doctrine of pure space and motion.

In the ancient world, science, as founded on a generalization of the experiences of art, was little prosecuted. It is only in modern times, that the science of experience has come to form an element of importance, in the general advance of invention.

It is clearly on the antecedent progress of art, that the foundation of the hopes of Bacon, for the future progress of science, rested. His philosophy may be fitly described, as a plan to reduce to method the chance processes that had been going on before, by which men, as we have seen, happening on one discovery after another, grope their way, as he expresses it, slowly, and in the dark, to fresh knowledge and power. The progress of the philosophy to which he has given his name, as well as that of the science of mathematics, have unquestionably discovered to us many general truths and theorems of art, and form therefore a new element influencing its progress. The great moving powers will, however, still, I apprehend, be found to proceed from the principles, the action of which we are now to attempt farther to trace through particular instances.

Men must have been very early led to the use of some of the farinaceous plants, and other vegetable matters, which, before they are fit for food, require to be reduced to small fragments. To effect this, they must either have rubbed them, or beat them, between some two substances. If stone were the material, they would rather prefer rubbing them, from the liability of that substance to break, and from its weight. It is thus that the rude tribes of southern Africa, to this day, lay their corn on one flat stone, and grind it by the help of another.¹ An improvement on this instrument, is to have the lower stone a little hollowed, and perhaps marked with transverse notches. In one form or other, this is a very general and ancient instrument, and, it may be observed, is probably the first machine in which a circular motion was introduced.

If wood be the material, then, to produce any effect, the substance to be comminuted must be laid on one piece, and another be struck against it. But thus, a large portion of the matter operated on would fly off, and be lost. The most natural mode of preventing this, is to hollow out the lower piece. The Indians of North America make an instrument of this sort very easily, by taking a portion of the trunk of a tree of hard wood, setting it upright, and burning and scraping out a hole in the upper end. They have then a large mortar, to which adjusting a wooden pestle, they produce the implement with which they pound all their corn. Such an instrument seems, like its fellow of stone, to have been in very general use, at one time or other, in most parts of the world.²

Tribes having learnt the use of such an instrument, on substances most easily comminuted, would be urged on to essay its powers on more cohesive matters. They might succeed in the attempt, at first, by simply increasing the size of the implement, and searching out the hardest and heaviest woods to construct it of; but, even these improvements would at length be insufficient for the enterprises to which their confidence in

¹ [So also peoples by no means altogether "rude," in Central and South America.]

² In a Scotch ballad, I believe in Allan Ramsay's collection, containing a catalogue of a peasant's furniture, perhaps two centuries since, "A timmer mell the bear to knock," is among the utensils enumerated. We yet speak of striking barley.

[The early frontiersmen of America, in the days of their extreme poverty before they set up water mills, adopted the Indian mortar and pestle described above, with the addition that the labor of raising the heavy pestle was greatly lightened by the attachment of a spring-pole. These were called "samping mills," and the loud noise made by their operation could be heard a long way through the forest, and announced to the traveller his approach to a clearing.

The introduction of water mills into many parts of the tropics is permanently opposed by great obstacles, owing to the extreme seasonal variations in rainfall. The device just described would seem to be the first and most natural advance upon the *tortilla* stone in these regions.]

their powers, or their necessities, might excite them. To overcome these increasing difficulties, it would require no great stretch of the inventive faculty, to hit on the expedient of placing a firm transverse bar, with a hole in it, for the passage of the handle of the pestle, across the top of the mortar, from side to side. Such a change in its construction, seems accordingly, to have been very generally effected. Simple as it is, it contained the germ of very many subsequent improvements. The force employed, acting thus not directly, but through the intervention of a fulcrum, may be so applied as to give either increased velocity, or increased power, and the regulated movement introduced renders mere power almost all that is necessary. The size of the mortar, and weight of the pestle, might, therefore, be increased indefinitely, and the instrument might be put in motion by men, or by cattle. The expression of the vegetable oils, was found to be the most difficult operation to be performed by instruments of this sort, and it is probable, that it was to effect it, that machinery, by which increased force might be employed, was first made use of. Oil mills, of this sort, are yet common in the east.

This construction rendered the union of the wooden mortar and pestle, with the parallel instrument of stone, almost inevitable. Hardness and heaviness, being the requisites in the pestle, and an equal resistance being necessary in the mortar, to bring about the junction, it would seem to have been only requisite, that the two machines should have met where there was a scarcity of wood of proper quality. The handle of the pestle, through which a cross bar was then thrust, became the axle of the upper mill stone, and the lower mill stone formed the bottom of the mortar. The movement then became altogether circular, and required small absolute force, but as much swiftness as could be given to it. The machine thus generated, by the passage of the one instrument into the other, was then a regular mill, to work which was the employment of cattle or slaves. As it united the advantages of the two original instruments, the capacity of the wood to receive and modify motion, and of the stone to bruise and comminute hard vegetable matters, its invention seems to have had considerable effect in advancing art still farther. The moving power, in one of the most laborious and common operations, was thus reduced to a simplicity of action, that paved the way for its being performed by an inanimate agent; such an agent was introduced into the process, through the intervention of another art.

In hot regions, water is very abundantly consumed, both as a necessity and luxury, for immediate use, and as the great fertiliser of the soil. In such regions, the raising it from wells and rivers has always been a very common and laborious process, and to facilitate it has given occasion to some of the earliest efforts of ingenuity. One of these consisted of a large wheel, placed upright, and to the circumference of which small buckets were affixed. It was put in motion by treading on it, and the buckets and it were so arranged, that they should just dip beneath the stream, in the lower part of their circumvolution, and, at the height of it, should empty themselves into a reservoir placed above. A considerable saving of labor was thus produced. Another improvement did entirely away with the necessity of employing it, in many situations. To the outside of the wheel, where there was a sufficient current, were affixed broad plates of wood, or other material, on which the strength of the stream acting, forced it round, and performed the office of the laborer. Such engines are of common use at present in China. They were known in Italy, in the time of Julius Cæsar, to which they probably found their way from Asia. They presented to the Romans a means of employing the power of water in the laborious operation of grinding,[1] which they had sufficient discernment to adopt. The motion of the water-wheel, was communicated to the mill, by the intervention of a toothed wheel.

[1] Fiunt etiam in fluminibus rotæ eisdem rationibus, quibus supra scriptum est. Circa earum frontes affiguntur pinnæ, quæ cum percutiuntur ab impetu fluminis, cogunt progredientes versari rotam; et ita modiolis aquam haurientes et in summum referentes, sine operarum calcatura, ipsius fluminis impulsa versatæ, præstant quod opus est, ad usum. Eadem ratione etiam versantur hydraulæ, in quibus eadem sunt omnia, præterquam quod in uno capite axis habet tympanum dentatum et inclusum; id autem ad perpendiculum collocatum in cultrum, versatur cum rota pariter. Secundum id tympanum, majus item dentatum planum est collocatum, quo continetur axis, habens in summo capite subscudem ferreum qua mola continetur. Ita dentes ejus tympani,

Thus, from the union of the productions of the inventive faculty exercised on at least three arts, came the rude model of the present water-mill. Its progress was at first slow. Such mills seem only to have been constructed, when there was a current of water suited to the purpose. The expense of forming artificial falls, seems to have been too great for the improvidence of the age. Though abundant materials existed, the accumulative principle of the people was too weak to work upon them. Cattle-mills, and mills driven by slaves, continued therefore to be generally preferred.[1] It was owing to an invention, like so many others, the result of necessity and genius united, that the use of water-mills became more general. When Rome was besieged by the Goths, in the time of Belisarius, they cut off the supply of water by the aqueducts. Among the other inconveniences arising from the measure, it stopped the mills driven by the water from these aqueducts. To remedy the evil, that general devised the scheme of anchoring barges in the river, in which he placed mills driven by the current. The plan met the immediate exigence, and, as such a construction suited the low strength of the accumulative principle of the age, it was generally adopted elsewhere. In the present times, such a plan would be rejected, because, though the first expense is comparatively small, the durability of the instrument is too short. We prefer the greater expense of making dams and sluices, on account of their greater durability. The cause leading to the construction of the one or the other, is the same as that determining the Chinese to the formation of floating gardens, where the Dutch would build dykes.

The invention maintained itself through the dark ages, and followed the improvement and extension of agriculture, and

---

quod est in axi inclusum, impellendo dentes tympani plani, cogunt fieri molarum circinationem, in qua machina impendens infundibulum subministrat molis frumentum, et eadem versatione subijitur farina.—Vitruvius, Lib. X. c. 10, as quoted by Beckman, Vol. I.

Si aquæ copia est, fusurus balnearum debent pistrina suscipere; ut ubi formatis aquariis molis, sine animalium vel hominum labore, frumenta frangantur.—*Pallad de re rust.*, lib. I. 42, edit. Gesn. II., p. 892.—*Ibid.*

[1] Three hundred years after Augustus, the number of cattle-mills in Rome amounted to three hundred.—Beckman.

facility of communication, which returning civilization and tranquillity gradually diffused. It seems to have spread very generally over Europe, about the beginning of the sixteenth century. The force of water being, by it, turned to the service of man, wind also was made to employ its powers to a similar purpose.

Important as these engines were in themselves, from their immediate utility, they were more so in their effects. Men's minds were directed to the advantage of what is termed machinery, instruments, that is, giving new velocity and direction to motion, and to the power of inanimate agents generative of motion, of both of which the mill afforded the first eminent instance. Examples of the possibility of executing by other powers than the human hand, or the strength of the inferior animals, one of the most difficult of the operations that the necessities of mankind called for, being brought freshly before the eyes of almost all Europe, naturally prompted the genius of reflective men to conceive the idea of applying them to other, and even more difficult processes. This general stimulus to the inventive faculty, conjoined with others, acting vigorously, but occasionally and partially, and already referred to, carried the improvement through a great variety of operations. Mills of all sorts, came to be constructed, driven commonly by water, as the more forcible, and manageable power. To trace the course of invention through these, were not to mark the principles regulating the progress of that faculty, but to enter on a description of European art. It may be sufficient to observe, that, in conformity to these principles, not only was each difficulty overcome by it, a benefit to the particular art it was meant to serve, but to art in general, each conquest extending its authority, not alone over the province where it was achieved, but over the whole region which it was its object to gain. If, for instance, comparing the ingenious and complete machinery of a well-constructed flour-mill of the present day, with a model of the rude and imperfect engines of the sort that existed two hundred years ago, we ask the cause of the difference, we shall probably be told, the improvement of mechanics; but, if we trace the progress of this improvement carefully, we will find that it was the fitting of the machinery of this very engine to other arts, that was one of the main producers of it. The productions of the union of arts also propagating others, like all generators, their increase goes on, when there are no retarding checks, to borrow a phrase of common use in inquiries connected with these, not in a simple arithmetical, but in a geometrical progression.

The effects produced, by the passage through different arts, of this improvement on a very ancient engine, important as they were, have been far exceeded in extent of consequences, by one of altogether modern invention. I allude to the steam engine, the progress of which, we will find to have regulated itself almost altogether according to the above principles.

As the progress of order, civilization, and art, covered the island of Great Britain with a numerous population, the stores of fuel which its cold and moist climate required, and its forests had at first afforded, were by degrees exhausted. Its situation prevented its receiving the supplies, which, had it made a part of the continent, might have been brought down rivers issuing from interior regions. Necessity thus taught its inhabitants the general use of coal, in which, happily, its territory abounds. But what of this material lay close to the surface, and the fields immediately beneath, having been wrought out, the miner was urged on by the increasing wants of his countrymen, and the abundant materials before him, to penetrate still deeper; and the labors of generations formed large excavations, in regions far beneath the surface. Here, however, he was met by an enemy continually gathering strength as he advanced on him, and threatening completely to bar his future progress. The farther he penetrated, water poured in upon him in greater quantity, while to free himself of it he had to elevate it to a greater height. A period seemed approaching, when very many of the mines must be abandoned. In this extremity, it was natural to the men engaged in this occupation, to cast about, and endeavor to discover some device, through help of which they might successfully continue its pursuit. The resources of all powers hitherto known having been tried, as far as in such situations they could be effectually employed, and seeming to be on the point of yielding, it could not but occur to attentive thinkers, that, if they were to succeed, the probability was it would be through some one hitherto unemployed. Of those, steam was perhaps the most apparent, and manageable. Its force must have been, at least in some measure, known to many, and had been previously pointed out by one distinguished individual, as capable of producing the greatest effects. The operation to be performed by it, too, seemed peculiarly fitted for its action. Water is moved in pipes, and, it is only in confinement that the power arising from the rarefication and condensation of steam becomes sensible. It appeared then by no means impracticable, to manage the condensation and rarification within metal pipes, so connected with those in which the water had to be raised, as to supply the force necessary to produce its elevation. On this principle the attempt was made, and succeeded in first practically establishing the power of an agent, destined, we cannot doubt, to produce effects far greater than any which has hitherto been placed within the hands of man.

The various circumstances conjoining to bring about this important event, are deserving our attention. 1st. The urgent demand for some powerful agent, however rude and unwieldly in action. Had the operation to be performed been in any degree complicated and nice in its nature, it would never probably have occurred to any one, that the expanse and collapse of a vapor, shut up in iron vessels, could be brought to execute it. 2d. The materials, metal, coal, and water, being in these situations abundant. 3d. The previous improvement of machinery in general. 4th. The want occurring to men of property, and of a class in general bold in enterprise, and accustomed to stake their funds freely.[1] Had any of these been wanting, this extraordinary invention might yet have slumbered, veiled in the darkness which had covered it for so many thousands of years. Perhaps it might have been stifled

---

[1] [To this catalogue should be added a fifth "circumstance," touched upon in part by Rae two pages back, and that is, the existence of a government strong enough to secure at least ordinary law and order, but not so strong as to crush out the spirit of individual initiative. Had the experience of Dud Dudley in iron smelting, for example, been universal and continuous in respect to all British industrial innovators in each generation, the whole course of modern economic history in Great Britain would have been vastly different.]

at its birth, for its first appearance gave but slight token of its inherent capabilities. The expenditure of fuel and of labor, necessary to the discharge of its functions, was excessive. It having, however, been thus established, that it was an agent within the compass of man's ability, to make a partner in the series of his operations, there was a strong stimulus to endeavour to render it a more economical agent. This was effected by a change in the construction of the apparatus, the leading feature of which is, the causing the steam to perform its operations, through the intervention of a piston. The instrument thus produced, was an effective and economical operator for the purpose designed. The improvement was important in itself, and far more so in its consequences. Had the machinery of simple pipes and valves been continued, under some improved form,[1] it might have appeared only fitted for propelling fluids, and been confined to that purpose; as through the aid of sails of some sort, wind has been made to propel vessels, from very early ages, though it is only of comparatively recent times, that it has been applied to give motion to mills. But, the introduction of the piston, and its adjuncts, showed the power in a familiar form; the handle of a pump was a thing well known as put in motion by machinery, and it was obvious that the movement had only to be reversed, to communicate motion to any machinery. Under this form, therefore, its progress as a power through all other machinery, may be said to have been inevitable. It possessed the important advantages of being always at command, uniform in action, and unbounded in force. In this progress it was assisted in one important step by science. The discovery of the doctrine of latent heat enabled it at once to surmount a great obstacle, which might otherwise have long limited the extent of its operations. It is perhaps not to be supposed, but that the general truth would have been itself at last made known by the continual groping after improvement, which the existence of such an instrument in the hands of men would of itself have occasioned; if however science advanced it by only a few years, the beneficial

---

[1] The formation and condensation of the steam, might have been managed in chambers, separate from the system of pipes and reservoirs elevating the water.

effects of such an anticipation, will be allowed to have been very great.[1]

In its course, two things seem specially worthy of notice, the additional freedom which it gave the inventive faculty, and the circumstances which existed to facilitate the progress of that faculty, and which it seized on for the purpose. The consciousness of the possession of an agent of unlimited and perfectly manageable power, which had escaped the attention of all preceding ages, seemed to have immediately more effectually broken the constraining and retarding influence of the propensity to imitation, than any preceding event. Whatever mere motion could do, if the sphere of its action could be contracted into small space, was conceived within the power of steam; and invention set to work with a determination, progressively to supply the means of its application. In these essays, it has been always ultimately successful. It is not necessary here to enlarge on the great changes it has hence effected, or on the important improvements it has introduced. It is to be observed, however, that, whatever it has performed, has proceeded in the order we have indicated, and which, I believe, almost all inventions have followed. The diversity of climates, territories, productions, and other circumstances of different regions and nations, has helped it, as them, forward, and been to it as it were steps, by which it has gained the rank it holds in the modes of human industry.

Thus the peculiar circumstances of the North American continent, may, with propriety, be said to have been the exciting cause producing steam navigation, one of the most important of these steps. That country is full of great lakes and rivers, affording the easiest, and often the only means for the transport of the large quantities of agricultural produce, that its interior sections yield. Such inland navigation is always exceedingly tedious; there were therefore peculiar reasons for the device of some new agent to facilitate it. An agent like steam, too, might evidently be employed with more safety and chance of success, in calm inland waters, than in the great

---

[1] Since the above was written, I have seen it stated, that Watt did not take the idea of his great improvement from Dr. Black's discovery, but that it was entirely the result of his own inventive powers.

ocean. If we consider, in addition to this, the greater play which, from circumstances already enumerated, the inventive faculty enjoys in that continent, we shall see that it was there, so to say, that this improvement ought to have taken place. The point, too, in North America, where it did first actually take place, is also, as it were, particularly marked out for it. The transport between New York and Albany, by sailing vessels on the Hudson river, was both very expensive, and peculiarly tedious. Steam has there changed a voyage of days, or weeks, into one of less than sixteen hours.[1]

The circumstances leading on to the invention of steam land carriage, may also be noted as exemplative of this view of the subject. There were first simply railroads, to facilitate heavy drafts for short distances, from coal mines; then there was a more general use of them in all heavy drafts; finally, there was the general application of steam, as the power to effect transport of all sorts, and with all velocities, along the smooth surface they afforded. All that was wanted for the last step was, that the mechanism should be rendered less heavy and cumbersome, and it may be remarked, so great confidence had been generated of the power of the inventive faculty, that the undertaking was commenced with full assurance that it would accomplish the desired improvement, although the manner how was not known. The result showed that the confidence was not misplaced.

Thus, such are the steps by which invention advances, that it would seem, had there been no country like Great Britain, the steam engine might not yet have been produced; had there been none like North America, steam navigation might not yet have been practised: and again, had not Great Britain existed, metal railways and steam carriage might have been still only in the category of possibilities.

---

[1] Since the passage in the text was written, the art of the application of steam, as an agent in transport by water, has made a farther step. It consists in a passage of the engine used in land carriage, to that used in water carriage. Besides this, however, the germ of some other principles has appeared, which, it seems probable, will ultimately produce a great and important revolution in the art. It is remarkable, that the site of this event is also the Hudson.

The invention of printing has often been cited as one of the most important of modern times. The steps by which it advanced were also of that gradual and easy nature, one leading on to another, and surrounding circumstances prompting to essay the ascent, as to take away all admiration of its progress, were it not that the constitution of man's nature renders the passing of any individual, coolly and deliberately, the least out of the circle of imitation, very often a proof of the strongest powers of mind. There was first the stamping with signets; then the transfer of this initial art, to stamping, instead of painting, playing cards; then the existence of a great and unceasing demand for one book, the Bible, the excessive cost of transcription, and the transfer of the art of stamping cards to stamping pages, first of the sacred volume, and afterwards of others; lastly, there was the passage of another art, that of casting dies for coining, to facilitating the formation of metallic types.[1] The art, thus perfected, was disseminated by the tyranny of a petty prince.[2]

The art which [while not itself a technical process] has most immediate connexion with the increase of wealth [in general], the business of banking, is itself in some measure illustrative of the influence of change in producing improvements in all arts. It commenced in countries where exchanges for large amounts were numerous. Venice, Florence, Genoa, Amsterdam, the great marts of commerce, were the first banking communities. In them, however, its operations were confined to

---

[1] In ascribing the invention of printing not to chance, but to the gradual progress of events, I am supported by the authority of Condorcet, and apparently also by that of Dugald Stewart. "L'invention de l'imprimerie a sans dout avancé le progres de l'espèce humaine; mais cette invention étoit elle-meme une suite de l'usage de la lecture répandu dans un grand nombre de pays." *Vie du Turgot*, Pref. to first dissertation to *Enc. Brit.*

[2] On sait comment l'imprimerie s'est répandue depuis 1462 par la révolution que Mayence éprouva cette meme année. Adolphe, comte de Nassau, soutenu par la Pape Pie II. ayant surpris cette ville imperiale, lui ota ses libertés et privilèges. Alors, tous les ouvriers, qu'elle avoit dans son sein à l'exception de Guttenburgh s'enfuirent, se disperserent et porterent leur art dans les lieux et les pays ou il n'étoit pas connu. C'est à cet événement que tous les historiers réunis à Jean Schœffer fils de Pierre et petit-fils de Faust, placent l'époque de la dispersion dont l'Europe profita. (*Encyclopedie*, Art., "Imprimerie.")

transfers of specie, and the benefits derived from them consisted chiefly in security given, and trouble avoided. It passed, at last, into countries where there were comparatively few actual exchanges, and where, in order to effect the passage, invention was obliged to develop its capacities for facilitating, and thus exciting and increasing exchanges. The following extract from the *Wealth of Nations* will render this apparent.

"The commerce of Scotland, which at present is not very great, was still more inconsiderable when the two first banking companies were established; and those companies would have had but little trade, had they confined their business to the discounting of bills of exchange. They invented, therefore, another method of issuing their promissory notes; by granting what they called cash accounts, that is, by giving credit to the extent of a certain sum, (two or three thousand pounds for example), to any individual who could procure two persons of undoubted credit and good landed estate to become surety for him, that whatever money should be advanced to him, within the sum for which the credit had been given, should be repaid upon demand, together with the legal interest. Credits of this kind are, I believe, commonly granted by banks and bankers in all different parts of the world. But the easy terms upon which the Scotch banking companies accept of repayment are, so far as I know, peculiar to them, and have perhaps been the principal cause, both of the great trade of those companies, and of the benefit which the country has received from it."

If we may judge of the progress of an art from its general success, the transfer of the business of banking to Scotland would furnish another proof of the benefits accruing to arts themselves, from their passages from country to country. Nowhere has banking been productive of more acknowledged advantages, [as is shown in another place], and nowhere have the evils occasionally attendant on it been fewer.

As also illustrative of the subject, I may call the attention of the reader to a fact often noted,—the small progress of the aborigines of the new world in art, when compared with that attained by the inhabitants of the old.

If we are to search for natural causes of the phenomenon, in my opinion we may find them, in the greater extent of continent in the eastern than in the western hemisphere, and, especially, of continent lying under the equatorial regions, the birth place in both of the arts they possessed. This extent of country, and diversity of materials, must have increased very much the chance of discovery in the arts, and tended greatly, on the principles we have just been considering, to push forward their improvement. To take as an example an art which has been particularly referred to,[1] that of domesticating the ox, and teaching him labor. To suppose that men, while the whole of that species of animals were yet wild, conceived the project of domesticating them, in order that they might apply them to the various purposes they now serve, were a conjecture altogether unwarranted by any event in the history of mankind and of art. We have rather reason to believe that in this, as in other instances, they must have been led on to the object gradually, by the intervention of circumstances, each carrying them a certain way towards this great end. But there must evidently have been a greater chance for the existence of such circumstances, in the great range of continent lying within, or not far from, the borders of the torrid zone in Asia, Africa, or Europe, than in the small part similarly situated in America. Without pretending to say what those circumstances were, it is at least probable that one may have been the keeping these animals in enclosures, merely to satisfy the curiosity, or to afford the amusement of hunting to the chiefs, or kings, of the agricultural nations. This we know, in more recent times, to have been a custom in some eastern countries.[2] There they would in time lose great part of their natural ferocity, and become, like deer in our parks, half tame. Now, it is evident enough, that the chances for this important step towards the accomplishment of the object being undertaken, would be directly in proportion to the number and extent of the agricultural countries of those ages, that is, to the extent of continent lying near the equator.

The period when the event took place marks a great change in the condition of man, for, independently of its immediate effects, it necessarily brought about the existence of a race of herdsmen, occupying regions, in the state of art at the time, not

[1] Dr. Robertson's *History of America*, Vol. II. [2] Xenophon, *Cyrop*.

coming within the range of the strength of the effective desire of accumulation of the neighboring people, as tillable land. Herdsmen once existing, it could scarce be but that they would spread themselves wherever they could find support for their cattle, and gradually exterminate the hunting tribes. There is, I think, reason to suppose that such a revolution occurred in Europe many ages previous to the time of recorded history. Its importance may be estimated from the observations that are made in a preceding part of this volume.[1]

We may, on similar principles, in part, account for the low rank in the scale of humanity occupied by the aborigines of Australia, that fifth and yet but partially explored continent. The uniformity of soil, climate, and natural productions, of that whole region is very great. This limited variety of materials would seem to have diminished the number of arts generated, and that of improvements arising from effects of changes, among those having obtained existence.

In conclusion I may observe, that I believe it will be found, that there is no art in existence which we may not find means to trace, with greater or less certainty, to the rudest and most simple principles; and which may not be shown to have attained perfection by continual changes from place to place, and material to material, and by encountering consequently alternate difficulties and facilities, the former developing its powers, the latter extending their field of action, and both, by helping to introduce general principles, weakening the restraining power of the tendency to servile imitation, and advancing the progress of science. This successive passage of the same arts from country to country, and from one into another, seems to be the great exciting cause of the progress of them all. The greatest improvement of British manufacture in recent times is, I may remark, [the result of] a passage of

---

[1] Page 84. Were this the place to enlarge on the subject, many circumstances confirmatory of such an event might be enumerated: as the traces of the existence of a race of mere hunters over all Europe; the roots of European languages being the same as those of central Asia; the form and constitution of the present domestic ox species, and of sheep, marking their gradual migration from a warm climate, into colder regions and more abundant pasture.

this latter sort. The cotton manufacture is a passage of the art of fabricating woollens, into that of fabricating cottons. It was the perfection of the former more easy art that showed the possibility of the existence, and eventually brought about the existence of the latter,—invention in this case, being excited by the higher wages of labor in Europe than in Asia. Improvement was the consequence. The peculiar difficulties the material presented being overcome, the facilities it possessed were experienced.

This view of the subject seems somewhat to illustrate the following reflections of Lord Bacon, concerning the early progress of art, and may satisfy us that, even yet, they are not altogether inapplicable. He observes, that, " although, when we first begin to consider the variety of necessaries, conveniences, and elegances, which the mechanical arts minister to life, we are rather struck with a feeling of admiration at the abundant wealth which mankind inherit, than with a sense of their poverty; yet, when we examine every thing, and consider through how many chances and revolutions these arts have been brought to their perfection, and through what simple and easy reflections they have been discovered, such sentiments will soon leave us, and we shall be inclined to commiserate the penury and barrenness of invention of the human race, which have taken so many ages to accomplish things deducible without difficulty, from facts neither very numerous, nor very hard to be ascertained."[1] It is indeed true that the philosophy, in the introduction of which he bore so eminent a part, has, in these latter ages, been a very effective promoter of the dominion of man, and, mixing with art, has much purified and dignified its spirit, and greatly increased its powers, turning invention in this department from particulars to generals, and converting art into science. This has more especially happened in the chemical sciences, and those connected with them, a sphere to which, I may be allowed to observe, his system seems particularly applicable. There, science begins to lead and direct art; in other departments she rather follows and assists it. But, with regard to the general progress of art, even its recent history

[1] *Nov. Org.*, L. 1, LXXXV.

evinces the justice of these observations, and shows that "men estimate falsely both their possessions and their powers, deeming of the first more highly, and of the last more lightly, than they ought."[1] We shall admit this, if we consider the vast number of qualities and powers, and of new practical combinations of them, that, in our days, have been discovered and applied to use, and reflect on the long series of ages during which they were hid in darkness, on the proximity of men to them, and the ease with which they might have lighted on them, would they have turned their eyes, ever so little, out of the busy circle of actual life and occupations. If, too, the history of the past tell us truly what the future will be, we may feel assured that, as it is not the powers of nature or of man, but the application of them, that is limited, if individuals be inclined by their own dispositions to apply themselves to purposes conducive to the general good, and if they be incited to do so by causes similar to such as have before operated, art and science will still stretch their capacities, until they may at length reach an extent of which it is impossible for us now to form any conception.

An attentive consideration of the history of art might also give rise to a series of reflections of another sort. It would show a purpose, which does not strike us on a first view of the creation. Nature, it would seem, if I may be allowed so to express myself, sensible of the combined pride and imbecility of man, has so arranged the world she has provided for him, as to make it the means of urging him on, in a continual progress, towards higher and higher attainments. Neither the defects of his limited and cloudy faculties, nor the intoxication of the vainglory, that, fed by his imitative propensities, is ever representing him to himself as having reached the summit of terrestrial perfection, can preserve him stationary. He is now impelled by necessity, now excited by hope, to attempt the amelioration of his condition, and thus gradually to develope the latent capacities of his own being, and of the sphere of existence in which he moves. By a diversity of climates, soils, and nations, steps are, as it were, arranged for him, up which he is gradually enticed, or compelled to mount,

[1] *Nov. Org.*, L. 1, LXXXV.

to fresh acquisitions of knowledge and power. He is never allowed to remain stationary. A portion, indeed, of the race may, and for a limited time, but ultimately they either improve, or yield their place to surrounding peoples who have improved.

Some philosophers urge it as an objection against the world's having been formed by a designing cause, that so large a portion of its surface is useless to man. According to them, had it been formed by perfect and beneficent reason, it should have been such a level garden, as a certain theorist supposed it originally to have been. Had it been so, we may safely assert, that man, as man, could never have inhabited it. He must either have been formed above, or sunk below, his present condition. Because we do not turn to any account the sandy desert, or rugged mountain, we are not entitled to look on them as blots on the general utility of the creation, or suppose, even, that they may not be put to use by succeeding generations. The savage of New Holland conceives every tree useless that does not soon rot, and so breed maggots for him. The ancient Romans scarcely conceived that the woods and morasses of Caledonia would, at any time, be abundantly useful. We judge rashly, then, in condemning as useless any portion of the earth. Even the barren deserts of Africa may, in after ages, be fertilized. Art and industry may, in time, draw water plentifully from the depths of the earth, and cover them with treple harvests. To do so, human art must make great advances, and these and the other obstacles it has met with, and will meet with, are stimulants to its advance.

War itself, so great an evil to the individuals within the scope of its ravages, is evidently the only manner by which, in certain states of society, an amelioration can be induced. The destruction of the Roman Empire, and almost of the Roman race, by the barbarians, was, perhaps, ultimately, the most beneficial revolution ever brought about. Even in its minor consequences, this apparent evil produces also much of real good. Without it, many of the most useful inventions might never have been either propagated, or improved.

We are ever ready to forget the part which nature thus

bears in our operations, and to lay the whole credit of our skill and industry to our own discernment. The slow and gradual manner in which she has led us on to the acquisition of every art, acting all along the part of the sagacious teacher, who puts before his scholar, at first, the most simple and easy lessons, and on his mastering these, by degrees, through the influence of suitable rewards and penalties, conducts him to more difficult efforts, meets not our notice, and rises not to our thoughts.

Were these or similar reflections fitly placed here, the subject might give occasion to many more of the sort. But, it seems to me, that we act always rashly and imprudently in bringing such disquisitions into inductive inquiries. They belong to another subject.

The aim of science may be said to be, to ascertain the manner in which things actually exist. The doing so, indeed, has been generally found to bring to light some useful purpose in their arrangement, and the proofs of benevolent design thus exhibited, are exceedingly interesting in relation to the evidence they afford us of the attributes of the great first cause. But, as science is only progressive, we are never certain of having ascertained the exact manner of the existence of any thing, and, therefore, we must often be mistaken in the ends for which we may conceive that the things we see are formed. The confident assumption, then, that we have exactly ascertained, in any case, the precise end, and the application of this assumed purpose, as a guide to scientific inquiry, has a decided tendency to retard the progress of science. For, the supposition that the actual arrangement is different from what it was conceived to be, is held to be inadmissible, as it would imply some deviation from the design for which we assumed it was devised. It is, as Lord Bacon expresses it, an improper blending of things human and divine, and a mode of reasoning which he, in my opinion, with much propriety repeatedly cautions his followers to avoid.

The reflections, therefore, as to the probable designs of nature, in the constitution of the world as the abode of man, which I have here introduced, would have been excluded, had it not been that Adam Smith, and many other popular writers on these subjects, sometimes indirectly, in their application of terms, sometimes directly, in their reasonings, assume, that the designs of nature are quite opposite to what I have represented, and make their conceptions of her purposes an argument in favor of their particular theoretical views.

The embryo doctrine is to be found in Virgil.

> "Nonne vides, croceos ut Tmolus odores,
> India mittit ebur, molles sua thura Sabæi?
> At Chalybes nudi ferrum, virosaque Pontus
> Castorea, Eliadum palmas Epirus equarum?
> Continuo has leges æternaque fœdera certis
> Imposuit natura locis, quo tempore primum
> Deucalion vacuum lapides jactavit in orbem."

> "Thus Tmolus is with yellow saffron crowned;
> India black ebon and white ivory bears;
> And soft Idume weeps her odorous tears.
> Then Pontus sends his beaver stones from far,
> And naked Spaniards temper steel for war:
> Epirus for the Elean chariots, breeds
> (In hopes of palms) a race of running steeds.
> This is the original contract; these the laws
> Imposed by Nature and by Nature's cause
> On sundry places, when Deucalion hurled
> His mother's entrails on the desert world."[1]

In the same manner as by the poet, the products of different regions are spoken of by political economists as bestowed on them by nature, are termed natural productions, and the attempt to transfer them to other sites, is held to be a procedure in opposition to the designs of providence, whose intentions, it is asserted, in giving them these productions, were, that the inhabitants of different countries should exchange the products of their several territories with one another.

There are, I conceive, two objections to this view of the subject, the first referring to the term, natural productions; the second to the purposes assumed to be the ends designed by nature.

If by the term, natural productions, we mean things produced without the aid of art, then no civilized country can be

[1] Georgic I. Dryden's Translation.

INVENTION ECONOMIC

said to have any natural productions, for to all that it produces art lends its aid. It were, therefore, I think, better to substitute for the term, natural productions, that of actual productions.

But, because one country alone now produces particular commodities, we are by no means warranted to conclude that nature intended they should be produced only there. On the contrary, if we may judge of a scheme by the mode in which its parts are arranged, and in which they act, her intentions were, that the variety of materials placed before man should generate the rudiments of arts at different points, but that these arts should be advanced from their first rough simplicity, and carried to greater and greater excellence, by passing from one region and people to another. If, therefore, we find any art confined to a particular region—the actual production of only particular communities,—the presumption is, that it is yet in its infancy, and that it will only be as it is carried to new countries and other men, and generally diffused over the whole globe, that it will advance towards maturity. Time has shown that the supposed laws and decrees of nature, which the poet declared to be of eternal power, are already abrogated by the progress of art, in most of the instances he adduces. The natural productions of Great Britain, serviceable to man, are certainly very few. The catalogue of her actual productions, even of those alone in which she preeminently excels, is greater than that of any region of equal extent. Were Virgil now alive, he certainly would not cite Albania for horses, or Spain for iron. These results are entirely the work of art, to the operations of which it is impossible to put any bounds. Who can positively say what fifty years hence will be the productions of any country?

It is the intention of the inventive faculty, when it applies itself to the arts of ministering to the necessaries, conveniences, or superfluities of life—the wants of our nature that the subject we treat of considers,—to increase the supplies which it is the aim of each to procure. If when it gains the ends it purposes, it really produces this increase, in doing so, it must render the labor of the members of the society in which it operates more effective, and enable them from the same outlay to produce greater returns, or from less outlay to produce the same returns, [or from the same outlay to produce the same returns in less time.] An improvement in the construction of a plough, enables the individual employing that instrument to plough a greater quantity of land with the same cattle and labor, or an equal quantity of land with fewer cattle and less labor. The use of water as a power diminishes very greatly the labor necessary to perform the operations in which it is employed, and, therefore, from a less outlay, produces equal returns. Were the assumption correct, on which we have been all along proceeding, that instruments compare with each other by the physical effects they produce, and, that, in proportion as the same effects result from less outlay, or greater effects from the same outlay, the ratio of the capacity of the instrument to its cost will be increased, and it moved to an order of quicker return; then the successful exertions of the inventive faculty would always be effective, and every discovery, directly or indirectly, lead to real improvement. This, as we shall presently see, is not always the case, because many commodities are not estimated by their physical effects;[1] but continuing for the present the assumption, which, for the sake of simplicity of exposition we have made, improvement, in this case, must carry the instruments improved by it to more speedily returning orders.

It is here also to be observed that, although any particular improvement, immediately, and at first, affects only the instruments improved, it very shortly diffuses itself over the whole range of instruments owned by the society. The successful efforts of the inventive faculty are not a gift to any particular artists, but to the whole community, and their benefits [are] divided amongst its members. If an improvement, for instance, in the art of baking bread were effected, by which, with half the labor and fuel, equally good bread could be produced, it would not benefit the bakers exclusively, but would be felt equally over the whole society. The bakers would have a small additional profit, the whole society would

[1] [Here Rae refers to his theory of luxury. See Article I. in the Appendix.]

have bread for the product of somewhat less labor, and all who consumed bread, that is, every member of the society, would from the same outlay have somewhat larger returns. The whole series of instruments owned by the society would be somewhat more productive, would be carried to an order of quicker return.[1]

In this manner, all improvements, by moving the whole stock of instruments belonging to any society, to more productive orders, increase proportionably its absolute capital and stock. Should a naturalist, in examining the nature of the surface on the farm of an individual in a small agricultural society, make the discovery, that beneath it there was a quantity of plaster of Paris; and should the farmer, in consequence of his recommendation, sprinkling a little of this reduced to powder on some of his fields, find that it caused them to yield double returns, his farm or the lease he held of it, might in his eyes be doubly valuable, and he might demand in exchange, and perhaps receive, two other farms of equal size in its place. Were it, however, found, that a stratum of this substance extended over the whole range of country possessed by the society, and was equally efficacious when applied to any portion of the surface, his farm would not be more valuable than other farms. The supply [provision], however, for future wants, possessed by the whole society, would be largely increased, and, the strength of their effective desire of accumulation remaining undiminished, their absolute capital would be proportionably augmented. But, as the whole stock of instruments [still] remained the same, with the exception of the difference made by the surface of the fields having been sprinkled with a quantity of this mineral powder, their amount, as measured by one another, [or by some particular instrument taken as a standard and to which all other instruments are referred (see Chapter VIII.)], would be the

[1] This follows from the nature of exchange, see pages 104-105.

[What Rae means by this reference to his theory of exchange in the eighth chapter, is somewhat obscure. It is, apparently, that the system of separation of employments and resulting system of exchange, with its phenomena of competition, forms altogether a benefit-of-progress diffusing mechanism.]

same as before. Some instruments might possibly exchange for a greater amount of instruments of another sort, than formerly, but this change could no more be considered an increase in the total value, than the fact of the latter instrument exchanging for a less amount, could be considered an indication of a diminution of the total exchangable value of the stock of the society. The relative capital and stock would thus remain unchanged [for the time being]. But, though this relative or exchangable value of the society's stock might remain unchanged, its absolute capital and stock would be [straightway] increased. The reality of such increase is marked, in all similar cases, by at least three [attendant] circumstances.

1. The members of the society possess, in general, a more abundant provision for future wants, the revenue of the whole society, and of each individual composing it, is increased.

2. The whole society, as a separate community, becomes more powerful, in relation to other communities. It can support the burdens of war, and the expense of all negotiations and national contracts with foreign powers, with greater ease. It can also, without inconvenience, execute a greater number of useful works and undertakings. The imposts which the state levies for such purposes, in a society where the stock of instruments is wrought up to an order correspondent to the average effective desire of accumulation of its members, must almost always occasion some diminution of that stock. The returns coming in from their industry, being only sufficient to reconstruct the instruments as they are severally exhausted, an additional drain made upon their funds must, in most cases, prevent the reconstruction of many of them, and consequently occasion a disappearance, to that amount, of a portion of the general stock. But, when instruments are of more productive orders than the effective desire of accumulation of the society demands, the abstraction of a part of their returns by the state, to supply its exigencies, only carries them nearer, or brings them altogether, to an order corresponding to the strength of that desire, and, therefore, interferes not with their reconstruction. Taxation [in that case] is paid out of revenue, not out of capital.

3. As it is the effect of improvement, to carry instruments into orders of quicker return than the accumulative principle of the society demands, a greater range of materials is brought within reach of that principle, and it consequently forms [eventually] an additional amount of instruments. The various agricultural improvements with which invention enriched that art in Britain, towards the conclusion of the last and commencement of the present century, occasioned a great amount of materials to be wrought up, which before lay dormant. The construction of the plough in Scotland, and generally over the island, was so improved that two horses did the work of six oxen. The diminution of outlay thus produced, giving the farmer, from a smaller capital, an equal return; he was encouraged and enabled to apply himself to materials, which he would otherwise have left, as his forefathers had done, untouched. He carried off stones from his fields, built fences, dug ditches, formed drains, and constructed roads.— Lime was discovered to be a profitable manure. The additional returns, which the hard clay thus converted into a black loam yielded, were spent in the cultivation of land before waste, in levelling and reducing to regularity, the rude ridges of antecedent periods.—The culture of turnips was introduced; and instead of useless fallows the farmer had a large supply of a nutritive food for his cattle. He erected better buildings for the reception of his stock, he improved their breed, he transported manure from great distances, he had his fields trenched deeply with the spade, fresh soil brought up, and all useless or prejudicial matters buried beneath. Each succeeding improvement gave a fresh stimulus to industry, and brought new materials within the compass of the providence of the agriculturist. Nor was this all; the stimulus reacted also on the inhabitants of the towns, and their industry was augmented by the increased returns yielded by the country, and by the new demands made by it. Improvements, too, in the branches of industry in which they were themselves engaged, of at least equal extent, carried them forward in a like career. Rocks were quarried; forests were thinned; lime was burned; the metal left the mine; large manufacturing establishments arose; wharfs, docks,

canals, and bridges were constructed; villages were changed into towns, and towns into cities.

It is thus that every improvement animates industry, and, though it cannot increase immediately the amount of instruments possessed by the society, or the sum of the values produced by measuring the one with the other, [or all relatively to the customary standard], shows that the members of the society really estimate them higher than they would thus be rated, by their instantly commencing to work up, into analogous instruments, inferior or more stubborn materials, or by their working up similar materials more laboriously. The amount thus wrought up, until the process stops, by the total instruments constructed arriving at an order correspondent to the effective desire of accumulation of the society, must depend entirely on the nature of those materials, and is, therefore, always a variable quantity, and one never to be ascertained previous to the event. Sometimes a very small improvement may put a large range of materials within reach of the accumulative principle, sometimes a very considerable improvement may not enable it to make much addition to the stock of instruments before constructed.

When misfortunes befall the general industry of a community, improvements, though they may not add to the national capital, prevent or lessen the threatened diminution of it. In agriculture, the introduction of the drill husbandry for grain crops, and the discovery of new manures; in manufactures and trade, the improved construction of steam engines, the discovery of railroads, and many other recent improvements, have taken off part of the weight of the heavy burden, that has of late years been imposed on the resources of Great Britain.

The high rate of profit, which, unless when counteracting causes intervene, follows [for a time] the introduction of improvement, is indicative of an immediate proportional augmentation of the absolute capital of the society, and produces a subsequent addition to its relative capital, the amount of which is determined by the additional capacity which the materials in possession of the community can receive, and by the quantity of materials of the next lower grades owned by it. That high rate of profits, again, which arises from a deficiency in the strength of the effective desire of accumulation, is essentially different. It indicates no increase of the absolute capital of the society, no recent increase of the revenue of its members, no greater ability to support public burdens, and no approaching increase of relative capital.[1] The want of a clear perception of this distinction, seems to have led Adam Smith, and some other writers, to speak of high profits as generally prejudicial.

In countries where the effective desire of accumulation is low, profits are of necessity [permanently] high. Such countries, too, from their inability to work up into instruments the same materials, must always be poorer than their neighbors. Hence high profits have been regarded as indicating, and producing poverty. This prejudice is one source of the errors of Sir Josiah Child on this subject, and it seems to have given rise to one or two rather declamatory passages in the *Wealth of Nations.* " Our merchants and master manufacturers complain much of the bad effects of high wages in raising the price, and thereby lessening the sale of their goods, both at home and abroad. They say nothing concerning the bad effects of high profits; they are silent with regard to the pernicious effects of their own gains; they complain only of those of other people."[2] Now I apprehend that high profits springing from improvement, can never lessen the sale of

---

[1] [It seems to the editor that the application of Rae's expressions "absolute" and "relative" capital or stock might, indeed, with greater propriety be turned right about. What he calls the absolute might be regarded as the relative, that is, in accordance with his own explanation, relative to the prevailing effective desire of accumulation in any society at any time, taken as a standard. And contrariwise, what he calls the relative might well be considered as the absolute, since its increase means the increase of the actual accumulations embodied in instruments in any society. When, for example, after a rapid advance of the arts in any country for ten or twenty years, its total stock of instruments comes to be priced, let us say, at $900,000,000 instead of $700,000,000, is not that an indication of an absolute increase of capital? The notion of permanency seems to go naturally with the notion of absoluteness, and, according to Rae's own showing, any increase, at least of what he calls absolute capital, is essentially ephemeral.]

[2] *Wealth of Nations*, Book I. c. ix. The paradox contained in the passage preceding this quotation is exposed by Mr. Ricardo.

goods either at home or abroad, for they do not occasion a rise in their price, but rather a fall in it.—" In countries which are just advancing to riches, the low rate of profit may, in the price of many commodities, compensate the high wages of labor, and enable those countries to sell as cheap as their less thriving neighbors, among whom the wages of labor may be lower."[1] In countries rising to riches, I conceive, on the contrary that profits will commonly be high. They will be higher than where, the principle of accumulation having had time to work up all the materials within reach of its strength, a stop is put to its farther advancing the stock of existing instruments, and the state of the society becomes stationary. If they be lower than in other countries, during the progress, it is from the greater strength of this principle.

In North America, profits and labor [wages] have been as a matter of fact permanently high, from the unintermitting transfer to that continent of European arts, and from the generation of new arts in the country itself. In Russia the passage, in like manner, of new arts has kept the rate of profits high. But, of all civilized countries of the present day, these, probably, are the most rapidly advancing to riches.

If, in any society, instruments be at orders of speedy return [and consequently the rate of profits high], and we have not the [ready] means of ascertaining whether or not this proceeds from the actual recent progress of invention, we may fairly conclude it does so, if, in that society, there be much economy, little luxury, good faith in exchanges, fidelity in the discharge of promises, credit consequently extensively prevailing, and few breaches in the peace, or transgressions of the laws of the community. If, on the contrary, there be little economy, much luxury, a want of good faith and fidelity, credit narrowed, frequent public and private crimes, we may certainly conclude that this position of instruments arises from a deficiency in the accumulative, not from recent progress of the inventive principle.[2]

It thus appears, that it is through the operation of two

[1] *Wealth of Nations*, Book I. c. ix.
[2] [This paragraph is an interpollation taken from p. 322 of the original.]

principles—the accumulative, and inventive,—that additions are made to the stocks of communities. It would contribute something to accuracy of phraseology, and therefore to distinctness of conception, to distinguish their modes of action by the following terms:

1. *Accumulation* of stock or capital, is the addition made to these, through the operation of the accumulative principle.

2. *Augmentation* of stock or capital, is the addition made to them, through the operation of the principle of invention.

3. Increase of stock or capital, is the addition made to them, by the conjoined operation of both principles.

Accumulation of stock diminishes profits; augmentation of stock increases profits; increase of stock neither increases nor diminishes profits.

["Accumulation" is the embodying of labor (and its equivalents) in new instruments; "augmentation," the embodying of ideas. With "accumulation" resistance in some form is encountered, and the rate of net returns declines; with "augmentation" resistance recedes and the net yield rises. With "increase" of capital there is no interval formed between the progress of the effects of the accumulative and the inventive principles (both advancing with equal pace), and hence a negative result as regards the basis of the general rate of profit in the community. The formation temporarily of an increased interval between the advance of the accumulative and the inventive principles, is what is called an increase of "absolute" capital or stock.

Rae uses the term "improvement" in this chapter loosely. Sometimes it is synonymous with invention, or the direct effects of invention; at other times it is the ulterior, collateral effects of invention,—as a particular manifestation of it passes from one art to other arts, both to those which are easier and to those which are more difficult.]

CHAPTER XI.

OF EXCHANGES BETWEEN DIFFERENT COMMUNITIES OF COMMODITIES OTHER THAN LUXURIES.

. . . .

WE are now able to enter upon the investigation of some phenomena, relating to the exchange of commodities, which we have not hitherto particularly noticed. As yet we have only attended to the laws finally regulating the exchange of commodities between individuals of the same society, but it is necessary that we should also ascertain the general conditions existing in those exchanges which take place between different societies.

In our view of the subject, every society considered apart, is a system within which all circumstances are common and similar; and all societies compared together, are systems in which all or many circumstances are proper to each and dissimilar to others. The wages of labor, orders of instruments, and profits of stock, in one society, for instance, are [approximately] the same; but in different societies, they are, or may be, diverse. When two persons in the same society exchange commodities, we have seen that the exchanges they make are for equal quantities of labor, reckoned according to the time when applied, and the actual orders of instruments. This happens because one man's personal labor, or the command of other men's labor which he may possess, is equal to another man's personal labor, or the command of other men's labor which he may possess. In separate societies, however, this law obviously no longer holds. An individual in one society, exchanging with another, in another society, cannot pretend to regulate the amount he is to receive in return by the power which he possesses, if he conceives too much demanded, of turning his own funds to the formation of that which he desires, for he has no such power. To form the commodities he in this case desires, it is necessary he should become a member of the society in which they are formed, and give up the place he holds in the community of which he now makes one. If the manufacturers of cloth in England find that the farmers do not give them, in the form of wheat, the same quantity of labor that they in exchange give them in cloth, they will turn their capital to agriculture, and so reduce the price demanded; but should they find that the American farmer puts less labor to the formation of the wheat he exchanges for their cloth, than that cloth costs them, they have not the same means of lowering his price.

As the exchanges, therefore, that take place between the members of different societies, cannot be regulated by the amount of labor embodied in the commodities fabricated by each, there would seem to remain, as the foundation of the principles of such exchanges, only the qualities of the articles exchanged. If the manufacturers in England find that, including the expense of transport, they can have wheat as cheap from the American farmers as from the British, they will be inclined to exchange, and if the American farmers find that, including also the expense of transport, they can have English cloth as cheap as American, they will be inclined to exchange. It is evident, too, that the British manufacturer will be more inclined to exchange, if the American wheat come cheaper than the British, and the American farmer, if the British cloth come cheaper than the American.

The commodities to be exchanged between any two societies, may either minister to use, or to luxury, or partly to both. The subject will present itself in the most simple form, by discussing separately the divisions of it thus indicated.

First, then, we have to consider the principles and effects of the exchanges of commodities which are in no degree luxuries.

If the members of one society, having before had no intercourse with some other society, become aware that in it there is a commodity of this sort, of which they would desire to have a supply, the question to be determined is, will they procure that supply, and if so, what will be the effect thence resulting. As they have hitherto done without the commodity, they must already possess some substitute for it. They will then only seek to procure it, if they can procure it for less labor than the substitute they already possess; and if they can procure it for less labor they will naturally be excited to do so. Were coal, for instance, the commodity which the members of one society A possess, and of which the members of another society B wish to procure a supply, there must be some means in existence in B, of more or less fully and easily satisfying the wants which that mineral can supply. It may be, for instance, that wood is the fuel there consumed. Let us suppose that three cords of the wood commonly burnt, are equivalent, in the heat given out by them, to one chaldron of coals; if, then, in the society B there be any commodity there equivalent to less than three cords wood, and which, transported to A, will in A be equivalent, considered as an utility, to one chaldron coals, the exchange will be possible, for this difference may pay, or may do more than pay, for the expense of transport. If, for example, in the society A timber for architectural purposes be more scarce than in B, it might happen that the wood used for fuel in B, when transported to A in logs, would be in estimation there. It might be that in A, owing to the general application of the soil to agricultural purposes, and the scarcity of forest, a quantity of timber, fit for the use of the builder, such as might be got out of a cord of the fire wood used in B, might exchange for one chaldron coals. Were, then, an individual of the society B, to transport to A a quantity of square timber equivalent in B to three hundred cords of wood, he might exchange it there for three hundred chaldrons coals, and might so return to B with a commodity there equivalent to nine hundred cords of fire wood, thrice the amount which he had transported from thence. Suppose that the expense of the transport of both commodities is equal to three hundred cords, then he will just have doubled the stock embarked in the enterprise. Were this the state of things, timber, instead of being consumed as fuel in B, would be transferred to A, and would return, in the form of coals, an equivalent, after paying the charges of transport, to double the labor expended in its formation. But in this state of things the whole advantage would fall to the society B; fuel would be more easily obtained there, but timber would not be more easily obtained in A. As, however, it would be equally in the power of the members of the latter society to send their coals to B, and there exchange them for wood, were other circumstances wanting, this alone would have the effect of equalizing the advantages, and in most cases, therefore, they would come to be nearly equally divided between two societies so situated. The first effects, therefore, would be that the same quantity of fuel which before cost in B three days' labor might now be obtained for two; and that the quantity of building timber that in A cost three days' labor, might also be obtained for two. The revolution effected might nearly compare to an improvement in both societies, by which, in the one, two cords fire wood might give equal heat to what three had done, and, in the other, two logs of timber might serve the same purposes as three. Like other improvements, they would not be confined in their operation to the particular branches of industry in which they had place, but would be diffused equally over both societies, carrying the whole instruments in each towards the more quickly returning orders. Profits would rise equally in all employments. The absolute capital of both communities would be increased in proportion to the augmented provision made for their future wants. This provision, indeed, would be so far uncertain, that it might be rendered inaccessible by war, or other causes interrupting the commerce between the two countries; and the whole industry and instruments engaged in it might, therefore, be compared to a stock engaged in some hazardous branch of industry, and running a chance of being wholly or partially lost, by the action of uncontrollably destructive causes. Abstracting, however, the chances to which they might thus be exposed, they would embody as real a provision for futurity as any other part of the stock of either society.

In all exchanges taking place between different societies, in commodities which are not luxuries, similar principles regulating them, and similar effects flowing from them, may be traced. For, if they derive their value not from the gratification they afford to vanity, but from their capacity to supply real wants, they may be compared with other instruments belonging to the society, satisfying more or less perfectly the same class of wants. And when, through the exchange of other commodities for them, they can be obtained for less labor than such instruments, they will naturally come to be so obtained, and will completely or partially fill the place of them. As coals will compare with cord wood, so indian rubber will compare with leather, New Zealand weed with hempen cordage, slates with thatch, copper with iron. In these cases, and in others where probably mere utility is sought for, there are means of comparing one thing with another; and the substitution of the one for the other, when in proportion to the labor necessary to obtain it, will more effectually supply future wants and is always a real improvement.

It will often happen that the process will engage in it more than two societies. Thus, the society B might exchange wood with C, C might exchange iron with A, and A coal with B. Similar principles would still, however, guide its progress, and similar effects result from it. While the exchanges were confined to commodities in no degree luxuries, an increased provision for future wants would result from them, and a general augmentation of the absolute capital of the societies receiving these new supplies, and quickening in them of the accumulative principle, would be experienced. They would in them all have the general effect of improvements, and would operate, in the case supposed last, in the same manner as would in B some discovery facilitating the transport of wood, in C some discovery facilitating the smelting of iron, in A some discovery facilitating the mining of coal. The fewer obstructions, therefore, that stood in the way of such transfers, the farther, in these cases, would the stock of instruments in those societies be carried towards the order A; as any obstruction that might occur would, on the contrary, have the effect of checking the progress towards the more quickly returning orders, and keeping them nearer the order Z.

The benefits to all parties, arising from such an interchange of commodities as we have described, would be liable to be interrupted by war or by legislative enactments. These disturbing causes we have afterwards shortly to advert to, but there is one arising from the progress of invention that may be properly noticed here.

As there are no limits to the inventive faculty, so no community can assure itself that any commodity which it now produces and exports to some other community, may not come to be produced in that community, and so be no longer exported there. It may be, for instance, that, to return to the supposed case we were just considering, in the society B, strata of coal are discovered so near the surface as to be as easily wrought as in A, and that the spirit of enterprise may there be sufficiently active, successfully to engage in the occupation of mining for them. In that case coals would there be procured for about five-sixths of the labor they had cost when brought from A. They would fall in relative value, the absolute capital of the society would be augmented, and profits proportionally increased. But while in the society B, the effects of the progress of invention would be thus beneficial, in A they might operate prejudicially. No exportation of coals could now take place from A to B, for being necessarily very nearly at the same price in the one as in the other society, there would be nothing to pay the expense of transport. Iron then could no longer be paid for in coals, unless that commodity sold at a lower rate. To pay for it, coals must be sold at B for less, or some other commodity must be resorted to. In the former case the society A would sustain a sensible loss, comparable to an increased difficulty in working its mines, and proportional diminution of the amount of its absolute capital. In the latter, though the loss might be less, it would nevertheless be real; for, by the supposition, coal was the only commodity exported, and it could only be so because it was the one bringing the best return. The necessity therefore of turning to some other article, implies the obtaining of a less return, and a consequent diminution of the absolute capital of the society, and, unless counterbalanced by the progress of improvement, or an increase in the strength of the effective desire of accumulation, a withdrawal from the reach of the accumulative principle of

O

its members, of some portion of materials before within its grasp.

. . . .

An interruption of the exchange of articles of real use between communities checks accumulation, by taking from it the materials on which it exerts itself; but it excites the inventive faculty, by prompting it to discover fresh materials, and new means of forming them into instruments. According, therefore, to the circumstances of the community, and the nature of the materials within reach of its members, it may come [in the end] either to be a good or an evil.

Were the intercourse between two communities, of which the one A exchanges coal for the wool of the other B, suddenly to cease, the event might be felt as a very great evil, and, at first, the substitutes for these materials requiring more labor to work them up into instruments of the sort required, the whole stock of instruments possessed by both societies might be carried on in the series some distance towards the more slowly returning orders. It might happen, however, that in the Society B importing coal, there were beds of coal [capable of being made] as easy to work as in A, and that in the other A importing wool, there were tracts of land as capable of feeding sheep as those employed for that purpose in B. In this case, it is probable that invention would apply to such materials, and that, in time, coal would be obtained in B, at as cheap a rate as in A, and wool in A at as cheap a rate as in B. Were it so, by the saving of labor and of time in the transport of the commodities from country to country, the stocks of instruments in both societies would be placed in orders of more quick return than they were at the commencement of the interruption. Whether the loss on the one hand, or the saving on the other, might, in the circumstances of either society, be fitly esteemed greater, would depend on whether or not there were materials in existence that by the power of invention might with sufficient ease, and within the requisite time, supply the particular wants in question. There might not be fit materials, or the time requisite to work them up might be too long.

Before the cession of Norway to Sweden, it was reckoned to

produce grain or vegetables for its inhabitants sufficient only for four or five months. Its supplies for the rest of the year were obtained from Denmark, to which country, in return for corn received from it, it exported timber. When the great powers had resolved on its annexation to Sweden, a British fleet blockaded its coast, the peasantry came in starving crowds to the towns, and a country from which the bravest race in Europe once issued, was compelled to yield without a stroke. The insult then received, and the hardships endured, had the effect of giving a great stimulus to agriculture. The more opulent formed themselves into societies for the purpose of improving the art, individuals skilled in its operations were engaged in Britain, and in a few years a great addition was made to the agricultural produce of the country.[1] The time in this case required [allowed] for the formation of instruments was too great [short], even supposing there had been a sufficiency of materials of which to construct them; and had not, therefore, the society submitted, it must have endured successive evils.

Many instances, however, might be cited, where the interdiction by war of the intercourse between different countries, has very speedily produced a supply of the commodities interdicted, and apparently without great injury to the nation possessing the materials necessary for their formation. "Upon the breaking out of the war with France," observes Mr. Gee,[2] "and prohibiting French commodities, encouragement was given for erecting several of those manufactures here, as the lustring, alamode, and other silk manufactures for hoods and scarves which the king's royal consort, the excellent Queen Mary, took no small pains to establish; for which article alone it is allowed France drew from us above £400,000 yearly. At the same time the manufacture of glass was established, which before we used to have from France, and also that of hats and paper. In his time also the manufactures of copper and brass were set on foot, which are brought to great perfection, and now in a great measure supply the nation with coppers, kettles, and all other sorts of copper and

---

[1] These facts I learned in a tour through that country in 1818. I have no means of ascertaining what is now the state of affairs there.

[2] *Trade and Navigation of Great Britain.* Lond. 1738.

brass ware. The making of sail-cloth was begun and carried on to great perfection, and also sword blades, scissors, and a great many toys made of steel, which formerly we used to have from France; in the manufacture of which, it is said, we now excel all other nations. The setting up of salt works and improving of salt springs and rock salt, hath proved very beneficial here, and saves a very great treasure yearly, which we heretofore paid to France for salt and a great many other things which I forbear to enumerate."

CHAPTER XII.

OF WASTE, OR PURE ECONOMIC LOSS.

THE causes arising from deficiencies in the moral and intellectual powers retarding the progress of improvement and accumulation, and diminishing the stocks of societies, which we have hitherto noticed, refer to the matter of which commodities consist.[1] There are others proceeding apparently from the same deficiencies, which create difficulties in the exchange and preservation of instruments, and may be said to relate to the manner in which exchanges are made and instruments preserved.

Every thing retarding, or interposing difficulties in the exchange of instruments, must have the effect of placing them in orders of slower return.[2] It must lengthen the period of exhaustion, or add to the labor of formation. Instruments may be exchanged, as we have seen, either by barter or cash, or, through the intervention of credit,—a promise to deliver an equivalent at some future time.

In the case of transfers by barter or cash, were the holders of instruments so exchanged to represent them exactly for what they are, all difficulties would be done away with, not arising from the nature of the things themselves. But it is the business of every exchanger to buy as cheaply, and sell as

---

[1] [That is, they work through the physical make-up of commodities, formed and used for different purposes.

In the original, the treatment of the subject of luxury preceded this chapter.]

[2] [This broad statement is of course subject to the limitations laid down elsewhere as to the contingent effects of restrictions upon foreign commerce, and as to the difference between trade in luxuries and other trade.]

dearly, as possible, and he very frequently, I might say generally, endeavors to do so by representing things to be other than what they are. Were any one, for example, desirous of purchasing a horse, morally certain to whatsoever vendor of those animals he applied, he would tell him, as nearly as he himself knew, the qualities of the horses he had on hand, and their just value, any purchase of this sort he might have to make would be made with facility and at once. The purchaser, however, can seldom depend on the accuracy of the statements he so receives. He is often obliged to take much trouble, and to spend no little time, before he makes his bargain, and, notwithstanding, is not unfrequently deceived. The time and money thus expended, both by the sellers and purchasers of horses, and other commodities, is so much dead loss to the community, and places the instruments on which they are expended in orders of more slow return. Indirectly, too, they may occasion still more serious losses. If a farmer be deceived in the purchase of a horse, it may very injuriously retard his operations at the moment when it is most necessary for him to advance them. If a builder be deceived in the timber he purchases, it may occasion the speedy decay of the whole fabric he erects.

The amount of loss arising, both directly and indirectly, from successful or unsuccessful attempts to pass off commodities for what they are not, is, I apprehend, determined by the weakness of the social and benevolent affections and intellectual powers. Where there is the most lively sympathy with the distresses and losses of others, one will be most restrained from being the cause of loss to another, both from the promptings of his own feelings, and from a consideration of the sentiments with which others will regard him. Where the tendency and consequences of actions are most clearly seen, one will be most cautious of doing any thing, which, by weakening general confidence and security, may prejudicially affect the interests of society. Such losses will therefore be least frequent where the accumulative principle is strongest, and most frequent where it is weakest.

In China every man who sells tells as many lies as he thinks have any chance of passing. He is never ashamed at being detected. When that happens, he merely compliments the person discovering the intended deception on his sagacity. Among the ancients, both Greeks and Romans, all sorts of trickery and artifice in purchasers and sellers seem to have been common. Plato makes Socrates say that, in traffic and commerce, there is no such thing as an honest man, and Cicero has a remark very similar. These, and the like assertions of classical authors, have indeed, now-a-days, been put down as mere prejudice; but, though we are doubtless a very acute and sagacious generation, I can scarce think but that Socrates and Cicero knew their own countrymen better than we can do. Mercantile honor and fair dealing are modern terms. Without much of the reality of what they import, the extensive transactions now carried on between individuals and communities could not exist. Nevertheless, the things to which they are applied want often not a little of being fitly so described, and the deficiency in all communities occasions a large portion of the outlay necessary to the formation of instruments.

Deceit, however, it is to be observed, when exercised in the exchange of mere luxuries, occasions an immediate gain, instead of loss, to communities. When there was a prohibition on French silks imported into Britain, they were particularly fashionable, their great expense rendering them a fit material for vanity. The British manufacturer could make fabrics not to be distinguished from them, but which of course as British goods would not sell. They were, however, readily vended as smuggled French goods, by individuals hired to hawk them about under that guise. The deceit was certainly an immediate loss to no one, and a considerable gain to the manufacturer.[1] The ulterior effects of all deceit, however, in weakening the moral principle, must ever be injurious to communities.

In exchanges effected by the intervention of credit the necessity of perfectly fair dealing is more apparent, and the losses occasioned by fraud and deceit still greater. The persons giving the credit must generally depend for repayment on the good faith of the persons receiving it. The extent conse-

---

[1] Hansard's *Debates*, March 8th, 1824.

quently to which these transactions can in any community be carried, must be measured by the general probity of its members. Where people are inclined to make promises which they have reason to fear they may not be able to fulfil, or which they know they cannot fulfil, the system of credit is confined or destroyed.

. . . .

[But "the formation of instruments is rendered difficult and costly to individuals," not only from the lack of a "spirit of integrity in credit transactions," and generally in that department of economic activities which is called exchange, but also from all forms of "frauds and violence punishable by law," in contrast to mere deceits, in every branch of business.]

To guard against them always requires some vigilance, and occasions some expense, and often demands a good deal of both. The loss hence arising may be very considerable. It is said that the cloth trade of Verviers, in France, was ruined from the number of thefts committed in various stages of the manufacture, occasioning a loss of about eight per cent. on the quantity produced.

The infrequency of crime will also, I apprehend, be found chiefly to depend on the same principles that give force to the effective desire of accumulation,—the general strength of the social and benevolent affections, and intellectual powers. Where a desire of promoting the common good prevails, and there is a clear perception of the means of doing so, infringements on the rights of individuals, or violence to their persons, will be rare. It is the strength of the moral feelings that is the safeguard of the laws. Where these are destroyed, or greatly weakened, as where a person has been cast out of the brotherhood of society by being marked as a criminal, the dread of corporeal pains is scarcely ever sufficient to deter from future trespasses.

The establishment of good laws and the security of the system of government, by diminishing the temptation to crime, and the chance of escape from its consequences, have also, no doubt, great effect. But good laws or government can neither be established nor maintained without good

OF WASTE

morals. When purely selfish feelings prevail laws have no power.

"Quid faciant leges ubi sola pecunia regnat?"

The [in]direct destruction and waste occasioned by wars make, also, no small item in the account of losses, to which the stocks of all communities are subject.

The loss occasioned by the deceits and frauds of individuals, and by the prohibitions and violence of states, may not unfitly be termed waste.

[The expression "Of Waste," which alone was the original title of this chapter, does not seem adequate. It does not give an impression sufficiently distinct from that conveyed by the term luxury. According to Rae's treatment of this last subject, and according also to the ordinary usage of language, wealth or industrial energy may be said to be misappropriated or wasted in luxury. The same takes place through the direct expenditure occasioned by war and preparations for war.

But what Rae deals with in the present chapter is indirect not direct causes of loss; not with wealth which is created and misapplied, but with wealth which is not created at all. This last is a thing which necessarily escapes the census-taker in every country, and is indeed the leading subject of our science. Economics is nothing if it does not develop an eye of the imagination to see that.

In modern civilized countries, after everything possible is done to minimize individual crimes and misdemeanors, it is "the prohibitions and violence of states" which constitute the chief preventable cause of pure economic loss.]

CHAPTER XIII.

OF THE EFFECTS RESULTING FROM DIVERSITIES OF STRENGTH IN THE ACCUMULATIVE PRINCIPLE, IN MEMBERS OF THE SAME SOCIETY.

THE mass of the individuals composing any society, being operated on by the same causes, and having similar manners, habits, and to a great extent feelings also, must approximate to each other, in the strength of their effective desires of accumulation. In the view we have hitherto taken of the subject, we have considered them, as not only approximating, but coinciding in this respect. In reality, however, they do not do so. Though the desire may be generally of nearly equal strength, throughout the bulk of the society, it cannot altogether be so, but must vary, in some, in degrees scarcely perceptible, in others, as in every community there will be men of characters opposite to their fellows, very largely. But there are nevertheless circumstances, which, notwithstanding these variations, restrain and confine the construction of instruments, either altogether to the same order, or to orders much more nearly approximating to each other, than would be indicated by the strength of the effective desire of accumulation, in the individuals forming them.

The accumulative principle of the different individuals composing the same society, may vary from the average strength, either by being above, or below it. There will, in every society, be some individuals not disposed to construct any instruments, but such as are of orders of more quick return than those generally formed; as there will be others, disposed, if they have no opportunity otherwise to make additional provision for futurity, to expend part of their revenue in working up materials even to orders of slower return, than the average of the instruments already formed.[1]

Persons of the former class, possessing any amount of funds presently available, would be inclined to apply them to the formation of instruments, could they obtain materials, returning so largely as to correspond to the estimate they make of the future and the present. But they will not be able to find any such materials, for they will have been previously appropriated, and wrought up more laboriously than they would be inclined to do, by other members of the society. If, again, the funds [accumulated means] of an individual of this class, consists of instruments whose returns are future, he will gradually transfer them to other members of the society, whose accumulative principle is stronger than his own; for, according to his estimate of the future and the present, he will receive more for them than they are worth.[2] It thus happens, that all the members of any society, whose accumulative principle is lower than the average, are gradually reduced to poverty. The same persons, moving to a community where instruments were of orders of quicker return than those correspondent to the strength of their own accumulative principle, would acquire property. Thus the artisan, or laborer, who, in England, never thought of saving, is excited to accumulate property, in North America. The Chinese, who, in Europe, would be very

[1] [This last class of accumulators receive an income which includes a clear bonus, comparing their psychological condition with that of the marginal savers. The sub-marginal constructors of instruments, and the savers of funds to invest in titles of property in instruments, are, of course, shut out altogether in the manner Rae goes on to describe.]

[2] [Restating the above in the everyday language of the market-place, it might read,—Persons of the former class possessing savable funds would be inclined to invest them, could they find safe investments returning so largely on the purchase price as to constitute a sufficient inducement. But all safe securities are selling at too high a price. If such persons happen to own paying property already, the "present value" in the market of the series of annuities yielded by it, is so much greater than their own valuation, according to their estimate of present and future (their own "discounting" of the future), that they part with their ownership.]

prodigals, are accounted frugal in the tropical regions of Asia, and there attain to considerable wealth.

Individuals whose accumulative principle, is, on the other hand, stronger than the other members of the community, would be inclined to construct instruments of orders returning more slowly than usual, rather than not devote a part of their present funds to additional provision for futurity. But this is not necessary.[1] They are the natural recipients of the funds passing from the hands of the prodigal, and their excess of providence, balances his defect, and maintains the whole mass of instruments in the society, at nearly the same orders.

It thus happens, that all instruments capable of transfer, are in the same society, at nearly the same orders.[2] Some instruments, however, cannot be transferred, for many of them that are of gradual exhaustion, and directly supply wants, must belong to the persons exhausting them. Wearing apparel, household furniture, and sometimes dwelling-houses, cannot be the property of any other individuals than those in whose service they are exhausted. Such instruments must often, therefore, correspond to the strength of the accumulative principle of their possessors. If they belong to persons in whom the strength of this principle is greater than the average of the society, they will not indeed vary much from the prevailing orders, the surplus funds of such individuals, going, as we have seen, to the acquisition of the stock of the prodigal. The difference is probably just sufficient to indicate the character of their owners. Thus, if we inspect the dwelling-houses and furniture of rigid economists, we generally perceive that they have an air both of durability and efficiency, distinguishing them from those of the rest of the community.

When, again, individuals, in whom the strength of the effective desire of accumulation is below the average of the society, have no other stock but what is embodied in instru-

---

[1] [That is, it is not necessary so far as the general situation existing at any one time is concerned. With the lapse of time strong savers may, and often do, descend to a lower margin of investment or accumulation.]

[2] [With those not capable of transfer there exists at any time all degrees of situation in respect to the series of "orders," and hence of differential gains and losses.]

ments of this sort, these instruments, in their exhaustion of them, will correspond to the weaker power of this principle. Such, unfortunately, is sometimes the case, with what are termed the lower classes of society; causes to which we shall afterwards advert, sometimes generate a spirit of improvidence among these classes, and diminishing the estimation in which they hold the interests of futurity, incapacitate them from expending any present funds, as a provision for these interests, if they do not return either very speedily, or very largely. The consequence is, that the instruments of this sort which they possess, have but a very small capacity for the supply of their coming needs, and that they are unable to extricate themselves from pressing poverty.

Thus, suppose that a man in this class, has two different hats offered him, the present appearance, and immediate comfort in the wear of which are nearly equal, but of which the one, from its being formed of better materials, and these wrought up with more care, is much more durable than the other, and cannot be afforded but at a higher price than it. Let it be that four days' labor is demanded for the one, and six and a half for the other, but that the former will last only one year, the latter two. It is evident, that, if the effective desire of accumulation of the individual is very weak, not carrying him beyond the order A, he will prefer the former, and at the expiration of the year will consequently have to expend again an equivalent to four days' labor, instead of having this want supplied by a previous expenditure of two and a half days' labor.[1]

We may, in most cases, judge very accurately of the strength of this principle among individuals of this order of society, peasants, mechanics, day-laborers, and domestic servants, by the qualities of the instruments of these sorts with which they provide themselves. By observing, for example, the kind of shoes, gowns, blankets, which a woman in this rank of life

---

[1] It is a matter of indifference, it may be observed, to the hat maker, which of the two he disposes of. Both hats are to him instruments for procuring labor, or some equivalent to it. Of all his stock, it is only the qualities of the one he makes choice of for his own wear, that can, in any degree, indicate the strength of his own effective desire of accumulation.

purchases, one may form a near guess of her character. Were she to make a point of selecting such as would wear well, though somewhat dearer, or less showy, we might safely conclude that the influence of the present, did not prevent the interests of the future from being carefully regarded. On the contrary, did she choose the unsubstantial, but more showy, or cheaper article, we might with equal certainty infer, that the present, in her estimation, far outweighed the future. All who have had opportunities of making such observations, must have remarked the influence, which the one line of conduct, or the other, exercises on such individuals. The difference between them constitutes the main distinction between thrift, and unthrift, the former of which is the only safe means that persons in the lower walks of life possess, through which they may give a beginning to their fortunes. The store accumulated by the exercise of the virtue of providence, which, as it shows itself in them, we thus denominate, enables them to turn the funds of their daily labor to the construction of other instruments than those, and, at length, to add largely to that stock which is destined to supply the future wants of the whole society. What is true concerning one individual, is true concerning many, and on this account, the degree of strength of this principle possessed by what are called the lower orders, exercises a great influence on the amount of the general stock, accumulated by the society. The influence, in this respect, of those who form that class, is, indeed, much more important than we might at first suspect. Their greater numbers would alone make up for the smaller power of each, but besides the weight which this consideration is entitled to, the amount of labor that may, with advantage, be accumulated by the mere working man, in instruments of this sort, is, in reality, very considerable. His dwelling and its contents may fitly be considered as a store that he possesses, for the supply of the future wants of himself and family, or, what is the same thing, for the abridgment of their future labor; and according as there is much or little of this provision wrought up in them, will the one be supplied or the other saved. First, the house itself, as the place in which he and they live, and pursue many of their various occupations, will not yield the advantages it ought, if the apartments be not so roomy and well lighted, as neither from the closeness of the atmosphere to induce debility or disease, nor, from their confinedness and obscurity, to cramp and retard the inmates in their several labors. Then, according to the compactness and finish that is given to the walls and other parts will the inclemency of the weather be more or less excluded, and a greater or less quantity of fuel, be in future requisite. The cupboards, where things may be readily put past, and as readily found, and where they are preserved from destroying causes and accidents, the cooking utensils, the bedding, and the numerous other articles of the sort, that enter into the domestic economy of a frugal and industrious family, are to be considered, in like manner, as so many means by which future labor, or future expense, may be prevented or diminished. The extent of the saving which the provident working man in this way effects, is sometimes very great. In a rude, or imperfectly finished fabric, fuel must be wasted; in one where there are not proper conveniences for preserving and cooking food, food must be wasted; and where there are not fit places for depositing articles of wearing apparel, they must soon get dirty, and receive much unnecessary damage. In a well finished, and convenient habitation, too, the inmates lose no time, either from torpor in winter's cold, or languor in summer's heat; they have space and comfort to pursue their various labors, and unless it be the periods given to repose, and to their meals, may employ the whole time they spend at home, in some useful or agreeable occupation. The animal frame, also, it is to be observed, when exposed to the extremes of heat and cold, and to damp, seems to require a greater supply of nourishment, than when properly sheltered and protected. This is seen in the inferior animals, and agreeing with them in other parts of his corporeal constitution, man does not here differ from them, and when comfortably lodged, is preserved in health and vigor, on a diet which he would else find too scanty. The amount of provision for future needs, that may, in a similar manner, be embodied by a laborer or mechanic having a family, in [superior] bedding, and other furniture, and in kitchen utensils, is very considerable.[1]

[1] If the reader be skeptical concerning the effects of a sufficient supply of

It is to be here observed, that the prevalence of a really economical spirit among the working class, implies no diminution of the [aggregate] purchases made by them. On the contrary, it being the desire of the laborer, under such a supposition, to turn every sixpence he can earn to some useful employment, either to the acquisition of necessaries, or other commodities, he must have as many demands on the capitalist [on the general market] as before. The change produced, would be, in the articles purchased. The proportion of those providing for the wants of futurity would increase, that of those ministering to the gratifications of the present, diminish.

Thus, such a spirit pervading the working classes in Great Britain, at the present period, would probably lead them to abandon all delicacies of fare, and would occasion a diminished consumption of alcoholic liquors, tea, coffee, silks, expensive calicoes, and the more showy articles of apparel. It would, on the other hand, increase the demand for the higher priced, and more substantial cloths, cottons, blankets, kitchen utensils, and articles of that sort, and for all matters used in the construction of dwelling-houses.

Neither, it is to be observed, would the prevalence of a contrary spirit among those orders, and a proneness to seize on the enjoyments of the present, occasion any immediate diminution of their demands on the capitalist. It would merely lead to his providing for them a greater amount of instruments of sudden exhaustion, contributing to the gratification of the instant, and a smaller amount of those of gradual exhaustion, providing for the wants of futurity; and to his giving a construction to the latter, that might make them correspond during the period of their exhaustion, to the lower degree of the accumulative principle of the individuals in whose service they were to be exhausted. Such a circumstance would, therefore, occasion the production of a larger portion of

materials and utensils, in diminishing the expense of diet, I would request him to read Count Rumford's *Essays*.

[It is apparent that the foregoing argument inculcating the virtue of thrift, is very different from the usual one. For poor people to save money, as they are commonly urged to do, often causes them to pursue a most uneconomical course of action.]

delicacies, of articles of nourishment more grateful to the senses, but not more nutritious or more wholesome than cheaper fare, of fewer substantial articles of dress and furniture, and more of those that are flimsy and showy.

The whole stock of instruments owned by the laboring population, would thus contain a smaller amount of the means of lessening future labor, or expense, as their effective desire of accumulation diminished in strength. Even instruments that they do not own, but of which they pay for the use, as dwelling-houses rented by them, are in a great measure, reduced to the same order as those which they would themselves form. In the rank of society above them, improvidence is long before it show on the dwelling, it attacks first other funds; but, as they have not these other funds, it necessarily shows itself in the funds they have. Thus, if a family of improvident habits get the use of the best finished dwelling, they soon so damage it, as to deprive it of its efficiency. Some manifestation of what we call careless habits, want, that is, of taking thought of the consequences of what one is doing, breaks, we shall say, a pane or two of glass, in some of the windows. To get these replaced is present expense, and trouble; demands, perhaps, the doing without a pot or two of liquor, or some other immediate enjoyment, and requires the trouble of going for the glazier, or acting for him. An old hat or two, or some bundles of rags, stuffed into the holes, shifts off this denial of present pleasure, or ease, to some other time, a time which, similar habits, while they render the arrival of it more needful, indefinitely postpone; and the window that had been formed to exclude wind and wet, and admit light, serves, at last, to let in the wet and wind, and shut out the light. Pursue the effects of these habits, this absorption in the present, and heedlessness of the future, as they show themselves upon the plaster, the floor, the ceiling, and we shall find them soon doing away with the efficiency of the whole dwelling, for procuring enjoyment, or saving toil, and reducing it, as far as it is a provision for the future wants of its inmates, to a condition little superior to that of the miserable mud hut.

The presence of this evil, to a greater or less extent, is

marked, by the high rates of interest given, for the petty sums borrowed by individuals of this class. The increase that is said to have taken place in the number of pawn-brokers' shops in England, and the high rate of interest there demanded, and given, by mechanics, for small loans afforded to one another, would seem to indicate its presence, to a degree sufficient to alarm a lover of his country.[1]

When we come to treat of the causes that seem the great agents in diminishing the stock owned by a community, the mode in which the strength of the accumulative principle is weakened, and extravagance introduced among the lower classes, and the effects arising from these circumstances, will present themselves to our notice. It will then appear, that this diversity of the orders of instruments owned throughout a community, can never exceed certain limits. On this account, and because the stock belonging to the lower classes, when the accumulative principle is much lower with them than with the higher ranks, is always inconsiderable, the orders to which instruments belong in the same society, and the [pecuniary] returns they make, or the ordinary profits of stock, may be said to be nearly equal throughout every community.

This uniformity in the orders of instruments, and in the returns made by them, in conjunction with the system of calculation, by which, as we have seen, transactions relating to the transfer and accumulation of capital are regulated, produces effects on the conceptions of the individuals concerned, worthy of being noticed.

The rules by which all persons regulate their proceedings in the construction of instruments, are drawn from the [pecuniary] returns made by them, that is, the profits yielded by them. If an instrument, or a series of instruments, which it is proposed to construct, promise to yield the usual profits, the enterprise is undertaken, and, if it make the anticipated returns, it is considered a profitable, or gaining business ; if it do not promise to yield, and do not yield the usual profits, it

---

[1] Pawn-brokers charge, I believe, about 20 per cent. The combinations of the working classes in societies, or unions, have lent their members small sums, if I well remember, at a rate nearly equal. I cannot, however, recollect my authority for these statements.

is considered an unprofitable, or losing business. Probably, too, it is not considered, that this mode of expression is correct, only as relative to a particular society, and not absolutely, to all societies, and that what in one country or time, may be an unprofitable undertaking, will, without any change of returns, be profitable in another country or time, and *vice versa*.

Thus, suppose an English land-holder, whose income far exceeded his outgoings, to be asked why he does not apply his means to enclosing and draining some sea marsh, his answer probably would be, " it would not pay : it would only yield me two per cent. when finished, and landed property ought to yield four; I can always find estates to purchase, which will produce that." Ask him, why, instead of stone fences round his fields, which decay, or hedges, which require constant trimming and dressing, he does not put iron railings, he will give the same answer, " it would not pay." Ask the house-builder, why this is not cut stone, instead of brick, that oak instead of pine, this again iron instead of oak, or that copper instead of iron, and consequently the whole fabric doubly durable, he also will reply " it will not pay." In all these cases, and a thousand others that might be put, the answer is abundantly sufficient as regards the individual, but is no answer at all as regards the society. The only answer that can be given, in old countries at least, for such or similar neglect of materials, is, that there, the effective desire of accumulation is not sufficiently strong, to reach them, in the present state of science and art. Were there fewer prodigal land-holders in England, estates could not be so easily got, and part of the funds of those who buy estates, would be laid out in improving land at present unproductive, and the salt marsh might be drained. In the same way, houses and other instruments would become more substantial, and better finished, were the strength of the accumulative principle throughout the whole society to advance.

In China, precisely similar replies would be made by capitalists, concerning the draining of marshes, the erection of more substantial buildings, and other enterprises requiring a large present expenditure, for a remote future return. There, such undertakings would be really unprofitable, not paying the usual profits of stock; and they can only in like manner become profitable, by the accumulative principle acquiring increased strength, and instruments being wrought up generally to orders of slower return.

This, however, is not the view which most readily presents itself to practical men. To a person engaged in the practice of an art, the particular mode which the circumstances of the country to which he belongs has rendered the most profitable, and best, is considered as absolutely the best, and most profitable; and if he remove to another country, he is apt to conceive not only that his knowledge of the art is superior, which may perhaps be true, but that the precise mode in which he applies that knowledge to practice, is also the best, that can anywhere be adopted, which is very possibly erroneous.

An English farmer, for example, who comes to North America to pursue his art, almost always commences on the same system which he followed in Britain. His agricultural implements, his harness, his carts, waggons, etc., are all of the most durable and complete, and, therefore, of the most expensive construction, and his fields are tilled as laboriously, and carefully, as were those he cultivated in his native land. Some time usually elapses, before he discovers that he may do better by being content with more simple, and less highly finished implements, and that it will be for his advantage to cultivate his land less laboriously, though not less systematically. His neighbours tell him, indeed, from the first, that if he expects the same profits as they have, he must have less dead stock on his hands, and must give more activity to his capital; but he is slow of believing them.

Similar observations might be made, concerning almost every other class of artists, who emigrate to the new world. They all, at first, give a degree of finish to the materials on which they employ their industry, that is unsuited to the circumstances of the country.

[But while individual or class divergencies from what may be called the standard of the effective desire of accumulation in any society, produce but relatively unimportant effects upon the character of the mass of instruments possessed by members

OF ECONOMIC STRATIFICATION 229

of the society, they produce effects of the utmost importance (as has already been suggested), upon the character of the population itself. Instruments at any time stand at approximately the same "orders," but the members of all advanced societies are stratified. To treat economic stratification adequately would necessitate a study of great complexity, since it comes about through the operation of several principles, in addition to the pure accumulative principle, "always acting in combination." Some further consideration of the subject is as follows.]

To add continually to the stock of any community, even sometimes to maintain it without diminution at its actual amount, is a process in the prosecution of which difficulties always oppose. While the funds of any society increase, the numbers among whom those funds are to be shared also [normally] increase. The greater annual revenue which invention and accumulation provide, though it must support a more numerous population, may not support a population having, individually, a greater share [amount] of the means of comfort or pleasure, than that possessed by the members of the society when improvement was yet in its infancy. To carry the community still farther onward, even perhaps to maintain it in its place, requires, therefore, generally, that the interests of futurity should hold the same relation to those of present time in the minds of the members of the society as ever. If, therefore, among any of the divisions of the body politic, futurity weighs more lightly when compared with the present than it did before, there there will be weakness,— an incapacity to advance or even to maintain the same position may be experienced, and, that which is defective drawing to it what is sound, from this point the progress from bad to worse may commence. The course of society may thus be said to be always against an opposing current, which, if it cannot be stemmed, sweeps downward with headlong force.

"Sic omnia fatis
In pejus ruere, ac retro sublapsa referri.
Non aliter, quam qui adverso vix flumine lembum
Remigiis subegit : si brachia forte remisit,
Atque illum in præceps prono rapit alveus amni."

As a foundation for the few observations which our limits permit me to make on this part of the subject, it is necessary to refer to a circumstance, the truth of which was assumed in an early part of the discussion. "The numbers of every society," it was said, "increase, as what its members are inclined to esteem a sufficient subsistence, is provided for them."[1]

The only classes in society which our inquiry has considered, are the two of capitalists and laborers. With regard to them we might *a priori*, and abstracting our attention from what we know to be the fact, be in doubt which of the following suppositions would be correct.

We might suppose that both classes would reckon that a sufficient subsistence which had supported themselves [in the past], and that the numbers of both being equally multiplied, the average revenues of the individuals composing both might remain the same; or we might suppose that neither class would reckon that a sufficient subsistence on which they had been supported, and that they would not add to their numbers but in a proportion less than the additional funds provided, so that the average individual incomes of both capitalists and laborers, would be equally and continually increased; or, finally, we might suppose that the capitalists would add more to their numbers than to their revenues, or that the laborers might do the same thing.

But though it might be difficult, *a priori*, to determine which of these would take place, yet, in fact, we generally find that, in the progress of society, the increase of the numbers of capitalists does not keep pace with the increase of their stocks and incomes, while that of laborers does keep pace, or does more than keep pace, with their incomes.

The cause of this circumstance may, I think, be shortly stated as follows.

Marriage may be desired both for the pleasures of sense, and for those of sentiment and affection. But, among men of even moderate fortune, it does not in general add to the sum of their purely sensual gratifications. It were obviously absurd, considering the lives which most young men in this class in

---

[1] See Chapter III.

OF ECONOMIC STRATIFICATION 231

Europe lead, to speak of celibacy as implying abstinence. Purely selfish motives will never, therefore, lead such men to form this connexion. They will rather keep them from it, vanity aiding, or prompting them to the resolution of refraining from any such union, until they have a prospect of raising their families above their own rank.

Among men in the laboring class, again, marriage generally adds to the amount of immediate sensual gratifications. Purely selfish motives, therefore, side with those of sentiment and affection in prompting them to it, and they are not so apt to entertain the ambition of raising their families above their own condition. Hence, while capitalists are inclined to think that only a sufficient subsistence for their offspring, which exceeds what they themselves were supported on, laborers are content if they leave their children in the same condition as themselves. It thus happens, that the one class has a tendency continually to rise above the other.

This separation has farther effects.

Vanity itself is sometimes a coadjutor to the accumulative principle. A man's pride is sensibly gratified by rising, as it is called, in the world, and placing himself on an equality with those to whom he was once inferior. But the further they are above him, the greater his difficulty in raising himself to their level, and the less his hopes of any gratification to mere vanity from this source. It is, I apprehend, in a great measure on this account, that as capital increases, there are fewer instances of laborers making vigorous efforts to accumulate property. Vanity, losing hopes of acquiring distinction by accumulation, is entirely occupied in exciting to [economic] dissipation. The laborer seeks preeminence in displaying his abilities to spend, and employs any spare funds he may possess in the purchase of fineries, in treating his companions at the ale-house, and in similar extravagancies.

The prevalence of such habits and sentiments among the laboring classes, produces various evils. Neglect to employ any part of the earnings of to-day, in making provision for the wants of to-morrow, every now and then, when that morrow brings nothing for itself, gives rise to severe suffering. The condition of the laborer fluctuates between abundance and dissipation, and want and misery. The society loses, first, the benefits of that stock, which the laboring classes accumulate in a better state of things. It loses, also, the amount requisite to keep the laborer from starvation when in necessity, or to raise up other laborers, to supply the place of those who perish from want, or the diseases consequent on it. These may be called direct evils; those which are indirect are much greater.

Waste [as previously defined and explained] accompanies dissipation. When laborers are in general improvident and extravagant, very many of them must be dishonest. Men are naturally suspicious of persons whose expenditure exceeds the bounds of prudence, and they have too often reason to be so. Honesty is at last the best policy, but it is only at last. Deceit and knavery very often succeed better at first, and, therefore, people who look not beyond what is present and immediate, are very apt to resort to artifice and fraud, to get rid of the necessities which their extravagance brings on them. Hence, such a state of things would imply much watchfulness, many checks and contrivances to guard against fraud and violence, and much loss, both from them and from the expensive machinery necessary to restrain them. The most prejudicial, however, of all the mischiefs that belong to our subject, brought on by vicious principles of action pervading the lower classes, is the gradual spread of similar manners and feelings through all the orders of the state. The middle and higher classes of society may be said to rest upon the lower; when decay, therefore, infects the foundation, the structure must fall. By looking back for a generation or two, we shall find that nearly all the capitalists in the nation have sprung directly from the people, and that to them we must finally trace the greater part of that honorable enterprise, frugality, and perseverance, which have given prosperity and power to the state. When the principles that actuate the great lower and sustaining mass have a large mixture of benevolence, self-denial, and probity, and when there is nothing in the institutions of the society keeping them down as a degraded caste, there is a constant mounting upwards of the elements of health and strength, giving firmness and vigor to the whole body politic. When, on the contrary, the proper vices of the higher ranks, luxury, extravagance, and their attendant evils, instead of being counteracted by a continual infusion of the severer manners, and more self-denying morals, that should belong to the lower, find those orders partaking as far as possible their follies and levities, admiring them, and if required ready to minister to them, we may assure ourselves that much unsoundness lurks beneath whatever show of prosperity the outward condition of national affairs may exhibit. It will, I believe, be found that, in civilized societies, decay has generally thus proceeded from below upwards, and that a deficiency in the lower classes, of the principles exciting to economy, has gradually checked accumulation and invention throughout the whole body, and at length produced universal degeneracy and decay, and introduced the reign of waste and violence. "Semper in civitate, quibus opes nullae sunt, bonis invident; vetera odere, nova exoptant; odia suarum rerum mutare omnia petunt."

The experience of all ages proves the justice of the observation of the Roman historian. That state can never enjoy tranquillity, which is oppressed by a crowd of

"Hungry beggars,
Thirsting for a time of pell-mell havock
And confusion."

But to trace at length the connexion between these [various social tendencies] is impossible, without reference to the subjects of rent, and of population, which are not embraced in our plan. I may, however, in conclusion, observe that though, for the sake of simplicity of exposition, I have assumed, all along, that the wages of labor constitute an invariable quantity, I yet conceive that, in a society making a steady and healthy progress, they should rather be continually increasing, the laborer as well as the capitalist, gaining something by the improvements which the progress of invention produces.

[A portion of Rae's *Essay on Education* (1843), mentioned in the biographical sketch, may be reproduced to advantage in this connection.]

"The unsatisfactory results on human happiness which the progress of civilization has hitherto exhibited, as measured by the visible condition of any ten thousand taken at random from the ancient and modern population of Great Britain, has given rise there to a feeling of despondency and alarm among a numerous and not uninfluential class, as to the results that are to spring from its farther advance. They dread any further progress. They would wish to stop where we are—even, if possible, to bring things back to the condition of the good old days of our fathers. It is a vain attempt, we are hurried forward by an irresistible impulse. All in our power to do is to use every effort to direct our onward course aright. Art and science, and with them wealth, must increase and advance. The sphere of real philanthropic exertion is confined to elaborating the possible good they may produce, restraining and extirpating their possible evils.

"Now, though the subject has given rise to many intricate and perhaps not very satisfactory discussions, there is one view that may be taken of this progress of science, art, and wealth, as affecting the condition of humanity, by no means difficult to seize, and which will sufficiently indicate one main cause of the evils that have overtaken, and those which yet threaten to overtake, our modern civilization.

"It is in the nature of this progress to convert the original simple and rude tools, first, into instruments of greater cost and efficiency, and these again into complex and difficultly constructed machines, still more costly and still more efficient. The distaff becomes a spinning wheel; and that, changing its form, and wrought by other powers, is made part of a woollen factory. The rough edged blade of the original knife is first cut into a regular saw, wrought by one hand; it is then put into a frame, which two men operate; and this, in turn, by means of crank and pinions, is made to go by water, and becomes a saw-mill. Even a farm, in this manner, with all its appendages, may be said to become a great machine or factory—a factory for the production of crops. What was before the work of the hands from year to year, is now, in such countries as England, brought about in a great degree by machinery and scientific processes, requiring a large surface to operate on, and many years for their completion.

"And so it is with all our implements, they are passing on to great machines. This progress can be averted by no conceivable process that would not have the effect of fettering all the active powers of humanity. It is the inevitable consequence of man's asserting and employing the dominion over the realms of nature which his Creator has bestowed on him. Placing ourselves in the position of the philosophers of the age of Bacon, it will be difficult for us to assign a reason why we would not have hailed the discoveries of which they are the results as great inventions, conferring benefits on the whole human race, without being a means of occasioning wrong or sorrow to anyone.[1] And yet there was a question which might by possibility have occurred to the philosophic philanthropists of that day. 'Who are to be the owners of these great machines? Will the mechanics and artisans who now wield the tools own the machines, or will they be the property of a distinct class?' We cannot ascertain how they might have *a priori* determined the question. It is most likely, perhaps, that they would have conceived that the owners of the tools, clubbing together to purchase machines, would have owned the machines. To us, experience has determined it. So constantly has it occurred that it may be said it has invariably happened, that the former artisans, in giving up their tools, have never become the owners of the machines that have succeeded them. These machines, manufactories, or whatever name may be given them, come to be owned by a distinct class. The operative has no property share in the industrial operation, he owns nothing but his hands and the art of using them fitly. For opportunity to use them, and for pay for their use, he depends on the owner of the machine. He suffers in consequence a degradation in the social scale. Formerly he was a small capitalist, now it is the characteristic of his condition to be a mere operative, destitute of capital. The difference may be seen by recalling the pictures left by Hogarth and Scott, when

[1] Etenim inventorum beneficia ad universum genus humanum pertinere possunt—inventa beant et beneficium deferent absque alicujus injuria aut tristitia.

the change was just coming over them. Compare the industrious apprentice and the father of Bailie Nicol Jarvie, with the present factory boy, or look at the fate which, in our conception, awaits any of our handicrafts when the revolution [through which modern industry seems destined to pass in all its branches is complete]."

CHAPTER XIV.

OF THE PRINCIPLE OF THE DIVISION OF LABOR.

NOT having been able without interrupting the course of investigation, to enter into a discussion of the principle of the division of labor, as viewed by Adam Smith, I have thought it better to place apart the observations I have to make on it.[1]

In the *Wealth of Nations*, the division of labor is considered the great generator of invention and improvement, and so [indirectly] of the accumulation of capital. In the view I have given, it is represented as proceeding from the antecedent progress of invention, and increase of stock, and as operating chiefly by quickening the exhaustion of instruments, and so placing them in orders of more speedy return. Now in reality, as far as its origin is concerned, the account of the matter which we find in the *Wealth of Nations*, is more favorable to the latter supposition, than to the former.

"In a tribe of hunters, or shepherds, a particular person makes bows and arrows, for example, with more readiness and dexterity than any other. He frequently exchanges them for cattle or for venison, with his companions; and he finds at last that he can in this manner get more cattle and venison, than if he himself went to the field to catch them. From a regard to his own interest, therefore, the making of bows and arrows grows to be his chief business, and he becomes a sort of armorer. Another excels in making the frames and covers of their little huts or moveable houses.

[1] [In the original this chapter was an "appendix" to the second "Book."]

He is accustomed to be of use in this way to his neighbors, who reward him in the same manner with cattle and with venison, till at last he finds it his interest to dedicate himself entirely to this employment, and to become a sort of house carpenter. In the same manner a third becomes a smith or a brazier; a fourth a tanner or dresser of hides or skins, the principal part of the clothing of savages."

If this be a true account of matters, it is evident, that it is the antecedent progress of invention, and the existence of the several arts of the bow-maker, the hunter, the carpenter, the brazier that is the real cause of the separation of the members of the society into artists of different sorts. I rather think, however, that it will be found, that separate artists have come to exist from the passage of individuals from one community to another, and there carrying with them the arts proper to each.[1] If, for example, in any particular tribe, the art of reducing from the ore and working up some of the metals, were well known, and were chance to throw a member of it among another tribe ignorant of this art, he might come to employ himself altogether in the smelting and giving form to metal, and there might come to be a class, whose chief employment were that of working in metal. But it is of little consequence how the separation of employments was brought about. The real question is, do the acknowledged advantages of it proceed directly from the increased efficiency of the labor of the workman; or from the stock of instruments of the society being thus in much more constant employment, and its being, therefore, in the power of the accumulative principle to give them a much more effective construction.

The efficiency of the labor of the workman may be advanced, either by his dexterity being increased, or by an improvement in the construction of the implements with which he works.

---

[1] [Rae is supported in this surmise by Bücher (*Industrial Evolution*), who maintains that the primitive division of employments was inter-tribal, rather than by classes and individuals within each tribe. From the earliest times there has been, however, a separation of employments as between the sexes, affording a point of origin of arts.]

1. As concerns his dexterity, it is to be noted that it is chiefly in the beginning of art that great manual dexterity is requisite. Then the hand is the great instrument. The manual dexterity of the savage in hurling his dart, or shooting with his bow and arrow, in guiding his canoe by the pole or paddle, in framing his fishing and hunting apparatus with the rude tools he possesses, far exceeds that necessary to the civilized man, not only in the common, but even in more delicate arts of civilized life; and, were we to take into the account things generally confounded with manual dexterity, quickness and accuracy of sight, and delicacy and flexibility of the other organs, the disparity between the two would be much greater. As art advances from its first rude elements, the hand does less, the instrument more. To acquire the manual dexterity necessary to guide a bark canoe with security and speed, requires the practice of years. To row a boat equally well might be learned in a few months. The mere manual dexterity necessary to move the different pieces of mechanism that govern the motion of a steamboat, might be acquired in a few days or hours.

It may be remarked, that the examples of this dexterity adduced in the *Wealth of Nations*, are from arts where the implements are exceedingly simple, and where, of consequence, the hand is the great operator. Were improvements taking place in the art of pin-making, or nail-making, that would be done by the instrument which is now done by the quick and complex motions of the hand. In fact, in the arts in which the greatest improvements have had place, such as in the cotton manufacture, the mere manual dexterity requisite is very easily acquired. In a few weeks, or months, the limit is attained. But, when the manual dexterity requisite for the practice of any art can be attained in so short a time, it cannot matter much to the society or to the individual, whether the workman have to learn one or several arts. Besides, the acquisition of any difficult art very much facilitates the attainment of any other. The great matter is to get, as a workman expresses it, the use of one's hands. To become familiar, that is to say, with handling matters of various sorts, judging of their forms and qualities, and acquiring the power of determining the movement to be given, and the habit of executing it quickly and accurately. When this is acquired, there is no great difficulty in the management of any common tool, if once the principle on which it operates be understood. Hence a good workman in any trade, displays comparatively but trifling awkwardness in applying himself to any other. Almost all he requires is to know how a thing is done, and to understand how the implements employed operate. This is very observable in the progress of new settlements in America, where I have seldom seen a good mechanic have much difficulty in turning his hand, as it is said, to any thing.

Agriculture, from its nature, is the art in which the division of labor has made least progress. Were it possible to conceive that, by the operation of any circumstance, it could there be carried to its full extent, whether would its benefits be felt, in the increased dexterity of the workman, or in the increased efficiency of the instruments employed? At present a man employed in such work, generally ploughs, harrows, reaps, mows, threshes, and drives as well at twenty-five, as at thirty-five, or forty-five. It seems not very probable, therefore, that, were he to confine himself altogether to one of these occupations, he would perform it better than he now does. On the other hand, it seems very likely, that, did the dependence of the several agricultural operations on the seasons permit the separation of occupations in this art, the implements employed in it would soon become much more efficient. We see, in fact, that it is the impossibility of this separation taking place, that does here retard or prevent improvement. Threshing-mills, for example, would be universally adopted were it not that, being nearly idle a great part of the time, the cost of construction is too great for the return. The machine is probably unemployed for nineteen days out of twenty, so that could this division take place in twenty adjoining farms, each of which has now its own threshing-mill, nineteen of those at present necessary might be dispensed with. The same thing may, I believe, be said concerning drilling-machines; it is their cost and the long time they lie idle, that prevents their general adoption.

Similar causes altogether prevent the introduction of many other ingenious machines and implements. As much ingenuity, indeed, has been displayed in contrivances for the purposes of this art, as for any other; but the instruments produced, though they would have been very effective aids in particular operations, have never come into use, because, unless for a few days every year, they would have lain idle on the hands of their owners. Were it possible for farmers to divide their employment, and, each taking to a particular department, were the distinct occupations of ploughers, reapers, harrowers, etc., to arise, none of the instruments employed lying idle, they would yield much more speedy returns; their construction, in all probability, would greatly improve, and the whole capital of the country would soon be very much increased. It is worth while observing, too, that in this sort of labor, the improved construction of instruments seems to lessen the quantum of manual dexterity necessary. The manual dexterity necessary for managing a threshing or a drilling-machine is very trifling.

It is chiefly in some very delicate arts, such as that of watchmaking, or in some in which, from their nature, the use of tools cannot be extensively introduced, as in printing, that the efficiency derived from long practice is very great, and where, consequently, the division of labor would seem in this way a direct improvement. These, however, make but a small part of the arts of any community.

2. Among the direct advantages derived from the division of labor, Adam Smith reckons the invention of many machines facilitating and abridging labor. It seems to me, that the facts are, on the whole, opposed to this idea. Whatever confines a man's faculties to one monotonous occupation, must rather dull and cramp, than quicken and expand them. "The understandings of the greater part of men, are necessarily formed by their ordinary employments. The man, whose whole life is spent in performing a few operations, of which the effects, too, are perhaps always the same, or very nearly the same, has no occasion to exert his understanding, or to exercise his invention, in finding out expedients for removing difficulties which never occur. He naturally loses, therefore, the habit of such

exertion, and generally becomes as stupid and ignorant as it is possible for a human creature to become. The torpor of his mind renders him not only incapable of relishing or bearing a part in any rational conversation, but of conceiving any generous, noble, or tender sentiment, and consequently of forming any just judgment concerning many even of the ordinary duties of private life. Of the great and extensive interests of his country he is altogether incapable of judging; and unless very particular pains have been taken to render him otherwise, he is equally incapable of defending his country in war. The uniformity of his stationary life naturally corrupts the courage of his mind, and makes him regard with abhorrence, the irregular, uncertain, and adventurous life of a soldier. It corrupts even the activity of his body, and renders him incapable of exerting his strength with vigor and perseverance in any other employment than that to which he has been bred. His dexterity in his particular trade seems, in this manner, to be acquired at the expense of his intellectual, social, and martial virtues."[1]

These being the direct effects on the intellectual and moral powers of the division of labor, it can scarcely be said to be the direct cause of invention in the artisan. The extended division of labor [in modern industry, however,] implies the existence of many arts, and of much intelligence [in some of the members of the society]. Where it exists, therefore, the inventive faculties will be generally active. But this activity, though a concomitant of the division of labor, is to be held as an effect, not of that division, but of other causes themselves producing the division of labor. It will appear, in short, to be, like most popular principles, a result, not a cause; and ranks properly, not as a prime mover in the course of human affairs, but as a consequence of the actions of the prime movers.

[For a much more vigorous treatment of the leading subjects dealt with in this Chapter the reader is referred to Lauderdale, to whom Rae is undoubtedly much indebted.]

[1] *Wealth of Nations*, Book V. c. I.

APPENDIX.

ARTICLE I.

OF THE NATURE AND EFFECTS OF LUXURY.

THE general tendency of all the circumstances, the nature and causes of which it has been our aim hitherto to investigate, is to advance the wealth of society, the capital and stock of communities. Were the operation of the principles of invention and accumulation to go on unchecked, the amount of the stock of all nations would be gradually and uninterruptedly increased; the one furnishing the means of providing additional supplies for the wants of futurity, the other giving the motives to make the provision. But there are opposite principles, the tendency of which is either to retard the progress of the general stock, or actually to diminish the amount already existing. To some of these we have now to attend.

As the prevalence of the benevolent and social affections, and the strength of the intellectual powers, are the great springs from which the increase of the wealth and prosperity of communities arise, so it might be expected, as I believe it will be found, that the diminution of that wealth is chiefly occasioned by the spread of contrary principles, by the ascendency of the purely selfish, and debasement of the intellectual and moral parts of our nature.

The first of these principles, of which we have to consider the operation, is vanity; by which term I understand the mere desire of superiority over others, without any reference to the merit of that superiority. A perfect being may be desirous of superiority in well-doing, not on account of surpassing others, but from pleasure in the good he does. A very evil being may derive satisfaction from a superiority in evil-doing, simply from the pleasure which the certainty of having been the cause of very great misery may give him. But there seems to be a feeling that finds its proper gratification in merely going beyond others, without reference to the path taken. It would be gratified by excelling in vice, were it not that the moral feeling restrained it; it would be gratified by excelling in virtue, were it not that immoral propensities incapacitate it from attaining an eminent degree of it. It is this which, for want of a better word, I distinguish by the term vanity. It is a purely selfish feeling; its pleasures centre in the individual; and if it does not endeavor to diminish the enjoyment of others, it is never directly its object to increase them. When, in the course of its action, pleasure is communicated to others, this arises from its being then blended with other feelings.

Its aim, in all cases that concern our subject, is to have what others cannot have. One of the most perfect instances of it ever exhibited was when Cleopatra caused a very precious pearl to be dissolved, that she might consume it at a draught. There could be here no pleasure in the taste of the liquor, that must have been rather disagreeable; the gratification consisted in having drank what no one else could afford to drink. The son of the famous Roman actor performed a similar feat.[1]

We learn from Pliny[2] that it became a sort of fashion at Rome as it seems to have been in the East.[3]

But it is seldom that this feeling fixes itself upon objects that gratify it alone, or objects solely desirable from the difficulty of obtaining them, and from the consequent [factitious] superiority which their possession implies. It rather prefers such as have also qualities capable of gratifying other desires, or ministering to other pleasures. The amount, however, of these other wants supplied by the objects it covets is often

---

[1] Filius Æsopi detractam ex aure Metellæ
Scilicet ut decies solidum exsorberet, aceto
Diluit insignem baccam.
Hor. *Sat.* II. 3. The value, 1,00,000 sestertii, was equal to about £5,000.

[2] Plin. IX. 59.

[3] Vis margaritarum aceto subactu. Quintus Curtius.

OF LUXURY

very small; if this be large enough to distinguish them from matters altogether useless, it seems very frequently sufficient for its purpose. The extravagances of the table in which the Romans indulged were of this sort. The enjoyment afforded by the articles consumed must evidently have arisen, almost altogether, from the high price they cost. A dish of nightingale's brains could scarcely be a very delicious morsel, yet Adam Smith quotes from Pliny the price paid for a single nightingale as about £66. For a surmullet £80 were given. According to Suetonius, no meal cost Vitellius less than £2000. The enormous prices paid for various articles of dress and furniture could have proceeded alone from the promptings of similar desires. Thus Adam Smith reckons the cost of some cushions of a particular sort used to lean on at table, at £30,000.

The things to which vanity seems most readily to apply itself are those to which the use or consumption is most apparent, and of which the effects are most difficult to discriminate. Articles of which the consumption is not conspicuous, are incapable of gratifying this passion. The vanity of no person derives satisfaction from the sort of timber used in the construction of the house he occupies, because the wood work is usually concealed by paint or something else. Again: if the effects produced by it can be ascertained with accuracy, the object seldom affords the means of sufficiently marking superiority. Thus coal is consumed for the heat given out by it, and the different quantitites of heat yielded by different qualities of coal are easily ascertained. One scarcely, therefore, prides himself on burning one sort, in preference to another. It is not equally easy to ascertan how much the marble of which his chimney is composed exceeds, or comes short, in the beauty, the variety, and arrangement, of its colors, the same sort of material made use of, for similar purposes, by his neighbors. Fancy here, stimulated by vanity, may raise the one more or less over the other, and according, therefore, to the strength of this passion will the assumed superiority be greater or less. Few things have qualities better fitted for the gratification of this passion than liquors. Their peculiar flavors and tastes are sufficient to distinguish them, and yet afford no room to determine how much the one exceeds the other. The imagination, also, seems to have a peculiar power over the organs of taste and smell, and to be able, through the instrumentality of habit, to bring them to receive pleasure from what at first was indifferent, perhaps even disagreeable. Hence it is impossible to set any bounds to the superiority which one may acquire over another, from the influence of this passion; and it may almost be laid down as a general rule with regard to them, that any one that is at all drinkable, becomes fit for being placed at the tables of the luxurious, by being carried a sufficient distance from the place of its manufacture. Thus, during the peninsular war, London porter was largely consumed in Spain by the very classes who, in England, reckon it a mark of vulgarity to drink it at all.

It is not, indeed, to be disputed, that the rarity and costliness of the liquors, and other similar commodities consumed by an individual, may heighten greatly the absolute pleasure he derives from them. This arises from a trait in the character of man, which we have every day opportunities of observing. The attention is always aroused in a greater degree by an object, when it excites more than one faculty. Two flowers together, the one having the beauty without the scent of the rose, and the other its scent without its beauty, would not afford so much pleasure as that plant. We prefer fruit that has a fine color; it absolutely tastes better. The taste is quickened by the additional stimulus which the eye being caught by the beauty of the color gives to the sensation, in the same way as a blow, long expected, is felt more than one coming unawares. In a similar manner, the mere costliness of wines, or meats, rouses the sense to a keener perception of pleasure, by awakening the vanity; and, when the individual is conscious of being a connoisseur in such matters, this very potent mover of our thoughts and sentiments is, besides, excited by the decernment shown in the discrimination, and by the familiarity thence implied with rare wines and meats, and, consequently, with what is called the best society. The slight, and, to another person perhaps, scarcely perceptible relish which the contents of the glass, or the dish, leaves on the palate, is seized and dwelt upon, and being associated and wrought up with more exciting and intellectual delights, is fixed in the mind of the sentimental epicurean as something infinitely surpassing what he would otherwise have conceived of it. Had pearls, when dissolved in vinegar, produced a beverage that the imagination could possibly have transformed into a delicacy, how would it not have been extolled by the Romans!

The general consumption of any commodity by the vulgar lessens, on the contrary, in many minds, the pleasure it would otherwise give. It brings down the individual, in this particular, to a level with the lowest. This feeling gave rise to the exclamation by a once celebrated northern Duchess, "What a pity that eggs were not a sixpence the piece."

The Roman moralists and satirists ground many of their invectives against the extravagance of the times, on the want of connexion between the qualities of the articles and the estimation in which they were held.[1] Heliogabalus confessed, that it was the relish which the dearness of the dishes gave to them, that led to the extravagance of his table, and liked to have the price of his food overrated, because this sharpened his appetite.

Were proofs wanting of how very slight grounds the taste has for its judgment, in declaring this to be delicious, and that beneath notice, we might find them in its variations in different times and places. It seems only constant in preferring what is expensive. Yet, however different, each society in perfect sincerity believes its system the best. Who could relish now-a-days a Roman feast? Certainly, however, they

---

[1] Laudas, insane, trilibrem
Mullum in singula quem minuas pulmenta necesse est.
Ducit te species, video. Quo pertinet ergo
Proceros odisse lupos? quia silicet illis
Majorem natura modum dedit, his breve pondus.
                                        Hor. *Sat.* L. II., II.
Interea gustus elementa per omnia quærunt,
Nunquam animo pretiis obstantibus; interius si
Attendas magis illa juvant quæ pluris emuntur.
                                        Juvenal, XI. *Sat.*

believed that in cookery, as in other arts, they had attained the summit of real perfection. Of their good faith in this belief they gave a singular instance. A very expensive and much esteemed sauce was made by them out of the probably half rotten entrails of certain fish.[1] So convinced, however, were they of its superlative delicacy, that they had the care to make a formal law specially prohibiting its being given or sold to the barbarians.[2] They were seriously fearful lest, should these rude warriors only taste it, it might so highly gratify their appetite, as to bring them down at once upon the empire. They came, notwithstanding, but neither they nor their more polished descendants seem to have found particular charms in the *garum*.

We find the estimation of every article, whether of dress, of furniture, or of equipage, if to be seen by many, regulated also, in a very great degree, by the gratification it affords this passion. "With the greater part of rich people, the chief enjoyment of riches consists in the parade of riches; which, in their eyes, is never so complete as when they appear to possess those decisive marks of opulence which nobody can possess but themselves. In their eyes, the merit of an object, which is in any degree either useful or beautiful, is greatly enhanced by its scarcity, or by the great labor which it requires to collect any considerable quantity of it; a labor which nobody can afford to pay but themselves. Such objects they are willing to purchase at a higher price than things more beautiful and useful, but more common."[3] Though its influence now, perhaps, is not so great as it was among the ancients, it is yet more apparent. The progress of art has been such, that there is scarcely any material, or fabric, or color, the production of which it does not so much facilitate as to bring it within the reach of a large mass of consumers.

---

[1] Aliud etiamnum liquoris exquisiti genus, quod garum vocavere, intestinis piscium cæterisque quæ abjicienda essent sale maceratis, ut sit illa putrescentium sanies.—Nec liquor ullus pæne præter unguenta majore in pretio esse cœpit. Plin. lib. 31. c. 8. *Nat. His.*

[2] The edict was in the time of the Emperors Valens and Gratian. Gold and wine were laid under a similar prohibition.

[3] *Wealth of Nations*, B. I. c. XI.

It then loses its value as a distinction, and ceases to serve the purposes of vanity. Hence arises the necessity for the variety, and seeming caprice, of fashion. What Adam Smith applies to one class of articles, will apply, in a great measure, to the whole expenditure of the opulent. "When by the improvements in the productive powers of manufacturing art and industry, the expense of any one dress comes to be very moderate, the variety will naturally be very great. The rich, not being able to distinguish themselves by the expense of any one dress, will naturally endeavor to do so by the multitude and variety of their dresses."[1]

To attempt to enumerate the modes in which fashion varies the fitness of things for the purposes of its votaries, were little profitable, and is, I apprehend, superfluous. Its extended influence will hardly be disputed. "What is the cause," demands Mr. Storch,[2] "that gives so high a value to the rare jewels with which opulence loves to deck itself? Is it the pleasure they give the eye, by the brilliancy of their reflected light? No; that slight enjoyment has no relation to their value; it is because they attest the wealth of him who wears them. Such are all the objects of this sort of luxury: the amount of enjoyment they give through the direct medium of the senses is nothing, in comparison of that which they yield by the display that can be made of them to others—even objects which seem by their nature to have no other end but to please the senses, are almost altogether estimated by the gratification this display produces. Consider a sumptuous repast given by opulence, separate from it, in thought, every thing that serves only to show the riches of him who gives it, and leave nothing absolutely on the table but what may gratify the appetite of the individual: what would remain? In short, if we take a general survey," continues the same author, "of all that expenditure which is made after the natural desires are satisfied, we will perceive that it is almost altogether occasioned by the desire to appear rich."[3] This desire of appearing superior to others thus keeps a vast

---

[1] *Idem.* B. IV. c. IX.
[2] *Cours d'Economie Politique,* liv. VII. c. V.
[3] *Traité d'Economie Politique,* liv. VII. c. IV.

number of things in a state of ceaseless revolution. All this domain is under the rule of fashion.

> Diruit, ædificat, mutat quadrata rotundis.

It destroys before its time, as Mr. Say complains, whatever it lays its hands on. "Any thing which a person has provided himself with, to serve some useful purpose, is preserved as long as possible, its consumption is gradual. An object of luxury is of no use from the moment it ceases to gratify either the senses, or the vanity, of its possessor. It is destroyed, at least in greater part, before having ceased to exist, and without having supplied any real want;—luxury has in abhorrence every profitable expense."

The expenditure occasioned by this desire falls on all classes of society. To supply it takes a large portion of the revenue of what are called the middle classes [that is, of those who are recognized members of the middle classes], of those who have difficulty to prove their claim to be so ranked, of those who are comfortable in the lower classes, and even of those who have difficulty in procuring absolute necessaries. "In all classes," says Mr. Storch, "the desire of show (*le luxe d'ostentation*) has been able to identify itself with whatever serves the comfort or the conveniences of life. It is this which borders with a narrow lace the head dress of the country girl, and gives to her whole attire colors and a shape foreign to its utility."[1]

I should wish to apply, to the expenditure occasioned by the passion of vanity, the term luxury. Though that word has properly a wider signification, it is perhaps the one that comes nearest to mark the thing we speak of.

It is somewhat difficult to define precisely how far the limits of luxury, so understood, extend. It is a point which, probably, different people would fix differently. Whatever amount of pleasure any thing gives, that is entirely distinct from its rarity, or any association with that circumstance,

---

[1] Liv. VII. c. V. [The dress of a girl has indirect as well as direct utility. The above was written before the discovery of the principle of sexual selection.]

certainly is not luxury. There is a pleasure in the sight of certain shapes and colors, and arrangements of them, which is quite independent of their cost; there is a fitness, also, in the texture of certain fabrics, to preserve from the extremes of heat and cold, to add to the beauties of feature or form, and to correct their defects, that, of itself, gives pleasure; there are pleasures, too, which the mind creates to itself, out of the associations of these. We feel pleasure, in a cold day, in looking at a person well wrapped up in warm furs, as in a hot day, in seeing that one has no lack of clean linen. A nobleman of a right mind experiences gratification from seeing the clean sheets and warm blankets of the peasant, as well as when he enters and looks round his own sedulously arranged chamber. It is this feeling we experience when we say that such a house, or dress, has an air of comfort about it. The term has properly reference to the sensual, and to the benevolent, not to the selfish feelings. The sight of statues, paintings, flowers, is also capable of affording a high degree of gratification to many minds. The degree of pleasure thus experienced is different in different individuals, and it is scarcely possible to ascertain what its exact amount is in any one; hence the difficulty, in most cases, of determining what is, or is not, luxury. Mr. Storch, in a chapter of his system from which I have already quoted, observes: " All the ornaments which decorate the apartments of the rich, that gilt work, those sculptures which art and taste seem to have formed solely to delight the mind, are nothing but a sort of magical characters, presenting every where this inscription: *Admire the extent of my riches.*" Vanity, there can be little doubt, is the predominating feeling prompting to the construction of such apartments; it is not, however, the only one. Well-executed statues, even elegant gilding, have certainly something in themselves pleasing to the eye, and to the mind of the beholder, whether owner or guest. The larger part of the gratification derived is drawn probably in most cases from vanity, and we occasionally meet with a character whose pleasures are altogether those of ostentation; like Pope's prodigal,

> Not for himself he sees, or hears, or eats,
> Artists must choose his pictures, music, meats;

> He buys for Topham drawings and designs,
> For Pembroke, statues, dirty gods, and coins;
> Rare monkish manuscripts for Hearne alone,
> And books for Mead, and butterflies for Sloane.

But, in most cases, real enjoyment [of an aesthetic nature or otherwise] mixes largely with mere vanity, in expenditure of the [luxurious] sort.

Adam Smith remarks, that "It is not by the importation of gold and silver that the discovery of America has enriched Europe. By the abundance of the American mines those metals have become cheaper. A service of plate can now be purchased for about a third part of the corn, or a third part of the labor, which it would have cost in the fifteenth century. With the same annual expense of labor and commodities, Europe can annually purchase about three times the quantity of plate which it could have purchased at that time. But when a commodity comes to be sold for a third part of what had been its usual price, not only those who purchased it before can purchase three times their former quantity, but it is brought down to the level of a much greater number of purchasers, perhaps to more than ten, perhaps to more than twenty times the former number. So that there may be in Europe, at present, not only more than three times, but more than twenty or thirty times the quantity of plate which would have been in it, even in its present state of improvement, had the discovery of the American mines never been made. So far Europe has, no doubt, gained a real conveniency, though surely a very trifling one. The cheapness of gold and silver renders those metals rather less fit for the purposes of money than they were before. In order to make the same purchases, we must load ourselves with a greater quantity of them, and carry about a shilling in our pocket, where a groat would have done before. It is difficult to say which is most trifling, this inconveniency, or the opposite conveniency."[1] I suspect there is also a little exaggeration here, as the words of the author in another place would prove. "If you except iron, the precious metals are more useful than any other. As they are less liable to rust and impurity, they can more easily be kept clean; and

---

[1] *Wealth of Nations*, B. IV. c. I.

the utensils, either of the table or the kitchen, are often, upon that account, more agreeable when made of them. A silver boiler is more cleanly than a lead, copper, or tin one; and the same quality would render a gold boiler still better than a silver one"[1] But, even if we should admit that silver, as a commodity possessing many useful qualities, is valuable on other accounts than its scarcity, we must also grant that a very large share of other departments of the expenditure of the wealthy consists of mere luxuries,—articles, the sole gratification afforded by which is, that they alone can afford to possess them. It is then, I apprehend with some truth, that, in another part of the *Wealth of Nations*, the author, in tracing the causes which brought on the diminution of the power of the great feudal lords, and ascribing them chiefly to their expending their revenues on the produce of foreign commerce and manufacture, instead of maintaining a large retinue, characterizes the bulk of the articles constituting this expenditure as useless for any other purpose than the gratification of a selfish vanity. "All for ourselves, and nothing for other people, seems, in every age of the world, to have been the vile maxims of the masters of mankind. As soon, therefore, as they could find a method of consuming the whole value of their rents themselves, they had no disposition to share them with any other persons. For a pair of diamond buckles, perhaps, or something as frivolous and useless, they exchanged the maintenance, or what is the same thing, the price of the maintenance, of a thousand men for a year, and with it the whole weight and authority which it could give them. The buckles, however, were to be their own, and no other human creature was to have any share of them; whereas in the more ancient method of expense, they must have shared with at least a thousand people. With the judges that were to determine the preference, this difference was perfectly decisive; and thus, for the gratification of the most childish, the meanest, and the most sordid of all vanities, they gradually bartered their whole power and authority. Having sold their birthright, not like Esau, for a mess of pottage in time of hunger and necessity, but, in the wantonness of plenty, for

---
[1] *Wealth of Nations*, B. I. c. XI.

trinkets and baubles, fitter to be the playthings of children than the serious pursuits of men, they became as insignificant as any substantial burgher or tradesman in a city."[1] Even here, too, there is some exaggeration; the seat of a wealthy modern nobleman exceeds the rude castle of his half barbarous ancestor, not only in the gratification it gives to the personal vanity of its possessor, but also in the refined enjoyments it affords its inmates. The exact proportion between the mere luxuries and the absolute enjoyments, in this as in other cases, is indeed impossible to ascertain. The former, however, undoubtedly make a very large portion of the total amount.

As we descend in the scale, from the persons and mansions of those who have the fortune to possess hereditary wealth and hereditary claims to good society, to those who have themselves accumulated, or are employed in accumulating riches, and raising themselves to distinction, from thence to the lower grades of life, and, at last, to the mere drudges of the community, we shall find every step we take marked by a greater prominence in two circumstances. The amount expended on what are neither the necessaries nor conveniences of life becomes less, but that expenditure is more decidedly mere luxury. Taste gives enjoyment even to the wildest extravagance of those whose chief occupation has been to devise means to enjoy life, and to make it agreeable to others; but he whose business has been, or is, to discover the best means of gaining wealth, though he may yield less to the desire of show, does so more thoroughly. He becomes a mere imitator, and, like most imitators, is apt to retain all the defects and to drop much of the graces of his copy.

Vanity is combated by the strength of the social and benevolent affections and intellectual powers. The former represent its excesses as hurtful, the latter as absurd. The same principles, therefore, which give strength to the effective desire of accumulation, diminish the sway of this passion. Hence, in all societies, where the effective desire of accumulation is high, and instruments consequently at orders of slow

[1] *Wealth of Nations*, B. III. c. IV.

return, or only kept at orders of quick return from the progress of improvement, vanity and luxury will prevail but little;[1] while, in societies where the effective desire of accumulation is low, and instruments, not in consequence of superabundance of materials or recent improvements, but of the inability of the community to work up any but the best materials, are at orders of very quick return, such a state of things, indicating a weakness in the social and benevolent affections, and in the intellectual powers, is generally accompanied by great strength, and the general prevalence of vanity and luxury.

Savages, in general, are remarkable for the influence which vanity has over them, and for their propensity to give up any provision they may have made for the future, or to suffer severe privations, to have the means of decking their persons or habitations with something rare and costly, distinguishing them from others. Beads, bones, plumes of feathers, porcupine quills, gay colors, and all the rarities of their native abodes, are sought out, and wrought up by them with great labor. They besides cut their flesh, or tatoo their skin. The operation costs severe pain and requires some skill, and the bearing the testimony of this outlay about with him is as real a gratification to the vanity of the savage as a diamond ring to that of an European. Their intercourse with civilized nations turns their desires towards fineries of European manufacture. Glass beads, trinkets of silver, or, if it be not to be had, of tin, fine cloths, showy cottons and silks, then make up a large part of their expenditure.[2]

---

[1] [This seems to be a debatable position. See the note at the end of this article.]

[2] I have seen many of the Indians in Canada, when in high dress, clothed in the finest English cloth, of which they are, I am told, excellent judges; certainly, however, in the way they wear it, the Indian blanket, one made thick for the purpose, with a broad blue border, makes a more convenient and more becoming robe.

The almost irresistible passion which these people have, for whatever they perceive esteemed precious by others, must have struck every one having had any intercourse with them. Perhaps the following anecdote may be worth relating, as in some degree illustrative of it. I was once voyaging with a friend in a small canoe, when we chanced to keep company for two or three days with

All travellers speak of the vanity of the Chinese, and of their propensity to show. Their glittering gilding, variegated silks, and crispy cows' hair dyed red, with them the most splendid of ornaments, catch the eye of every stranger, and contrast strongly with the squalid poverty and misery that is the constant portion of a considerable part of the population, and occasionally invades the whole mass. One of the father Jesuits, in speaking of the necessity of his brethren changing their habits and style of living, observes, that, "besides other reasons, they are obliged to conform to the general custom of the country; that even individuals of the common people, when they go to visit any one, dress themselves in silk, and have themselves carried in a chair. This does not pass with them for vanity, or affectation of grandeur, but for an evidence that they esteem the persons whom they visit, and that they themselves are above absolute want, and are not in a despicable condition.[1] This attention to a showy exterior seems to have led Mr. Ellis to form too high an estimate of the general opulence and comfort of the people, "I have been much struck," he says, "in all Chinese towns and villages with the number of persons apparently of the middling classes; from this I am inclined to infer a wide diffusion of the substantial comforts of life, and the consequent financial capacity of the country."[2]

The Romans are still more conspicuous instances of the extravagance into which this passion betrays nations. Vanity reigned throughout their expenditure. The decorations of

---

some Indians in another, one of whom a severe intermittent had reduced to a mere skeleton. One forenoon when we stopped for a little, they requested us to come close to them, and open a case we had, to let the sick man examine it. Having done as they desired, the invalid seemed sadly disappointed, "I thought," he said, "when I saw it at a distance yesterday, that the inside was silver, and it seemed to me it would do me good to look at it, but it is only tin." The expression of his countenance and voice showed that he fancied the sight of so much silver, would have acted like a cordial, and so I dare say it would. It is to be observed that it is not the custom of Indians to make requests having an air of impertinence of strangers, or to express disappointment.

[1] *Lettres Edifiantes*, Vol. IX. p. 531.

[2] *Embassy to China*, Phil. edition, 1818, p. 237.

their persons and mansions were a show of the most costly luxuries.

> "Gemmas, marmor, ebur, Tyrrhena sigilla, tabellas,
> Argentum, vestes Gætulo murice tinctas."

The head, the neck, the arms, the fingers, of a Roman lady were loaded with jewels. Pliny relates that the jewels which Lollia Paulina, the wife of Caligula, even after her repudiation, carried on her person when attired simply for paying visits, were worth forty millions of sesterces, upwards of two hundred thousand pounds sterling. According to the same author, women of the greatest simplicity and modesty durst no more go without diamonds than a consul without the marks of his dignity. The men, also, he tells us, wore on their fingers a variety of the most expensive rings, rather loading than adorning them. It was common to have tables and other articles of ivory, or of the precious metals. The plate and tables of Heliogabalus were of pure gold. Examples of their excessive luxury in articles for the table have been already given, and many more might be added, were it necessary to repeat what has been often narrated.[1]

The magnificence of the eastern Empire was perhaps even greater than that of Rome itself. It reflected something of the excessive splendor of the Babylonish and other Asiatic monarchies. Chrysostom thus describes the palaces of the nobles. "The roofs made of wood were gilt. The doors, even the long folding doors, were of ivory. In all the chambers the walls were incrusted with marble. If they were only of common stone, it was covered with plates of gold. The beams and ceilings were gilt, and the apartments were inlaid with small stones, and often with precious stones. Over the floors were sometimes spread very rich carpets. Their taste for magnificence could bear nothing of the ordinary kind. In the rooms were great pillars of marble, with their chapiters gilt, and sometimes the whole pillars were gilt, statues by the most excellent artists, pictures and mosaic work. The beds were usually of ivory or of wood, gilt or covered with silver plates, and sometimes of solid silver decorated with gold. All

[1] The reader may consult Gibbon, or the work of M. d'Arnay *sur la vie privée des Romains*.

the furniture was surprisingly rich. The chairs and benches were of ivory; the pots and other vessels, even for the meanest uses, were of gold and silver."[1]

Mr. Say has remarked, that there is a large part of the consumption of the French, which is occasioned by their excessive attention to mode and fashion, and that, in this respect, they contrast disadvantageously with the English, who pay more attention to comfort and convenience, and less to the changing fancies by which vanity seeks to distinguish itself. Instruments have never, in France, been wrought up to orders of so slow return as in England.

I believe it will be found that the strength of the effective desire of accumulation, is higher among the working classes in North America than in Europe. The influence of vanity in many cases, is certainly less. The consumption, for instance, of coarse unbleached cotton, for shirting, is very great; this is certainly a more comfortable wear for a working man than the finer sorts. It washes more easily, and endures more fatigue.[2] The finer cottons, also, of American manufacture, are of a stouter and more substantial fabric, indicating that the American purchaser looks more to the wear of the article, the European to the delicacy of the fabric. The same thing may be said of woolens. A substantial farmer in England would scarcely, as one of the same class in North America, think himself decently clad in a winter's suit of which the cloth cost only a dollar per yard, though a comfortable and durable dress.

It is to be observed, that, as vanity is opposed by the social and benevolent affections and intellectual powers, according as the one or the other of these preponderates, the manifestations of that luxury which yet remains, are modified into some resemblance to what it approves. When the intellectual powers are strong, this passion endeavors to elude them by attaching itself to objects that it can represent as of permanent excellence. When the benevolent affections are

---

[1] Chrysostom, quoted by Jortin, *Ecclesiastical History*, Vol. II. p. 359.

[2] Until about two years since almost all upper Canada and the eastern townships of lower Canada, were supplied with American cottons of this sort smuggled over. Patterns were sent to Manchester, and imitation American cottons got out, which now supply the Canadian side of the line; they do not, however, as far as I have been able to learn, pass to the other.

powerful, it endeavors to gain its ends, by representing them as proceeding from a wish to gratify others, and to share with them things, which are at least generally esteemed rare and valuable. In the former case it escapes opposition, and finds vent in expensive buildings and decorations; in the latter in sumptuous entertainments, and luxuries of the table. "In Holland," says Mandeville, "people are only sparing in such things as are daily wanted and soon consumed; in what is lasting they are quite otherwise; in pictures and marble they are profuse; in their buildings and gardens they are extravagant to folly. In other countries you may meet with stately courts and palaces of great extent that belongs to princes which nobody can expect in a commonwealth, where so much equality is observed as there is in this; but in all Europe you shall find no private buildings so sumptuously magnificent, as a great many of the merchants' and other gentlemen's houses are in Amsterdam, and some other great cities of that province, and the generality of them that build there, lay out a greater proportion of their estates on the house they dwell in than any people upon the earth."[1] Something of the same genius may, I think, be observed in the expenditure of the North Americans. Their houses are frequently larger than they have use for, so that part of them remains unoccupied. They are, also, often built with a greater regard to show than comfort. There is little substantial difference between a gold and silver watch, but that the former costs double of the latter. Gold watches are perhaps more common in North America, than in any other part of the world. It is pure vanity that leads to so general an adoption of this luxury, by classes who in England would not think of it, but it is a vanity that fixes itself on something permanent. In the end, there is no cheaper way in which man can write, "I am rich, or at least, I am not absolutely poor," than to carry a gold watch. It is ready to meet all occasions, and all persons.[2]

[1] Remark Q, *Fable of the Bees*.

[2] These observations apply to the population of British descent or birth on both sides of the line. [Rae overlooks here that the possession of a gold watch, or any sort of valuable jewelry, constitutes a hoard of wealth which may be of great use in certain emergencies. It is like the gold chain of the knight of the Middle Ages, of which he speaks elsewhere.]

In Britain, on the other hand, the luxuries that mix themselves with the virtues of hospitality are more apt to prevail. There rare wines, and refinements in the dainties of the table are more common.

Besides the varied character with which the various strength of the passion stamps different peoples, there is a difference, in this respect, in the same people, between the agricultural population and the inhabitants of cities, which the following sagacious remarks of Montesquieu seem to me sufficiently to explain. "The extent of luxury farther depends on the size of towns, and especially of the capital. In proportion to the populousness of towns, the inhabitants are filled with notions of vanity, and actuated by an ambition of distinguishing themselves by trifles. If they are numerous, and most of them strangers to one another, their vanity redoubles, because there are greater hopes of success. As luxury inspires these hopes, each man assumes the marks of a superior condition. But, by endeavoring thus at distinction, every one becomes equal and distinction ceases; as all are desirous of respect, nobody is regarded."[1]

In the country it is different; every one is known, and no one can succeed in passing himself off for other than he is. In town Molly Seagrim would have been admired as a fantastical fine lady; in the country she got herself mobbed. To account for the difference, which we every where see between the dissipation of the town and the economy and frugality of the country, we have only to consider, in addition to this, that in the country there are always considerable facilities and encouragements, for even the poorest to form instruments, unless in very anomalous cases, such as that which the abomination of the poor laws has introduced into England. In the country the poor man can devote all his spare time, which perhaps is his only disposable [savable] fund, to the cultivation of some plot of ground, to repairing his house, working in his garden, and procuring food for his cow or his pig. He is induced and enabled to place out[2] all

---

[1] *Esprit des Lois*, B. VII. c. II.

[2] One who has happened to reside in any part of Scotland, where facilities of this sort exist, must have had opportunities of observing very remarkable

his little savings, as they come in, on some profitable investment. Similar circumstances operate similar effects on the man in middling circumstances, and even on the rich man. It is the town, especially the metropolis, that is the ruin of landed proprietors.

We may also, in a similar manner, explain the tendency of new countries to engender industry and frugality. The very scattered state of the population effectually keeps down vanity; the absolute necessity of working up the materials within reach, rouses the accumulative principle to action, and the abundance of these materials stimulates it to unremitting exertion. There is hence no better school for the dissolute European than the back woods. After a dozen years' residence in them, or in the clearings to which he has helped to convert them, he comes out a completely altered man.

It is perhaps proper to observe here, that no blame can attach to individuals, for compliances [within reasonable bounds] with the follies to which the passion of vanity prompts. It were a great mistake to imagine that even its absurdities are easily avoidable. It is in vain for any one man to oppose general opinions and practices, however ridiculous. If he does so, he is sure to encounter greater evils than a compliance with the customs of the society would inflict. It is the business of the poor man to stand well with the world, else he would scarcely make his way through it. It is his business, too, to avoid a display of poverty. One is sure to have most friends when they least need them. " Pour s'établir dans le monde," says Rochefoucauld, " on fait tout ce qu'on peut pour y paroître établi."

instances of the indefatigable industry they excite. Tracts of land, so very barren and impracticable as to seem condemned to perpetual sterility, may be seen in process of being converted into fertile soil, by being let out in small patches at very long or perpetual leases. A portion of the estate of Pilfoddles, near Aberdeen, almost a continuity of rock, was, I recollect, so reclaiming about fifteen years ago. Those small feus, as they are termed, are taken by laborers, who work on them at spare hours when their other occupations fail them.

[This sort of procedure is the original and elemental method of "accumulation" or growth of capital. "Saving" proper, or the putting by of funds in the form of money to be either expended in hiring labor or in buying titles to property ("investing" proper), is an historical category.]

"Notwithstanding my poverty," writes a Jesuit missionary from China, "I have yet been able to relieve the extreme misery of two poor Christians. The one had his house, his furniture, and his implements of trade, destroyed by fire. The other was by profession a physician, and some thieves had in the night carried off his silk dresses; they might as well have stolen his profession and his reputation; for here a physician, unless dressed in silk and cow's hair, passes for ignorant, and is employed by no one." The doctor who had lost his silken robes was probably worse off than the mechanic; the former was still in a condition to find work, the latter was not. He probably, indeed, had nankin left; but had he dressed in it, especially had he pretended to say it was the more comfortable wear, he would have acted about as wisely as would a poor young M.D. in England who should, in cold winter days, attire himself in dreadnought. Who would trust a case to so absurd a mortal?

The man of independent fortune, again, though he need fear no very serious evils from setting himself in direct opposition to received modes of extravagance, will yet certainly incur the charge of eccentricity, perhaps of niggardly parsimony. These are small inconveniences, but he consults his ease in avoiding them.

A person is then only properly guilty of inflicting an injury on the community, when he runs into both acknowledged extravagances and real luxuries. He is censured by some, but envied and followed by others. An individual may, on the other hand, somewhat advance the prosperity of the whole society, or at least of the order in it in which he is himself ranked, by checking his vanity when it urges him to adopt luxuries, permitted to his fortune, though not demanded by it. The nobleman who, in equipage and lackeys, keeps somewhat within the limits which his revenues would afford; the tradesman's wife, who dresses in calico instead of silk, are both, to a small extent, public benefactors. Luxury, indeed, generally advances or recedes slowly, and can scarce be successfully encouraged or opposed but by degrees. There is always, and in every society, one line, to go beyond which is acknowledged extravagance, and another, not to come up to which is accounted sordid parsimony. Crassus was ashamed to use some of his plate, the cost, even to him, appeared too great.[1] It is invidious to run to expenses which others cannot follow, and his guests would have felt themselves too much outshone. He would have been more severely censured, had he ventured to entertain them in the simple style of their ancestors.

It were very difficult to discover a society where vanity does not more or less direct the necessary expenditure. Could this be done, we should there find things estimated solely by their physical qualities, and as these differ greatly, there would be great differences in the estimate made of each. Whatever could really set forth to advantage the beauty or grace of form or feature, would be proportionally prized, as would real beauty in articles of furniture, and in the form and decorations of apartments. But under this supposition, other circumstances being equal, that would always be preferred which was cheapest. If two articles, therefore, were presented, of which the one was of much greater real beauty than the other, but also much more expensive, though it might be that the former would be preferred, its high cost would be esteemed a defect, and would proportionally diminish the pleasure yielded by it. Very expensive articles would, if possible, be avoided. A very costly dress, for instance, would affect the mind of such spectators disagreeably, as auguring either a want of taste, or a want of beauty in the wearer, requiring much adventitious aid to help out the deficiency. It would produce a disagreeable feeling, somewhat similar to that caused by the view of a profuse expenditure of animal power, bringing about only a small effect, and impressing, therefore, with an idea of defective mechanism. In such a society the notions of most people, and therefore the general rules of conduct, would in this respect be completely different from what they generally are.

Sometimes, though rarely, this passion instead of leading to dissipation [of industrial energy], has an effect similar to an enlarged providence, and causes the formation of instruments

---

[1] L. vero Crassus orator duos scyphos Mentoris artificis manu cælatos—sestertiis C.—Confessus tamen est, nunquam se his uti propter verecundiam ausum. Plin. *Hist. Nat.* XXXIII. c. 11.

of slowly returning orders. This is chiefly remarkable in buildings intended to be permanent. If the materials and workmanship of these are not substantial, and such as insure durability to the edifice, the defect is commonly perceptible, and is ridiculed as proceeding from poverty, or from dread of expense. The vanity of the rich man, therefore, here excites him to work for succeeding generations, that he may give the present a high idea of the extent of his resources. He besides, in this way, hopes to make it apparent to his contemporaries, that a monument of his prosperity and magnificence will descend to future times. The same observation will apply to public works undertaken by a proud and extravagant government. Vanity is always an operator in their formation, and therefore their construction is never altogether regulated by the [prevailing or standard] strength of the accumulative principle, nor are they instruments of the orders which it would indicate. "The proud minister of an ostentatious court may frequently take pleasure in executing a work of splendor and magnificence, such as a great highway, which is frequently seen by the principal nobility, whose applause not only flatters his vanity, but even contributes to support his interest at court. But to execute a great number of little works, in which nothing that can be done can make any great appearance, or excite the smallest degree of admiration in any traveller, and which, in short, have nothing to recommend them but their extreme utility, is a business which appears in every respect too mean and paltry to merit the attention of so great a magistrate. Under such an administration, therefore, such works are almost always entirely neglected."[1] It is, however, to be observed, that in regulating public works, and other public affairs, men ought to pay more attention to the concerns of a distant futurity than in the management of their private affairs. A century is a small part of the existence of a nation,

---

[1] *Wealth of Nations*, B. V. c. I. [The above statement in respect to "little works" has little applicability under present day conditions of government in Western Europe and America. One of the leading drains everywhere on public resources is the great multitude of petty undertakings extravagantly carried out. The appropriations for really great public works, for buildings which should indeed have "splendor and magnificence," are frequently unduly cut down because the revenue of the state has been thus frittered away.]

though it includes that of several generations of individuals. In statesmen, therefore, in the affairs of states, the accumulative principle should be strong. Great durability, consequently, in public works, is always desirable. In like manner governments should borrow on different principles from individuals. No one, for instance, now disputes that it should have been the policy of Great Britain to have borrowed as much on long annuities as possible. The misfortune is, that statesmen generally think of themselves more than of their country, and instead of grappling with present evils, let them grow, content if they grow quietly and imperceptibly, and do not threaten to deprive them of the gratification of maintaining the pride of their power for a few years' political triumph. This consideration may in part explain the cause of the great durability of public works in China. It shows that the paternal character of the government is in some measure a reality. I suspect, however, that the contrast between the construction of public and private works there, is more apparent from the diminishing strength of the accumulative principle in that great Empire. I shall presently have occasion to adduce some reasons for this conjecture.

It is perhaps here worthy of remark, as serving to show that ostentation and extravagance have very little connexion with any other species of enjoyment, but that which places its gratifications in some superiority over others, that in proportion as nations are addicted to vanity and luxury, their range of bodily enjoyments seems to become less. Cleanliness, for instance, may be said to be a refined sensuality; it is a real enjoyment, on which the self-mortified ascetic wastes not his care; and we find that least attention is paid to it by the vain, and most by the provident, so that other things being equal, where the effective desire of accumulation is high, there it is most scrupulously observed; where it is low, it is little regarded.

The North American Indians seem really not to have any notion of its existence. It appears to them, in other people, as an affected and unaccountable scrupulosity.[1] The Chinese are described as disgustingly filthy. The Romans were cer-

[1] See "Note J" in the Appendix.

tainly, as may be gathered from various passages in the Latin writers, far from being what we would esteem cleanly. An English gentleman would not think of writing to his friend that if he dined with him he should find well-washed dishes.

———— Ne non et cantharus et lanx
Ostendat tibi te ;[1]

Horace introduces a fanciful epicure, complaining of unwashed goblets, want of table napkins and sawdust, as taking away from the pleasures of a sumptuous feast.[2] In modern times Holland has been esteemed the country of cleanliness; England perhaps ranks next.

Improvement can never facilitate the production of mere luxuries. It cannot do so because it is not the thing itself, but merely the quantity of labor embodied in it that vanity prizes. Diminish the labor necessary for its production, and you take away what this passion covets. It will, therefore, [thereafter] either consume a proportionally larger quantity of the commodity, or will turn itself for its gratification to other commodities of greater rarity, which a greater amount of labor, or some equivalent to it, is necessary to purchase.

Pearls, as ornaments, probably derive nearly their whole value from their scarcity. Reduce their price to one half, and the quantity worn to produce the same effect would require to be doubled. Render them obtainable for a trifle, and they could be no longer worn. It has been more than once attempted to cultivate them, that is to make the oyster that produces them, bear them universally and plentifully. Linneaus conceived it practicable by pricking the animal, and other managements, but the scheme has never succeeded. Had it done so fully, it had certainly been useless. Suppose it had diminished the labor necessary to procure them by one half, then a lady to be as richly dressed as before, would just have had to carry double the number. Had the facility been farther increased, so that they became as plentiful as glass

---

[1] Hor. *Epist.* Lib. I. V.

[2] *Sat.* IV. L. II. The Romans, it is true, bathed frequently, but then they had neither soap nor linen, and woollens were high priced.

beads, they would then have become as useless. If every peasant girl could afford to have a string of them, no lady would wear them, and when ladies ceased to wear them, peasant girls would lay them aside.[1] It is the same with all other articles that are mere luxuries. As they only serve for marks of the riches of the individuals possessing them, every diminution made in the labor embodied in them diminishes, in a proportionate degree, their fitness for the purpose for which they are employed. Should topazes become as plentiful as cairngorms they would be no more esteemed.

There are few commodities, however, in which utility, as well as vanity, has not a considerable share. On such the effects of improvements are twofold. As far as they possess inherent utility, it tends to carry them first, and subsequently all other instruments in the society, towards the more quickly returning orders. In so far again as they are mere luxuries, it renders a greater quantity of them necessary, or unfits them altogether for the supply of the demands of vanity. There is hence a sort of strife between the two principles, the one seeking to disparage and discard such commodities, the other to retain them. The result seems mainly determined by the proportion of the one, or the other sort of qualities, existing in the article in question, and by the degree in which its consumption is apparent. It may have so many useful and agreeable qualities, that however easily obtained, or however openly consumed, it cannot be driven out of use. All that vanity can do with regard to such articles, is, to consume them when they are most scarce. Some of the Romans never ate fish but when at a distance from the sea, nor flesh but when on the sea-shore. Green peas become luxuries at Christmas. Should the best flannel cost only two pence a yard, it would still be worn by all who now wear it, and by many who do not. Its consumption is not conspicuous. On the contrary, were any particular fine fabric of cotton at present used for gowns, and costing two shillings per

---

[1] "The price of pearls in modern times has very much declined; partly, no doubt, from change of manners and fashions; but more probably, from the admirable imitation of pearls that may be obtained at a very low price." McCulloch's *Dictionary of Commerce*. They are also less worn.

yard, in consequence of improvement to be sold for two pence per yard, it could no longer be worn. It would no longer be dress for any rank, and its consumption would therefore diminish or cease. About ten years ago, what are called leghorn bonnets were fashionable and much worn in Canada and the United States. They then cost three or four pounds. They may be had now for a few shillings, and no one wears them; straw which were then disused but by the less wealthy, are now preferred; they are dearer and less durable.

People who regard appearances, and are accustomed to see and be seen, can scarce expect that any improvement will materially diminish their yearly outlay for dress, for themselves or families. Whatever proportion of their revenues they may have found it necessary so to expend, in order to maintain the appearance their rank required, they may fairly reckon they will have to expend in future. The gentleman, the tradesman, the lady, the servant girl, must alike obey the laws which the strength of this principle imposes on the society. Whatever advance improvement may make, they must still lay their account with being looked down on by their respective associates, or having to wear garments just as expensive as ever, without being better looking, or more comfortable, in a degree answering by any means to the facilities of fabrication effected by the successful efforts of invention. In so far as their dress is a mark of their riches, a sort of inscription they bear about with them, as Mr. Storch expresses it, serving to impress others with a belief of their possessing a certain amount of wealth, or holding such a rank in society, it is exactly analogous to coin. Double the faculty of production, the quantity carried about, to answer the same purpose, must be doubled, or recourse must be had to some other material. Purple or scarlet, served among the Romans for a mark of this sort; only the rich could afford to wear it. Although still admired as a color, it no longer serves the purpose, and is comparatively little used. Lace, among the moderns, was once a mark of the same kind. Invention has so far facilitated the production of some sorts of it, that the wearing them no longer confers distinction. Increase that facility, till a yard of the finest sorts may be had for a few half pence, and it is questionable if the beauty of the fabric would preserve it as an article of dress wearable by any one.[1]

To articles of furniture, of diet, to the equipage of the rich, and to the whole apparent expenditure of every class, similar observations will apply. A greater or less part of the effects of improvement, is absorbed by vanity in them all, and consequently lost.

In as far again as any article is not a luxury, in as far as it is beyond the reach of vanity, and consumed to supply some real want, not to display superiority, in so far improvement is really felt. Were invention to discover some substance having all the properties, and the exact appearance

[1] "At Honiton, in Devon, the manufacture had arrived at that perfection, was so tasteful in the design, and so delicate and beautiful in the workmanship, as not to be excelled by the best specimens of Brussels lace. During the late war, veils of this lace were sold in London from twenty to one hundred guineas; they are now sold from eight to fifteen guineas. The effects of the competition of machinery, however, were about this time felt; and in 1815, the broad laces began to be superseded by the new manufacture. Steam power was first introduced by Mr. John Lindsey, in 1815-16; but did not come into active operation till 1820. It became general in 1822-23; and a great stimulus was at this period given to the trade, owing to the expiration of Mr. Heathcoat's patent, the increased application of power, and the perfection to which the different hand frames had by this time been brought. A temporary prosperity shone on the trade; and numerous individuals—clergymen, lawyers, doctors, and others—readily embarked capital in so tempting a speculation. Prices fell in proportion as production increased, but the demand was immense; and the Nottingham lace frame became the organ of general supply, rivaling and supplanting, in plain nets, the most finished productions of France and the Netherlands. Lace, having become a common ornament, easily accessible to all classes, has lost its attractions in the fashionable circles, by which it was formerly patronized, so that very rich lace is no longer in demand. And many articles of dress, which in our drawing rooms and ball rooms, lately consisted of the most costly and tasteful patterns in lace, are now either superseded or made of different manufacture.—Many of the embroiderers in Nottingham are at present unemployed; and even for the most splendid and beautiful specimens of embroidery, some of which have occupied six weeks, working six days a week and fourteen hours a day, the young women have not earned more than one shilling a day. The condition of the plain lace workers is still more deplorable—they cannot obtain more, on an average, than two shillings and six pence a week, and working twelve or fourteen hours per day, for their anxious and unremitting labor."—McCulloch's *Dictionary of Commerce*.

of good leather, and capable of being formed for one sixth of the outlay, it would be an effort of that power very sensibly felt. Boots would probably indeed cease to be worn by the higher classes, unless when on horseback, but good shoes cannot be dispensed with by any class. They are worn for comfort, not for show, and the diminution in the outlay necessary to procure them, would constitute a real improvement. Improvements in mining and modes of transporting coals, diminishing the labor necessary to bring them to market, are also sensibly felt, they facilitate the supply of real wants and move instruments towards the more quickly returning orders. Improvements in the manufacture of iron, also escape vanity and are real. Could ingenuity discover a method of quarrying stones and reducing them to shape, or of making bricks at one half of the present outlay, it would be a real improvement: only a small part of it would be lost in vanity; for, unless in the highest classes, a dwelling-house is much more for comfort than for show. Could the substance of potatoes be converted into an article exactly similar to wheaten flour, and requiring only half the outlay, that would also be a very great improvement. Improvements, too, in the fabrication of articles of glass, and earthen ware, are in a great degree real. Could the manufacture of plate glass be so facilitated, that it might be had for only double the price of common window glass, the substitution of the one for the other could not be called a luxury, but a real improvement, an increased provision for the supply of future wants. In Great Britain ingenuity has succeeded, in recent years, in very greatly facilitating the manufacture of cotton fabrics. The increased facility of production has in part effected a real improvement, but certainly has in a great measure also been absorbed by vanity. Much less labor is now necessary to produce articles of dress of this material which are not seen, or are but little seen; but for dresses worn in public, the expenditure is certainly not diminished, or the beauty or comfort of the article increased, in proportion to the increased facility of production. The finer sorts of these stuffs are perhaps produced with ten times the facility they were twenty years ago, yet probably the whole annual expenditure which a young female makes for such part of her apparel as is formed of these stuffs, is little less than what her mother, twenty years ago, was accustomed to make, and certainly she is not ten times more becomingly or more comfortably clad. The great cheapness indeed of even the finest and most delicate of these fabrics, is such that vanity seems to be discarding them. The utmost efforts of ingenuity can scarcely embody a sufficiency of labor in them, or vary them so as to make them a fit full dress for even a tradesman's wife.

All luxuries occasion a loss to the society, in proportion to their amount. The industry employed in their formation, generates no provision for future wants, and may be said to be expended in vain. Taking the whole society as a body, it supplies no wants. It gives no absolute enjoyment, it is all relative; as much as one is raised by it, another is depressed, the superiority of one man being here equivalent to the inferiority of another. To increase the facilities of production of luxuries, therefore, brings no addition to the absolute capital. It is precisely analogous to increasing the facilities for the production of the metals used for coin, merely adding to the bulk circulated, and not enabling it in any degree to perform its office better. The expense, too, occasioned by keeping up the circulation of the one and the other, and consequent diminution of the national revenue, is equally a loss. It is much greater, however, in the case of luxuries than of coinage, because the whole amount of the former, in all societies, is probably much greater than that of the latter; and because it consists, in general, of materials far more easily destroyed. To the loss thus occasioned by vanity the term [economic] dissipation may be applied. Its amount cannot, for reasons already stated, be easily ascertained, nor is it necessary for our purpose that it should. It is sufficient to observe, that, in all societies which have hitherto existed, it has been considerable; and that it seems to be determined, in every society, by the strength of the selfish, and weakness of the intellectual powers and benevolent affections; and, consequently, that it is inversely as the strength of the accumulative principle.

Though vanity, in this way, operates directly to retard the increase of the stock of the society, some of its indirect effects have, notwithstanding, an opposite tendency. As an antagonist to the restraining influence of the spirit of imitation, it is often a very useful auxiliary in the spread of inventions. These, without its aid, might perhaps have been shut up in the countries where they were discovered; certainly they would not have passed from region to region, so rapidly as they have sometimes succeeded in doing. Under the guise of foreign rarities, and consequently luxuries, they have made their way easily; and the mask rubbing off in time, a substratum of utility has been found under it.[1]

Soap seems to have been first made in the midst of the ashes and tallow of Germany and Gaul. It came to Rome as a luxury, in the shape of a pigment for the hair. In the course of time, its superior detergent qualities becoming apparent, and the manufacture being introduced, this article so essential to the comfort of the modern European, passed entirely out of the rank of luxuries. Vanity also brought silk to Europe. At first it was almost entirely a luxury. As a garment it often has more beauty than [material of] any other texture; but when it exchanged for its weight in gold, its beauty must have constituted but a small part of the enjoyment derived from the wearing of it. In some fabrics it is now scarcely a luxury; its qualities of durability and beauty seem to give it a real superiority, sufficient to render the superior price paid for it no dissipation. Increase that facility very much, and some of these fabrics would be [altogether] discarded by vanity, [but retained by true economy]. Were velvet to become as cheap as cloth, it would not be worn by the higher classes; its greater durability would make it too economical for them, and its adoption by the lower would render it vulgar. Fabrics of cotton were at first luxuries. They would not, perhaps, have been worn [at all in Europe] had they not had rarity, and consequently vanity, to recommend them. Cashmere shawls are so now; in time they too may cease to be so. The process, indeed, has made some progress in France, where, I have been told,

[1] [Compare Article VIII., p. 415.]

the breed of the animal yielding the wool has been introduced, and the manufacture considerably advanced.

Vanity, also, [besides aiding in the spread of established arts] sometimes facilitates [the creation of wholly new forms of] real improvement, by the high estimate it gives to articles that are mere luxuries, but which contain the rudiments of extensive utility. It thus stimulates invention to facilitate their production, develop their utility, and put them out of the class of luxuries.

Glass was at first a pure luxury. It was prized by the Romans for show, as glass beads are now by savages. Ingenuity at length perfected the various processes of the manufacture, and made it an article extensively supplying real wants. The diamond is at present chiefly a luxury; should art ever succeed in giving at will a crystalline structure to simple carbon, so as to convert it into that substance, it would pass from the rank of luxuries, and would, too, contribute largely to the supply of real wants. The high estimation in which it is held serves at present to turn the attention of ingenuity strongly to such a project.

These, however, are indirect, and, as it were, accidental effects of luxury; its direct operation is always to dissipate a part of the national funds proportioned to its strength.

The different effects arising from the action of the inventive faculty, as it operates on utilities or luxuries, afford a means of distinguishing the one from the other. The progress of invention extends the consumption of utilities; it diminishes the consumption of pure luxuries. Were steel, platina, or plate glass, produced by one tenth of the labor they presently cost, their consumption would be very much increased. Were pearls, or lace, to be got for one tenth of the labor that must now be given for them, they would go completely out of fashion. The additional amount of utilities produced, occupying the place of instruments that cost more labor, and did not return more abundantly, their consumption implies a diminution in the cost of the whole stock of the society as compared with the returns made by it, and consequently the progress of that stock to an order of quicker return. The facility given to the production of luxuries has rather a contrary effect, exciting to the greatest outlay of labor of which the accumulative principle is capable, previous to the abandoning of the manufacture.

.   .   .   .

[In the last few pages of the foregoing Article, Rae takes some account of the indirect and contingent effects of luxury (as elsewhere of wars, persecutions, and the like), but he does not carry this line of speculation far enough. His handling of the subject as a whole is, consequently, much inferior to that of Hume and some others. It may be said, I think, to lack generosity ; and hence its error. Such a sweeping indictment cannot issue against the whole human race.

Rae's teaching here, on its purely economic side, needs to be supplemented by the following from Bagehot's *Economic Studies*, London edition, 1880, p. 172.

"But we must observe what is incessantly forgotten, that it is not a Spartan and ascetic state of society which most generates saving. . . . Without the multifarious accumulation of wants which are called luxury, there would in such a state of society be far less saving than there is. If you look at the West-end of London with its myriad comforts and splendors, it looks at first sight like a mere apparatus for present enjoyment. And so far as the present feelings of those who live there go, it often is. Very many of the inhabitants are thinking only of themselves. But there is no greater benefit to the community for all that than this seemingly thoughtless enjoyment. It is the bait by which the fish is caught ; it is the attraction by which capital is caught. To lead a bright life like that, at least that his children may lead it or something like it, many times as many as those who now live it, spare and save."]

ARTICLE II.

OF EXCHANGE BETWEEN DIFFERENT COMMUNITIES
OF COMMODITIES WHICH MINISTER TO LUXURY.

WHEN luxuries, the produce of foreign art, present themselves to a society, where they had before been strangers, their [true] value cannot be [readily] ascertained by comparing them with commodities of domestic formation, for it is not indeed the really useful qualities of commodities [which are readily comparable], that fit them more or less perfectly to gratify the passion of vanity, but solely the difficulty of procuring them. Were a quantity for example of the article used for hemp in New Zealand, shown to a person in England, who had never before seen it, and was totally ignorant of its price, on being made accurately acquainted with its strength, durability, weight, absorbing qualities, and pliancy, as compared with real hemp, he would be able, knowing the value of the latter, to state pretty nearly what it actually sold for. But were a person, in the same country, perfectly ignorant of the value of pearls, and never having seen any, to be shown a string of them, and made acquainted with their qualities in relation to artificial pearls, and glass beads of various sorts, though knowing well the price of the latter, he would certainly be unable to assign the sum to be got for the former. Were a variety of alcoholic liquors to be presented to an individual quite ignorant of them, and of their value, and were he, changing from one to another, to partake, occasionally, freely of them all for months and years together, all other circumstances concerning them but their sensible qualities and effects being concealed from him, he would certainly be unable to fix their relative value. Were, in like manner, specimens of all the different fabrics used for female attire for the last ten years, with their relative durabilities ticketed on them, presented to a person of good taste, but perfectly ignorant of these matters, he would certainly also be quite incapable of coming near their actual relative cost [to purchasers in the market.] The same observation will apply to all other luxuries. As they compare with each other, not by their inherent qualities, but by the difficulty in procuring them, unless the comparative labor necessary to procure them be known, there is no means of fixing their relative price. It affords a rule, too, by which we may test what are, or are not, luxuries. Thus, I apprehend, that were a silver spoon, or sauce-pan, or vase, shown for the first time, to any person in the middle ranks of life, though ignorant of its value [selling price], yet seeing its beauty and susceptibility of receiving the most delicate impressions of the workman, and being informed of its durability, safety, and the saving of labor attending its use, on a fair estimate of these qualities, he would place it not very far below its present relative value to copper. He might, it seems to me, considering merely the qualities inherent in it, be willing to give for it twenty or thirty times what he would for the same article wrought in copper. He would, however, I should apprehend, be far from estimating similar articles fabricated of gold, at sixteen times the price of the same in silver. Supposing him possessed of real taste and accurate judgment, the difference between his estimate, and the actual comparative value [market valuation] of these metals, would mark how far they were, or were not, luxuries to people of his fortune.

The only rule, then, which people desirous of possessing luxuries can adopt for measuring what they will give for them, is the degree of difficulty of procuring them, the amount of labor which must be given for them. When they are satisfied that any particular article of the sort they are in quest of is used by other people, and that it cannot be had for less, they will pay the price demanded. They do not seek for the grounds of their determination in the utility of the commodity, but in its scarcity. Let a farmer go to lay out three pounds on lace for his wife, if he is assured that the dealer in that article to whom he applies will not charge him more than others, and that Mr. A's wife and Mr. B's wife wear the same sort, he will care little whether he gets for his money six or twelve yards, or whether it be two or three inches broad. All that he is concerned about is that he should get as much as other people. Let the same farmer think of purchasing some new manure for his land, he will conceive it necessary to ascertain both the effects of the article upon the soil he farms, in comparison with other manures, and its cost also compared with them. If he find that, compared with them, the cost is no greater, he will be inclined to purchase; if he find it less, he will conceive it so much gain; while it lasts it will be equivalent to a marle pit discovered on his own farm.

If a dealer imports a commodity having a shade of distinction scarcely perceptible considered in relation to the degree of enjoyment it gives, but sufficiently marked to distinguish it from other commodities of the sort, and if half a dozen people of rank adopt the use of the article as a sign of their superiority, it has all chances to enter into the consumption of every individual in the community who can afford it. In such cases, the price of the commodity depends [at first] altogether on the venders of it. But, as each of these wishes to sell as much as possible, and as he can do so most readily by underselling his neighbors, the price gradually falls under a free competition, until the dealers in it receive only the profits that the effective desire of accumulation, and the progress of improvement in the society measures out to them. At the end of the process the whole difference observable, if the article be completely a luxury, is a change of fashion. The principle of accumulation has not been led to grasp a greater compass of materials, nor has any addition been made to the general stock of the society: there has been merely the introduction of a new set of marks of distinction. The property in circulation is not augmented, but the coin has received a new impression, or got increased weight. It may, however, happen and very often does happen, that, during the process, a sort of factitious improvement is introduced, which, while it lasts, is sometimes nearly equivalent to a real improvement.

Suppose a merchant, seeking to strike out a new branch of trade, exports to some distant country, and sells there to advantage, an article of luxury the produce of the community to which he belongs, and in return receives for it a commodity, a simple utility in demand among his countrymen. Let the former commodity be lace, and the country to which it is exported E, and the latter commodity barilla, and country to which it is imported D. In process of time the trade increases, until a large quantity of lace is exported, and a large quantity of barilla imported. Suppose, farther, that the steady demand for the lace, joined to other circumstances, animates ingenuity to facilitate the process of manufacture, and that the article is before long produced at half the outlay it cost when first exported. In the ordinary course of matters, the diminished cost of production should be followed by a correspondent reduction in the price it is sold at in E. Two circumstances, however, may prevent this. The intercourse between D and E may be very difficult, and clogged by many obstructions, and the community E may be very numerous, and may easily absorb a large amount of the article. Both circumstances would help to diminish the effects of competition; the former by lessening the number of competitors, the latter by preventing the actual competition induced from operating fully. It might in consequence happen, that lace, though produced with double facility, [still] sold in E at nearly the same price as at first. If we suppose that commodity to be a pure luxury, this would be no disadvantage to E, for the quantity actually used at that price would serve exactly the same purpose as double that quantity at a price reduced one half by reason of the diminished outlay of labor: while, on the other hand, it would be so far an advantage to D, that it would place somewhere there the command of all the labor which in E was actually paid for. Among the members of the society D, double the quantity of barilla that the labor [indirectly] expended in procuring it was [equitably] entitled to, would somehow or another be shared. The advantage would not certainly, of necessity, have that healthy and vivifying effect which real improvement occasions, for it might not spread through the whole community, but might be dissipated in luxuries by the merchants, manufacturers, and artisans engaged in acquiring it. If, however, in other branches of trade and of manufactures for exportation, similar facilities were [generally] introduced, and similar large returns obtained, and if in all the departments of domestic industry great real improvements take place, the advance of the whole society would be uniform, and not much unlike what would flow from a universally real improvement.

Should two societies in the same way trade together in mere luxuries, a sort of factitious improvement [for them both] might be created by the effects of [an artificially] restricted competition. The merchants who engaged in the trade would, in the first place, acquire [the equivalent of] all the labor saved by the overcharge of the commodities they bought and sold, and these benefits might be in both societies more or less generally diffused.

When, on the other hand, by the removal of [such] restrictions, and the increased capacity of industry to fabricate the goods in request as luxuries, a free competition is induced, all these factitious advantages disappear. Each adventurer endeavoring to beat down his opponent in the foreign market, the productions of the industry of remote countries come to be offered there, for the lowest amount at which the strength of the principle of accumulation can permanently continue to produce them. They may even pass much below this; for vanity, capricious in its tastes, soon begins to despise altogether what may be every one's purchase, and leaves what it once highly prized as now vulgar and unworthy of regard. In the supposed case of the exportation of lace, that commodity might have triple the labor expended on it, and its quantity might be increased sixfold, and yet might bring in a smaller return than it did before. The ample revenues which the merchant, the manufacturer, the artisan, [previously] derived from the fabrication of such articles, become reduced to the lowest amount that may suffice to move their respective productive faculties. Other branches of manufacture share the same fate; the whole machinery of industry is clogged and encumbered by the heavy additional burden thrown on it, and distress and discouragement pervade the community.

. . . . . .

[To sum up this particular phase of our subject.] Restrictions [of any sort, brought about by wars or otherwise,] operate quite oppositely on the exchange of [pure] luxuries between communities, from what they do on the exchange of utilities. Their first effects are beneficial, while their ulterior effects may be injurious. The interdiction of a pure luxury occasions no loss whatever to the whole society. It can scarcely fail to produce a gain. If it diminish the whole amount of luxuries consumed in the society, that is evidently so much saved. If, as is more likely, the force of vanity be not weakened, it must at least be directed to other objects, probably to some domestic imitation of the foreign article. In such cases the successful imitators will demand and obtain prices yielding much larger profits, than their capitals would give in any other employments. The saving of labor, either in checking vanity, or in supplying it with less outlay, is gain to some individuals, loss to none. Competition, however, will in time reduce the price paid for luxuries, to the lowest amount for which the laborer and capitalist will exert their energies. As improvement can have no effect on domestic luxuries, and as they must always be rated by the real labor bestowed on them, they are ultimately the productions of all others least profitable to the society.

. . . .

There are, however, very few, if any, commodities which are purely luxuries. Although vanity is in part the cause of the estimation in which very many are held, and though it gives to some perhaps nearly their whole value, nevertheless it seldom exists in any alone. It almost always applies itself, as I have already observed, to something ministering in some degree to real wants or pleasures. There is beneath almost every luxury a substratum of utility of greater or less depth.

The effects, consequently resulting from the exchange between different communities, of very many commodities, are compounded of the results produced by the traffic in articles of utility and of luxury. As it is impossible in almost any case to determine accurately how far any article is or is not a luxury, there is proportional difficulty in ascertaining what are the precise effects resulting from the exchanges actually carried on between any two communities. There is one principle which may, in some instances, help to guide us. Almost all articles of which the consumption is conspicuous, the precise effects resulting from their physical qualities difficult to ascertain, and which, from their novelty, have not yet been subjected to the effects of a free competition, may be presumed to be in a great degree luxuries. In them, we may be sure, vanity has found a material on which she could easily fix, and from which there has been no opportunity of dislodging her.

The relative effects of restriction, and free competition, when opportunities have presented themselves of observing them, enable us, however, with some certainty to determine, how far the commodities subjected to their operation have been luxuries, or real utilities. In regard to articles supplying real wants, the more easy and unconstrained the communication, the more extended the production, the freer the competition, the farther, as we have seen, are the stocks of instruments of the societies exchanging carried towards the more quickly returning orders. Every step in advance in the course is equivalent, subject only to the risk of the communication being interrupted, to a real improvement. With regard to such commodities, any general evil resulting from overproduction is quite impossible. A partial glut, as it is termed, may indeed occur; but this, although a slight partial evil, [although an evil to particular persons], must be a general good. The commodity produced satisfying real wants, an increased supply of it must diffuse a general and sensible plenty. In regard to such commodities the reasoning of Mr. Say is, I conceive, conclusive. A general overproduction is an absurdity, for it implies the means of a general consumption, and would, in fact, be a general improvement. It would be as if the materials which nature has given to man were to receive powers in addition to those which they already possess, for satisfying his wants; as if the grain of the fields, the grass of the meadow, the trees of the forest, advanced more rapidly to perfection, as if the ore yielded up its metallic treasures with greater facility, the sun diffused a more genial warmth, and the earth rejoiced in universal and exuberant fertility. The increased provision for wants thus presented, must either be consumed, or applied to the formation of instruments to supply the demands of a more distant futurity.

But though these are the effects of increased facilities in the exchange of commodities in as far as they are real utilities, it is exactly the reverse in so far as they are luxuries. Restriction in the exchange of luxuries may be, and often is felt, as no diminution of enjoyment, but a great saving of labor, and the removal of that restriction may almost immediately oblige all, or many of the communities exchanging, to expend the whole amount of labor they had before saved. If then we find that increased facility of exchange, instead of diffusing plenty, spreads poverty, instead of carrying the stocks of the communities exhanging towards the more quickly returning orders, places them in those of slower return, we may assure ourselves that vanity must have been a very potent agent in giving to the commodities exchanged the estimation in which they were held.

Perhaps the most remarkable example that was ever presented, of general and long continued restrictions being at once and completely removed, is that which occurred in consequence of the general peace succeeding the final defeat of the Emperor Napoleon. A power which modern times cannot parallel, had been long exerted to bind up the commerce of Europe. It had been exerted in vain, for that commerce still moved, though it moved in shackles. The termination of the war undid them at once. The ships of the merchant again securely passed from land to land, and he again, without fear, exposed his wares in every market. Had the commodities thus largely exchanged, been altogether utilities, it is impossible but that a vast improvement must have been universally experienced, an augmentation of the resources of society every where felt. The havock and insecurity of war, and the waste of stock and labor attending it were done away with, and the whole energy and intelligence of the most powerful and intellectual race which possibly the world has as yet seen, were turned to the arts of peace, and the amelioration of the condition of man. Instead, however, of having to mark the progress of abundance, prosperity, and happiness, we are rather called on to note the prevalence of poverty and distress. It is, I apprehend, impossible, to explain the far extended oppression under which capital and industry have labored, but by admitting that they have applied themselves largely to objects, the direct effects of the attainment of which are worse than useless to society. Misery it is true is clamorous, happiness is quiet, and therefore the amount of the actual distress may sometimes have been made to appear greater than the reality; but admitting a large deduction for misrepresentation thence arising, there remain too many well authenticated facts and statements to doubt, that if freedom of intercourse and competition has produced good, it has also produced evil, and hence that luxuries have made a large part of the commodities in the production of which that competition has exerted its powers. We may observe, too, that countries producers of articles which cannot be accounted luxuries, have in fact derived great advantages from the facility of intercourse and increase of exchanges. Russia seems never to have made so rapid advances, as within the last twenty years, while in Great Britain protracted misery and distress were never so rife as they have been for the greater part of that period. Were European nations ranged according to [the character of] their productions, those two countries would probably be at opposite extremities of the scale of industry.

ARTICLE III.

OF THE OPERATIONS OF THE LEGISLATOR ON LUXURIES.

The legislator is always called on to provide a considerable annual revenue. He has to provide for the expenses incident to the conduct of present wars, to the burdens imposed by those of preceding times, to the construction and maintenance of public works, to the encouragement of science and art by premiums and otherwise, and to various other outlays. If any part, therefore, of this necessary annual expenditure, can be drawn from funds naturally dissipated in luxury, the art of the legislator will here effect a saving to the community to that amount.

Commodities which are mere luxuries, derive their value, as we have seen, from the difficulty of obtaining them. The amount of labor [and other costs of production] necessary to procure them, and which thus may be said to be embodied in them, is what makes them esteemed. It is through it that they become fit objects of vanity, marks of riches, things distinguishing their possessors from other men. It is of no consequence how this labor has been expended. It may have been given to ransack the depths of the earth as for diamonds, or of the sea as for pearls. All that the possessor of the luxury desires, is, to have a means of showing that he has acquired the command of a certain amount of the exertions of other men. It is a matter of indifference to him, what the difficulty is, to surmount which these exertions are necessary. Thus, were we to suppose that diamonds could only be obtained from one particular and distant country, and pearls from

OF LUXURIES AS OBJECTS OF TAXATION 287

another, and were the produce of the mines in the former, and of the fishery in the latter, from the operation of natural causes to become doubly difficult to procure, the effect would merely be that in time half the quantity of diamonds and pearls that it had before been necessary to employ for that purpose, would be sufficient to mark a certain opulence and rank. The same quantity of gold, or some other commodity reducible at last to labor, would be required to procure the now reduced amount, as the former larger amount. Were the difficulty interposed by the regulations of the legislators of the distant countries, it could make no difference to the fitness of these articles to serve the purposes of vanity. As in the case of a natural difficulty, an additional quantity of labor would be requisite to procure [on the market] the commodities in question, and they would, therefore, equally serve the purposes of vanity. Nor would it seem to alter the case, were the difficulty interposed by the legislator of the society consuming [but not producing] the articles.

For the sake of illustration, we may suppose that some particular society is possessed of a pearl fishery, from which its members are supplied with the pearls they use, and farther, that the case may assume the simplest form, that this society has no communication with any other. The fishery is situated in a particular bay, where alone, it is found, the animals yielding these concretions can live. The labor annually expended in procuring this luxury, amounts to a million days, or reckoning each day at two shillings, to one hundred thousand pounds. Each day's labor procures one hundred oysters; from which, on an average, one pearl is procured. In this state of things a discovery is made, similar to that which Linnaeus conceived probable. It is found, that, by a particular process, the diseased action in this creature, which, like ossification in the human body, produces a deposition of calcareous matter in its fleshy substance, instead of on the sustaining earthy portion of its frame, may be induced *ad libitum*. The effect of this discovery is to diminish very greatly the labor necessary to procure these substances. In process of time, every hundred oysters, instead of one, yield, on an average, five hundred pearls, consequently the amount of labor expended in procuring each might be little more than the five hundredth part of what it was.

The ultimate effect of such a change would depend on whether the fishery were free or not. Were it free to all, as pearls could be got simply for the labor of fishing for them, a string of them might be had for a few pence. The very poorest class of women in the society could, therefore, afford to decorate their persons with them. They would thus soon become extremely vulgar, and unfashionable, and so at last valueless.

If, however, we suppose that instead of the fishery being free, the legislator owns and has complete command of the place, where alone pearls are to be procured, as the progress of discovery advanced, he might impose a duty on them equal to the diminution of labor necessary to procure them. They would then be as much esteemed as they were before. What simple beauty they have would remain unchanged. The difficulty to be surmounted in order to obtain them, would be different, but equally great [would be less for the producer, but equally great for the consumer], and they would, therefore, equally serve to mark the opulence of those who possessed them. If we suppose the yearly expense of obtaining the pearls, and of collecting the duty on them, to amount to twenty thousand pounds, there would then remain to the legislator, a clear annual revenue from this source of eighty thousand pounds. This revenue would not cost the society any thing. If not abused in its application, it would be a clear addition of so much to the resources of the community.

Were the precious metals in reality, as Adam Smith seems to have conceived, mere luxuries, a tax imposed on them at the mines would have a similar effect to the hypothetical tax on pearls, which we have been considering. It would make a real addition of so much to the revenue of the community possessing the mines. In this case the tax imposed by the king of Spain on the gold and silver obtained from America amounting at first to half of the whole quantity annually procured, would not, unless among the first adventurers, have caused any diminution of the revenue of individuals, and its produce would have formed a large real addition to the general revenue of the society.

OF LUXURIES AS OBJECTS OF TAXATION 289

Neither in this case, however, nor perhaps in any other, have commodities altogether luxuries presented themselves to the operations of the legislator. They all, probably, derive part of their value from their utility, although in many instances the part it makes up may be very small. Hence a general tax upon almost any class of commodities, is a tax in whole, or in part, upon some utility, and abstracts something from the revenue of its consumers. All silk goods are perhaps in part luxuries to the majority of those who consume them. They are also, however, in a very great degree, and to all classes, utilities. There is a real beauty and durability in such fabrics, probably in many cases sufficient to warrant the higher price paid for them. A general tax, therefore, upon silks, though it would in part be a tax on luxuries, and, in so far, occasion no diminution of the [real] revenues of any one, would also in part be a tax upon utilities, abstracting a real amount from the funds [pleasures] of individuals. The same things will hold true concerning a great number of commodities. Pure vanity, and real enjoyment, have each a place, as we have seen, in the general expenditure of almost every person.

But though this is true of taxes levied generally on any class of commodities, it yet not unfrequently happens, that taxes on commodities of the same class may be so ordered as to fall nearly, or altogether, on luxuries. It may be, though a whole class of commodities have, under the appearance of luxury they exhibit, a considerable substratum of real utility, that yet individuals of the class, not differing from others in the quantum of utility they possess, may have some peculiarities serving to afford a hold to vanity, and to enable that passion to raise their value very high, by making them pass as marks of the superiority of one man over another. As these, therefore, differ from other commodities of the sort, merely in the amount of luxury embodied in them, a tax on them may be considered as altogether a tax on luxuries, giving a revenue to the legislator, and taking nothing from the society.[1]

[1] [The managers of the passenger traffic on European railways, and the managers of city theatres everywhere, make use of the principle here set

Alcoholic liquors, considered as a class, are probably, in a great degree, luxuries. They may in part be really useful, but certainly, speaking in the general, their consumption is not measured by the utility resulting from it. Some of them, however, agreeing with each other in the amount of utility they may possess, differ yet largely in the quantum of luxury embodied in them. Thus it is, I apprehend, very difficult to say whether rum, brandy, whisky, or gin, considering each with regard to its intrinsic qualities, is the preferable liquor. It seems probable that they are nearly alike in most respects, save their being more or less luxuries. In Great Britain rum is, I believe, at least double the price of whisky, and brandy still higher, the consumption, therefore, of the dearer article instead of the cheaper, must arise nearly altogether from vanity. In Canada, again, the price at which Scotch whisky is sold, is double the price of rum, and considerably above the price of brandy. The excess of its price above these other liquors must, therefore, be considered a luxury.[1] The chief part of the high price in England of rum and brandy, is made up of the duty paid to the government. In this case, therefore, the legislator would seem to derive a revenue from mere luxuries. Were such duties withdrawn, and were not the measure to lead to an increased and extravagant consumption of alcoholic liquors in general, it would have the effect of changing the sort of liquors consumed. Rum and brandy being as cheap as whisky, would come, with many people, to occupy the place of it, they would no longer afford a peculiar gratification to vanity, and that passion would fly off to some other article, fitted for its purpose, in all probability, not by the operations of the legislator, but by the real expenditure of labor or some equivalent to it. The society, considered as

forth. The "substratum of real utility," in the one case, is to see the play, and in the other, to be transported from one place to another. The managers artfully combine with these "utilities," through a system of classification, a means of attainment of social distinction.]

[1] The quantity consumed is small. It would in all likelihood be much greater, were it not for the difficulty of distinguishing it from whisky of the country, which sells at less than one fourth of the price. Scotch whisky brings 10s. per gallon; Canadian, from 2s. to 3s.

OF LUXURIES AS OBJECTS OF TAXATION 291

a body, would lose the advantages of the revenue before at the command of the legislator, and, considered as individuals, they would gain nothing. Certain classes among them would merely change the form of some of the characters, by which they marked to others their relative means and stations.

It would appear, then, that the powers of the legislator, when prudently directed in the taxation of luxuries, may be so exercised as to raise a considerable revenue, without trenching at all on the incomes of individuals. It is to be observed, that his proceedings in this way have a greater chance of success, when he levies duties on foreign, than on domestic commodities. Almost all commodities of home manufacture form large classes, running gradually into one another, and so not easily discriminated, or affording any very striking characteristics to serve the purposes of vanity. If we examine, for instance, the manufactures in Britain of cloths, or of malt liquors, we shall find in them all a great number of commodities differing very little from each other. If a heavy duty be then imposed on any of them, there is a considerable chance of its consumption greatly diminishing or ceasing altogether. Were porter taxed more highly than other malt liquors, there are so many sorts of ales which very nearly resemble it, or might be made to do so, that instead of being converted by the tax into an especial luxury, it is probable the consumption of porter would nearly cease. The imposition of a high duty on any particular sort of foreign wine, has not so great a tendency to diminish its consumption ; people would still drink claret, however highly it were taxed, because it has qualities sufficiently marked to distinguish it from other wines, and to make, therefore, its consumption capable of denoting a degree of present opulence, proportioned to the price it costs.

Some commodities of domestic manufacture are, nevertheless, much better fitted for the operations of the legislator than others. A duty, for instance, on the finer textures of cottons and linens, might perhaps be so levied as to make it nearly altogether a tax on luxuries. The fineness of the thread in these fabrics, affords a pretty conspicuous mark, and by raising the impost gradually in proportion to it, the more delicate sorts might, perhaps, come to be esteemed as adequate marks of a capacity to expend largely and so be converted into especial luxuries. In this case part of the expenditure of individuals, which is now dissipated in changing fashions, would be made over to the legislator, and might suffice to sustain some part of the public burdens.

All such duties, however, require to be laid on very gradually, else the consumption of the commodities on which they are imposed may very probably be stopped. Men have generally a very high opinion of the reasonableness of their conduct, and the correctness of their taste. They are apt to fancy that there is a real and very great enjoyment in expenses, which, in truth, have scarce anything to recommend them but the gratification they afford to vanity. In like manner, when any article rises suddenly and greatly in price, when in their power, they are prone to adopt some substitute and relinquish the use of it. In such cases the observation is forced on them, that the commodity is no better than it was before, and that, if then they sometimes used another for it, the best thing for them now to do is to confine themselves altogether to that other. Hence, were a high duty at once imposed on any particular wine, or any particular sort of cotton fabric, it might have the effect of diminishing the consumption very greatly, or stopping it entirely. Whereas, were the tax at first very slight, and then slowly augmented, the reasoning powers not being startled, vanity, instead of flying off to some other objects, would be apt to apply itself to them as affording a convenient means of gratification.

The chief practical objection to such imposts, as a source of revenue, is the expense of collection and the attempts generally made to evade them. The former diminishes the amount yielded by them, the latter is injurious to the morals of the people. Both are greater in commodities of domestic, than of foreign manufacture. In articles produced within the country, it is necessary to watch the whole progress of manufacture, and to guard against imposition at every stage. Commodities, on the other hand, imported from abroad, have only to be watched at the time and place of importation.

There is a case in which duties imposed on foreign commodities, have particular advantages. It not unfrequently happens that in manufactures which it is the object of the legislator to introduce, and carry to perfection within the society, the chief, perhaps the only difference, between the enjoyment afforded by the foreign and by the domestic article lies in the gratification the former affords to vanity. This is very generally the case in all commodities affording materials for such articles of dress as are seen by many, these being always in a great degree luxuries. I very much question, for instance, whether the passage of the manufacture of calicoes from Britain to America, has occasioned the wearers of calicoes in the United States any sensible diminution in the comfort, or in the pleasure arising from the perception of beauty, afforded by such articles. The standard is in such cases altogether relative, the pleasure given by any particular dress of this sort arising from its being as fashionable, and as becoming as the dresses of other persons, or more fashionable and more becoming than theirs, and the chief requisite for rendering any fabric fashionable, seeming to be that it be costly, and have novelty. The unrestrained introduction of British or other foreign calicoes would, therefore, in all probability, have been felt, merely as a change in fashion, not as an increase of pleasure or diminution of cost.

There are very many similar cases. As the great mass of commodities are in part utilities, in part luxuries, so, in transfering the manufacture of any of them from one country to another, it very frequently happens that, in as far as the article in question has real utility, the domestic soon equals the foreign variety. It is chiefly in a laborious finish, for the most part the result of the demands of vanity, that the former falls behind the latter. In such instances the operation of transferring the art from one country to another, by means of a protective duty, takes either very little, or nothing, from the revenue of individuals, and makes, it may be, a considerable addition to that of the legislator. Its general effects on the funds of the community, are [accordingly] directly and indirectly, to advance the absolute capital of the society by the introduction of a new art, and, during the process, to give a considerable revenue to the legislator for the attainment of public objects, without encroaching at all, or but in a very slight degree, on the returns made by the industry or stocks of individuals.

. . . .

[The leading objection to the foregoing, founded on the principles of Adam Smith,] proceeds on the assumption, that what is true concerning the wealth of individuals, and sufficiently explains its increase and diminution, is also true concerning the wealth of societies, and fully explains the causes of its increase and diminution.

If, other circumstances remaining unaltered, a single individual in a society acquires the power of purchasing some article entering into his system of consumption, at less cost than before, he is by so much a gainer, and the change is equivalent to a proportional increase in [his] revenue.[1] Transferring this fact to societies, it is held that the revenue of every society is increased in exact proportion to the diminution in the cost of any article entering into its system of consumption, and diminished in proportion to the increase in the cost of any such article. By how much, therefore, any operations of the legislator add to the price of any commodity, by so much, it is said, they always, and in every case, take from the revenue of the society. When, therefore, by taxing foreign luxuries, the legislator raises their price, it is asserted that he proportionally diminishes the general revenue; [and thereby the general stock or capital, since capital can only augment by accumulation from revenue].

The answer to this objection is, that though as every commodity consumed by an individual, derives the estimation in which it is held from something in some most complicated system of persons and things constituting the society of which he is a member, while that system remains in all its parts unchanged, whatever gives him the command of a greater portion of the particular commodity than before, necessarily increases the amount of commodities, which, compared with others, he possesses, and thus makes him, as compared with them, so much richer; yet, if any commodity become universally cheaper throughout a whole society, as this implies a change to a certain extent in the system of things, comprehended

---

[1] [See the first paragraph of Number 9 of the Residua.]

with persons in the term society, it may be that the revolution may affect the causes giving estimation to the commodity in question, and that, until we know whether or not this be the case, and how it operates, we act with unwarrantable rashness in transferring rules true concerning individuals, to societies, and in asserting that a general diminution in cost, is, in all cases, equivalent to a general increase of revenue, or a general augmentation of cost, to a general diminution of revenue. That if there be any class of commodities, the estimation of which depends wholly, or in part, on their power to mark the possession of a certain relative superiority, or a command greater or less of the labor of other men, then the generally diminished cost of such commodities, lessening their power to mark the desired distinction, and taking thus in a like degree from that for which they were altogether, or in part, esteemed, either makes no change in the general revenue, or a smaller change than that indicated by the amount of the diminution. That as regards commodities serving merely, as Mr. Storch expresses it, for marks of opulence, their fitness for the purpose is diminished as their cost becomes less, and, therefore, a diminution of their cost produces no increase, or no proportionate increase, of general revenue, and an increase of it, no diminution, or no proportionate diminution of general revenue.[1] That thus, though, were the power of procuring a string of pearls for a few hours labor given to any individual European, it might very greatly increase his wealth, yet, the same power given to all Europeans, would produce no increase,

[1] It is remarkable that neither Adam Smith, nor Mr. Say, nor Mr. Storch, although they have stated distinctly enough in various places, that many commodities derive their whole, or the greater part of their value, from the gratification they afford to vanity,—their power to mark the superiority of one man over another,—seem to have perceived that the admission was fatal to the majority of their theoretical conclusions. They consequently have not thought it necessary to adduce any reasons to show that the operations of the legislator, on such commodities, may not have the beneficial effects indicated in the text. Mr. Say, indeed, has the following passage.

"De ce que le prix est la mesure de la valeur des choses, et de ce que leur valeur est la mesure de leur utilité, il ne faudrait pas tirer la conséquence absurde qu'en faisant monter leur prix par la violence, on accroît leur utilité. La valeur échangeable ou appréciative n'est une indication de l'utilité donnée de la production réelle, qu'autant que cette valeur est abandonnée à elle même

or no proportional increase to European wealth, and, on the contrary, as the facility of purchase by putting the wearing of pearls out of fashion, would probably render the stock of these articles in the possession of individuals, valueless, it would, in all probability, proportionably diminish the amount of wealth actually existing.[1]

. . . .

et que l'action des hommes qui font un marché est entièrement libre ; de même qu'une baromètre n'indique la pesanteur de l'atmosphère, qu'autant que le mercure peut s'y mouvoir avec facilité." p. 5. vol. I.

So far as the above is applicable to luxuries, it is evidently nothing but an *ipse dixit* dressed in a metaphor,—a sort of argument too *economical* to admit of an answer. If luxury, "Luxe de l'ostentation," be, as Mr. Say himself says, "une consommation qui n'a pour objet que cette dépense même ; une destruction de valeur qui ne se propose d'autre but que cette destruction" (vol. II. p. 225), it surely matters not to the consumer how this value be given to the commodity.

[1] [See " Note M " in the Appendix.]

[We get in the above statement of principles an important suggestion as to the erroneous tactics hitherto pursued by most advocates of unimpeded foreign trade. The mistake has been made of taking up the defence of the consumer—of commiserating him for the burdens he has to bear because of tariffs. We now see that such is the nature of expenditure for consumption (a large part of it) that he is going to be burdened in any event. If the government does not tax him he will tax himself.

The line of battle should be drawn not in the realm of exchange but in that of production. The question should be asked, how does the protective policy as actually carried into practice affect the forces of production—the prime movers of industry. Does it promote or hinder them ?]

ARTICLE IV.

OF THE ART OF THE BANKER.

PART I.—OF BANKING IN GENERAL.
PART II.—OF PARTICULAR SYSTEMS OF BANKING.

PART I.[1]

THE business of banking, seems to owe its foundation and extension, to its capacity for giving room for the developement of the benefits, and for restraining and remedying the evils of the system of credit. The operations which the banker executes in a great society, have more than the advantages of those performed by the system of *virements* in France, or Russia, and by the petty store-keeper in a remote American settlement, and avoid many of the inconveniences of both. He is the instrument, through which the mass of the exchanges, taking place in the community, is performed. It is his business to furnish the means of transacting all exchanges that the condition of the society requires, and it is the business of all individuals having many such exchanges to effect, to make application to him for the means of transacting them.

In a great society, a person extensively engaged in business, may, in a short time, have transactions with twenty, thirty, or a hundred individuals; his circumstances can be known but to a few of them, nor is it possible for him to produce to each satisfactory evidence of his own capacity to discharge his

[1] [This is the omission from Chapter VIII., where Rae began his discussion of the subject of credit.]

engagements, or to give him the security of others for their performance, and even could he do this, it would be insufficient for the purposes of the greater part of them. If such a person, however, really possessed funds in trade and manufacture, if he really owned a stock of instruments requiring a constant change and transfer with those in the hands of others, he might find means to satisfy one individual, the banker, of his capacity to execute these exchanges in reasonable time, or procure others to be responsible for his doing it. It is then the business of the banker to give him the means of doing so, and he accordingly lends him money when he requires to add to his stock of instruments, that is to buy, and receives money from him again, when he transfers instruments to others, that is, when he effects sales. Every person engaged in business doing the same, the banker is the general lender, and receiver of the society.

The mechanism of banking is managed in two ways. The one is by discounting bills, that is, by giving money immediately, for the obligations by which one man contracts to pay money to another, at some future time, deducting a part, the proportion of which is determined by the order in which instruments stand in the society, and by the length of the period. This method is analogous to that of *virements*, but far preferable. Thus, an individual who holds an obligation by which another binds himself to pay him the sum of two thousand pounds in six months, were he in some parts of Russia, would be justifiable, were he confident of the solvency of his debtor, to contract obligations to that amount, and payable at the same time. Were he then desirous of having something transferred to him, of the value of two thousand pounds, his granting an obligation to that amount, and payable at six months, might help to make the two transactions of easy arrangement. But, supposing that he were desirous of having a number of small transfers made to him, that he were to grant a proportional number of obligations, that the persons to whom he granted them were again to grant others, still smaller and more numerous, and that these were again to be subdivided and reunited, it is evident that the mass of affairs, would become so complicated, and the number of individuals concerned in them so large, that the trouble of arranging them would be excessive. This system is of consequence, as has been already observed, of limited application. But when an individual gets a bill discounted, the transfers he effects with the bank bills he receives, occasion no future trouble to himself or others.

The system of bank credits is the second mode, in which the business of banking is managed. It is somewhat analogous to that carried on, through the aid of the books of the North American store-keeper. The banker gives the means of effecting any purchases which those dealing with him are desirous of making, and, when they sell, gives them immediate credit for the amount they receive. He is not, however, like the store-keeper, urged on, by the dread of a stock of goods lying on his hands too long, to allow people to run accounts with him, whose credit is in any means doubtful. He is a dealer simply in credit, and it is his business, before giving credit, to demand such security as may satisfy him that he can sustain no loss, and this being granted, to afford the requisite accommodation on reasonable terms.

The advantages which the banker derives from being the general lender of the community, arises chiefly, from the peculiar sort of money he lends. It is not specie, but merely an obligation to pay in specie. But as all who engage in business have to return cash to him, it is equally good to them as specie, and through them is equally well received among the other members of the community. Thus the money of the banker comes to make a great part, or nearly the whole, of the circulating medium.

The benefits which the society receives from the system, when there are no defects in the conduct of it, seems to be threefold.

1st. As far as it extends, the expense of the circulating medium, the expense which men in business must otherwise be put to by being obliged to have a quantity of cash always lying by them to meet sudden emergencies, is done away with. When a man wants cash, he goes to the bank for it; when he has cash, he carries it to the bank. Money never lies idle.

2d. It does away with all deficiency in the circulating medium [in respect to the individual].[1] When the system of instruments which belong to an individual, is defective in any part, he can at once supply the defect, and when it is redundant, he has no difficulty in disposing of the superfluity where it may be usefully employed.

3d. It does both, without the evils otherwise attendant on the substitution of credit for coin. The dealings of men of prudence and character, are not so mixed up with those of improvident and suspicious persons, as to make the one bear the burden of the losses sustained through the folly or dishonesty of the other. Every instrument, as its formation is pushed on by the industry of the members of the society, is moved directly to its proper station. It neither runs the risk of being subjected to remain useless, owing to the expense of moving it, nor of being misplaced or destroyed in the process of moving it.[2]

The tendency of these three effects, flowing from the banking system properly conducted, is to carry the instruments subject to the operation of exchange, to orders of more quick return, than they would otherwise have occupied. The outlay expended on them is not so great, and they sooner make the expected returns. The accumulative principle receives in consequence, a stimulus, that enables it to embrace a larger compass of instruments, and the general stock of the society is soon proportionally increased. Greater facility is also given to the division of employments, from there being no extraneous obstruction to the additional exchanges required, and hence new branches of business arise. From both these circumstances, the number and amount of exchanges increase.

The money of the banker, compared with gold and silver, as a medium of exchange, would thus seem to be not only less expensive, but more efficient. When the circulating medium in

---

[1] [That is, the solvent individual never finds himself without the means of making a purchase which comes within his general financial ability. See *passim.*]

[2] [The statements in this last paragraph are obviously an exaggeration. But the burden of business risk is certainly greatly mitigated under a régime of banking.]

any country is specie, probably far the larger portion of it lies idle. Every merchant, in such a country, has a quantity of gold or silver, proportioned in amount to the business he carries on, doing actually nothing, but only waiting to do whatever may offer. The strong boxes of all the merchants in the country, always hold, therefore, a large portion of its capital in inactivity. In a country, on the other hand, where the bills of the banker form the circulating medium, the quantity of money lying for any time idle [outside the reserve of the bankers themselves] is insignificant. No money is retained, but for a specific purpose. In Scotland, for example, every merchant places in the hands of the banker, all the cash for which he has not immediate use.

Were we, therefore, to confine the advantages derived from the institution of banks, in any community, to the substitution of a cheap medium, for a dear one, we should make an imperfect estimate of them.[1] If, for instance, the circulating medium in any country be one million in coin, and if that be superseded by paper, should the quantity of paper in circulation be found to amount also to one million, it would indicate a great increase in the transfers effected, and would show, either that a larger compass of materials had been brought within reach of the accumulative principle, or that employments had been more subdivided, or that both these circumstances had occurred.

From the same causes, the effects of a recurrence to a metallic currency, and the compulsory substitution of one million of specie, for one of paper, would be far from being limited to the expense of the bullion employed in the operation. It would, besides this, render impracticable a multitude of transfers, that might otherwise have taken place, disorganize the whole system of exchange, place the stock of the society in orders of slower return, and put a mass of materials, which the accumulative principle had before been able to grasp, beyond its reach.

The extent to which the banking system may, in any country be carried, seems to depend on four circumstances.

1st. The amount of the science, skill, and population exist-

---

[1] [This is a covert criticism of Adam Smith. See Part II. of this article.]

ing in the country, to work up the materials it affords, and the abundance of these materials.

2d. The strength of the accumulative principle, the opportunity it has had to operate, and consequent division of employments, approach of instruments to the more slowly returning orders, and accumulation of stock. These two circumstances determine the amount of the possible exchanges, and, consequently, [at any given level of prices] of the [amount of] money [of all kinds] that may be employed in effecting them.

3d. The general intelligence, sagacity, and integrity of the members of the community. A person greatly deficient in any of these respects, is one with whom a banker would not wish to deal. But, these qualities are of those giving strength to the effective desire of accumulation; this circumstance, therefore, may be considered as merging in the last, the general strength of the accumulative principle.

4th. The efficiency and security of the system of banking adopted.

On the other hand, the benefits to be derived from banking, in proportion to its extent, would seem to be greater, the nearer instruments are to the more quickly returning orders, and the greater consequently the scarcity of specie. Where, therefore, the accumulative principle being strong, and from the implied intelligence, and honesty of the community, the system of banking extensively practicable, but from want of time to work up materials to more slowly returning orders, instruments are at those of quicker return, there the operations of the banker are peculiarly beneficial.

We have, perhaps, sufficiently enlarged already, on the three first of the circumstances referred to. It only remains, to show the chief points of connexion of the last of them, with the principles it has been attempted to explain. To do so, it is necessary to refer to the occasional evils resulting from the system of banking, diminishing its general utility. They may be reduced to two.

1st. The money which bankers circulate, must be the representative of real property. It must be exchangeable for some commodity, or commodities, equal to the amount at which it is rated. If it may be always exchanged for specie, or for some proportion of the general revenue abstracted for the purposes of government, it will be a representative of something real. But it sometimes happens that bankers squander, or waste, the funds provided for payment of the demands to which they are liable, and this being discovered, their money becomes valueless, and those holding it as an equivalent to capital, sustain loss to the amount they hold.[1] The loss thus sustained, both in itself, and in the general diminution of confidence in banking transactions and retardation of exchanges consequent on it, makes it a matter of great importance to every mercantile community, to have banks of indubitable solvency established throughout it. (It were beyond the present purpose, to inquire into the particular system and regulations that may best produce such a result. There are, however, two general observations, arising from the nature of things, which naturally present themselves.

When capital is largely accumulated, and at orders of slow return, there will be very many, who will be disposed to allow their funds to remain in that employment, and be content with the moderate revenue thus produced to them. When, on the other hand, they are at orders of quicker return, there is a great temptation to divert the fund, set apart for these purposes, to speculations promising great gain, but sometimes producing great loss. Banking will consequently be in general safest, where capital is most largely accumulated.

Again, as no possible precaution can prevent a company of bankers from acting dishonestly, who are willing to combine for such a purpose, for they can only be required to produce statements drawn up by themselves, where there exists a great deficiency of real principle, and a proneness to defraud, banking becomes dangerous or impracticable.)

2d. The second evil arising from the practice of banking, has its origin, in the system of credit itself; and the shock

---

[1] [That is, those holding a claim on the bankers as an equivalent to real funds. "Capital" of course with Rae means instruments other than the peculiar instrument of exchange, money. The proper term for an accumulated stock of money is funds. Sometimes in this Article Rae uses this term, but more often falls carelessly into employing the term capital.]

which, as it is founded on prevailing opinion, it is liable to receive from whatever shakes public confidence.

Every person engaged in the formation and transfer of commodities, and adopting the system of credit as the medium of transfer, is indebted to some individuals, as, in turn, other individuals are indebted to him. The stock also of instruments he has on hand, allows him to offer a certain amount of commodities for sale, and requires him, if he continue his business on the same footing, to purchase certain other commodities, and pay for certain amounts of labor. What is owing him, and payable within a given time, may exceed what he owes others, payable within the same time, or may equal it, or come short of it. What he is able to sell others within a given time, may also exceed what he requires to buy within the same time, or may be equal to, or less than it. It will always be the case, too, that individuals will look forward for the means of discharging the debts they have contracted, not only to the debts owing them by others, but to the sales they expect to effect. Were this to happen only to persons of really abundant capital, there would be no reason to fear the non-performance of engagements contracted. But it also happens to those, whose capitals have been reduced by misfortune or imprudence, and therefore, there are always many in every mercantile community, whose ability to discharge their obligations is more or less doubtful. When, therefore, any cause operating extensively, and prejudicially, on mercantile transactions occurs, it generally happens, that there arise cases of incapacity to meet engagements, and, as one man depends for the means of discharging his debts, on the debts others owe him, that embarrassment and distress spread throughout the whole mercantile body. The experience of the misfortunes attending this state of things, leads every one engaged in business, when he thinks there is reason to fear its approach, to endeavor to withdraw himself from the danger, by avoiding to contract obligations to pay. There is consequently a general diminution of purchases, and a general temporary fall in prices.[1]

---

[1] Market price, which is fluctuating, is here spoken of. What is termed the natural price of things, or their general average price, is that alone treated

OF BANKING

But while prudent people are thus able to secure themselves from evil, they increase the difficulties of those, who have contracted obligations to pay, in dependence on the proceeds of sales to be effected; and some of these becoming incapable of obtaining the means of meeting their engagements, their failure increases the general distress, and farther lessens the number inclined to purchase.

At this juncture, the affairs of the banker undergo a revolution. For, as the number of buyers diminishes, there is less money requisite for transacting the business of the community, and this overplus naturally returns on him. But while less money is really wanted to execute the business of the society, he is called on to furnish as much, or probably more. The debts those dealing with him formerly contracted have to be paid, while the sales of commodities, the means by which it was anticipated that part of the funds for that payment would be procured, have much diminished.

The situation of the banker becomes therefore at this crisis, very critical. He cannot, in justice to himself, grant all the requisite accommodation, and yet, his refraining from doing so must aggravate existing evils. As specie is, in such a state of things, the most desirable of commodities, he has reason to fear that a large portion of his money will be returned on him, which he will be required to replace with gold or silver, and he knows that if a suspicion of his solvency arise, he may be required thus to replace the whole of it. If he be unable to meet these difficulties, his failure adds very much to the general mass of misfortune, and farther diminishes public confidence.[1]

The natural termination to such a state of things, would

---

of in other parts of this inquiry, it being only the permanent causes affecting the increase and diminution of stock, that it was proposed to investigate. On this account, the view here given of phenomena resulting in a great measure from the operation of temporary causes, is somewhat confined and imperfect.

[Hence, for example, the subject of pure profit is almost wholly neglected by Rae; that being essentially a matter dependent on "temporary causes."]

[1] [It is noteworthy that Rae had so grasped the situation even at the early time at which he wrote, that he represents that it is a different sort of pressure than a "run," which a solvent banker first experiences in times of crisis.]

U

seem to be the diminution of contracts, and consequently of debts, progressively diminishing the amount of payments, for which it is necessary to provide. This termination is retarded by the struggles of those whose real funds, in proportion to the extent of their business, are smallest, and whose motives to engage in fresh transactions, are chiefly the hopes of extricating themselves from the embarrassments in which present transactions have involved them. It is also more injuriously retarded, as has been observed, by the failure of those engaged in the business of banking.

The liability of the mercantile community to be largely affected by such sudden pressures, must depend, in a great degree, on the peculiar circumstances of the country, and nature of the employments and trades carried on in it.

It must also be dependent on the system of banking, that is there pursued, and its capacity to furnish funds where there is real capital; to check unsafe and gambling transactions by withholding funds from those desirous of extending hazardous speculations, though deficient in capital; and to pursue its operations steadily and confidently notwithstanding any general embarrassment. To attempt, however, an enumeration and comparison of the different systems of transacting the business of banking, which have been adopted in different times and places, would involve us in inquiries of so complicated a nature, that while to discuss them partially would be unsatisfactory, to do so fully would lead too far from our present object. I reserve therefore the few observations I have to make on the subject, to another place.

PART II.

According to the view of banking given in the foregoing outline, it is an art which time, and what we call chance, have wrought out of the circumstances of European society, and the use of which is to quicken the exhaustion of instruments, by facilitating exchanges. But, according to this view of the subject, the consideration of two circumstances generally combined with banking transactions, is omitted. The business of banking has been very often combined with the payment and receipt of the revenue of the state. Whatever the government receives, in lieu of the precious metals, or other commodities, in payment of the imposts it levies, will have the value of that for which it is taken in exchange. Government may so give the value of the precious metals to paper, or any other material, and, for its own convenience, may circulate the money which it in this manner issues through the medium of a bank. Thus the Bank of England may be said to be founded on the transactions of this sort, of the British government. This is, however, a circumstance by no means necessarily connected with banking. Indeed, I think there is reason to believe, that, from the great fluctuations thus introduced into what is called the money market, by the magnitude of the transactions of the state, the union of the two, when it takes place, operates injuriously on the general system of exchange of the country.

The other circumstance to which I allude, is the exchange of the precious metals between different countries. Banks, as the great dealers in these metals, are necessarily exposed to the inconvenience of having to provide a supply for the demands occasioned by fluctuations in the business of different countries. Although, however, this circumstance is always more or less intimately connected with the business of banking, it is not necessary for our purpose to examine the effects resulting from it.

We may confine our attention, therefore, altogether to the consideration of the art, as a means of facilitating exchanges within any society. A brief statement of its condition in Scotland, a country in which, to judge from the circumstances attending its introduction, and the practical benefits arising from its operation, it has probably arrived as near perfection as any where, may sufficiently serve the purpose of showing the manner in which the mode of its operation may be explained by the principles I have endeavored to develop, and how it seems to attain the power of communicating the advantages it is capable of bestowing, and of avoiding the evils to which it is sometimes liable. The Scotch banking system is also better fitted for an example, both as it was the one directly presented to the observation of Adam Smith, and from which, accordingly, his ideas on the subject seem to be chiefly taken, and because it is not directly connected with the issue of government paper, or with the passage of coin or bullion from country to country.

Banks in Scotland are both what are termed banks of deposit, and of circulation. They are the receivers and transferrers of the money, or what is equivalent of the capital of others, and they are issuers of paper money of their own. Their business is confined to what is the proper occupation of bankers, transactions springing from the exchanges effected through the medium of credit. They avoid, therefore, to grant loans, unless for the purpose of facilitating exchanges. Previously, however, to examining the operation of the system, it may be well to direct our attention to the circumstances of the parties with whom bankers everywhere have to deal.

When, in consequence of the business of banking being established on a sure basis, in any community, the system of credit comes extensively to prevail, the owners of the whole stock of the society are divided into two classes, the one consisting of those having in their possession a greater stock of instruments than what actually belongs to them, the other having a less stock than what belongs to them. The larger proportion of the owners of stock, belong sometimes to the one, sometimes to the other class, but the circumstances of many place them permanently in the one or the other.

Individuals engaged in the forming, transporting, and exchanging of instruments—the farmers, manufacturers, and merchants of the community—have occasion to employ in their different businesses, sometimes a larger, sometimes a smaller stock of instruments or capital. At one time, for example, the state of the land the farmer cultivates, requires a great outlay for seed-corn, for tilling, and manuring it and for wages paid to laborers. At another time the returns from it in the shape of grain, fat cattle, and other instruments and commodities are proportionally great. At the former period the farmer may not have a sufficient stock of his own, and may wish to borrow certain instruments [or rather, the means to purchase them], at the latter he is in a condition to lend.

In a similar manner, the fluctuations of business render a merchant sometimes a borrower, sometimes a lender. For example, two merchants in Great Britain are engaged in the timber trade, the one in that carried on with Prussia, the other in that with Canada. A change takes place in the business, from the duty on Prussian timber being lessened. The Canadian timber trade being thus no longer profitable, the merchant whose capital [funds] was embarked in it, withdraws it from that trade. He employs a portion in an experimental adventure to Prussia, but the larger part he has no immediate use for, and is, therefore, in a condition to lend to others. On the other hand, the merchant who had been accustomed to trade to Prussia, knowing the details of that business, and having a correspondence established there, is able to employ with advantage a much larger capital than he possesses. He wishes to borrow instruments, that is, commodities to export to Prussia, and to have the use of ships for the double transport. Fluctuations, such as these, and innumerable others, occasion continual variations in the stock which every merchant, or other individual engaged in any sort of business, is capable of employing with advantage. Sometimes, therefore, the business of every one is expanded much farther than his own stock would permit, at other times it is contracted into so narrow limits, as not to give employment to the whole of it.

Again, in every society there are many individuals who cannot themselves employ the instruments they own. A merchant, for example, dies, leaving a large stock of instruments of one sort or other to his widow, and young children. These they cannot employ. They must either convert them into cash, which, placing in security, they may gradually expend as their occasions require, or they must lend them to others who will pay for their use. On the one hand, young men of ability, who have been bred to any business, although, perhaps, they may have very little or no capital, may yet be able to put instruments with which they may be entrusted, to so active use, that they may yield more than the ordinary returns, and so, after paying for the usual profits, may leave a considerable surplus as the reward of their exertions.

The Scotch system of banking seems well calculated for admitting the easy passage of individuals from the one to the other class. Its distinguishing characteristic is that the banker allows interest on all sums deposited, from the moment of deposit, and that, on sufficient security, he is always ready to grant the loan of as small, or as large an amount, as may be required. When he lends to individuals, by discounting bills, or by what are termed bank credits, he becomes the real owner of a proportional amount of the stock of instruments they hold, and in this way may be said to be the owner of a part of the general stock of instruments of those dealing with him, equal to the amount of what he has lent. In reality, however, it is not altogether he who owns them, but rather they who have given him the larger part of his funds in the shape of deposits. These have all come to him with money in the form of coin, of paper money of other banks, or of his own money, or of an order for his own money, and in place of it have been content with a pledge that it shall be returned on demand, and that in the interim interest will be allowed on it. By this arrangement the banker, in effect, transfers to them a portion of his claims on the instruments held by those who are debtors to him, and part of his right to a portion of the returns made by them. Thus, while the merchant formerly trading to Canada, instead of employing the money he receives for sales of his existing stock of timber in purchasing other goods, and in freighting other ships for that market, pays it into the bank, the merchant trading to Prussia is drawing money out of the bank, for the purpose of extending his trade with Prussia. The effect produced is, in so far, similar to that which would have resulted from the Canadian trader lending part of his capital [directly] to the trader to the Baltic. It differs from such a transaction, however, in three respects: 1st. These two individuals might be unknown to each other, and might have no means of ascertaining their respective plans; 2d. The merchant trading to Canada would probably have either less or more spare funds, than the merchant trading to Prussia required; 3rd. He might, also, probably have occasion to call for them, for his own purposes, at a time when it might be inconvenient, or impossible, for the other to replace them. The banker, on the contrary, is always ready to receive or to lend.

Throughout all the occupations carried on by the different members of the community, similar circumstances occur. One tradesman, or mechanic, is laying by funds for building a dwelling house, another is expending all the funds he has laid by, and, perhaps, borrowing a little more, for the purpose of finishing a dwelling house. While the farmer is depositing in the bank some part of the proceeds of his sales of grain and cattle, the corn merchant and the butcher are drawing funds from the bank, for the purpose of assisting them to purchase these commodities.

It will thus be found, that the person making the deposit, is one who has just transferred to others, who can employ them at the moment to more advantage than he, some instruments which he held, and that in return he receives a claim to that amount, on the funds [assets] of the bank, and of interest on it till paid. These funds, [assets] however, consist chiefly of debts owing to the bank by the community at large, and that interest is drawn from the profits arising from the stock of instruments effectively owned by the bank, and lent by it to the individuals with whom it deals. Hence the person making the deposit is one having transferred a part of his stock of instruments to an individual, and receiving in lieu of it a share of the claim of the bank, on the general stock of instruments owned by those indebted to it. In this way the bank may be considered as a broker negotiating between those, the condition of whose business requires them to borrow, and those, the condition of whose business disposes them to lend, and generalizing the transactions of both. It is not by any means, however, only a broker. Besides the fluctuating deposits, it has a large capital of its own embarked in the business. This is chiefly owned by individuals whose circumstances place them permanently in the class of lenders, persons retired, or retiring from active business, or widows, etc., who, selling off their stock, employ their funds in this manner.

This system probably yields as many advantages as any hitherto discovered, and avoids, as well as may be, the chief evils to which the business of banking is subject.

1. By means of it all possible exchanges are made at the least expense; and with the greatest facility. Every person is prompted to sell because the money he receives yields an immediate return. Every person having it in his power to turn any commodity to good account, has the means afforded him of obtaining possession of it.

2. The capital [funds] which bankers own, or hold, is liable to be embarked and lost by them in imprudent speculations; or, through partiality, to be lent to a few individuals who may squander it in the same manner. This seems to be best guarded against by there being many stock holders, and a large capital. In the banks to which we refer, this is generally, though not always the case.

The knowledge which the banker acquires, by means of the system of bank credits, of the state of the affairs of those dealing with him, is probably somewhat greater than can be obtained by the mere discount of bills. It gives him the sort of information, which one would acquire of the affairs of another, by having the care of his purse. I believe, also, that persons dealing with the Scotch bankers, are somewhat more strongly excited than those dealing with other bankers, to vigilance in providing funds to meet positive engagements with them, as the slightest failure of any individual in any such transaction, occasions his sureties being called on to pay up his cash account, ruins his credit, and renders it impossible for him to continue his business. It is probable, therefore, that this system has considerable efficiency in checking rash and imprudent speculations, by withholding funds from those most likely to run into them.

3. The large amount of stock subscribed, and the subscribers being severally responsible to the amount of all the property they possess, give so great confidence in the stability of the banks, that nothing but some very great revolution in the affairs of the society, or some great convulsion in the money market, would be sufficient to shake it. Owing to the system pursued, the possibility of any great disturbance of the money market is prevented. This forms the fourth circumstance to be noted.

4. I have observed in the preceding part, that, when any

reverse happens to the trade of a community, the diminution of sales which is the consequence of it, while it renders it necessary for those, whose business, as compared with their capital [ready money], is much expanded, to borrow money to meet the engagements which they have entered into, gives a redundancy of money to those whose business, as compared with their capital [ready money], is small, and who have contracted to receive a great amount of money, and to pay only a small amount.

According to the system of banking which prevails in England, and in most countries, all individuals in the latter class will have a greater or less amount of cash lying by them useless. They are afraid to lend it, owing to the prevailing embarrassments, and, where the banker allows no interest on money deposited with him, they have no particular motive to induce them to lodge it in any bank. But, when a person intends to keep money lying by him, he will be apt to prefer coin, to paper, the former is the securest of any sort of property, the latter may possibly be insecure. He will more especially be inclined to prefer the former, if he have the least suspicion of the stability of the bank issuing the paper. It is thus that, at such seasons, what are called runs upon particular banks, are very apt to arise, and both to bring ruin on the bank, and increase the general embarrassment. But wherever, as in Scotland, the banker allows interest on all sums deposited, no one thinks of keeping money by him. The very classes too, it may be remarked, who are most apt to commence these runs, petty shop-keepers and tradesmen, have in Scotland, in general, bank credits, and are continually striving to put as much money into the bank with which they deal, as the necessity of their business will permit. In Scotland, therefore, the banks, owing greatly, no doubt, to the guarantee of a very large capital prudently managed, but, also, as I conceive, in no inconsiderable degree, to the tendency of the system to bring into them all the spare funds of the society in the shape of deposits, have not for fifty years been exposed to any dangers or inconveniences of the sort, and in the midst of the severest commercial distress, and the ruin of the banking establishments of the sister kingdom, have always maintained their course steadily, and been able to apply the resources of the community to carry those through the crises, whose embarrassments had arisen, not from the bankrupt state of their affairs, but from the pressure of the times.[1]

5. Banks have very often issued an overabundant supply of their particular money, and it has been depreciated. An effectual remedy for this, one would be inclined to conceive, would be their being obliged to convert it, on demand, into gold or silver. Many persons, however, do not think that this is sufficient, and believe, that, notwithstanding, an over issue may take place. If so, the Scotch system, by its tendency to return on the bank all money not in immediate use would seem to be a pretty effective check on the occurrence of such an evil.

Banking may be fitly described, as a generalization of individual credit transactions. Every system of banking generalizes them to a greater or less extent. The more complete the generalization, the more completely does the system perform its functions, and the nearer it comes to the perfection of art. The Scotch system, viewed as an art of this sort, seems to discharge its function well. Whatever spare capital [funds] the turns of business may there throw into any individuals hand, he finds it for his advantage to place in the bank; whatever additional capital [funds] they may require of him, he easily procures from the bank. The facility with which it operates may be best seen, by contrasting it with the English system.

In England, an individual dealing with a banker, is expected to leave in his hands an amount of capital [funds] as a deposit, for which he receives no interest. It is from this that the profit of the banker is derived. When, therefore, a person in the course of business has a greater portion than usual of unemployed capital [funds], he finds there no immediate advantage in placing it in the banker's hands. He, therefore, probably, will not place it there so promptly, as he would in Scotland. The effect of this tardiness is more especially felt at those critical periods to which I have referred

---

[1] See the correspondence between Lord Liverpool and the Chancellor of the Exchequer and the Bank of England, in 1826, in Hansard's *Debates*.

in the preceding part, when, in consequence of a general decrease of the amount of sales, persons whose means [affairs] have been most expanded, are under the necessity of borrowing to a larger extent than they had anticipated. If, on such occasions, they whose business has been contracted within narrower limits than their capitals [means] would have admitted, and who, in consequence of avoiding to purchase, have a larger surplus capital [purchasing power] than usual in their hands in the shape of money, retain it there, instead of placing it in the bank, the banker is restrained from making the advances he otherwise would, and a violent check is given to the operation of the credit system, sufficient to give a beginning to convulsions more extensively deranging it.

This system, also, as compared with the English, adjusts itself with greater precision to the actual circumstances of the two great classes of the community, the lenders and borrowers, to whose transactions it serves as the instrument. When, in consequence either of the progress of accumulation, or of misfortunes befalling the industry of the country, instruments are placed in more slowly returning orders, and profits fall, borrowers should pay less, and lenders receive less, for the use of capital. And reversely, when profits rise, more should be paid by the one class, and more received by the other. This is naturally brought about where a certain rate is paid for funds deposited, as well as for those drawn. Under such a system the banker cannot afford to have any capital [any money beyond the necessary reserve] lying dormant. He must, therefore, preserve the proper proportion between the funds deposited in his hands, and those drawn out of his hands. When the former become too great, which will be the case when trade is dull, he lowers the rate of interest which he charges his customers, and, also, that which he gives them, and thus diminishes the amount deposited, and increases that drawn. He does just the reverse and produces directly opposite effects, when trade becomes more lively, and profits rise. In England, on the contrary, the state of trade has no direct effect on the interest which bankers charge, and the due proportion between borrowers and lenders is not so well maintained.[1]

[1] Joplin on *Currency*, p. 108.

APPENDIX

The advantages derived from any system become apparent, by considering the consequences that would result from its being abolished, or from its actions being impeded. On this account I shall state three hypothetical cases, with regard to the system which we are now considering, as an example of the effects of banking in general.

In the year 1826 it was proposed in the British Parliament, to enact a law putting a stop to the circulation of one pound bank notes, the chief money of Scotland. The bankers maintained that in this case they would no longer carry on business. Let us suppose, that the proposal had been adopted, and the effect had really been utterly to abolish the business of banking in that country, and unless in barter, to make all buying and selling to be transacted in coin, either in ready cash, or in cash paid when the period, to which credit had been limited, expired.

In considering the effects of such a change, we may divide all transactions now taking place in Scotland, and concerned in the question, into those effected by bank bills, or as they are termed, bank notes, and those effected by checks on some bank.

1. Of those now effected by bank bills, of which the majority are what are called one pound notes, [it may be said that without these bills,] every purchaser, that is, every person in business, would be obliged to have continually lying by him, to answer occasional demands, a certain sum [of actual money] proportional to the extent of his business, and when preparing for some extraordinary occasion, for a length of time previous he would be collecting and hoarding up funds sufficient for the purchase or purchases he intended making. A large part of the money of the country, would, therefore, be constantly lying idle, doing nothing, but waiting for something to do. Let us suppose that we are in Scotland at the present moment, and that bank notes being able to hear and answer questions, we take at random a parcel of one pound notes, and interrogate them as to what their employment is, and how they discharge it. They would doubtless answer: "the service we render is to pass from hand to hand, for the purpose of making exchanges." "Do you ever lie idle for any time?" "No. Every one that gets hold of us immediately passes us

to some other person, either to pay some debt, or to make some purchase, or if not, carries us to the banker, who sets us out again on the same round. Sometimes, indeed, we get a few days, or a few weeks rest, in the desk of a small country dealer, or some such person, who has to wait that time, perhaps, before he can collect a dozen of us to send to the bank, but this is seldom, and as it were by chance." Let now the banks be done away with, and, instead of bank notes, let us have to ask the same questions of sovereigns. Their answer would be, " we are employed in the service of people who collect us for the purpose of buying some thing, or things, with us, when the chance presents itself. We are lying continually idle, therefore, for longer or shorter intervals, waiting till this chance cast up. Sometimes we are collected in money bags for weeks, sometimes for months, and unless when we get into the hands of very necessitous persons, we each of us expect to be put by in some place of security, along with others of our brethren, and with them to wait the chance of being called out to effect some exchange, after which we again return for a time to inactivity."

What in the supposed cases must be true of a particular set of bank notes, or a particular set of sovereigns, would be true of all bank notes, and of all sovereigns, and hence the amount of exchanges effected in any particular year, by means of three and a half millions of bank notes (about the present circulation of Scotland), must be far greater than would be effected in the same time, under the suppositions we have made, by three and a half millions of sovereigns. The latter could not both be effecting exchanges, and lying idle.

2. But, besides the exchanges made by means of bank notes, a great amount of exchanges are effected by orders or checks on the banker. Were there no banking system there in existence, these, also, would have to be effected by the medium of money, either ready money, or money paid after a certain time, but certainly, in some way or other, through the instrumentality of money. There would require, then, to be a farther provision of sovereigns, to effect the large amount of exchanges now managed by a few strokes of the pen of a banker's clerk.

What would be the addition which these two circumstances would render it necessary to make to the circulating medium, in order to bring sovereigns to approximate in efficiency to the bank notes, the place of which they occupied, might be difficult to determine. The proportion of the one to the other, might be as 3 to 2, as 4 to 2, as 6 to 2, or as 8 to 2, or perhaps still higher; it is very certain, however, that the one would be much greater than the other. After all, it would only be an approximation. As what will happen can only be conjectured, not known, every person engaged in business would occasionally err in his calculations, and would sometimes have commodities offered him which he would wish to purchase, but for want of cash would be unable to purchase. The two circumstances referred to, the additional expense of exchanges, consequent to the additional money [specie] necessary to effect [any given amount of] them, and the diminution of exchanges consequent to the want of the money [conventional means of payment] necessary to effect them [expeditiously], united, would mark the direct loss the community sustained by the abolition of the banking system. The indirect loss would arise from the check given to the accumulative principle, by the diminished quickness of return of instruments—by what would be termed the dullness of trade—and the diminished accumulation of stock consequent to it.

But such a supposition as that we have made, could not possibly come to be a reality. When the art of banking has once been introduced into a country, the advantages resulting from it, are too great to admit of its being altogether abolished. There will always be some generalization of credit transactions, some recognized mode of transferring from hand to hand, promises to pay, made by one individual to another. The enactments of the legislator may act on the art so as to make it more or less effective, but they cannot prevent the practice of it. I shall, therefore, make another supposition, and assume that the measure proposed having been adopted, sovereigns took the place of bank notes, and that, notwithstanding, the banks continued their operations as before.

In this case the banks, by the supposition, giving sovereigns out, and receiving them again, in the same manner as they had their own notes, the community in general would have been sensible of no other alteration but that of handling gold instead of paper, and they would have had the advantage of some additional security against the danger of the failure of the banks, and against disorders consequent on drains of gold from abroad. But this supposition, also, is inadmissible. The diminution of the paper money issued by the bankers, would have proportionably diminished their profits. The amount of one pound bank notes there circulating, being something over two millions, their circulation would probably have been curtailed by the measure by nearly two millions. This at five per cent. is not much short of half of what they make by the whole funds deposited in their hands, which have been estimated at about twenty millions, and on which they gain one per cent., the difference between what they charge those who borrow from them, and which they give those who lend to them. Their profits must, therefore, have been greatly diminished by the measure, and unless we suppose that bankers in Scotland have more than the ordinary profits of stock, which, where there is so active a competition, cannot well be, capital would have been withdrawn from the business,[1] or the business would have undergone a change. It is probable that the latter circumstance would have happened. The banks would either have made more than one per cent. difference between what they allowed and what they charged for money, or, as is more likely, they would have changed the system of bank credits. The business of the small dealers, tradesmen and farmers, who have credit with the banks, is transacted mostly by one pound notes. Bank bills exceeding five pounds rarely pass into their hands. Under the supposition, therefore, this class would have circulated but very little of the banker's paper; he, consequently, would have declined granting them credit, in this way, and confined his credits of this

---

[1] It may be observed, that there is a great difference between Great Britain and the United States in this respect, because in Great Britain the government funds [debts] afford an advantageous investment for the capitals of individuals, widows, etc., who in this continent are under a sort of necessity of placing it in banks. In this, and in many other respects, as in the distance from other nations, and the increased difficulty in replenishing the stock of bullion when exhausted, the situation of the two countries is very different.

sort to merchants and others, whose transactions being large, made them the circulators of the paper to the issue of which he was confined, and whose business, consequently, would have been more profitable to him. The facility of exchange among the small dealers would have been greatly abridged, and through it, that among the whole community would have been somewhat lessened. The real amount of loss that would have been in consequence sustained, it is not necessary to our purpose to attempt to fix. Almost all persons practically acquainted with the business of the country, believed that it would have been very considerable, and, in consequence of their urgent representation, the measure in contemplation was abandoned.[1]

If I have succeeded in placing clearly before the reader my ideas concerning this somewhat intricate subject, he will, I think, perceive, that there exists an essential difference between the nature and operation of the money of the banker, and that of other money.

In communities where the art of banking has no existence, money may be defined to be a commodity, of which every person in the habit of making [many] changes, keeps a [considerable] supply by him, for the purpose of effecting them.

In a community, again, where the art of banking has been established, as in the instance of Scotland, if we confine our attention to those who have dealings with the banker, the money he issues[2] may be fitly described as counters which he gives them for the purpose of arranging their transactions with one another, and which they return to him immediately they are arranged, that they may be rated on his books

---

[1] [Rae neglects to mention one circumstance much emphasized by recent writers, that is, that the one-pound note in Scotland is quite necessary to enable the banks to maintain their extensive system of branches, which carry reliable banking facilities even into the smallest hamlets. The small bank-note furnishes a cheap "till-money," without which branch banking on any large scale is too expensive.]

[2] [That is, the money which he pays out and receives. "Bank money" in this paragraph is not "banker's money," that is, bank credit currency which we ordinarily speak of as being "issued"; it is actual money, specie, as used in connection with a system of banking. See below.]

according to the place they occupy as borrowers of part, or as owners of part, of the general funds which he holds. An individual who has a deposit in a bank draws from it, we shall say, the sum of £1,000, and lessens by that amount the deposits in the bank, and for which it has to pay interest. But, of course, he intends to put it to some use, that is, to make some purchase or purchases with it, or pay for some before made. The person or persons to whom, for this purpose, he transfers it, by the supposition dealers with the bank if they have no immediate use for it, will directly carry it to the bank, and then the general deposits and loans of the bank will be the same as before, but the bank accounts of the particular depositors and borrowers engaged in the transaction will have suffered an alteration. If, on the other hand, any of those individuals, among whom the £1,000 is distributed, or all of them, have use for the sums they receive, that can only be to make some immediate purchases, or to pay for some before made. In this way, after passing through a less or greater number of hands, the £1,000 the banker has issued finds its way back to him, and, as far as his business is concerned, he is exactly in the same situation as before he issued it. The situation of the person who took out the money, and that of them who return it, is altered. One holds a greater stock of instruments, and the debtor side of his bank account is proportionally greater, the others hold a less stock, and the credit side of their bank accounts are proportionably greater. The former has transferred a part of his claim on the general stock of instruments, and has in lieu of it the possession of some particular instrument or instruments, and the latter have done the reverse. The bank money, therefore, has merely served the place of counters, by aid of which the customers of the bank settle their transactions, and finally determine their relations to its stock. During the time these transactions were in progress, there was a proportional diminution in the amount of interest which the bank had to pay its customers, and, if the counters it gave them were merely pieces of paper costing it little or nothing, this would be so much clear gain to it: if they were gold, the expense of procuring them would exactly balance the gain.

If there be a plurality of banks, as the bankers in that case exchange their notes with one another, the series of transactions produced are substantially the same, unless in so far as the business of one bank may be extending, that of another contracting, a circumstance which is generally of little moment to the community.

It is only when the banker's money passes out of the range of those having transactions with him, that it comes to hold the place of other money. While it is in their hands, it performs the office that other money would, and in this respect, if it be paper money, he gains an advantage not directly springing from the exchanges managed by his funds. Individuals, however, who do not deal with any bank, where banking is properly managed, are persons whose affairs do not require them to keep [much] money by them, and by the agency of both classes, it is, therefore, preserved in continual motion and employment.

I have entered into a longer detail on this subject than I had intended, from my desire to make apparent the distinction stated above, in regard to the superior efficiency of the money which the banker puts into circulation,[1] whether paper or gold, as compared with that which exists where the art of banking is unknown, and where there is either no generalization, or an imperfect generalization of transactions performed through the medium of credit.

It will be seen, that the view I have attempted to give of the whole subject of exchange, is quite opposed to that exhibited in the *Wealth of Nations*. Adam Smith sets out from exchange, and makes it, and the division of labor consequent on it, the source of stock, whereas I have endeavored to show that exchange is the result of the increase of stock, and subsequent division of employments, that the necessity for its existence is a circumstance retarding the increase of stock, and that the benefits of the art of banking spring from the facility which that art gives to the process.

---

[1] [Apparently John Stuart Mill followed Rae in that passage of his *Principles* (Bk. III. c. III. sec. 3), where he speaks of the "efficiency of money" as an expression in some degree preferable to "rapidity of circulation."]

As exchange may be said to be the commencement of Adam Smith's system, and as money is the instrument of exchange, he assumes it as a first principle, that while the exchanges remain the same, the same amount of money is necessary to transact them. Bank paper, he, therefore, concludes, will exactly equal in nominal value the specie circulated before its issue. If it exceed this amount, it will return upon the bank, if it fall short of it, the vacancy will be filled by specie. This principle, which Adam Smith, as is observed by Mr. Say, has introduced into speculations on this subject, is thus epitomized by the latter author:

"Taking it for granted, then, that the specie, remaining in circulation within the community, is limited by the national demand for circulating medium; if any expedient can be devised, for substituting bank notes in place of half the specie, or the commodity, money, there will evidently be a superabundance of metal money, and that superabundance must be followed by a diminution of its relative value. But as such diminution in one place by no means implies a contemporaneous diminution in other places, where the expedient of bank notes is not resorted to, and where, consequently, no such superabundance of the commodity, money, exists, money naturally resorts thither, and is attracted to the spot where it bears the highest relative value, or is exchangeable for the largest quantity of other goods; in other words, it flows to the markets where commodities are cheapest, and is replaced by goods, of value equal to the money exported."[1]

He goes on to prove that the national capital must be augmented by the specie exported, and fixes the utmost quantity by which it can so be increased, at one tenth of the annual product or revenue of the nation.

Now I maintain, that to effect the same transactions, it requires far less banker's money, whether that money be paper or specie, than was required of the money in existence before the establishment of banks, the celerity of motion making up for the deficiencies of quantity; that what Adam Smith asserts concerning the comparative efficiency of the two kinds of money circulated by consumers and dealers, holds true of

[1] Say, B. I. c. XXII. Am. edit. Vol. I. p. 246.

that money [even though it be specie alone] of which the bank forms the centre of circulation, as compared with that, which, where there are no banks, circulates slowly and after intervals of inactivity between dealer and dealer; that the one by "a more rapid circulation, serves as the instrument of many more purchases than the other"; and, consequently, that if the same number of transactions only takes place after the establishment of banks, as before their introduction, then much less money will be necessary, and if the same money be circulated, the fact indicates, that a great addition has been made to the business transacted, and still more if the money circulated exceeds that formerly circulated. It is this last event, that, I conceive, generally takes place. In this, as in other instances of real improvements, the [ultimate] effect is contrary to what might have been anticipated, the greater facility in performing the operation bringing so much greater a compass of materials within its reach, that the occupation given to the art, instead of diminishing, increases, and by the subdivision of employments, and abandonment of barter, money comes to be so much more used as an instrument of exchange, that on the whole, the quantity of it employed is augmented, in the same way, as when a road is much improved, though one horse may be sufficient to transport what three did before, yet the commodities transported so increase, that there are, notwithstanding, thrice the number of horses employed.[1] This is especially the case in new countries, where, from causes already specified, money before the existence of banks is excessively scarce.

If the reader have still any doubts on the subject, he may, I conceive, satisfy himself of the accuracy of this view, by reference to the pages of the *Wealth of Nations* itself. Adam Smith, by no means, limits the advantages of banking as practised in Scotland, to the substitution of paper for specie, and the direct fictitious capital thus created. On the contrary, he thinks that every person dealing with the banker, that is,

---

[1] [This theory of displacement and expansion respecting employment for actual money in a community making extensive use of banks, may be further developed. See the article on the "Distribution of Money," by Prof. O. M. W. Sprague, in the *Quarterly Journal of Economics*, for August, 1904.]

every person engaged in business, derives individually very great advantages from the system. These advantages are resolvable into the circumstance, that every such person is free from the necessity of keeping any money by him. Whatever demands are made on him he answers by means of his cash credit, or by discounting a bill, or bills. In this way " partly by the conveniency of discounting bills, and partly by that of cash accounts, the creditable traders of the country are dispensed from the necessity of keeping any part of their stock by them unemployed, and in ready money, for answering occasional demands."[1] Now it is certainly very remarkable, that it did not strike Adam Smith, that if all the creditable dealers in the community, that is, the great majority of those who before the establishment of banks would have kept money by them, will by the facilities given by the art, be dispensed with the necessity of doing so, and can still carry on equally extensive transactions, the money requisite to transact the general business of the country must be diminished by that amount. If, for example, according to the estimate he makes, the specie in circulation in Scotland before the introduction of banking was about one million sterling, after the establishment of that art, had the exchanges effected remained the same, a much less sum than one million would have been sufficient to perform them; for all that money would have been useless which it had before been necessary to keep in the coffers of the different dealers, and which formed the great mass of the then circulating medium, or rather of the medium [half circulating and half stagnating] through the intervention of which exchanges were transacted. If, then, a million had been still employed,—if a million of the banker's paper had superseded a million of coin,—it would have indicated, as I have stated above, a great increase in the transfers affected, and would have shown, either " that a larger compass of materials had been brought within reach of the accumulative principle, or that employments had been more subdivided, or that both circumstances had occurred."

According to Adam Smith, the bank saves each dealer from keeping by him in ready money, all that amount which it

[1] Book II. c. II.

advances him by means of the cash account it opens with him, or by discounting the bills he presents. What in this way, then, all the banks advance to all the dealers, deducting from it the amount of paper circulated, must be so much which they save them from being obliged to keep by them. But this is the employment to which, where banking is properly conducted, bankers devote their whole funds, and by this mode of reckoning, the saving effected by them in Scotland might be made to appear equal to thirty millions of specie. Were banking, however, as a distinct business, totally abolished in that country, the event certainly would not bring into it thirty millions of specie. The effects produced by such an event would consist in a diminution of the number of exchanges, and, consequently, of the division and subdivision of employments, and of the capacity given to materials; [and also the bringing about of] the transaction of many exchanges by barter, and the generalization of a large amount of them by transfers from hand to hand. Specie would only come in, in sufficient abundance to make up the balance.[1]

To conclude; in my opinion the notion from which Adam Smith sets out, and which, since his time, has kept possession of all speculations on this subject, and been the foundation of many important practical measures,[2] is essentially erroneous. According to him, there is always a certain sum of money necessary to carry on the transactions of every society, the amount of which is proportioned to the transactions carried on. This is termed the circulating medium, and, whether it be bank paper, or specie circulated by the banker, or coin used for the purposes of exchange where there is no bank, it is reckoned always in quantity proportioned to the transactions carried on. On the contrary, it seems to me, that when once a bank is established in any community, the money circulated

[1] [Of course these last statements are exaggerated. Not the same amount of business, to be sure, but something like the same amount would still be transacted on a lower range of prices. But it is nevertheless true that one effect of the supposed occurrence would be to introduce barter to some extent, along a margin of the use of money, where barter did not before exist.]

[2] As for instance, the contraction of issues by the bank of England in 1826, (the immediate cause of the disasters of that year,) and the legislative enactments on British currency for the last twenty years.

among those who are its customers, serves merely the purpose of counters for arranging their transactions, performing the same part as a multiplicity of checks, operating upon their several accounts, might accomplish. It is not a fund *kept* for making exchanges, but an instrument applied for [and brought into use] at the time exchanges are to be made, and operating upon the real fund kept for that purpose, viz., the claim which the bank has on the general stock of the community, the specie deposited in its vaults, and the other items making up its capital [assets], which, like the coin in the old deposit banks of Italy and Holland, constitute that part of the general stock, really performing the function of exchange.

If this be the case, it follows that the more perfect as an art banking becomes, the less, *other circumstances being equal*, is the amount of the circulating medium required, and the greater the saving to the community. It also follows, that a system of banking, considered merely as a means of transacting exchanges taking place in the ordinary course of affairs within the community, approaches nearest to the excellence of art, when it most effectually secures its funds from being squandered, and when the counters employed by it in its operations, issue from it, pass through the hands of its customers, and find their way back to it most easily and quickly. The former circumstance diminishes the risk of loss from this mode of effecting exchange, the latter diminishes the expense of it.

It may farther be observed that the popular notion, that the advantages of banking are limited to the substitution of paper for specie, and the creation to that amount of a fictitious capital is altogether erroneous. The advantages derived from this source are rather contingent, than essential. They fall chiefly to the banker, and, as he may be considered as a broker having the care of the funds of certain of the lenders of the community, for the purpose of distributing them among the borrowers, and having to be paid for the trouble, the expense, and the risk of loss attending his business, this mode of paying him may be the most convenient that can be devised. The real advantage however of the art, arises from its [efficient] application of the floating loans [that is, the funds possibly available for making loans] of the society to the purposes of exchange; and, instead of the paper money issued being the cause and the measure of the good derived from it, the less the quantity of such money, in proportion to the business transacted with it [that is, the greater the amount of transfer of credits on the books of the bank in place of issue of notes], the smaller the expense of the business of exchange to the trading community, and the greater the benefits the banker bestows on it. And, again; in cases where bank paper makes the general currency, instead of the partial or total abolition of banking, only requiring the substitution of a quantity of specie equal to the paper withdrawn from circulation, it would, in proportion, as it were partial or total, compel the substitution of a much larger quantity of specie, or a proportional diminution of the exchanges before transacted; and, in either case, would place the instruments belonging to the society in more slowly returning orders, lessen the amount of materials within reach of the accumulative principle, and eventually occasion a proportional diminution of the national stock.

ARTICLE V.

OF THE *WEALTH OF NATIONS* AS A BRANCH OF THE PHILOSOPHY OF INDUCTION.

[OF THE SPIRIT AND METHOD OF SCIENCE.]

It will be perceived that there is an essential difference between the modes of investigation which I have followed in the preceding pages, and those guiding the speculations of the celebrated philosopher, from whose opinions I venture to dissent. Where the principles of investigation are different, the conclusions arrived at can hardly agree; and I scarce think, therefore, that I should assist the reader in forming an opinion on the subject, by entering into a particular discussion of the points in which we are at variance. The views I have endeavored to unfold must, in so far, stand alone.

It so happens, however, that concerning the principles of investigation themselves, there is a common standard to which the disciples of Adam Smith refer, and on the rules drawn from which, I also conceive, the determination of the questions debated must ultimately rest. Adam Smith has been said to have made political economy a science of experiment, a branch of the inductive philosophy.[1] Now, I apprehend, that the spirit of the philosophy of the author of the *Wealth of Nations* was completely opposed to the inductive philosophy—the philosophy of Bacon, and that he never intended that that work should be received as if established on it. If the reader

[1] Say's Introduction and note on Storch, p. 23, tome I.

agree with me, he will probably consider that the whole discussion here, in a measure terminates. In placing before him the reasons for my belief, I shall confine myself, as much as possible, to transcribing the words of the *Novum Organum*, on the one side, and those of Adam Smith, in some of his speculations, on the other.

Lord Bacon affirms, that there always have been, and must be, two sorts of philosophy—the popular, and the inductive; or, as they might perhaps be denominated, the philosophy of system, and of science. In the one, the mind explains natural phenomena according to its preconceived notions, in the other, it traces out, by a careful interpretation, the real connexions between them.[1] The former will always be the more popular,

---

[1] "Nos siquidem de deturbanda ea, quæ nunc floret, philosophia, aut si quæ alia sit, aut erit, hac emendatior aut auctior, minime laboramus. Neque enim officimus, quin philosophia ista recepta, et aliæ id genus, disputationes alant, sermones ornent, ad professoria munera, et vitæ civilis compendia, adhibeantur, et valeant. Quin etiam aperte significamus, et declaramus, eam quam nos adducimus philosophiam, ad istas res admodum utilem non futuram. Non præsto est; neque in transitu capitur; neque ex prænotionibus intellectui blanditur; neque ad vulgi captum, nisi per utilitatem et effecta descendet.

Sint itaque (quod felix faustumque sit utrique parti) duæ doctrinarum emanationes, ac duæ despensationes; duæ similiter contemplantium, sive philosophantium tribus ac veluti cognationes; atque illæ neutiquam inter se inimicæ, aut alienæ, sed fœderatæ, et mutuis auxiliis devinctæ; sit denique alia scientias colendi, alia inveniendi ratio. Atque quibus prima potior et acceptior est, ob festinationem, vel vitæ civilis rationes, vel quod illam alteram ob mentis infirmitatem capere et complecti non possint (id quod longe plurimis accidere necesse est,) optamus, ut iis feliciter et ex voto succedat, quod agunt; atque ut quod sequuntur, teneant. Quod si cui mortalium cordi et curæ sit, non tantum inventis hærere atque iis uti, sed ad ulteriora penetrare; atque non disputando adversarium, sed opere naturam vincere; denique, non belle et probabiliter opinari, sed certo et ostensive scire;—Atque ut melius intelligamur, utque illud ipsum quod volumus ex nominibus impositis magis familiariter occurrat; altera ratio, sive via, *anticipatio mentis*; altera, *interpretatio naturæ*, a nobis appellari consuevit." Præf. II. *Instaur.*

"Utcunque enim varia sint genera politiarum, unicus est status scientiarum, isque semper fuit et mansurus est popularis. Atque apud populum plurimum vigent doctrinæ, aut contentiosæ et pugnaces, aut speciosæ et inanes; quales videlicet assensum aut illaqueant, aut demulcent." Præf. *Inst.*

"Quinetiam significamus aperte, ea, quæ nos adducimus, ad istas res non multum idonea futura; cum ad vulgi captum deduci omnino non possint, nisi per effecta et opera tantum." Lib. I. c. xxviii.

OF SCIENCE *VERSUS* SYSTEM-BUILDING 331

and on account of its facility of explication, and its fitness for the purposes of argument, will maintain its place in the discussion of all subjects of general interest; while the latter must be confined to a few, its spirit being difficult to seize, above the grasp of the commonalty, and only to be comprehended by them in its effects.

It is not difficult to perceive the foundation on which each of the two systems rests.

Necessity obliges men to attend to the phenomena around them, to mark their actual successions, and to name them. They have thus a store of general facts, and of regular expressions for them. These, however, refer not to the laws of the general system themselves, but to the phenomena or events, the consequences of those laws.

Their farther discussion regarding them may be undertaken for the purpose either of *explaining*, or of *investigating* them. If for the former, they will refer to principles already admitted; that is, to known modes of succession. If for the latter, they will search for the causes on which those common successions proceed. An example will render this plain.

In the earliest stages of society, and before speculation commenced, men would make some general observations concerning the motions of the different bodies about them. They would observe, for instance, that, unless prevented by some obstacle, most bodies fall to the earth. Adopting this observation as a general rule, when they saw one so falling, they would conceive of the event as a usual or natural occurrence. A savage, when, in traversing the forest, he sees a rotten branch break off and fall to the ground, thinks of it as an event which is a necessary consequence of its nature, and, if his language furnished the expression, might say it was a natural motion in it as a heavy body. Were he to see the same broken branch moving rapidly through the air upwards, or horizontally, he would conceive of it as not proceeding from its own nature, but from some disturbing cause, and might call it a motion produced by violence. He would observe, too, that some substances, as air, and what he calls fire, rise upwards. He would so conclude, that all light bodies ascended. In the same manner, the heavenly bodies seem to him to have naturally a circular motion.

Let us now suppose that the two sorts of philosophy: 1st. the explanatory or systematic, and 2d. the inductive or scientific, in pursuit of their respective objects, apply themselves to the consideration of the complicated series of phenomena, connected with sensible motions of all sorts.

As what is conceived to be already known requires no explanation, the philosophy of system takes things which, because familiar, are admitted as obvious, as the media for explaining all other things. To do otherwise, were to undertake a work foreign to its objects. In this way, under its hands, the practical rules of the observer, become the speculative principles of the philosopher. Motion is divided into natural, and violent. Certain bodies have a natural tendency downwards, others upwards, others to move in a circle. From these principles, the whole phenomena are explained in a plausible manner, and arranged in a systematic form. Such was the plan of the philosophers of Greece, and such their pseudo science of motion. It is evident, that however it might systematize and explain facts already known, it could not conduct to new truths. It could not lead farther than the principles from which it set out, and these evidently embraced not the laws of the general system of things, but only circumstances, the results of those laws.

The philosophy of induction has for its object the discovery of truth. It seeks for the laws regulating the general system. As it is the aim of the other to explain plausibly, its aim is to investigate strictly. What, consequently, are to the one ultimate principles, are to the other collections of facts, the causes of which are to be inquired into. When, therefore, this philosophy applied itself to the consideration of the phenomena of motion, it pronounced the whole antecedent system factitious and foreign to its objects, and commencing their investigation sagaciously and diligently anew, it discovered the real and simple laws regulating the various series of these events.[1]

---

[1] Etiam quum de causis motuum aliquid significare volunt, atque divisionem ex illis instituere, differentiam motus naturalis et violenti, maxima cum

To which of those opposite sects does Adam Smith belong? and on which of these two modes are the principles guiding his speculations framed?

To me it appears that his philosophy is that of explanation and system, and that his speculations are not to be considered as inductive investigations and expositions of the real principles guiding the successions of phenomena, but as successful efforts to arrange with regularity, according to common and preconceived notions, a multiplicity of known facts.

My reasons for this opinion are drawn, 1st. from the object at which his philosophy aims: 2d. from the methods which he adopts to attain it: 3d. from the consequences which have resulted from his labors. I shall arrange the proofs for the justice of this conclusion, which I purpose submitting to the reader, according to these three heads; contrasting in each the spirit and consequences of his speculative principles with those of the inductive philosophy.

I. According to Adam Smith "Wonder, and not any expectation of advantage from its discoveries, is the first principle which prompts mankind to the study of philosophy, of that science which *pretends* to lay open the concealed connexions that unite the various appearances of nature;[1]—philosophical systems are to be considered as mere inventions of the imagination to connect together the otherwise disjointed and discordant phenomena of nature."—"A philosophical system is an imaginary machine invented to connect together in the fancy, those different movements and effects, which are already in reality performed."[2]

---

socordia, introducunt; quæ et ipsa omnino ex notione vulgari est; cum omnis motus violentus etiam naturalis revera sit,—ista mere popularia sunt, et nullo modo in Naturam penetrant. *Nov. Org.* Lib. I. lxvi.

[1] Διὰ τὸ θαυμάζειν οἱ ἄνθρωποι καὶ νῦν καὶ τὸ πρῶτον ἤρξαντο φιλοσοφεῖν, etc. Arist. Lib. I. Cap. 2. Metaph.

[2] These passages are quoted from one of his posthumous works: "The Principles which lead and direct Philosophical Inquiries, illustrated by the History of Astronomy, of Ancient Physics, Logic, and Metaphysics." It may perhaps be thought that in this work he represents only what he conceives to be the actual path of philosophy, not that which it should pursue. I do not think so, because the declarations of his particular friends intimate the contrary; thus his editors say, in reference to the fragment on Astronomy, that it

It is needless to say that this account of the object of philosophy is quite opposite to that given in the *Novum Organum*. The passages already quoted may show this and many others might be adduced. It is throughout the endeavor of the founder of the experimental philosophy to hold out truth itself, and the benefits to be derived from it, as its object; to show that this we can never reach by any effort of the mere reasoning and imaginative faculties, or in any other manner than through patient induction;[1] and that that framing of systems explanatory of things already known is foreign to its purposes.[2]

II. Philosophy being thus, according to Adam Smith, an art addressing itself to please the imagination, it gains its end by searching for some common and familiar observation, and making it serve as the means of connecting any series of interesting events, to the consideration of which curiosity may direct the attention. "In the mean time it will serve to confirm what has gone before and to throw light upon what is to come after, that we observe, in general, that no system, how well soever in other respects supported, has even been able to gain any general credit on the world, whose connecting principles were not such as were familiar to all mankind."[3] It is by this circumstance that he judges of the merit of all philosophical systems, and the superiority of Sir Isaac Newton over Des Cartes, consists, according to him, in his discovering that

---

is to be viewed as an additional illustration of those principles of the human mind, which Mr. Smith has pointed out to be the *universal* motives of philosophical researches. Dugald Stewart, also, in his life and introductory dissertation intimates the same thing. The best proof, however, is in the course he actually himself pursued.

[1] Etenim verum examplar mundi in intellectu humano fundamus; quale invenitur, non quale cuipiam sua propria ratio dictaverat.—Itaque ipsissimæ res sunt (in hoc genere) veritas et utilitas. *Nov. Org.* Lib. I. cxxiv.

[2] Rursus, si alius quispiam fortasse veritatis inquisitor sit severior, tamen et ille ipse talem sibi proponet veritatis conditionem, quæ menti, et intellectui satisfaciat in redditione causarum, rerum quæ jampridem sunt cognitæ; non eam quæ nova operum pignora, et novam axiomatum lucem assequatur. Itaque si finis scientiarum a nemine adhuc bene positus sit, non mirum est, si in iis, quæ sunt subordinata ad finem, sequatur aberratio. *Nov. Org.*

[3] *History of Astronomy.*

OF SCIENCE *VERSUS* SYSTEM-BUILDING

he could join together the movements of the planets by so *familiar* a principle of connexion as that of gravity, which completely removed all the difficulties the imagination had hitherto felt in attending to them.[1]

No doctrine, certainly, can be more opposed to the spirit of the philosophy of Bacon than this. It is this propensity to generalize immediately from a few familiar notions, that he all along represents as the vice of the antecedent system-builders, and the error which his followers have to guard against. "There have been, and can be," he says, "but two modes of searching after truth. The one commencing the chain of reasoning with some familiar conception of things, flies from them immediately to general axioms, and from these, and their assumed incontrovertible truths, judges of all particulars. A way of philosophizing brief, but rash; easy and well fitted to conduct to disputes, but not leading to a knowledge of nature. This is the common mode. The other rises gradually and slowly from fact to fact and only at last arrives at the most general conclusions. These, however, are not notions, the products of the imagination, but real laws of nature, and such as she herself will acknowledge and obey.[2] Of the two, the former, the explanation of things according to preconceived notions, much more easily gains assent than the latter; its principles collected from a few facts, and these of familiar occurrence, seize on the judgment, and fill the imagination. Whereas, on the other hand, a real interpretation of nature must find its materials in things very various in themselves, and gathered together from different quarters, cannot make a

---

[1] *History of Astronomy*. Pessimum enim omnium est augurium quod ex consensu capitur in rebus intellectualibus. Nihil enim multis placet, nisi imaginationem feriat, aut intellectum vulgarium notionum nodis astringat, ut supra dictum est. *Nov. Org.* Lib. I. lxxvii.

[2] ——"a sensu et particularibus primo loco ad maxime generalia advoletur, tanquam ad polos fixos circa quas desputationes vertantur; ab illis cætera per media deriventur; via certe compendiaria, sed præcipiti; et ad Naturam impervia, ad disputationes vero proclivi et accommodata. At secundum nos, axiomata continenter, et gradatim excitantur, ut nonnisi postremo loco ad generalissima veniatur; ea vero generalissima evadunt, non notionalia, sed bene terminata; et talia quæ Natura ut revera sibi notiora agnoscat, quodque rebus hæreant in medullis." *Nov. Org.* Præf. et lib. I. xviii. xix.

forcible impression on the mind, and must necessarily appear to it as something harsh, unusual, and mysterious. Hence in all chains of reasoning, having for their object not to gain a knowledge of nature, but to direct the opinions of men, the mode of philosophizing which proceeds by arguing from preconceived notions, will always be the most successful."[1]

I believe it will be found, that the practice of the author of the *Wealth of Nations*, every where agrees with his theory, and that he has himself, in all his speculations, adopted the explanatory and systematizing form of philosophizing, instead of the scientific and inductive, conforming himself to those principles which he has pointed out as leading and directing philosophical inquiry, and according to the accuracy of their agreement with which, all systems of nature have constantly, he tells us, "failed or succeeded in gaining reputation and renown to their authors"; and that, his object being every where to build common facts and familiar observations into a system, not to inquire into the causes or real laws from which they spring, he takes those things for fundamental principles which would present themselves to the inductive inquirer as phenomena, the principles of which his manner of philosophizing would call on him to investigate.

In the catalogue of our author's works, the *Theory of Moral Sentiments* ranks next to the *Inquiry into the Nature and Causes of the Wealth of Nations*. On what is it founded? A generalization from what is termed sympathy—a principle than which there is perhaps no one more sensible to every individual, more capable of serving as a familiar bond of connexion between the phenomena of the moral world, or better fitted therefore, for the purposes of the systematic philosopher; but than which, also, there is, probably, no single circumstance in the combined actions of the mind and body, that would

[1] Quin longe validiores sunt ad subeundum assensum *anticipationes*, quam *interpretationes*; quia ex paucis collectæ, iisque maxime quæ familiariter occurrunt, intellectum statim perstringunt, et phantasiam implent; ubi contra, interpretationes, ex rebus admodum variis et multum distantibus sparsim collectæ, intellectum subito percutere non possunt; ut necesse sit eas, quoad opiniones, duras et absonas, fere instar mysteriorum fidei videri. In scientiis, quæ in opinionibus et placitis fundatæ sunt, bonus est usus anticipationum et dialecticæ; quando opus est assensum subjugare, non res. *Nov. Org.* Lib. I. xxviii.

OF SCIENCE *VERSUS* SYSTEM-BUILDING

appear to the inductive philosopher more deserving of being itself investigated.

A person enters for the first time an hospital, and the spectacle is presented to him of an individual undergoing a severe operation. As at each cut of the knife he sees the flesh divided, the muscles, vessels, and nerves exposed, the blood flowing from the large, gaping, quivering wound, and as he hears the stifled groans of the sufferer, he is conscious of a strange, tremulous sensation, stealing rapidly over his frame, a cold dew stands on his forehead, his features contract, he breathes with difficulty, his limbs sink under him;—in fact, he will be found to be in the very same state with the person operated on, in all respects, but that he feels not the acuteness of torturing pain, and is not subject to the quickening reaction produced by it. The vital powers therefore very possibly yield for a little, he faints, is carried out to the fresh air, and in a few minutes walks off astonished at the strangeness of the occurrence. When he reaches his home, he learns that an intimate friend has suffered a great calamity, and the intelligence deeply afflicts him. In both cases he suffers, or sympathizes, with another person. But are the two precisely alike? are we warranted to assume, with Adam Smith, that the laws governing them are the same? and is there not a singular blending in both of mental and corporeal phenomena, all the circumstances of the actions and reactions of which are deserving of the minutest investigation from one, who would set about an inductive inquiry into the principles of our compound nature?

The picture, which, adopting the common notion of sympathy as the point of view, he has given of the phenomena of the moral world, is exceedingly interesting and comprehensive, and as a system regularly arranging a vast mass of facts, is very valuable. Here, however, its merits cease. No one, I apprehend, will now cite it, as truly developing the nature of our intellectual being, as an addition to the *science* of mind.[1]

Similar observations will apply to his fragments on the

---

[1] See the account given of it by his admirer and disciple, Sir James Mackintosh in his *Ethical Systems*.

imitative arts. He adopts in them the hypothesis that the pleasure they give arises from some difficulty in the execution being overcome, and it seems to have been his intention to build up a whole system of art on this principle. Perhaps no circumstance can be found, running more through all the arts, and, therefore, better fitted for the connecting purposes of the system-builder, or, on the other hand, more curious in itself, and which, therefore, the inductive philosopher would be more inclined to inquire into. How is it, that the images of the poet come upon us with most force, when he puts his words into measured cadence? How is it that an ideal form, if struck out of marble, affects us so much more than if moulded in wax? Is it that the spirit, when fully roused, and striving to embody some great sentiment, or strong emotion, naturally seizes on the materials which may best betoken energy, and thus contrives to give an additional air of intellectuality to mere matter?—This, or a series of such questions present themselves to the inductive inquirer. What to the systematic philosopher affords the means of explaining other things, is to him the subject itself of inquiry.

But, of all his speculations, there is none in which he seems to be more completely the philosopher of system and explanation than in the *Wealth of Nations*. It is a system entirely founded on the most common and familiar notions, and proceeds altogether on the generalization of them. *Value, riches, stock, capital, wealth, profit, self-interest,* [*competition*], *the desire of bettering one's condition,* are evidently of this sort. They are manifestly terms of ill-defined import, referring to notions drawn hastily, and confusedly, from the course of passing events; "notiones confusæ, et temere a rebus abstractæ." And the strain of his reasoning upon them is that proper to the philosophy of system, which, taking from experience the most common and familiar observations, applies itself not to inquire into them, but to form a theory out of them. "Rationale enim genus philosophantium ex experientia arripiunt varia et vulgaria, eaque neque certo comperta, nec diligenter examinata et pensitata; reliqua meditatione, atque ingenii agitatione ponunt." If we, therefore, view his work as an attempt to establish the *science* of wealth, on the principles of the experimental or

OF SCIENCE *VERSUS* SYSTEM-BUILDING

inductive philosophy, it is exposed to the censure of trangressing every rule of that philosophy.

"Men are inclined to think that it is not necessary to inquire into the causes of events that are common and happen every day, but, taking them for things too evident and manifest to require explanation, assume them as causes sufficiently accounting for phenomena, that are not of so frequent and familiar occurrence. Whereas, in reality, no judgment can be formed of events which are rare and remarkable, nor can any thing new be brought to light, without an accurate investigation of the causes, and even the causes of the causes of things, that are the most common and familiar."[1]

The reason of this will be evident, by referring to the example before adduced. If a man, as in the case of the savage, who is totally unacquainted with the system of things but as they present themselves to the eye of the practical observer, be asked why a stone falls to the ground, he would answer, "it is its nature, all heavy bodies fall to the ground." "Why does smoke ascend?" "It is its nature, all light bodies mount upwards." "Why, when a stone is seen flying through the air, do you look about to find out the reason of it?" "Because it is against its nature, and I know, therefore, it must

---

[1] Atque de istis rebus, quæ videntur vulgatæ, illud homines cogitent; solere sane eos adhuc nihil aliud agere, quam ut eorum, quæ rara sunt, causas ad ea, quæ frequenter fiunt, referant et accommodent: at ipsorum, quæ frequentur eveniunt, causas nullas inquirant, sed ea ipsa recipiant tanquam concessa et admissa.

Itaque non *ponderis*, non *rotationis cœlestium*, non *caloris* non *frigoris* non *luminis*, non *duri* non *mollis*, non *tenuis*, non *densi*, non *liquidi*, non *consistentis*, non *animati*, non *inanamiti*, non *similaris*, non *dissimilaris*, nec demum *organici* causas quærunt; sed illis tanquam pro evidentibus et manifestis receptis, de cæteris rebus, quæ non tam frequenter et familiariter occurrunt, disputant et judicant.

Nos vero, qui satis scimus nullum de rebus raris aut notabilibus judicium fieri posse, multo minus res novas in lucem protrahi, absque vulgarium rerum causis et causarum causis rite examinatis et repertis; necessario ad res vulgarissimas in historiam nostram recipiendas compellimur. Quinetiam nil magis philosophiæ offecisse deprehendimus, quam quod res, quæ familiares sunt et frequenter occurrunt, contemplationem hominum non morentur et detineant, sed recepiantur obiter neque earum causæ quæri soleant; ut non sæpius requiratur informatio de rebus ignotis, quam attentio in notis. *Nov. Org.*, I, cxix.

have been produced by violence—by some external force." Thus, too, among mere practical observers of events, there would come to be the terms gravity, levity, natural and violent motion. Now all these words and phrases, if correctly interpreted, are perfectly correct, according to the measure of the knowledge of the individuals, and assume nothing but what their experience warrants. When it is said that smoke ascends in consequence of its levity, or because it is the nature of it and other light bodies to ascend, nothing more is necessarily implied in the words than that there is something,—what is not known,—arising from the general constitution of things, from the system of nature itself, causing that ascent, and that, while this general constitution of things remains unaltered, all such bodies will ascend. So it is when it is said that it is against the nature of a stone to move in any direction but downwards, and that its other motions must be violent. The expressions, in strictness, mean nothing more than that unless acted on by some extraneous cause, while the present condition of things lasts, if it move at all, its motion will be directly downwards. All these are conclusions drawn from experience, and form general rules of real practical utility. Science will never teach the savage to shape, to trim, or to preserve the poise of his canoe, better than observations similar to these have already taught him.

When now the systematic philosopher applies himself to account for, and range in regular order, the various phenomena referable to matter and motion, his object being merely explanation and arrangement, he naturally sets out from common and familiar notions, and principles which no one doubts of, and applies all his powers to tracing out from their operation some explanation of the phenomena in question. " Reasoning on these familiar notions, from a few particulars, and perhaps some generally admitted maxims, he rises immediately to the most general conclusions, and from their fixed and immutable truth judges all other particulars. If some of them seem contrary to his theory, he employs his ingenuity to explain them away, or to make them appear coincident, or removes the difficulty by terming them exceptions; while such particulars as are not opposed to his principles, are laboriously and artfully

OF SCIENCE *VERSUS* SYSTEM-BUILDING 341

arranged, according to his system."[1] Omitting, for the present, the consideration of what he actually accomplishes, let us attend to that wherein he fails.

The familiar notions of the common observer become his connecting media, and he pretends to account for the whole phenomena of matter and motion, on the principles, as he calls them, of *gravity, levity, natural* and *violent* motion. Now it is obvious that, by this application of the terms, he completely, though imperceptibly, changes their meaning. As employed by the man of practical observation, though perhaps somewhat confusedly conceived, they necessarily and really mean nothing more, than certain known consequences, the results of some unknown laws or powers regulating the system of things. As employed by the systematic philosopher, they, on the contrary, are assumed to be the very laws, powers, or principles, themselves governing and sustaining the mundane system. The change in signification is not perceived, for the generality of mankind are incapable of any thing like metaphysical accuracy of conception, and are led away very easily by the fallacies of language. Its consequences, however, are important, for if we understand by science the knowledge of the real laws of nature, —the laws governing the general system,—this assumption completely diverts from their discovery, for it induces the belief that they are already reached. It seems to be on this account. that Lord Bacon so often points out the errors arising from the hasty adoption of preconceived notions, "anticipationes," the greater part of the first book of the *Novum Organum* consisting,

[1] Formam enim inquirendi et inveniendi apud antiquos et ipsi profitentur, et scripta eorum præ se ferunt. Ea autem non alia fuit, quam ut ab exemplis quibusdam et particularibus (additis notionibus communibus, et fortasse portione nonnulla ex opinionibus receptis, quæ maxime placuerunt) ad conclusiones maxime generales sive principia scientiarum, advolarent; ad quorum veritatem immotam et fixam conclusiones inferiores per media educerent ac probarent, ex quibus artem constituebant. Tum demum si nova particularia et exempla mota essent et adducta, quæ placitis suis refragarentur; illa aut per distinctiones, aut per regularum suarum explanationes, in ordinem subtiliter redigebant; aut demum per exceptiones grosso modo summovebant. At rerum particularium non refragrantium causas, ad illa principia sua laboriose et pertinaciter accommodabant. Verum nec historia naturalis et experientia illa erat, quam fuisse oportebat (longe certe abest;) et ista advolatio ad generalissima omnia perdidit. *Nov. Org.* L. I. cxxv.

in fact, of an exposition of them.[1] Acuteness of reasoning, and reach of thought are thus, he observes, rendered useless, for they come too late. The place for them is examining and weighing experiences, and from these deducing first principles.[2] If this be omitted no subtilty of definition, or logical accuracy of deduction can avail. The remedy is too weak for the evil, nor is itself void of evil. The instrument employed is not fitted to reach the depths of nature, and, by catching after what it can attain to, is rather calculated to establish error, than to open up the road to truth. The definitions may indeed sufficiently mark the sense, and from these definitions the conclusions insisted on may be logically deduced; nevertheless there is this of deceit in the procedure, that the notions themselves may be taken up hastily, and carelessly from common observation, and may, therefore, be confused, and loose, and afford no solid foundation for the edifice which it is attempted to rear."[3] Such was the system of physics which the Greeks raised from these principles. Being built on common and familiar notions—a conversion of general practical rules into speculative general principles—whatever its merits were as a system, explaining according to popular notions, the various phenomena of nature, and ranging these in regular order, it had no pretensions to merit as expository of the real science of nature.

It was not until attention was directed to the examination of things before supposed to be known,—motion, natural and violent, gravity, levity, etc.—and inquiry made into the prin-

---

[1] "Non, si omnia omnium ætatum ingenia coierint, et labores contulerint et transmiserint, progressus magnus fieri poterit in scientiis per anticipationes: quia errores radicales, et in prima digestione mentis ab excellentia functionum et remediorum sequentium non curantur." *Nov. Org.* Lib. I. xxx.

[2] *Ibid.* c. xxi.

[3] "Verum infirmior omnino est malo medicina; (*Ars dialectica scilicet*) nec ipsa mali expers—naturæ enim subtilitatem longo intervallo non attingit; et prensando quod non capit, ad errores potius stabiliendos, et quasi figendos, quam ad viam veritati aperiendam valuit—hoc subest fraudis, quod syllogismus ex propositionibus constet, propositiones ex verbis, verba autem notionum tesseræ et signa sint. Itaque si notiones ipsæ mentis (quæ verborum quasi anima sunt, et totius hujusmodi structuræ ac fabricæ basis) male ac temere a rebus abstractæ, et vagæ, nec satis definitæ et circumscriptæ, denique multis modis vitiosæ fuerint, omnia ruunt." *Nov. Org.* Præf.

OF SCIENCE *VERSUS* SYSTEM-BUILDING 343

ciples by which they themselves are regulated, the laws, that is to say, according to which the phenomena, so denominated, are produced, that a beginning was given to real science. Then the laws regulating the universal system were gradually unfolded, and things seemingly forever hidden in the depths of the immensity of space and time, brought clearly before the intellectual ken of man.

As in the system of things making up the world of mere matter, certain terms are employed to denote general facts and rules, which [common] experience has taught, so, in the compound system of men and things making up the world of civilized life, certain other terms are employed to denote the general facts and rules, which [common] experience also has there taught; and as in a department of the one, we have *heaviness, lightness, natural,* and *violent* motion, etc.; so in a department of the other we have *capital, value, profit, a due regard to self-interest,* etc.; in both, too, it is to be observed, such popular and familiar phrases and notions, correctly interpreted, express, not the general laws of the system, but the usual and expected results of those laws.

Thus, if in any particular society, one were to be asked, what the capital of some other person were, he might answer, " about a thousand pounds." If farther requested to state his reasons for saying so, he might reply, " the property he holds would fetch that in the market, he has been offered that for it," or, " I know it cost him that, and that he laid out his money judiciously." These are all the answers he would think of giving; for common purposes they are all he requires to give, and they are all that his notions actually embrace. If asked again, " what revenue does this person derive from his capital ? " he might answer, " I suppose about that which such a capital generally yields, the usual profits of stock—a fair, reasonable, mercantile profit, neither much above or below par." If questioned farther, as to the nature of this capital, and its return, which he terms profit, he would answer, if simply a practical observer, " Really as to this I have never inquired, I know that where I have lived, and I believe in all civilized societies, certain things, if sold, have certain values, bring certain sums of money, and if kept and judiciously employed, yield certain amounts of money, or moneys' worth. Why they do so, though it must arise, no doubt, from the circumstances and actions and reactions on each other of the various things and persons forming these societies, I have not examined into, and do not pretend to know." His answer, in short, would be that he knows them only as results of the laws governing the general system of which he makes a part.

By taking, therefore, these, and such like common and familiar notions, as the foundation of his reasoning, Adam Smith made his work an explanatory system, not an inductive inquiry. The principles of the inductive philosophy would have led him to inquire into the nature of those familiar notions,—into the laws or causes of those common occurrences; and he would have set out with the question, What is it, in the nature of man and matter, that makes any thing constitute a capital, or yield a profit? In the words of the *Novum Organum*, already cited, he would have considered, "that no judgment can ever be formed of things that are rare and remarkable, much less can any thing new be brought to light, unless the causes, and even the causes of the causes, of occurrences the most common and familiar, be rigidly examined and clearly discovered."

It is, therefore, an abuse of words to say, that the publication of the *Inquiry into the Wealth of Nations*, rendered political economy a science of experience.[1] It made it so in no other manner than as every philosophical system is, of necessity. They are all, of necessity, founded on some observations, the fruits of experience.[2] The difference be-

---

[1] "Une science expérimentale," Say. See note on Storch, p. 24, Vol. I. of the *Cours d'Economie Politique*, where he declares it to be precisely similar to modern mechanical science, "la mécanique analytique." The comparison should have been, as we have seen, with the ancient mechanical philosophy.

[2] "Neque illud quenquam moveat, quod in libris ejus (*Aristotelis*) de animalibus, et in problematibus, et in aliis suis tractatibus, versatio frequens sit in experimentis. Ille enim prius decreverat, neque experientiam ad constituenda decreta et axiomata rite consuluit; sed postquam pro arbitrio suo decrevisset, experientiam ad sua placita tortam circumducit, et captivam; ut hoc etiam nomine magis accusandus sit, quam sectatores ejus moderni (scholasticorum philosophorum genus) qui experientiam omnino deseruerunt." *Nov. Org.* ib. L. I. lxiii.

tween them is, that those observations which men make concerning the general results of the laws of the universe, and to which convenience leads them to give names, are assumed by the systematic philosopher for the laws themselves, and that the scientific inquirer examines them patiently, and perseveringly, and ascending gradually, from one thing to another, endeavors thus at last to reach the real laws of nature. While the one assumes phenomena for principles, the other applies to the things giving rise to those phenomena, and collecting, comparing, and arranging these, traces out the real connexions between them, the real principles governing nature.

We may easily satisfy ourselves of the difference of the principles which true science reaches, and those employed in the *Wealth of Nations*, by taking any of the latter and seeing how it agrees with the rules by which the former may be tested. Thus the principle, that self-interest is the great and all-sufficient cause of the increase of wealth, both private and public, is evidently nothing else than an application of the common assumption that a man's fortune and his interest are the same, and a generalization of the observation that he, therefore, who understands his interest best and takes best care of it, will get rich the fastest. But if self-interest be, in the scientific sense, the cause of wealth, both public and private,[1] (the law according to which it either is, or is not produced,) whenever self-interest, (the desire of bettering one's condition) manifests itself in action, it must tend to the increase of public wealth.[2]

Do the labors of the cool, calculating, gambler, or of the sharper, add to public wealth? Does the spirit of keen bargaining, and taking every possible advantage of those with whom transfers are effected, that sometimes pervades classes, and communities, add to public wealth? Assuredly not; yet in all these self-interest is the ruling motive of action. Let it not be said, that these are exceptions to a general rule.

---

[1] Désir de l'homme d'améliorer son sort: principe qui est au monde moral, ce que la gravitation est au monde phisique. Storch.

[2] It will be observed that I here, and throughout, speak of self-interest in the common and familiar sense. The author of the *Theory of Moral Sentiments* was not an utilitarian. If the reader happen to be so, he will perceive that the argument is not altered, the names only have to be so.

Though there may be exceptions to general rules, there are no exceptions to scientific principles. " Wherever a scientific cause, or law, or principle operates, there the thing itself, of which it is said to be the cause, is necessarily produced. And it may be universally affirmed that, where this the form is, there the thing sought is also, and where it is not, there the thing cannot be.[1] Nothing is to be received for the true scientific cause, unless the thing of which it is the cause, increases and decreases along with it.[2]

This difference, indeed, between common practical observations and rules, and general scientific principles must always exist, for it springs from the different nature of the one and the other. The observations which the man of practice makes, as has been already remarked, are on phenomena, the results of the play of real principles, and as these principles may vary in their proportions to each other, and in the modes in which their powers are exerted, the results produced by their action must occasionally vary. The principles themselves, however, never vary ; and, therefore, one observation or experiment concerning a real principle, if there be no inaccuracy in it, has always in science been esteemed as good as a thousand. The whole inductive philosophy may, indeed, be said to rest on the impossibility of the occurrence of exceptions to real laws. Hence the extensive use of *negative instances*, determining, at last, what is a principle by pointing out what it is not.

Again ; it is far from being the case, that a regard for self-interest, a desire of bettering one's condition, prompts always to a course of action leading to an increase of even private fortune. This must depend on what is esteemed the best condition,—on what one's happiness rests.[3] Hence what has

---

[1] Etenim forma naturæ alicujus talis est, ut ea posita, natura data infallibiliter sequatur. Itaque adest perpetuo, quando natura illa adest, atque eam universaliter affirmat, atque inest omni. Eadem forma talis est, ut ea amota, natura data infallibiliter fugiat. Itaque abest perpetuo, quando natura illa abest, eamque perpetuo abnegat, atque inest soli. *Nov. Org.* Lib. II. iv.

[2] Omnino sequitur ut non recipiatur aliqua natura pro vera forma, nisi perpetuo decrescat quando natura ipsa descrescit, et similiter perpetuo augeatur quando natura ipsa augetur. *Nov. Org.* Lib. II. xiii.

[3] Le désir d'améliorer son sort—le désir d'etre heureux. Storch, Vol. I. p. 44, 45.

been regarded as the most enlightened self-interest,[1] has often led, as we have seen, to a course of action the very reverse. The Romans, under the emperors, were assuredly as earnest in their quest after happiness, as were ever any race, yet their manners, and their whole practical morality tended to the diminution of wealth previously accumulated, and they swallowed up, in extravagant dissipation, the riches of kingdoms. Nor let it be here answered, that facts applicable to the Romans, or other people of habits and modes of thinking and acting unlike those characterizing the civilized world of modern days, cannot be fairly adduced in investigations concerning existing systems of society. This is indeed true, if the reasonings in the *Wealth of Nations* be admitted to be of the systematic and explanatory cast, but not if that work he maintained to be an inductive inquiry. These remote and heterogeneous instances, are the very ones which experimental science most prizes,[2] and this, for the reason just adduced, that real principles being constant in their action, what are, and what are not the principles inquired after, are thus tested.[3]

[1] [That is, the current self-interest of the educated classes, at any time or place; not the long-run, really "enlightened" self-interest, as tested by the experience of nations and of ages.]

[2] Nemo enim rei alicujus naturam in ipsa re, recte aut feliciter perscrutatur. *Nov. Org.* Praef.
Instantias remotas et heterogeneas, per quas axiomata, tanquam igne, probantur. *Ibid.* Lib. I. xlvii.

[3] Perhaps it may be said, that the strictness of the inductive method can only apply to the sciences treating of mere matter and its affections. This were to declare the same thing to be, and not to be, a science of experiment, and is besides in opposition to the authority of the founder of the inductive philosophy.
"Etiam dubitabit quispiam potius quam objiciet; utrum nos de naturali tantum philosophia, an etiam de scientiis reliquis, logicis, ethicis, politicis, secundum viam nostram perficiendis loquamur. At nos certe de universis hæc, quæ dicta sunt, intelligimus: Atque quemadmodum vulgaris, logica, quæ regit res per syllogismum, non tantum ad naturales, sed ad omnes scientias pertinet: ita et nostra, quæ procedit per *inductionem*, omnia complectitur. Tam enim historiam et tabulas inveniendi conficimus de *ira, metu,* et *verecundia,* et similibus: ac etiam de exemplis rerum civilium; nec minus de motibus mentalibus *memoriæ, compositionis* et *divisionis, judicii,* et reliquorum, quam de *calido* et *frigido,* aut *luce,* aut *vegetatione,* aut similibus." *Nov. Org.* Lib. I. c. cxxvii.

III. The actual history of what is termed the science of political economy, is another mode of ascertaining the justice of its pretensions to that appellation. By comparing it with the generic character of the history of philosophical sects of the explanatory and systematic form, given by the founder of the inductive philosophy, as contrasted with what he pointed out was to be expected from that philosophy, and time has shown it has accomplished, we might have farther grounds to come to a conclusion on the question. To do this at length, however, would lead us too far beyond limits, which I have already exceeded. I shall, therefore, confine the few farther observations I have to make, to one circumstance, which Lord Bacon gives as characteristic of the two sects. In his figurative language " the path which the inductive philosophy takes, is at first steep and difficult, but leads to an open country, while that adopted by the explanatory and systematic, though at first easy and inviting, is at last lost in deserts or conducts to precipices."[1]

The doubts and difficulties in which the progress of those has been involved, who have advanced farthest along the apparently safe and easy road that Adam Smith seemed to have opened up, indicate it not to be the path of science. Of these I shall adduce a few instances.

Capital is uniformly treated of in the *Wealth of Nations*, as a thing homogeneous in its nature, having always the same qualities, (according to the definition of Mr. Say, an amount of values), and any increase or diminution of it, as a mere alteration in quantity. This being taken to be the case, as like causes produce like effects, it seems very evidently to follow, that the only manner in which a change can be produced in the returns yielded by it [to the owner], must be by the labor that it employs, absorbing a larger or smaller part of them. This result is not uniformly kept in view in the *Wealth of Nations*, though it is very frequently brought forward.[2] We are often told, that, as the wages of labor fall,

[1] —" Via altera ab initio ardua et difficilis, desinet in apertum ; altera primo intuitu expedita et proclivis, ducet in avia et præcipitia."

[2] [" What is the nature of the profit of stock ? and how does it originate ? are questions the [real] answers to which do not immediately suggest themselves.

profits rise, and as profits fall the wages of labor rise, but other causes besides the proportion of its returns paid to the laborer, are conceived to operate on it. Thus a simple increase in its quantity is assigned, in one part of the work, as sufficient of itself to occasion a fall in profits. "When the stocks of many rich merchants are turned into the same trade, their mutual competition naturally tends to lower its profit; and when there is a like increase of stock in all the different trades carried on in the same society, the same competition must produce the same effect in them all." Mr. Ricardo has, however, pointed out, from Adam Smith's own principles, that no such effect would ensue, and insists on it as a general principle that wages alone vary profit. Profits, according to him, are increased or diminished, exactly as the maintenance of labor is easy or difficult, from fertile land being abundant or scarce. Admitting the popular notion of capital, that serves as the basis of Adam Smith's reasonings, to be of a sort on which true science may be built, the theory of Mr. Ricardo seems to me hard to be controverted, and has certainly the merit of giving uniformity and regularity to the system. It has accordingly been acquiesced in very generally in Britain, by men who are given to this department of inquiry, and has been adopted and defended by many writers of unquestioned ability. Nevertheless, it may well be doubted, if it has added to the general confidence in the science. The conclusions to which it leads have in them something so extraordinary, as to exceed the strength of any common measure of faith in such abstractions.

Thus, according to the principles of this school, no extension of foreign trade, however advantageous, and no improvement in domestic industry, however great, can in the least increase profits; [unless they cheapen food, and so multiply laborers, and so bring down money wages]. On the other hand, no diminution of foreign trade can, of itself, lessen profits. It follows also, from the same principles, that colonies give no commercial advantages to the mother country, and, therefore,

. . . The author of the *Wealth of Nations* appears to consider the profit of stock, as paid out of and therefore derived from, the "value added by the workman to the raw material." (Lauderdale, *Inquiry*, p. 149.)]

that being in general expensive, they ought to be shaken off as a burden on her resources. Sir Henry Parnell observes, and quotes Mr. Mill in his support, that, "The capital which supplies commodities for the colonies would still prepare commodities if the colonies ceased to purchase them; and those commodities would find consumers, for every country contains within itself a market for all it can produce.[1] There is, therefore, no advantage derived under freedom of competition, from that part of the trade with a colony which consists in supplying it with goods, since no more is gained by it than such ordinary profits of stock as would be gained if no such trade existed."[2]

These, and similar doctrines, have something in them so strange, so contrary to experience, and seem so paradoxical, that they have in most people rather the effect of exciting surprise, than producing belief. They are exceeded, however, by what a writer in the *Edinburgh Review* [McCulloch] has proved, and in my opinion satisfactorily proved, from the principles of his school, concerning the effect of Irish absenteeism. He shows that it can have no disadvantageous, and possibly may have an advantageous effect, in that it can only cause capital to pass from one employment to another, possibly from a less, to a more advantageous employment. That, as it is the capital of the artisan, the tradesman, and shop-keeper, that yields them their revenue, were all their customers annihilated, they would still live equally well on their capitals. That so, were all the landlords in Ireland to leave it, and were their rents to be sent them, to a distant kingdom, in the shape either of cash or agricultural produce, it could not possibly be of any detriment to the country they abandoned.

Though the argument is skilfully conducted, and though it is in perfect accordance with the leading principles of the science—for, if capitalists are dependent on their customers,

---

[1] [This last clause pertains to the theory of reciprocal demand, not to the theory of the general profit-yielding power of capital—two very different concepts.]

[2] [If the colonies were "in the deep sea sunk," as Bentham put it. There was, indeed, in the colonial speculations of several writers of this period, a most extraordinary exemplification of a lump-of-capital theory.]

OF SCIENCE *VERSUS* SYSTEM-BUILDING 351

what becomes of the all-sufficiency of capital?—and, if the British Government could advantage Ireland by taxing absentees, what becomes of the principle of non-interference? —yet there are perhaps few people, on whom it has had the effect the author probably desired. It has the disadvantage of proving too much. When it is shown, that, according to received principles, two large classes so intimately dependent on each other, as are the landlords of a great country, and the mechanics and capitalists that they employ, can be completely severed, without injuriously affecting the whole system of things in the society, we are rather inclined to doubt of the principles, than to acquiesce in the conclusion. However skilfully the argument may be urged, or however closely one part of it may seem joined to another, it has rather the effect of inducing skepticism than conviction. We still figure to ourselves that there is a loss to Ireland, a gain to some other place. We cannot get rid of the imagination, that, if the landlords were all to go in a body, for instance, to Brussels, and spend their rents there, they would give profitable employment, in some way or other, to a vast number of laborers, tradesmen, and artificers, and that the population and wealth of that town would be largely augmented, that of Ireland proportionally diminished.

These, and many such like instances, seem to us contrary to the usual progress of real knowledge. The experience of what true science is, has accustomed us to expect that in this, as in other branches of inquiry, the farther we advance the larger and larger a compass of undeniable facts should present themselves, that we should be able more and more evidently to connect phenomena, that seemed at first disjointed and isolated, and that, the indistinctness of distance being removed, truth should stand clearly before us. Deceived in our anticipations, we feel like travellers who find the straight and well-beaten path on which they entered, becoming more devious and faint the farther they journey, leaving the habitations of men, and leading to barren and dangerous wastes. Though we can trace no error, we begin to suspect that there is one, and that somehow or other, we have taken the wrong direction.

Dugald Stewart has a remark on the abstract philosophy of David Hume, that seems not inapplicable to this, so termed, abstract science. It is well known, that that skeptical philosopher deduced, pretty clearly, from Mr. Locke's principles, that the human mind was a mere bundle of sensations. The professor observes, that, before any formal refutation of the doctrine appeared, it might have been sufficient answer to it, that it was so contrary to the experience of every one, as to make it more reasonable to suppose an error, either in the premises or deduction, though that error might not be discoverable, than to believe that the metaphysicians were right, all the rest of mankind wrong. Such an answer is, I suspect, that which is now present to the minds of very many, in regard to the strange dogmas of the prevailing school of political economy. They regard them as a sort of practical *demonstratio ad absurdum* of some fundamental fallacy in the science.

Reasoning from Adam Smith's principles, his followers, in more than one instance, have arrived at conclusions differing considerably from his. He looked on parsimony as the great generator of wealth; they rather hold an opinion similar to that of Mandeville, that to consume largely is an essential part of the process, consumption and reproduction being represented by them as the two springs, by the rapid play of which the general prosperity is advanced.[1]

. . . .

I shall conclude these remarks, by observing, that in my opinion the disciples and followers of Adam Smith, in claiming for the speculations contained in the *Wealth of Nations*, and for the doctrines they have founded on them, the rank of an experimental science, the conclusions of which are entitled to the same credence with other experimental sciences, act injudiciously, and by insisting on pretensions which are unfounded,

[1] [No English writer actually reproduces the teaching of Mandeville; but certainly Malthus in his *Political Economy* represents exactly that progress is made by the "rapid play" on each other of supply and demand.

The opinion respecting English classic economics which Rae still held thirty years later, is to be found in a fragment of his manuscript published in the *Quarterly Journal of Economics* for November, 1901.]

injure the cause of that philosopher and conceal his real merits. If we view his philosophical system of the *Wealth of Nations*, or indeed any of his philosophical systems, as he views every such system, "as an imaginary machine invented to connect together in the fancy those different movements and effects which are already in reality performed," nothing of the sort can be more beautiful. A clear, orderly, and extensive view is given of a vast number of interesting and important facts, connected by a few familiar principles. A great body of knowledge is thus brought before the mind in a shape which it can readily grasp, and easily command. The object being not to discover, but to arrange and methodize, all the subordinate principles of the system are artfully bent so as to embrace the phenomena, and care is taken that the imagination be not shocked by a view of matters that shall seem irreconcilable to the aspect of affairs which the [mere] contemplation of the world of life itself presents. Nor is it to be disputed that a general system of the sort, besides the pleasure and the advantage derived from it, is likely to be nearer the truth than speculations of the same nature, confined to particular parts.

The case, however, is completely altered, when the loose and popular principles on which such a system proceeds, are adopted as demonstrative axioms, the discoveries of real science, and are carried out to their extreme consequences. Their original purpose is then altogether changed, and instead of serving to bring before the mind a collection of facts, they lead it farther and farther away from truth and reality, into the barren and wearisome regions of mere verbal abstractions.

ARTICLE VI.

THE THEORY OF POPULATION.[1]

THE laws of true inductive science are of universal application and admit not of exceptions. If even a single manifest exception occurs it ought to invalidate the law. If, for instance, a new compound were found that obeyed not the chemical law of definite proportions, it would rightly occasion an uneasy feeling in the whole chemical world, and there would be no rest there till the apparent anomaly was explained. Considered in this way the laws of population as expounded by Malthus will be found to fail. His error arises from the fact that he assimilates man to the inferior animals. This was also the practice of the elder Mirabeau [who maintained that wherever there was subsistence, the human species would multiply " like rats in a barn."]

Now the nature of the two is different; and if you assume that two things of unlike nature obey the same laws, you are guilty of a rashness that almost infallibly vitiates your conclusions. The inferior animals are led by mere instinct, whereas man is guided by reason, by fancy, and by that changeful thing we call moral feeling. Moreover, man and the lower animals are different physically. With the latter the female

---

[1] [From Rae's manuscript written in the Sandwich Islands, with the exception of the last three paragraphs which are taken from p. 323 of the *Political Economy*.

Two rather more elaborate versions of Rae's final position on the subject of population have already been printed in the *Economic Journal* for March, 1902.]

admits the male only when she is in a condition to conceive; with man it is otherwise. There are still other important points of difference under this head which you will find set forth in the *Memorabilia*, where Socrates is enumerating the particulars of man's superiority. [But the more significant differences are not those which are solely or chiefly physical; but those which are psychological and moral.] Man is the child of art, of phantasy, and of reason full of freaks.

The rapid depopulation of these islands is, in itself, a curious circumstance, and highly interesting as connected with the probable fate of other rude nations, the mass of the earth in fact, if subjected to similar influences. [It is, moreover, a phenomenon which does not square with the Mirabeau-Malthusian doctrine.] Subsistence is easily procured here, there being an abundance of vacant, fertile land, two hours daily labor on which would give every man ample support for a large family. Cattle, goats, and horses (the latter eaten by the natives and preferred to beef), have been added to the resources of former times. One would expect, therefore, on Malthusian principles, an increase of population instead of this fearful diminution.

Vice is put down by Malthus as one of the checks to population; and here it is true of recent years vice, in the form of drunkenness and licentiousness especially among young females, has greatly increased. [But with Malthus vice is treated as specifically "a check" to the pressure of a growing population upon the means of subsistence, and arising out of that pressure. Here, as has just been observed, there is no pressure of population.] Those other forms of vice, and things analogous to vice, which are the positive checks of a growing population in straitened material circumstances—wars, epidemics, human sacrifice, infanticide, inconstant marriages, and intercourse between males (which last was formerly an established institution), have all since the coming of the missionaries been greatly lessened or done away with altogether.

[The fact is that the Malthusian philosophy of population accounts for the vital phenomena of healthy societies only, not at all for that of sick societies, such as the one in these islands has become (notwithstanding the efforts of the missionaries),[1] and such as Rome was in the days of her decline.

A scientific theory which does not explain the totality of the phenomena with which it is concerned, is manifestly insufficient; at best, it may be half right.]

A truly philosophical Essay on Population, fearlessly embracing the whole subject, might proceed thus. Man is an animal and more. Being an animal he must in each generation exercise his powers of propagation to the extent of somewhat more than reproducing himself, else accidents would diminish and ultimately destroy the race. He resembles the inferior animals also in this, that the act of propagation is attended with vehement pleasure. But he differs from them in this, that he knows the probable results of this act (which they do not), and in dread of these results may altogether refrain or take measures to negative them. He may employ the organs for mere pleasure or as a means of gratifying and confirming the affections. He has in short the capacity of diminishing his numbers by abstinence which his reason, either when on the right road or when a wandering, may teach him; or by other modes in which the appetite is abundantly gratified. For the reason that man is more than an animal, therefore, to increase, or to merely preserve, the numbers of any society, it is necessary that there exist an *effective desire of offspring*.[2]

This last in some respects coincides with the effective desire of accumulation, since if a man desire offspring he will generally effectively desire the means of supporting them [and advancing their position in the world]. But it is, never-

[1] [See the article in the *Economic Journal* for the causes which Rae assigns for this social degeneration.]

[2] [The reader may be surprised at first sight that in this summary Rae makes no mention of man's need for food, seeing that in so far as he is an animal, that is a manifest requirement. The reason for the omission is that Rae is dealing here primarily with the specific principles of human propagation, not with their combination with other principles ("diminishing returns," "invention," and the like) which have to do with wealth production. In other words, throughout this Article he is concerned with setting forth not the complete doctrine of the actual multiplication of the human species, but with the pure theory of population itself.]

theless, regulated by different principles. These are mainly certain sentiments pervading the society, and which we may term instincts of Society. There is great difficulty in assigning a cause for these instincts, much the same as that we experience in accounting for the instincts proper of animals. We may rest on this without going farther, that in any particular species of animal and in any particular society, they conduce to their respective well-being in some particular phase of their existence.[1]

[But though in consequence of having been "hammered into the race," these social instincts respecting population are relatively permanent, they may, nevertheless, change. And thus it comes about that we tread on dangerous ground whenever we preach Malthusianism to any people.] The peculiar nature of the human mind, rather excited to action by motives, than passively operated on by them, and moulding, therefore, its energies to suit the course it adopts, occasions a difference between phenomena influenced by it and all others. Hence, according to the preponderating motive, and the course of action followed, the same powers and principles take opposite directions, and the will is able to draw to its purposes and make allies of those which would seem naturally opposed to it.

Thus in an intelligent and moral community, the vanity of the mother is gratified in the well-being of the child, and she prides herself in the proofs of her having been an affectionate and careful parent. In a vain and dissipated community, on the other hand, she would be ashamed of devoting her attention to the homely and unostentatious cares to which solicitude for the welfare of offspring prompts. In the one case vanity excites parental affection, in the other it stifles it. The movement of the mind, in these instances, is somewhat analogous to that of those balances, in which the poise, if in the least inclining to one side or the other, hurries it down with a rapid and continually increasing preponderance.

[1] [Rae believed that the strenuous warfare in which for many centuries the northern races of Europe were engaged, produced in them strong "instincts of society" respecting the desire for offspring and the sanctity of marriage, which still persist though threatened by modern conditions.]

This proneness in humanity to advance or recede with a speed accelerated by the subjugation of opposing motives, helps to afford an explanation of what I conceive to be one of the main causes of the decay of states.

[In the Article in the *Economic Journal* mentioned above, Rae goes more extensively, than in this brief outline, into the nature and causes of what he calls the "instincts of society" touching matters of marriage and procreation. He develops there at some length the idea that the effective desire of offspring depends not only upon individual psychology (as we ordinarily set bounds to that order of facts), but also upon a general hopeful, optimistic outlook on life pervading the whole social group. When a society gets on the downward road, and its members feel a sense of depression and lack of self-respect, men cease to breed. Under such conditions there is no agreement between material circumstances and the propagation of the species. The effective desire of offspring means, of course, not merely the desire to bring children into the world, but the taking satisfaction in them, and the desire to rear them to maturity. On these points, and generally on the whole subject of the theory of population, powerful support is afforded Rae by Bagehot in his *Economic Studies*.

In one particular, it seems to the Editor, Rae is not altogether correct; and that is in the position he takes here and elsewhere with respect to the relation between the principle of the effective desire of offspring and the principle of the effective desire of accumulation. They may be often opposed to each other. In a healthful society, indeed, for general sociological reasons, both will be strong; and in a sick society, on the other hand, both will be weak. But in a society which is neither wholly well or wholly sick (as is the state of most societies), a strong effective desire of accumulation with many individuals, or with certain sections of the society, may go along with a weak effective desire of offspring, and *vice versa*. Rae seems to have been led into this position, involving some degree of error, through his disposition to over emphasize social solidarity for the purpose of getting strong contrasts, as wholes, between the different communities.

But however this may be, it is certain that we cannot dogmatize for all times and places and classes in respect to population, in the Malthusian fashion. And it is also clear that in the principle of the effective desire of offspring we have the true centre of gravity, so to speak, of this complex and difficult subject,—the starting point for fresh and more fruitful studies.]

ARTICLE VII.

OF THE DOCTRINE OF *LAISSEZ FAIRE*, WITH SPECIAL REFERENCE TO THE OPERATIONS OF THE LEGISLATOR IN BRINGING THE ARTS OF FOREIGN COUNTRIES TO HIS OWN.

WHEN men unite in large societies, they cannot each take an active part in what concerns the common good. They are obliged to delegate their individual powers and rights to act, in things relating to it, to several, or to one. This body of men, or this man, acting and making laws for the supposed advantage of the whole, may properly be termed the legislator. It is, therefore, the capacities and powers of the whole, as far as they make one, turned to this sphere of action, and designated by this term, that we have now to consider.

"Man is generally considered by statesmen and projectors, as the materials of a sort of political mechanics. Projectors disturb nature in the course of her operations on human affairs; and it requires no more than to let her alone and give her fair play in the pursuit of her ends, that she may establish her own designs." "Little else is requisite to carry a state to the highest degree of opulence from the lowest barbarism but peace, easy taxes, and a tolerable administration of justice; all the rest being brought about by the natural course of things. All governments which thwart this natural course, which force things into another channel, or which endeavor to arrest the progress of society at a particular point, are unnatural, and to support themselves are obliged to be oppressive and tyrannical."[1]

[1] *Account of the Life and Writings of Dr. Smith*, by Dugald Stewart, p. 104.

APPENDIX

The principle [of economic politics] here set forth by Adam Smith, though not formally announced in the *Wealth of Nations*, runs, nevertheless, through the whole work, and in its particular application to this science, forms the most important of the conclusions to which his [purely economic] reasonings tend. It is very frequently, also, expressly brought forward by the supporters of his opinions, as an argument against the interference of the legislator, and of all those they employ, none perhaps, is more popular, or has had greater influence in giving currency to the system. A brief examination of its merit may not, then, form an improper introduction to the particular subject of this book.

In strict philosophical accuracy, the whole of every political system is certainly natural. Every political system must be allowed to have proceeded from the operation through long extended time, of the things without, and the things within man, acting as the powers and principles which nature has given them, cause them to act. Every such system has many parts, but they all belong to a great whole, and from their action and reaction on each other the movements of that whole proceed. It seems not, therefore, to me, that we can take any of those parts separate from the others, and with propriety say, that it acts in opposition to the designs of nature, for that cannot well be said to be in opposition to the designs of nature, or to thwart her operations, which proceeds from principles that she herself has established. Least of all can statesmen be taken separate from the rest of the frame of society, and the actions they generate considered as unnatural, or operating contrary to the order of things which nature has established, for, to speak in the general, they are all moulded after the form and character of their time and nation, and instead of giving laws to the age, must rather be regarded by the philosopher as emanations of its genius, and organs by which its voice is uttered. Were the whole present race of politicians swept from the earth, so little essential difference would there be between them and their successors, that the change hence resulting to human affairs could not, probably, be traced a century afterwards. Napoleon, when speaking on this subject to one of his generals, is somewhere reported to have expressed himself in nearly the following terms. "We are apt to think that we have done much more than we really have. It is the march of events that has made us, and makes us, what we are. Had you and I never existed, our places would have been held by others, and were we now to cease to exist, the blank would be so filled as not to be perceptible:" It must be allowed that this was with justice said of himself, even by such a man. Already we perceive that all the apparently mighty changes, referable to his personal agency, were rather undulations on the surface of the tide of human affairs, than alterations in its course.[1]

When we speak of the course of the operations of nature on human affairs, philosophical accuracy would, I think, imply a reference to the whole course, and all the springs and principles, that actuate and guide it. These springs and principles, discordant and jarring as they may appear, may, nevertheless, have been so adjusted by the hand of nature, as to have a tendency gradually to bring the whole system nearer and nearer perfection and happiness,

> "From seeming evil still educing good,
> And better thence again, and better still,
> In infinite progression."

This is a pleasing and no improbable theory, but, in this view of the subject, it is the tendency of the whole of these springs and principles that we have to consider, not some taken apart from others. Indeed, if we reason analogically, concerning the apparent action of these different springs and principles, so far from its appearing probable that the direct interference of the legislator in endeavoring to give an advantageous direction to the course of the national industry, in its efforts after the production of wealth, is a principle unlikely to further that production, the presumption rather is, that it will farther it.

To perceive this, it is necessary particularly to attend to the distinction which Adam Smith makes between nature and art as applied to the progress of human affairs. When we say,

---

[1] [These last statements seem to go badly with Rae's doctrine of invention.]

a thing is produced by art, we mean, that it is the result of the agency of man, designedly directed to its production. When we say, a thing is produced by nature; we mean that it is produced either without the agency of man, or, if by his agency, without its being his intention to produce that, which he, nevertheless, produces. Thus the fruit, which a tree cultivated with care in an orchard yields, is an artificial production, that yielded by another growing spontaneously in some wild, is a natural production. A path between two points marked out by rule and line is artificial. A footpath formed by the mere unconstrained passing of many people from one point to another, is natural, because, though equally with the former the work of man, it is not designedly formed by him. In this case it was his intention merely to pass from place to place, not to form a path by so passing. It is in this latter sense, that the production of national wealth is said to be the work of nature. It is said to be the intention of each individual in a nation, to advance merely his own wealth, and the tendency which the actions of all the individuals in a nation have to advance the sum of the national opulence, as it is said to make no part of their motives to action, is esteemed a work of nature, in the same manner as we may esteem a footpath, formed by the continual passing of people over some moor or heath, to be the work of nature. According to this view of the subject, it is the legislator alone, who can, of design, act with the view to advance the national opulence. It is held, however, that as this interference of the legislator disturbs the course which events would otherwise have taken, it acts in opposition to the course of nature, and, therefore, that the presumption is that it will be injurious. On the contrary, I hold, that a just analogy would rather lead us to infer that it will be beneficial.

It must be acknowledged that when man acts most successfully, it is thus that he does act. He never, indeed, seeks to conquer nature otherwise than by obeying her, but his aim, nevertheless, always is to conquer her. By observing the order of events, he acquires the power of changing that order. He does so, by that which distinguishes him from other animals, the reasoning faculty, which so directed we term art and without the aid of which so directed, we scarce attain any object.

But though art and nature are thus put in opposition to each other, the form of expression is more popular than correct. Were the changes which man every where produces on the course of events, contrary to the designs of nature, we may rest satisfied that she would not have given him powers sufficient to effect them. What we call a conquering or governing of nature, is to be held, in a more enlarged and truer sense, an acting in obedience to her designs; and man, as a reasoning animal is rather to be considered as an instrument in her hands, through which she effects much of that change in the order of events, and consequent progress from good to better, that we may fairly hope is going on, than as a separate agent acting in opposition to her. In this sense, all art may be said to be nature, as in another sense all nature may be said to be art.[1]

Is it then a thing to be assumed, *a priori*, as next to demonstrable, that art, the art of the legislator, cannot operate so as to advance the prosperity of nations? That, of all the springs and principles actuating the movement of societies, it is the only one powerless to do good, or whose power can no otherwise be advantageously exerted than in checking its own propensity to act? That though in every other department of human action it is called on to lead, yet here it must impose chains on itself and sit still? That though every where else nature willingly submits herself to its government, nay, seems to court it, yet here she commands it to rest a mere spectator, beholding her " working out her own ends in her own way ? "

The presumption, it seems to me, would rather be, that, though neither here nor elsewhere can man in wisdom oppose

---

[1] [In the words of Edmund Burke,—"Art is man's nature"; or, as another has expressed it,—"man is the executive organ of nature."

All this may be fully admitted and yet bring us no nearer the answer to the practical question,—how much beside maintaining simple law and order (setting up the "common Judge," in Locke's phrase) had the State in general better undertake to do? This is mainly not a question of economics but of politics; and it is not answered in the least by arguments drawn from analogy.]

nature, yet here, as elsewhere, he is called on to direct her operations. That the result of a successful inquiry into the nature of wealth, would terminate in affording the means of exposing the errors that legislators had committed from not attending to all the circumstances connected with the growth of that wealth, whose progress it had been their aim to advance, and would so teach them, not that they ought to remain inactive, but how they may act safely, and advantageously; and that thus, it would maintain the analogy running through the whole of man's connexion with the trains of events going on about him, the course of which he governs by ascertaining exactly what it is. That here, as elsewhere, his advance in knowledge would show him his power, not his impotence.

According to the view of the nature of stock, and of the causes generating and adding to it, which has been given in the preceding book, it would seem that its increase is advanced:

I. By whatever promotes the general intelligence and morality of the society; and that, consequently, the moral and intellectual education of the people makes an important element in its progress:

II. By whatever promotes invention;

1. By advancing the progress of science and art within the community;

2. By the transfer from other communities of the sciences and arts there generated:

III. By whatever prevents the dissipation in luxury, of any portion of the funds of the community.

A full investigation of the modes in which the legislator may promote the increase of the stock of the community, would comprehend an examination of the manner in which he may operate in these several particulars, of the rules necessary for him to observe in each case, and an enumeration of instances, in which, according as his efforts have been judiciously or injudiciously exerted, he has succeeded or failed in his enterprises.

. . . .

When we examine the arts practised by the members of any of the numerous societies, among whom the surface of the earth is divided, we find that there are very few which have arisen among themselves.[1] Unless in some rare instances, they have been all brought from abroad. Inventions appearing at various points in their rude elementary state, have gradually spread themselves far and wide, and, as they have spread, have improved. These passages from place to place, seem to have been generally brought about by violent causes—by wars, internal disturbances, and revolutions. But, as society assumes a more settled form, it is to be hoped that reason will rise superior to force, and that changes produced by violence will diminish; that wars and tumults will become less frequent, or will altogether cease, and that thus a great portion of the evils which have afflicted humanity will be removed. But if the direct evils brought about by the reign of violence, be removed by the ascendency of reason over passion, must the indirect good also produced by it be abandoned? or, is it not the place of the intellectual part of our nature, watching in this, as in other instances, the progress of events, so to influence that progress, as that the good may be brought to pass, the evil prevented?

The answer to these questions is, I conceive, too obvious to require a formal enunciation. If this be the case, it would not seem necessary to recommence a discussion concerning the apparent propriety of assistance being in many instances given by the legislator to the passage of the useful arts from country to country. This, as a general practical conclusion, must be granted. The question again resolves itself into particulars, and the investigations of the political economist, would seem to be confined to the tracing out, from the principles of his science, rules determining when the passage of any art is practicable, and when the benefits derived from it will exceed, or fall short of the necessary expense of effecting the passage. It is not my intention to attempt a full discussion of these various particulars. It will be sufficient for the object in view, to enumerate the general advantages which such transfers produce, and to state some of the chief circumstances favorable, and some of the others adverse to their success.

[1] [See "The Transplantation of Arts and Institutions," Appendix to the second volume of Cunningham's *Western Civilization*.]

When these measures are completely successful, that is, when the commodity, the product of the art in question, comes to be made at the same cost in the country to which its manufacture is transferred, as in that from which it comes, or at less cost than there, the advantages which the community derives from them are various, but, as concerns commodities, not luxuries, may be reduced to three heads.

1. The saving of the expense of transport of the foreign commodity. This, as is shown elsewhere, is often very great. It may be remarked, too, that some articles are so perishable, or so difficult of transport, that they cannot enter into the system of exchange of two societies. They are produced, or may very easily be produced in the progress of the construction and exhaustion of other instruments, but from its being found very difficult or impracticable to transport them to places where they might be exchanged for valuable commodities, they want the whole, or a great part of the utility they would there possess. A farmer, for instance, in the interior of some great agricultural country, say North America, has almost always a large mass of commodities which are nearly, or altogether, valueless to him. Great part of the timber he cuts down he is obliged to burn up on the ground, and much of the produce of his orchard, of his dairy, and of his poultry yard and garden, is either entirely, or in a great measure, lost. No little part of the direct produce of the farm, is also lost. His working cattle are idle for weeks or months in the course of the year, and any superabundance of the more bulky articles, such as turnips, potatoes, oats, or hay, lies nearly useless on his hands. When a manufacturing village is established in his neighbourhood, all such productions become valuable, and are transferred to the artisan, and master manufacturer, as returns for the products of their art. The pine of the forest goes to build their houses, the maple, the birch, and the walnut to make furniture for them, all potatoes and other vegetables of the sort, that can be spared, are consumed by them as articles of food, the working cattle get employed at all times, and there are none of the returns of the industry of the agriculturist, but find a ready market. The advantages hence resulting

to the parts of the country where the new art fixes itself, may be estimated by observing the great rise in the value and rent of land which follows it. We have also a good measure of them, in the difference between these in the neighbourhood of manufacturing towns and villages, and in places distant from them.

The direct effect, therefore, of these general and partial improvements, is to carry instruments, generally or partially throughout the community, to orders of quicker return, and so increase the absolute capital of the society.[1]

2. They have also a large indirect effect in carrying instruments to orders of quicker return, by stimulating invention, and diminishing the propensity to servile imitation. Every useful art is so connected with many, or with all others, that whatever renders its products more easily attainable, facilitates the operations of a whole circle of arts, and introduces change —the great agent in producing improvements—under the most favorable form. Thus the recent improvements in the iron manufacture, have in Great Britain had no inconsiderable share in effecting the general improvement in the mechanical arts which has there taken place. Arts, too, as we have seen, when brought together pass into one another, and thus also improvements in old arts are produced, or new arts generated. Even their very existence in any society gives a powerful stimulus to the ingenuity of its members. This has been well noticed by Mr. Hamilton: "To cherish and invigorate the activity of the human mind, by multiplying the objects of enterprise, is not among the least considerable of the expedients by which the wealth of a nation may be promoted. Even things in themselves not positively advantageous, sometimes become so, by their tendency to provoke exertion. Every new scene which is opened to the busy nature of man, to rouse and exert itself, is the addition of a new energy to the general stock of effort.

---

[1] [The foregoing seems to be the basis for an argument for "internal improvements" rather than for protection. Undoubtedly a community is held back economically by lack of "power of association," and this last depends chiefly on means of transportation. But so far as products of domestic agriculture cannot be exported by reason of excessive cost of transportation, this very circumstance constitutes indirectly a natural protection for manufactures.]

"The spirit of enterprise, useful and prolific as it is, must necessarily be contracted or expanded in proportion to the simplicity or variety of the occupations and productions which are to be found in a society. It must be less in a nation of mere cultivators than in a nation of cultivators and merchants, less in a nation of cultivators and merchants, than in a nation of cultivators, artificers, and merchants."[1]

3. The supply of any commodities which one society is in the habit of receiving from another and independent society, is liable to be suddenly interrupted by wars, or other causes. Hence arises [not infrequently] great waste of the resources of the community. In many cases the whole system of instruments it possesses is at once disjointed, and it is long before the society recovers from the shock. The deficiency is at last supplied, it may be in a more effective manner than before, but in the interim there is great waste. Communities dependent on others for the supply of commodities for which they cannot readily find substitutes, must [therefore] necessarily, every now and then, be subjected to great diminution of their funds from such causes. There are few extensive wars that do not furnish instances of it. It is probable that the absolute loss so caused to the present United States, from the interruption of their intercourse with Great Britain, at the commencement of the war of the revolution, equalled the whole expense of that war. The loss which many of the continental nations experienced from the sudden interruption to the supply of British manufactures, during the progress of the war against Napoleon, was also excessive. Great Britain herself, on the same occasion, suffered very severely from being at once deprived of the supply of materials necessary to many branches of her industry. Thus the cutting off the supply of Baltic and Norwegian timber, was for some years very sensibly felt by her.

It is no doubt true, that, on such occasions, the necessity which arises to procure substitutes for the commodities which are deficient, largely stimulating ingenuity, often ultimately produces real benefit. Wars and similar interruptions to intercourse, as has been repeatedly observed, are, in fact, one of the chief agents by which the arts have been made to pass from

[1] *Works*, Vol. I. Report on Manufactures.

country to country. But the same benefits might have been produced by the gradual operations of the legislator, without the sacrifice in this way required; and it is the business of reason, watching events, to separate the good from the evil, and to search for plans of obtaining the one, and avoiding the other.

But, while the legislator is called on to act, he is also called on to act cautiously, and to regulate his proceedings by an attentive consideration of the progress of events. He is never justifiable in attempting to transfer arts yielding utilities from foreign countries to his own, unless he have sufficient reason to conclude that they will ultimately lessen the cost of the commodities they produce, or are of such a nature, that the risk of waste to the stock of the community, from a sudden interruption to their importation from abroad, is sufficiently great to warrant the probable expense, both of the transfer and of maintaining the manufacture at home. It is his business first to ascertain these points, and to regulate his proceedings accordingly.

When there are circumstances particularly unfavorable to the practice of the art, and no countervailing circumstances particularly favorable to it, the first introduction of it must always cost the society high, and the subsequent maintaining of it will in all probability be a burden on the common industry and stock. Among unfavorable circumstances may be noted a strength of the effective desire of accumulation, less than that of a foreign country, and instruments consequently remaining at orders of quicker return. This is a circumstance lying beyond the reach of the legislator, and which he cannot hope to change. If then there are no other counteracting favorable circumstances, the art cannot be transferred and preserved, but at great and continual expense. Examples of injudicious conduct of the legislator from inattention to this particular have been not unfrequent. As an instance, may be noted the attempts of Louis XIV to make France a maritime and commercial nation. To do so, it only required that the principle of accumulation should have existed in sufficient strength among the people of France, to carry them to the construction of instruments of the same orders as were formed in England, and other maritime and commercial nations. The French at that time had ships and commerce, and had their accumulative principle been so strong as to lead them to construct instruments returning as slowly as those formed by the English and Dutch, their commerce and navy would easily have rivaled those of these nations. The attempt of the British, in some instances, to supplant the Dutch in their fishery, was liable to a similar objection.

Among circumstances particularly favorable to the transfer of a foreign art, may be noted the raw materials of the manufacture existing within the territory of the society in abundance. The acquisition of the art in this case saves the expense of a double transport. On this account, the bringing the woollen manufacture to England was a very happy measure.

Great strength of the accumulative principle, is also another particularly favorable circumstance. This rendered the efforts of the English in the beginning of last century, to acquire many foreign manufactures, prudent and successful.

The legislator effects his purposes by premiums for successful individual imitations of the foreign article; by general bounties on the home manufacture; or by duties on that imported from abroad. Of these, premiums take so little out of the common funds, that their amount forms an item too small to enter into the calculation, in questions of national policy. They are useful as testing the practicability of the transfer. That having been done, it having been made sufficiently apparent that nothing prevents the branch of industry in question being established, but the difficulties attending new undertakings, the want of skilled labor, and a sufficiently accurate knowledge of the properties of the materials to be employed in the formation of the new instruments, it is then proper to proceed to direct and general encouragements by bounties or duties. In this way real capital, and healthy enterprise are directed to the art, the difficulties attending its introduction overcome in the shortest possible space, and the commodities yielded by it are produced at less outlay, and afforded at a less price than that, at which they were before imported.

. . . .

It appears, therefore, that the legislator can effectively

advance the general stock of a society, by effecting the passage of the useful arts from foreign countries to his own.

To this position several objections may be made, of which some are founded on the nature of things, others arise almost entirely from the ambiguity of language.

It may, probably, occur to the reader, that I have considered the legislator as always endeavoring to act for the good of the society, and capable of understanding what is for its good, whereas, in reality, the individual or individuals in whom the legislative power is vested, very often neither understand what is for the general welfare, nor act so as to promote it. This objection carries us to the nature of laws and government, and can, therefore, be only very generally answered.

I would observe, then, that though in other matters, as in projects of distant conquest, or in intrigues for changing the constitution, the legislator may act in opposition to the common interests, yet, speaking generally, in all his proceedings relative to the wealth of the community, it is his aim to act in accordance with them. In despotic governments this is the case, because there the legislator looks on the wealth of the people as his own; in free governments because in them his interests are identified with theirs. It may be that he does not adopt judicious measures for the purpose, but if so, it is his judgment, not his will that is in fault.[1]

Again, it must be granted that the perfection, or imperfection of action of the power invested with legislative authority, depends chiefly on the prevalence or defect, of intelligence and public spirit throughout the community. Every government rests on opinion. Whenever the majority are thoroughly convinced that they would derive advantages from a change in the constitution, or in the person or persons administering it, the time of a revolution approaches. It is only from the members of any society not perceiving what would be for their good, or not believing they can find among them men sufficiently honest or intelligent to execute what would promote it, that the legislative power can be greatly or permanently vicious or

[1] [Compare Article I. p. 267.]

defective. There is always a close connexion between the nature of the people and of the government. Despotism and anarchy imply a general debasement in the intellectual and moral powers; freedom and order, an elevation of them. The more despotic the government the more dependent on the will or caprice of a single person, the more it is subject to error in all legislative measures. The more despotic the government, however, the less also the intelligence, and the greater the selfishness, and consequently the vanity of the governed. The less, also, the inventive power, and the advance in science and art, and the greater the addiction to luxury. But the less the comparative advance in science and art, and the greater the addiction to luxury, the greater facility is given to such operations of the legislator as have for their aim to increase the wealth of the community. The farther any society is behind others in a knowledge of the useful arts, the greater the number of new arts that may be introduced; the larger the amount of luxury that prevails in it, the greater the revenue that may be raised by taxation without interfering with individual income. Hence, speaking generally, if legislators in despotic governments, were other circumstances equal, would be more prone to go wrong; they have there so great facility in acting, that they have greater chance to go right.

A reference to examples will make this apparent. If, for an instance of one of the most ignorant and slavish of existing societies, we turn to some one of the islands of the South Sea, it will be allowed that a legislator of intelligence and perseverance might there effect much good by introducing among them the arts of men farther advanced in the career of improvement. Though we cannot expect to find such a legislator there, one would be inclined to augur favorably of the effects likely to result from the unskilful efforts of even any of their barbarous chiefs, directed to so praiseworthy an object. We should not conceive he wasted the resources of his country, by turning part of the national funds to such purposes. Of extensive countries where unmitigated slavery and despotism prevail, Egypt is perhaps most under the eye of Europeans. It is not, however, commonly believed by them, that the projects of its present ruler for the introduction into it of modern science and art, are inconsistent with the dictates of sound policy. Facts would demonstrate the fallacy of any such supposition. Errors, no doubt, may have been, and may be committed, but the good assuredly overbalances the evil. The revolution wrought in Russia by Peter the Great, is another instance of the same sort. In such cases the power of the legislator to effect beneficial changes is so great, that even his most blundering efforts are seldom altogether successless. A fruitful soil yields large returns, even to a very unskilful husbandman. If we pass from them to governments, of which freedom, intelligence, and public spirit, are the moving powers, we find there, that though the capacity to produce good is diminished, the liability to error is also diminished. It were folly in the legislature of the United States, to imagine itself capable of giving an impulse so sudden and great, to the resources of the country, as that brought about in Egypt by the present Pacha, or in Russia by the first Peter. It has the advantage, however, of being much less liable to error. Every important measure there agitated, before it can be adopted, is subjected to the scrutiny of great numbers of intelligent and well informed individuals, stimulated alike by their regard to their country and to themselves, to trace out with accuracy its future operations and effects. By this means the greatest security, of which the nature of human affairs admits, is given against the adoption of impolitic or hurtful schemes. With such cautions, the legislator may with prudence undertake a series of measures, that, under other circumstances, were of very doubtful expediency.

In one sort of government, therefore, the facility of action gives warrant to act, and in another the probable freedom from error. In both it is the part of the legislator to act, but to act in conformity to the laws arising from the constitution which nature has given to man and to matter. In doing so instead of acting in opposition to nature, he fills his natural place in a system established by nature. In both, also, it is the part of the inquirer into the principles of politics, to endeavor to throw light along the path of the legislator, not vainly to attempt to persuade him, that an insuperable obstacle blocks it up.

Finally, concerning this objection, it may be observed, that it refers to casual ills connected with what is in itself an acknowledged good, and is of a character altogether different from those springing from the doctrines of the followers of Adam Smith. They hold up legislative interference as necessarily and essentially evil.

The second objection I have to note, as resulting from the nature of things themselves, is the possible evil effects of an excessive revenue accruing to the legislator, from protecting and encouraging the industry of the society and turning into his own coffers as much as possible of the amount otherwise dissipated in luxuries. A superabundant revenue in the hands of the legislator, though directly a great good, is sometimes, indirectly a great evil. It may enable him, without any expense to the society, to carry on projects that must otherwise have pressed heavily on its resources, but it also places an instrument of great power in his hands, and one which, in certain circumstances, he may turn to very pernicious ends. It may have an effect similar to that which the discovery of the western continent produced on Spain. The direct effects of the riches that flowed in from the new world, were mightily to increase the power of the Spanish monarchy. Indirectly, however, their effects were to corrupt the court and the nobles, and to spread wide, through the higher classes, a dissolute, and yet a mercenary spirit. The objection, however, only refers at all to countries where there are no public burdens to absorb the surplus public revenue. Is is, consequently, totally inapplicable to Great Britain. It also chiefly refers to countries where there are no efficient checks to abuses of the legislative or executive powers. This, too, it may be observed, is an objection which, as far as I know, has not been urged by modern political economists.

The objections, which have their foundation in the views of the subject presented by Adam Smith, and which are urged by his present followers, depend mainly on the nature of words, and the sophisms produced by a generalization from names instead of things—from preconceived notions which verbally, but not really, embrace the phenomena. Terms, and so, also, reasonings, fitly applied to the operations of individuals in the preservation, enjoyment, and increase of wealth, are transferred immediately to societies, and the [economic] rules and principles which hold good in the one, are assumed to be exactly applicable to the other. If what is thus taken for granted be admitted, farther discussion is unnecessary, for the truth of the proposition to be proved, is implied in the terms in which it is enunciated. It has been my aim, throughout the preceding pages, to expose the fallacy of these assumptions, and, consequently, of the arguments resting on them.

. . . .

[The position of the upholder of *laissez faire* is precisely that "the nature of human affairs," respecting things political, does not admit of sufficient "security" against grave abuses in complicated business, unnecessarily undertaken by government. As an editorial writer has recently expressed it—"A great gulf is fixed between the theory and practice of civil government. Theoretically, the legislature expresses the will of the people. As a matter of fact the laws enacted have all sorts of origin. Most of them are carried through in the interest of a small number of persons." That this applies in a special degree to protection, even under the purest and most free governments, is due to the fact that "every important measure" of that sort "resolves itself into particulars" about which few people, except the interested beneficiaries, inform themselves and take action. But we have before us a broader question than that of protective tariffs alone.

On both sides of this controversy of individualism *versus* collectivism (I have in mind now especially the opening paragraphs of this article), there is the fallacy of metaphor. "Nature" is personified by one side and represented as doing things. The idealized abstraction of the all-wise "legislator" (in recent literature called "the State") is set up on the other side. But it is in fact many men of many minds who do things,—ordinary men always possessing some knowledge and some good will, but also always prone to intellectual and moral error. The question is, by which general plan can society best get the work of the world done : is it by the relatively inflexible, preconceived, centralized methods of the governing power of organized civil society ; or by the comparatively flexible, spontaneous, decentralized methods of individuals and voluntary associations of individuals? Is it, in short, by the impatient plan of compulsory regimentation ; or by the slow-moving methodless method of freedom?

"The inquirer into the principles of politics" has indeed the high office to throw such "light" as he may possess "along the path" of the many-headed legislator. It is his duty to say not pleasant things, but true things. Not at all in the spirit of a mere obstructionist, he may point out that certain specific "ills" connected with "legislative interference" along many lines, are not "casual" but permanent, and that they clearly outweigh the possible "acknowledged good" to be derived. And speaking generally, he may teach that no refined policy based on the theory of economists, is ever likely to be carried into practice under the conditions which obtain in government. Such a policy, merging with other policies, is almost certain to be compromised completely out of shape. Only the private manager (with all his short-comings) is eye-single to the economic, business-like execution of any piece of work.

All this, and other aspects of this great subject, belong to an "order of facts" with which Rae does not seem to have been at all acquainted. Clearly, politics was his blind side. In these matters his great adversary was vastly his superior.]

ARTICLE VIII.

OF THE SUPPOSED IDENTITY OF THE CAUSES GIVING RISE TO INDIVIDUAL AND NATIONAL WEALTH.[1]

PART I.—WHEN ASSUMED AS A SELF-EVIDENT TRUTH.
PART II.—WHEN DEDUCED FROM AN INGENIOUS THEORY.

PART I.

WHEN wealth, considered in the general, is conceived to be a thing either so clear as to require no definition, or so simple as to be fully grasped by any definition, two different and opposing systems naturally seem to arise concerning it.

The wealth of all the individuals in a state being, it may be said, of necessity measured by the amount of the national

---

[1] [The title of Rae's first "Book" in the original edition was "Individual and National Interests are not Identical." The idea accords with his leading concept on the side of man's association with his fellow men, which is that the sociological principle of the "social and benevolent affections" takes precedence over the purely economic principle of individual profit. The social virtues of the individual, embodying the "instincts of society," maximise prosperity through stimulating all the fundamental productive forces, and further the real, long-run, economic interests of the individual as well as those of the society.

On the other hand, it is certain that the direct, short-sighted attempts of individuals (actuated by "isolation of thought and feeling") to increase their advantage, often miss their aim as regards the individual, and cause loss to the social body as a whole. (Compare Article V.) There is, therefore, always room for efforts of society to compel its delinquent members to observe their real, long-run interests. But the argument elaborated in this and the foregoing Article,—that organized civil society is itself called upon to play the part of *entrepreneur* and be progress-maker in the realm of industry, is no necessary part of Rae's general system of speculation.]

wealth, whatever adds to the wealth of the nation must increase the stocks of individuals. But it has always been found that nations have become most wealthy when they have engaged most extensively in commerce and manufactures. To encourage commerce and manufactures by every possible means, should, therefore, be the great aim of the legislator; and every enactment and regulation of his conducing to this effect, as it cannot but tend to the increase of the general funds, must ultimately add to the stocks of individuals. This view of the matter leads directly to a system of unceasing regulation and restraint.

Again, on the other hand, it may be said, that, as the wealth of the nation is necessarily made up of the riches of the various individuals in it, so the national wealth would grow as each individual adds to the portion of it which he possesses. But every restraint is a hindrance to a man's acquiring wealth, and he always gains by evading it. As, therefore, all interference on the part of the legislator, operates as a restraint, he never in any case ought to interfere.

As the former view of the subject produces a system of general regulation and restraint, this teaches the doctrine of complete inaction on the part of the legislator, of the removal of all restraint, and of perfect freedom of trade.

Both systems proceed on the assumption of the exact identity of public and private wealth; of wealth, as it is the same word, being always the same thing, whether applied to individuals or communities, and being in its increase and decrease subjected in all cases to similar laws;—an assumption flowing easily from the conception that its nature is very simple and may without difficulty be apprehended.

The latter of these systems, that adopted by Adam Smith, we might expect, would at present be most popular in Europe. Institutions and forms very often endure after the circumstances that had originally called them forth have disappeared, and when, consequently, their operation injuriously restrains the movements of some new order of things. Such seems the condition of most European kingdoms at present. The frame of their existing constitutions and laws was moulded in remote times, in ages of comparative barbarism and stern military rule, and is, therefore, in many parts, unsuited to the circumstances of the present period. It is perceived that a multitude of abuses exist, and the efforts of the majority are directed to detect, expose, and do away with them. The prejudices of men of liberal minds and enlarged views, for even such men have prejudices, run consequently, rather towards overthrowing and rooting out, than to establishing and maintaining. A system of political economy, the fundamental principles of which inculcated the doctrine that every attempt of the ruler to direct the industry of the community was injurious, and that all laws having this tendency should be abrogated, fell in with the current of public opinion and could not but draw to itself a large body of zealous and able advocates. It is in this temper that Mr. Bentham addresses its author. " On this subject you ride triumphant, and chastise the impertinence of kings and ministers with a tone of authority, which it required a courage like yours to venture upon, and a genius like yours to warrant a man to assume." [1]

It may be remarked, also, that as the circumstances of Europe, in remote ages, produced the former system, in the present give popularity to the latter; so in North America, where a new form of government suited to the state which society has there assumed, has been established, we might expect, as is the case, that a medium would be taken between the two extremes.[2]

My main object, in this book, is to show that that notion of the exact identity of the causes giving rise to individual and national wealth, on which the reasonings and arguments of Adam Smith all along depend, is erroneous, that consequently the doctrines he has engrafted on it, cannot be thus maintained, and are inconsistent with facts admitted by himself.

I have already observed that through every part of his work, in the conduct of all his reasonings and arguments, Adam Smith blends together the consideration of the processes by which the capitals of individuals and nations are increased, and always treats of them as precisely identical. Sometimes this

[1] *Defence of Usury.*
[2] [See "Note C" in the Appendix.]

is assumed as a self-evident truth, sometimes it is a deduction from an ingenious theory; but, in one shape or other, it forms the basis on which his whole system is built. If this simple view of the subject be admitted as correct, it may very easily be made to lead to the conclusions at which he is desirous of arriving.

The axiom which he brings forward, that the capital of a society is the same with that of all the individuals who compose it, being granted, it follows that to increase the capitals of all the individuals in a society is to increase the general capital of the society. It seems, therefore, also to follow that as every man is best judge of his own business and of the modes in which his own capital may be augmented, so to prevent him from adopting these modes is to obstruct him in his efforts to increase his own capital, and, in so far as his capital is a part of the general capital of the society, to check the increase of that general capital; and hence, that, as all laws for the regulation of commerce are in fact means by which the legislator prevents individuals conducting their business as they themselves would deem best, they must operate prejudicially on the increase of individual and so of general wealth.

In pursuance of the same idea, of the perfect identity of the means by which individual and national capitals are increased, the argument is thus further enforced. Accumulation is the means by which individual capital is augmented. We know very well that if any person spend as fast as he makes, he can never get richer. Whatever his gains are he must save some part of them, else he can never add to his capital. The amount also of his savings for any period of time must measure the addition, which, during that time he makes to his wealth. As, therefore, the capital of a single individual is increased by his continually accumulating and adding to it whatever he saves out of his revenue, so the national capital, or the capital of all the individuals in a nation, is increased by these individuals continually accumulating and adding to it what they save out of their respective revenues. Hence whatever prevents them from making the most of their respective capitals, or drawing from them the largest revenue, in so far as it deprives them of the power of laying past so large a portion of that revenue as they otherwise would, must in a like proportion diminish their individual accumulations, and consequently the sum of all their accumulations, or the amount added to the national capital. But all laws for the regulation of commerce, and all encouragements given to particular branches of industry, do in fact prevent individuals from turning their capitals into the channels which, but for these regulations, they would prefer as offering the largest returns. They must, therefore, it is said, to a certain extent, diminish individual accumulation, and consequently, in an equal proportion, the increase of national capital.

Viewing, then, the subject in this simple light, and taking as undoubted truths the assumptions of our author, that individual and national wealth increase in the same manner, and that the manner in which individuals increase their riches is by saving from their revenues, we would easily arrive at the doctrine he inculcates, that as every man is the best judge of his own interests, so he should be left to pursue them in his own way, without the legislator at all interfering with his operations, or pretending to aid or direct them.

This very simple view of the subject would, however, be defective in two respects.

1. Though it is, in the general, true that individuals may find some employment, by the prosecution of which they may procure a revenue, and so, by saving from this revenue, acquire wealth, or add to what they have before acquired, yet it seems not so clear that it is by this means alone that nations advance, or can advance, in the acquisition of wealth; because it must occur to us that materials on which the national industry may be employed are to be provided, and often are or may be wanting.

2. It is not altogether correct to say that the sole means which an individual employs to add to his capital, is the process of saving from revenue. It is very evident he must first gain this revenue, and that the amount he gains, and consequently the amount he can save, must in general depend on the talents and capacities he possesses for the prosecution of the particular employment to which he devotes himself. As

an inquiry, therefore, into the manner in which an individual might most rapidly accumulate wealth, would in part resolve itself into an examination of the modes by which he might acquire the greatest perfection of knowledge, skill, dexterity, and other talents and capacities, tending to the successful prosecution of his business; so an inquiry into national wealth, even supposing the process by which nations and individuals add to their riches to be the same, must partly resolve itself into an examination of the modes by which the knowledge, skill, and dexterity of all the individuals in a nation, in the various businesses and professions that may be carried on in it, may be raised to the highest pitch.

These two circumstances render the subject more intricate, than the first simple view we might be inclined to take of it, would lead us to suspect. An attention to the operation of either of them will be sufficient to show that that identity of the interests of individuals and states, which is assumed throughout the *Wealth of Nations*, is not a self-evident principle. In the following observations, I shall, however, confine myself to the former of them.

Individuals, it is very clear, in general, increase their capitals by acquiring a larger portion of the common funds. While one man is growing rich, another is becoming poor, and the change produced, seems not so much a creation of wealth, as a passage of it from one hand to another. These transfers have been going on in all ages of the world and have existed equally, in what has been called the advancing, the stationary, and the declining stages of society. Everywhere this means of acquiring wealth is open to individuals, and they everywhere avail themselves of it. Let any one in any country, in Great Britain for instance, trace backwards for fifteen or twenty years the mutations that have occurred in the fortunes of the persons with whom he is acquainted, and he will find that there are few, whose circumstances are not very much changed from what they then were. Good conduct, good fortune, and frugality have made many rich who were then poor; imprudence, misfortune, prodigality have made many poor who were then rich.

But while that man has thus been adding house to house,

and farm to farm, and this has been giving up one portion of property after another, till he finds all he once possessed in the hands of others, the whole mass of houses, lands and wealth, has undergone but little alteration; the national capital itself, remains, comparatively, but little changed. It is not by thus acquiring wealth previously in the possession of others, that nations enrich themselves. But a very small part of the capital of any community, can, I suspect, be accounted for, by tracing its passage from any other community. Instead of one nation growing rich, and another poor, we rather see many neighbouring nations advancing at the same pace towards prosperity and affluence, or declining equally, to misery and want. As individuals seem generally to grow rich by grasping a larger and larger portion of the wealth already in existence, nations do so by the production of wealth that did not previously exist. The two processes differ in this, that the one is an *acquisition*, the other a *creation*.

Ex nihilo nihil fit. Nothing can spring out of nothing. Every thing that exists must have a cause. As we do not see that individuals increase their wealth by creating new wealth, we do not think of inquiring how the riches of an individual came to exist, but how they came into his possession. But as we do not see how nations can increase their wealth, but by creating new wealth, we naturally inquire, what are the causes of the wealth of nations.

Adam Smith asserts, and as I think truly asserts, that these causes are to be found in the improvement of the productive powers of human labor. Men, and therefore nations, are said to be rich or poor according to the degree in which they can afford to enjoy the necessaries, conveniences, and amusements of human life. But as it is the annual labour of the nation which supplies these necessaries, conveniences, and amusements; so as this labor is well or ill directed, the supply it affords must be great or small. The skill, dexterity, and judgment with which labor is applied; that is, I presume, the facility of the operations which it employs for executing its ends, and the accuracy with which it conducts them, must consequently mainly regulate the amount which it produces. Thus the increase of the skill, dexterity, and judgment with which the national labor is applied, furnishes us with a cause for the increased productive powers of that labor, and so for the increase of the national wealth.

This account of matters will be found sufficiently to agree with the ideas which the contemplation of their progress forces on every one. When we are told that an individual this year employs in agriculture double the capital which he employed last year, the conception which most readily presents itself to us is, that he now farms double the land which he then farmed, owns double the number of horses, cattle, farming utensils, etc. and has double the number of barns and other necessary buildings. When we are told that a country has double the agricultural capital which it had a century ago, we cannot, of course, conceive that its farms are double the extent they then were; neither do we conceive that its farmers have simply double the number of barns and other buildings, of cattle, ploughs, harrows, and other farming utensils, which they then had. We conceive a change in the mode in which its fields are laid out and tilled, in the form and qualities of the stock, in the construction of all the implements of husbandry, in the size and arrangement of the barns and other buildings; and that through these changes the national agricultural labor produces at least double the products it formerly did. It is this change necessarily involved in our conception of the process by which nations increase their capitals, and not necessarily involved in the process by which individuals increase their capitals, that constitutes the difference between them.[1]

Though they are thus essentially different, there are nevertheless two points in which they agree. When estimated in gold, silver, or any other instrument of exchange, the sum at which the agricultural property presently possessed by the individual would be rated, would be double that at which what was formerly in his possession was rated. The sum, also, at

---

[1] As here I merely aim at giving a very general view of the subject, I only refer to what generally occurs. In this and some other instances the text does not apply to new countries. Communities commonly occupy the same territories unchanged. The growth of such communities as increase by occupying a larger and larger extent of territory, must be regulated in part by laws which are exceptions to those that apply to the rest of mankind.

which the present agricultural property of the nation would be rated, would be double that at which it was formerly rated. The things, too, that so estimated formed the increase in both, would have been produced by man: they would be his works. But though two things may both be estimated as worth a sum of money, and may both be works of man, it follows not that the principles which have produced them are perfectly similar. The poem of Childe Harold cost the publisher a certain sum; so did the paper on which it was printed. They both, too, were works of man, and required mental and corporeal energy to produce them; but we should not, therefore, say the principles that produced them were precisely similar.

Within a few centuries the national capital of Great Britain has increased tenfold. Could we imagine that we could tell this fact to some one of the men of the olden time, waked from the slumber of the tomb and raised up to us, we may suppose he would ask how it could be; how there could have been produced so mighty a change; or from whence so full a tide of wealth could have flowed in upon us. But were we then to take him abroad and show him the wonders and achievements of art with which the land is overspread; the various processes carried on in our manufactories and workshops; the scientific labors of the agriculturist; the curious mechanism with which the vast bulk of our ships is put together and guided; fire and water transformed into our obedient drudges, excavating harbors and draining mines for us, carrying us over the land with the speed of the wind, bearing us through the ocean against tide and storm; he would no longer wonder whence the wealth was that he saw around, or that the land yielded tenfold what it had done of old, though he might well demand how the power had been acquired that had wrought so great a change.

Were such a thing possible as we are thus imagining we can scarce suppose that any one would be found to reply,—"the whole process is nothing extraordinary; it is just the same as you must have seen in your own days, when, by continual parsimonious saving, an individual accumulated ten times the capital he once had; he began, perhaps, with one house, and died owning ten." Such an assertion would evidently be absurd.

Invention is the only power on earth, that can be said to create. It enters as an essential element into the process of the increase of national wealth, because that process is a creation, not an acquisition. It does not necessarily enter into the process of the increase of individual wealth, because that may be simply an acquisition, not a creation. The assumption, therefore, that the two processes are perfectly similar is incorrect, and the doctrine which I have designated as that of the identity of the interests of individuals and communities cannot be thus established.

The ends which individuals and nations pursue, are different. The object of the one is to acquire, of the other to create. The means which they employ, are also different; industry and parsimony increase the capitals of individuals; national wealth, understood in its largest and truest sense, as the wealth of all nations cannot be increased, but through the aid also of the inventive faculty. Though each member of a community may be desirous of the good of all, yet in gaining wealth, as he only seeks his own good, and as he may gain it by acquiring a portion of the wealth already in existence, it follows not that he creates wealth. The community adds to its wealth by creating wealth, and if we understand by the legislator the power acting for the community, it seems not absurd or unreasonable that he should direct part of the energies of the community towards the furtherance of this power of invention, this necessary element in the production of the wealth of nations.

In the following cases it would at least seem not improbable, that the power of the legislator so directed, might be beneficial.

I. In promoting the progress of science.

II. In promoting the progress of art.

1. By encouraging the discovery of new arts.

2. By encouraging the discovery of improvements in the arts already practised in the country.

3. By encouraging the discovery of methods of adapting arts already practised in other countries, to the particular circumstances of the territory and community for which he legislates.

In the attainment of all these objects, the aid of the inventive faculty is required. Our judgment of their propriety or impropriety, as far as this is determined by their direct tendency to promote the wealth of the community, would seem to depend on two circumstances. 1. On the probability of their success, and of this success enabling the industry of its members to acquire with increased facility some of the necessaries, conveniences, or amusements of life, the capacity for producing which, measures the general revenue and riches. 2. On the probability of the future wealth to be derived from this new source, being sufficient to repay the expenditure of present wealth necessary to open it up.

As far as any considerations, which I have as yet presented to the reader, warrant us in forming a conclusion, it certainly does appear not impossible, or unlikely, that there might be instances in which the legislator might, with advantage to the progress of the wealth of the community, direct the energies of some of its members towards discoveries in all these different departments of knowledge and action.

But in doing so, he always acts contrary to the doctrine which teaches that he ought never to disturb the natural course of events; that is, the course which the efforts of individuals, uninterfered with, by him, would give to these events. His agency so directed, according to this doctrine, must be injurious; because, in every instance, it in part changes the direction, and in part retards the progress or the natural course of events. In every such instance, he directs the industry of some of the members of the society from gaining a revenue by the practice of old arts and so accumulating capital, to the discovery either of materials for new arts, or of means of adapting old ones to new countries. By doing so, he takes from the national revenue, and retards, consequently, the accumulation of the national capital.

This doctrine, as given by Adam Smith, is in general, blended with theoretical principles afterwards to be considered. The following is an abstract of it, in his own words, from different parts of his system, separated from these principles.

"The capital of all the individuals in a nation is increased in the same manner as that of a single individual, by their continually accumulating and adding to it whatever they save out of their revenue.[1] As the national capital is thus increased

[1] *Wealth of Nations*, B. II. c. IV.

by parsimony, so it is diminished by prodigality and misconduct. The conduct of those whose expense just equals their revenue, without either accumulating or encroaching, neither increases nor diminishes it. It can seldom happen that the circumstances of a great nation can be much affected by the prodigality of individuals; the profusion of some, being always more than compensated by the frugality and good conduct of others. Men are prompted to expense, by the desire of present enjoyment, a passion only momentary and occasional. They are prompted to save by the desire of bettering their condition, a passion which comes with them from the womb, and never leaves them till they go to the grave. In the whole course of life of the greater part of men, therefore, though the principle of expense prevails occasionally, yet the principle of frugality predominates, and predominates very greatly."[1]

" The principle exciting to frugality, the uniform, constant, and uninterrupted effort of every man to better his condition, produces both public and national, as well as private opulence, and is frequently more than sufficiently powerful to counteract the extravagance of government, and the greatest errors of administration. Like the unknown principle of animal life, it frequently restores health and vigor to the constitution, in spite, not only of the disease, but of the absurd prescriptions of the doctor. Alone and without any assistance, it is capable, not only of carrying on the society to wealth and prosperity, but of surmounting a hundred impertinent obstructions with which the folly of human laws too often encumbers its operations."[2]

The reader will perceive, that the whole force of these arguments lies in the assumption, that the process of the increase of national capital, is precisely the same as that of the increase of individual capital.

. . . .

The principle, therefore, of the identity of the interests of nations and individuals is by no means a self-evident principle. The identity of their interests can only follow from the identity of the ends which they pursue; but these ends being, as far as we can see, identical only in name, and in reality not identical,

[1] *Wealth of Nations*, B. II. c. III.
[2] *Idem*, B. II. c. III. and B. IV. c. V.

the presumption rather is, that the means also by which they are arrived at are not identical.

It seems to me, that it requires very little pausing upon the examination of this principle to perceive its inconclusiveness as an argument. It is a principle, nevertheless, which, like other popular doctrines founded merely on the ambiguity of a word, has been very much insisted on, and meets one in all variety of shapes. On this account, the reader may perhaps excuse me, for detaining him a little longer on the consideration of it, by bringing before him a passage from our author, which may serve to expose its unsoundness, by showing how easily it may be made to lead to the most obvious fallacies. "The annual produce of the land and labor of England is certainly much greater than it was more than a century ago at the restoration of Charles II. It was certainly much greater at the restoration than we can suppose it to have been about a hundred years before, at the accession of Elizabeth. At this period, too, we have reason to believe, the country was much more advanced in improvement than it had been about a century before, towards the close of the dissensions between the houses of York and Lancaster. Even then it was probably in a better condition than it had been at the Norman Conquest; and at the Norman Conquest, than during the confusion of the Saxon Heptarchy. Even at this early period it was certainly a more improved country than at the invasion of Julius Cæsar, when its inhabitants were nearly in the same state with the savages in North America.

"In each of these periods, however, there was not only much private and public profusion, many expensive and unnecessary wars, great perversion of the annual produce from maintaining productive to maintain unproductive hands; but sometimes, in the confusion of civil discord, such absolute waste and destruction of stock as might be supposed not only to retard, as it certainly did, the natural accumulation of riches, but to have left the country, at the end of the period, poorer than at the beginning. Thus, in the happiest and most fortunate period of them all, that which has passed since the restoration, how many disorders and misfortunes have occurred, which, could they have been foreseen, not only the impoverishment, but the total ruin, of the country would have been expected from them. The fire and the plague of London, the two Dutch wars, the disorders of the Revolution, the war in Ireland, the four expensive French wars of 1688, 1702, 1742, 1750, together with the two rebellions of 1715 and 1745. In the course of the four French wars the nation has contracted more than £145,000,000 of debt, over and above all the other extraordinary annual expense which they occasioned; so that the whole cannot be computed at less than £200,000,000; so great a share of the annual produce of the land and labor of the country has, since the Revolution, been employed upon different occasions in maintaining an extraordinary number of unproductive hands. But had not those wars given this particular direction to so large a capital, the greater part of it would naturally have been employed in maintaining productive hands, whose labor would have replaced with a profit the whole value of their consumption. The value of the annual produce of the land and labor of the country would have been considerably increased by it every year, and every year's increase would have augmented still more that of the following year. More houses would have been built, more lands would have been improved, and those which had been improved before would have been better cultivated; more manufactures would have been established, and those which had been established before would have been more extended; and to what height the real wealth and revenue of the country might by this time have been raised it is not perhaps very easy even to imagine."[1]

These conclusions would indeed all follow did individual and national capital augment on precisely the same principles; but as the progress of the inventive faculty, an essential element in the increase of national wealth, is here left out of the calculation, we have good reason to doubt its accuracy.

Before the time of the *Essay on Population*, arguments and conclusions very similar to these were brought forward concerning the waste of human life in wars, and the consequent amazing diminution of the greatness and prosperity of nations. Perhaps the fallacy of the one doctrine may be best exposed by stating the other.

[1] *Wealth of Nations*, B. II. c. III.

"Nations, it was said, can only advance in greatness and prosperity as the numbers of their inhabitants increase. Whatever the natural fertility of the soil, however genial the climate, and however well fitted the whole country may be for the practice of every species of industry, yet, if it be deficient in population, these natural riches can never be elaborated, and it must hold a poor and inconsiderable rank in the scale of nations. A confined and comparatively barren territory, filled with a numerous, industrious population, exceeds the most fertile and extensive country scantily peopled. It is the people that make the state, its real riches lie in its inhabitants.

"But as population increases, and can only increase, by more coming into the world than go out of it, every man who marries and raises a family is a public benefactor, and the practice of celibacy, so far from being a virtue, is, in reality, a great public crime. The number, however, of those who marry, and have children, in all tolerably quiet and peaceable times, much exceeds that of those who remain single; and, consequently, the number of all the inhabitants of the earth has continually augmented, and, had it not been for the wars which the ambition of princes has stirred up, would have been still much farther augmented.

"The population of England is now much greater than at the Restoration. It was greater at the Restoration than at the accession of Elizabeth, and then than during the great civil wars. Even then it was greater than at the Conquest, and at that time, than at the invasion of Julius Cæsar.

"In each of these periods, however, there were not only many private feuds and public dissensions; many bloody and harassing wars; great perversion of the powers of the inhabitants from the production to the destruction of life; but sometimes such dreadful massacres and bloodshed, so great multitudes perishing by the sword, and by famine following up its ravages, as might be supposed not only to have retarded the increase of the numbers of the inhabitants, but to have left them fewer at the end than at the beginning. Had it not been for these events, the greater part of those whom they carried off would have married and had children, whose whole numbers would naturally have been greater than that of the parents who procreated them. In this manner every generation would have exceeded proportionably the one preceding it. The number of industrious hands thus produced would have built more houses, would have improved more lands, and would have cultivated better those which had been improved before; more manufactures would have been established, and those which had been established before would have been more extended, and how far the population of the country, and its real wealth and strength, might have been carried by this time, it is not perhaps very easy to imagine."

The error of both reasonings arises, in the same manner, from taking what is merely a necessary concomitant, for a cause. It is perfectly true, that the real wealth, strength, and prosperity of a country, cannot advance, but as its population advances, and that population can only advance by more being brought into the world than go out of it. It is also true that they cannot advance but as its capital advances, and that its capital can only advance by more being saved than is spent. But when it is said in either case, that as they can only advance as population advances, or as accumulation advances, we have only to allow population to go on unrestrained, or only to allow accumulation to go on unchecked, we are deceived, and led to unwarrantable conclusions, by a sort of sleight in the use of words.

The contemplation of a couple contending with unremitting labor against the evils of poverty and want, and, however occasionally pinched by them themselves, warding them off with care and success from their offspring, and rearing up a numerous and industrious family, is a very pleasing sight. It is pleasing as an evidence of the existence of some of the best and purest affections of our nature; it is pleasing, also, from the mere view of the healthy addition thus made to that surest stay of a state, an industrious and frugal population. But when it is hence assumed, that nothing is wanting to augment the numbers of the community, and carry it forward to greatness, than that similar principles and conduct should be allowed to go on in all its members without restraint, a hasty and inaccurate conclusion is drawn from a partial view of a complicated subject. The numbers of a state can never exceed, what its resources can support. When these resources are augmented, the principles which tend to the preservation and multiplication of the species are, in all well regulated communities, sufficiently active speedily to fill up their numbers to the amount of the increased supply.

In like manner, the contemplation of honest industry, and patient frugality, not only manfully bearing up against present necessity and want, but repelling them, and accumulating a plentiful store to answer the demands of futurity, is also no unpleasing spectacle. But for such principles neither public nor private comfort or affluence could exist, or be preserved. But, when it is hence also assumed, that nothing else is wanting to carry the community forward to the highest degree of affluence and power, than that similar principles and conduct, through all its members, should be encouraged, and allowed to go on without check, a conclusion equally unwarranted and equally inaccurate, is drawn from a like hasty and imperfect view of a great subject. The capital of a state is a mere instrument in the hands of its industry, to enable it to draw forth the riches, with which the conjoined powers of nature and art have endowed it. A multiplication of instruments is of no avail, unless something additional be given on which they may operate. When invention succeeds in discovering these additional riches, the mere view is sufficient, in every well regulated community, to induce its members to form the new instruments, necessary to draw these riches forth.

There must be some strong inherent vice in any community, where the certain prospect of plentiful subsistence does not produce an abundant population. It can only be, also, from the effects of some great inherent vice, that, in any community, a very profitable investment for capital can be held out, and yet capital not accumulate with rapidity. Where there is no sufficient prospect of subsistence, people may be restrained from marriage by the dread of their families suffering want. Where there is no sufficient prospect of profit, people may be withheld from accumulating capital, because they may see no sufficiently profitable adventure open to them that they would not fear to embark in. But the fact is, that people, rather than live single, are inclined to marry at all risks, and hence population is kept down by misery, and premature death; and they are also, rather than do nothing, inclined to embark in adventures where the chances are against their success; hence the vast numbers of unsuccessful projects that in most communities are continually dissipating previous accumulations of capital. To form a right judgment of the power of any community, under the most favorable circumstances, of increasing its population, we must consider the additional marriages which would take place, and the greater numbers that would be reared to maturity from such as do take place, if plentiful subsistence were provided. In like manner, to form a right judgment of the powers of any community, under the most favorable circumstances, to increase its capital, we must consider, that, if abundance of secure and profitable investments for capital were presented, its members would be more eager to possess additional capital, and, therefore, would be more prompted to accumulate it; and the capital they possessed would be more productive, and would not be subject to be risked and lost in imprudent speculations.

From the inconsiderable rudiments of population and capital, which Great Britain furnished to North America, is to be traced the great amount of both, of which that flourishing division of the globe at present boasts. The former has increased so greatly, because plentiful subsistence has been afforded it: the latter, because profitable and secure investments have been presented to it. Had it been possible to have afforded, and had the same abundant subsistence been afforded, to the population, and the same profitable and secure investments to the capital remaining within the kingdom, they would have both augmented, we have every reason to believe, in a ratio equal to that at which the fragments of both that went to North America have augmented. It certainly was not the voyage across the Atlantic, but the rich soil on which they fell on the other side of it, that excited them to so luxuriant a growth.

This great productive power of both the population and capital of a country, when room is afforded them to shoot, seems so easily to fill up any gap which is made in the national numbers or stock, that a calculation founded on the assumption, that any loss in either which a nation may sustain, necessarily occasions a proportionably permanent diminution of its funds must evidently be inconclusive. It is very doubtful if the population of London or England would have been greater than it is at present, had there been no plague. It is very doubtful also if the capital of London or of England would have been greater than it is at present, had there been no great fire. The additional demand for labor and capital, which these disasters created, may very well be supposed soon to have brought both up to the amount they had previously attained.

In all instances of such, or even far greater calamities, destroying a part of the population or capital of a country, while the principles and elements, through and from which they sprang, are not consumed along with them, we see them quickly reproduced. When, for example, the great destroyer War holds his course through a country, and clearing wide his path with fire and sword, leaves property and life a wreck behind him, we see not that the traces of his wrath are long perpetuated; in the midst of the ruins of what were, lie the germs of what are to be, and seizing on the elements of existence that lie waste around, they expand with a vigor proportioned to the magnitude of the void that has been made for them, and speedily replenish it. Like the track of the whirlwind through the forest, the present desolation is quickly covered up and obliterated by the freshness of the new growth, to which that very desolation gives light, and air, and the means of existence. We should think the calculation rather fanciful, which, estimating the trees overborne by the blast for centuries, and reckoning the increase that might have possibly come from each of them, should bring out as a correct result, that all this would have been a clear addition to the vegetable life of the forest; and that so much greater it must have been to-day, had not these disasters had place. Calculations proceeding on the assumption of the indefinite increase of population or capital, without showing also that there will be room for them, are but little more logical.

Before population can advance, there must be something on which it can subsist; before capital can increase, there must be something in which it may be embodied. Produce subsistence, and, if vice prevent it not, population will follow; show that if capital did exist, it would produce great profits, and, if vice prevent it not, capital will be accumulated. But, until there be some means of subsisting the population, and employing the capital, they can never, by simply urging on their production, be rationally expected to be much augmented.

It is invention, which showing how profitable returns may be got from the one, and how subsistence procured for the other, that may most fitly be esteemed the cause of the existence of both; and hence this power has most title to be ranked as the true generator of states and people. It is certainly, therefore, very far from being a self-evident truth, that the legislator, by employing the resources of the country in rousing this principle to activity, necessarily retards, instead of advancing, the increase of wealth and the prosperity of the state.

PART II.

Though the doctrine of the identity of the interests of individuals and communities cannot be established as a simple and self-evident principle, from the assumption that the objects which individuals designedly pursue, for their private emolument, are precisely those which most promote the progress of the general opulence; and though in this sense, as we have seen, the identity of the ends which they pursue is nominal, not real, yet it follows not from this that the doctrine is necessarily erroneous. Many doctrines which are far more simple or self-evident are nevertheless true. Many, which at first sight seem even contradictory to experience, are found, by closer examination, to be legitimately deducible from it. It is manifest that the general opulence, however brought about, results, in some way or another, from the action and reaction on each other of the whole system of persons and things, which constitute communities, or belong to them. It is then at least possible to conceive that it is entirely produced by the efforts of individuals to advance their private fortunes. That, though it is the object of individuals to acquire wealth, and of nations to create it, yet that the series of actions which the former generate, in endeavoring to make the acquisition, are precisely those which are best calculated to forward the creation; and that thus, unconsciously to himself, each member of the community, while seeking merely his own benefit, necessarily adopts the very course which is most for the advantage of the society, and, to use our author's words, " is led in this, as in many other instances, by an invisible hand, to promote an end that was no part of his intention."

In this view of the subject the doctrine would put off the shape of a simple principle, and assume that of a theory deduced from an examination of the whole series of actions that are concerned in the production of the wealth of communities; and in this way we may conceive that it might be satisfactorily proved by an extended inquiry into the " Nature of the Wealth of Nations."

Such is the theory of this department of human action, which the author gives. If it be found not to be inconsistent with the phenomena, but fairly deduced from them, the truth of the peculiar doctrine, which it is the aim of his work to maintain, would be established by it.

Before endeavoring to explain it, or attempting to show wherein it fails, it is proper to remark that it is blended, throughout the whole work, with that notion of the exact identity of the ends which nations and individuals pursue, the fallacy of which I trust I have, in some measure, exposed in the preceding chapter. I shall afterwards have occasion to show that this arrangement of his materials sometimes renders his arguments illogical. I am led to notice it at present, because I wish to account for the appearance of this assumption, unremarked by me, in the analysis of the theory I am about to give.

It must be apparent to every one acquainted with the system, that its parts would not in any way hang together, if deprived of the support which this popular notion gives to them. Indeed, I conceive that the truest account that could be given of it, would be to say, that it is altogether founded on the assumption that national and individual wealth and prosperity increase, and must increase, in precisely the same manner; and that the theoretical part of it merely serves to show how the increase of individual wealth does, in reality, produce the events which we see accompanying national wealth; that the former is the cause, and the sole cause, of the latter, and must therefore produce all the phenomena attendant on it, being taken for an undeniable fact, and the author seeming merely to have proposed to show how it may be supposed to produce those phenomena. Thus, were what was once the popular doctrine concerning population still held to be the correct one, and were we to take it for granted as an undeniable truth, that, as the national strength, and revenue, and wealth can only advance as the number of industrious hands that form them is increased, so every augmentation of the population of a nation is an addition to the national funds, and that, therefore, things ought to be allowed to take their natural course, and all restraints on marriage be done away with, the assumption and doctrine might be supported by a theory, showing, or endeavoring to show, how all the phenomena attending the advance of mankind towards prosperity and affluence do, in fact, result from their increasing numbers.

It might, perhaps, in support of such a view of the subject, be said, "that, as necessity is the mother of invention, so, unless pressed by want, or the dread of it, mankind might never have exercised their ingenuity in discovering even the rudiments of the arts; and certainly would not have advanced them beyond the most unformed and imperfect elements. That, while in genial climates the spontaneous fruits of the earth afforded them abundant nourishment, they could have had no motive to tax the labor of either their minds or bodies to produce that for which they had no need. That it was the increase of their numbers, which, rendering the supplies that nature had dealt out to them insufficient, imposed the task on them of searching out the means of procuring additions to them: and that thus necessity,

'Curis acuens mortalia corda
* * * * *
Ut varias usus meditando extunderet artes
Paulatim, etc.—'

'Whetting human industry by care
That studious need might useful arts explore,'

is in truth the divinity that taught mankind the most essential arts.

> 'Primo Ceres ferro mortales vertere terram
> Instituit ; cum jam glandes atque arbuta sacræ
> Defecerunt sylvæ et victum Dodona negavit.'

> 'First Ceres taught the ground with grain to sow,
> And armed with iron shares the crooked plough ;
> When now Dodonian oaks no more supplied
> Their mast, and trees their forest fruit denied.'[1]

"That this urgent necessity, this imperious mistress, which nature caused to spring from their increasing numbers, made them spread themselves over the earth, and people even the most rigorous climates. That the 'rigid lore' of the 'stern rugged nurse' thus imposed on them, though harsh, was healthful ; as a proof of which we may observe, that men in general subsist in greatest comfort and abundance, where the climate is most forbidding, and the soil most stubborn, because there, that they may subsist at all, they have been obliged to call to their succour the most ingenious arts, and the most indefatigable industry,

> 'Labor omnia vincit
> Improbus et duris urgens in rebus egestas.'
> 'What cannot endless labor urged by need?'

"That, as it is the action of this principle which has given rise to all the arts, so it is it which has brought them to perfection. That, while a territory is scantily peopled, and its inhabitants spread over it at a great distance from each other, they can never subdivide themselves into different trades and employments, and each devoting himself to a particular business and art, exercise his whole ingenuity to bring that particular occupation to perfection ; and that hence arts are in general in the most flourishing condition, where the population is the most dense.

"That to these causes, thus necessarily proceeding from this great principle, we are to ascribe in particular both the opulence and prosperity of our own nation, and the necessary diffusion of the arts, manners, language, and race, with which they are connected, and in which they are embodied, over the remotest

---

[1] [Virgil, *Georgics*, I. 149 f (Dryden's *Trsl.*).]

regions of the globe. That thus, although men in marrying seek only their own good, they nevertheless adopt that course which is most to the advantage of society; and here too, as in many other instances, are led by an invisible hand to promote an end which was no part of their intention. That, therefore, as the revenue and power of a nation can only increase as its population increases, and as the increase of population tends to give a beginning to every useful art, and to carry it to the highest perfection, legislators act a very absurd and culpable part in attempting, in any instance to restrain it, or to check what is undoubtedly the natural, and apparently the most beneficial course of events."

Such a theory, like almost every other view of only one side of a complicated subject, would probably be partly correct, and partly erroneous; but it might be possible to embrace in it a great mass of facts, and perhaps to give it considerable plausibility.

In examining the soundness of the doctrine founded on it, it might first be expedient to allow the assumptions necessarily involved in it to pass unnoticed, and to test its accuracy by an application to facts. Such is the course which I mean to follow in this introductory examination of the somewhat similar theory, as it seems to me, which is the groundwork for the vast and varied accumulation of facts and opinions embodied in the *Wealth of Nations*. I shall allow the author's assumptions to pass unquestioned in all cases where they are mixed with the explanation of real events, though I may esteem that explanation erroneous; and it is only where, alone and unconnected with facts, they are brought forward for the purpose of arguments—as incontrovertible truths in order to establish the particular doctrine which I combat,—that I will feel myself called on to expose the fallacies into which they lead.

The celebrated author remarks, "that it is from his labor alone that man can draw the necessaries, the conveniences, the amusements of human life, from the materials which nature has placed around him. As the amount of these necessaries, conveniences, and amusements, which any man can afford to enjoy, constitutes his riches; so the amount of them which all the men in the nation can enjoy constitutes the national riches.

Labor, then, being the first price, the original purchase money, that is paid for all things, an inquiry into national wealth is, in fact, an inquiry into the means by which the labor of the individuals composing a nation may produce, from the materials they possess, the greatest amount of necessaries, conveniences, and amusements.

"These may either be the immediate produce of that labor, or what is purchased with that produce from other nations. Hence such an inquiry may be divided into two parts; the first treating of the means by which the produce of the national labor becomes greatest; the second, of the manner in which the part transferred to other nations procures for them, in return, the greatest amount of necessaries, conveniences, and amusements.

"First, then, may be considered the sources of wealth that lie altogether within the society, the means of bringing, by the labor of its members, out of the materials which it possesses, the greatest amount of products; that is, of articles affording, necessaries, conveniences, or amusements.

"This, in any particular nation, must be regulated by two circumstances. First, by the skill, dexterity, and judgment with which its labor is generally applied; secondly, by the proportion between the number of those who are employed in useful labor, and that of those who are not so employed." It is to the first of these circumstances, which he observes is of much the greater influence, that our author's reasonings chiefly refer, and to the consideration of it, therefore, we may altogether confine ourselves.

"The chief cause operating on this, the main source of the productiveness of labor, is capital. Without capital, industry could scarce at all exist. While a man is executing a piece of labor, he must have, to maintain him, a stock of goods, and he must have ready provided for him the tools and materials necessary for performing the work. These are all procured by capital. A weaver, for instance, could not apply himself to manufacture a web of cloth, unless there were stored up for him a supply of food, and other necessaries, sufficient to maintain him till he complete and sell it, and were he not provided beforehand with a loom and other requisite tools and materials.

It is capital which provides all these, either his own or that of some other person.

"As capital is thus the most essential element in setting industry in motion, so it is by the amount of it, that the productiveness of that industry is chiefly determined.

"Every man having capital naturally endeavors to make the most of it; that is, to cause the labor which it puts in motion to yield the greatest amount of productions. This he effects by the division of that labor; that is, by separating the operations it has to perform into as many distinct parts as possible, and allotting each of them to one man, or one set of men, as a peculiar employment.

"The increase arising to the productive powers of labor, from this division of it, is owing to three different circumstances. First, to the increase of dexterity in every particular workman; secondly, to the saving of the time which is commonly lost in passing from one species of work to another; lastly, to the invention of a great number of machines which facilitate and abridge labor.

"First, the improvement of the dexterity of the workman necessarily increases the quantity of the work he can perform; and the division of labor, by reducing every man's business to some one simple operation, and by making this operation the sole employment of his life, necessarily increases by much the dexterity of the workman. A common smith, for instance, will scarce make more than three hundred nails a day, and those very bad ones. A boy who has devoted himself entirely to the business of making nails, can make upwards of two thousand.

"Secondly, time is not wasted in passing from one work to another, and the indolent sauntering habits induced by the frequent change of employment are avoided.

"Thirdly, the invention of all those machines by which labor is so much facilitated and abridged, seems to have been originally owing to the division of labor. In consequence of it, the whole of every man's attention comes naturally to be directed to some one very simple object. It is naturally to be expected, therefore, that some one or other of those who are employed in each particular branch of labor should find out easier and readier methods of performing their own particular work, wherever the nature of it admits of improvement. In this mode a great number of such improvements on the productive power of labor have been made.

"The other improvements in machinery and manufactures [1] have been also owing to the division of labor. Many of them have been made by the ingenuity of those, who, from this separation of employments, have taken up the trade of making such machines; others, by that class of citizens of whom also philosophy or speculation becomes the sole trade and occupation.

"The perfection to which this division of labor may be carried depends on the amount of capital that sets it in motion; because the same number of workmen, executing a greater quantity of work in proportion as they are better classified and divided, require consequently, when so classified, a larger stock of materials, and the extent of the stock of materials provided must be regulated by the amount of capital accumulated. Again, when so divided, they both require and cause to be invented many new machines. These machines, also, can only be procured by a capital previously stored up. Not only, however, does the accumulation of capital, by providing more abundant materials and better machines, enable the same number of workmen to be better divided, and to produce more work, but it also may be observed that the number of workmen in any branch of business increases with the division of labor in that branch. Thus the increased accumulation of capital, by effecting a more and more extended division of labor, not only increases the productiveness of the labor of the same number of workmen, but adds to that number. By both means, therefore, it greatly augments the total riches of the society, the amount of necessaries, conveniences, and amusements produced by its members, and consequently enjoyed by them.

"These productions which labor by the aid of capital effects, have to be transported to the places where they are to be consumed, have there to be stored up till they may be wanted, when they have to be divided into small portions, suited to the convenience of the persons who are to use them.

[1] I add this word because the chain of reasoning seems to require it.

The dealers in wholesale and retail are enabled to perform these useful offices by the instrumentality of capital, and the greater the amount of that capital the more easily and effectually they can perform them. Hence, every addition their economy makes to that amount, tends also to the increase of the general prosperity.

"The division of labor is limited by the extent of the market. Before any man, or any set of men, can in common prudence devote themselves to any particular employment, they must be assured that they can dispose of the commodity which their exertions in the prosecution of that employment will produce. In situations where there is not a sufficient number of customers near at hand to consume the manufactured article, or where it cannot with advantage be transported to those at a distance, the making of that article can never become the exclusive employment of any man, or set of men. When, therefore, there is not a sufficiently extensive market, labor cannot be so much subdivided as it otherwise would, and its productive powers are cramped for want of room in which to exert themselves. The increase of capital extends the market by adding to the numbers and general opulence of the community, and by facilitating the modes of communication between all parts of the territories which it possesses; and this extending market gives, in turn, additional celerity to the increase of capital."

To this accumulation of capital, this continual parsimonious saving out of revenue, the principle that, according to our author, animates the whole progressive movement of the society, he assigns the following limit.

"When the stocks of many rich merchants are turned into the same trade, their mutual competition naturally tends to lower its profit; and, where there is a like increase of stock in all the different trades carried on in the same society, the same competition must produce the same effect in them all. As, then, the profits of capital continually lower with its augmentation, there must arrive a period when they will be so diminished as to render it no longer possible to save any part of them." When this period arrives, the country would then, I think, according to our author, have acquired its full complement of riches; every branch of business therein having the greatest quantity of capital that could be employed in it.

"But besides the immediate produce of its own industry, a country that has made any progress in the accumulation of capital, and consequent division of labor and facility of production, comes to furnish other countries with many articles, and, in exchange, to receive from them many other articles. This forms another source from whence the necessaries, conveniences, and amusements of nations may be supplied. A country is enabled to do this from two causes. The soil, climate, and natural productions of countries are various. Hence one country has generally peculiar advantages over others in manufacturing certain articles. Again, one country exceeds another in the amount of capital it possesses, and consequently in the skill with which its industry is applied; hence, also, there are articles which it can produce in greater perfection than other countries, with greater facility, or both.

"This is the origin, and these are the advantages, of foreign trade. By means of it two or more nations are enabled to exchange with one another what would otherwise have been to each superfluous for what, through these exchanges, procures to each an additional amount of the necessaries, conveniences, and amusements of life.

"It is capital which enables them to effect these beneficial exchanges, and the amount of them must be limited by the amount of capital that can be embarked in the employment." What quantity of capital this employment may absorb, what quantity of productions may thus be exchanged between different countries, is a problem which our author has not, as far as I perceive, given us certain data for solving. Some of his followers think it illimitable, but it is clear that this was not his opinion, and that, though he did not assign the limits, he nevertheless believed there were limits to it. Accordingly he makes another channel, through which, when these are filled, it may flow, gathering still volume to itself, and adding to the national prosperity as it proceeds.

"This is what is called the carrying trade, the carrying the surplus produce of one nation to another. Two countries may have products which it would be advantageous for them to exchange, but they may not have capital sufficient to provide the means necessary for effecting this exchange. In such case, another nation having a superabundant capital may embark part of it in performing this office for them, and into this employment a country so circumstanced naturally directs such a capital. When the capital stock of any country is increased in such a degree, that it cannot be all employed in supplying the consumption, and supporting the productive labor of that particular country, the surplus part of it naturally disgorges itself into the carrying trade, and is employed in performing the same offices to other countries."[1]

It may be observed, however, with regard to this last employment, which our author assigns to capital, that it implies a superiority in the progress of the productive industry of the country enjoying the trade, which cannot be calculated on beforehand. A nation can only possess a carrying trade, from other nations wanting foreign trade. Though it may, therefore, form a source of gain to a particular nation, it seems not so properly to be reckoned among the causes of the wealth of nations; for, with the general progress of that wealth, according to the theory of our author, it would decay.

The ingenious theory, of the main elements of which, I have thus attempted to delineate the outlines, its eminent author has illustrated with a felicity of observation, and laboriousness of research, which it were as vain to attempt to depreciate, as superfluous to praise. He conceives that it establishes the following conclusions.

"The natural effort of every individual to better his own condition, when suffered to exert itself with freedom and security, is so powerful a principle, that it is alone, and without any assistance, not only capable of carrying on the society to wealth and prosperity, but of surmounting a hundred impertinent obstructions with which the folly of human laws too often encumbers its operations; though the effect of these obstructions is always, more or less, either to encroach upon its freedom or to diminish its security."[2] That "every system which endeavors, either, by extraordinary

---

[1] *Wealth of Nations*, B. II. c. V.   [2] B. IV. c. V.

encouragements to draw towards a particular species of industry a greater share of the capital of the society, than what would naturally go to it, or, by extraordinary restraints, to force from a particular species of industry some share of the capital which would otherwise be employed in it, is, in reality, subversive of the great purpose which it means to promote. It retards instead of accelerating, the progress of the society towards wealth and greatness; and diminishes, instead of increasing, the real value of the annual produce of its land and labor." And therefore, that "all systems, either of preference or restraint, being completely taken away, the obvious and simple system of natural liberty establishes itself of its own accord. Every man, as long as he does not violate the laws of justice, is left perfectly free to pursue his own interest his own way, and to bring both his industry and capital into competition with those of any other man, or order of men. The sovereign is completely discharged from a duty, in attempting to perform which he must always be exposed to innumerable delusions, and for the proper performance of which no human wisdom or knowledge could ever be sufficient; the duty of superintending the industry of private people, and of directing it towards the employments most suitable to the interest of the society."[1]

I expect in the sequel to show that the system contains certain fundamental errors invalidating very many of the conclusions, which the author desires to establish. In the mean time, passing all such discussions, and viewing the subject in something of the light in which it seems to have been contemplated by Adam Smith himself, I would observe, that his system, if correct, must be consistent with itself, and with admitted facts. His theory pretends to show, that the source of the wealth of nations, the abundance, that is, of all the materials of comfort and enjoyment, the necessaries, the conveniences, the amusements of life which men possess, is to be found in the gradual accumulation of capital by the undisturbed industry and economy of individuals, continually through the division of labor, introducing improvements in the modes in which this labor operates with that capital, and,

[1] *Wealth of Nations*, B. IV. c. IX.

consequently, increasing with the greatest possible rapidity the returns from them. His doctrine is, that the accumulation of capital by individuals, being thus the only thing required to produce that abundance with the greatest possible rapidity, ought never to be interfered with by the legislator; and that, if he does so, it must necessarily be to the detriment of the society for which he legislates. If, therefore, even according to him, there are other sources, than the mere accumulation of capital, and consequent division of labor, on which nations are dependent for turning their labor and capital to the best account, and thus drawing from their resources the most abundant returns of necessaries, conveniences, and amusements, that is of wealth; in so far, his theory would seem imperfect, and his doctrine inapplicable. If we now turn in particular to the part of the system with which we are specially interested, we find, in reality, that as far as it is concerned, the theory is thus inconsistent with events admitted by its author, that hence this portion of it is contradictory to itself, and to admitted phenomena, and that consequently the doctrine drawn from it cannot here be maintained.

In the account of the progress of opulence, given in the *Wealth of Nations*, we find assigned, as one of the causes of it, the introduction into a country of new manufactures. "According to the natural course of things," we are told, "the greater part of the wealth of any growing society is first directed to agriculture, afterwards to manufactures, and last of all to foreign commerce."[1] "After agriculture, the capital employed in manufactures puts into motion the greatest quantity of productive labor."[2] The utility of such manufactures is enlarged on in many parts of the work. "They give a new value to the surplus part of the rude produce by saving the expense of carrying it to the water side, or to some distant market, and they furnish cultivators with something in exchange for it, that is either useful or agreeable to them, upon easier terms than they could have obtained it before. The cultivators get a better price for their surplus produce, and can purchase cheaper other conveniences

[1] *Wealth of Nations*, B. III. c. IX.   [2] B. II. c. V.

which they have occasion for. They are thus encouraged and enabled to increase this surplus produce by a farther improvement and better cultivation of the land; and as the fertility of the land had given birth to the manufacture, so the progress of the manufacture reacts upon the land, and increases still farther its fertility. The manufacturers first supply the neighborhood, and, as their work improves and refines, more distant markets. For though neither the rude produce nor even the coarse manufacture could, without the greatest difficulty, support the expense of a considerable land carriage, the refined and improved manufacture easily may. In a small bulk it frequently contains the price of a great quantity of rude produce."[1] "The revenue of a trading and manufacturing country must, other things being equal, always be much greater than that of one without trade or manufactures. By means of trade and manufactures a greater quantity of subsistence can be annually imported into a country than what its own lands, in the actual state of their cultivation, could afford. The inhabitants of a town, though they frequently possess no lands of their own, yet draw to themselves, by their industry, such a quantity of the rude produce of the lands of other people as supply them, not only with the materials of their work, but with the fund of their subsistence. What a town always is in regard to the country in its neighbourhood, one independent state or country may frequently be with regard to other independent states or countries.[2] Commerce and manufactures gradually introduced order and good government" (into Europe), "and with them the liberty and security of individuals among the inhabitants of the country, who had before lived almost in a continual state of war with their neighbors, and of servile dependency upon their superiors.[3]

"No foreign war, of great expense or duration, could conveniently be carried on by the exportation of the rude produce of the soil. The expense of sending such a quantity of it to a foreign country as might purchase the pay and provisions of an army would be too great. Few countries, too, produce much more produce than what is sufficient for the subsistence of

[1] *Wealth of Nations*, B. III. c. III.   [2] B. IV. c. IX.   [3] B. III. c. IV.

their own inhabitants. To send abroad any great quantity of it, therefore, would be to send abroad a part of the necessary subsistence of the people. It is otherwise with the exportation of manufactures. The maintenance of the people employed in them is kept at home, and only the surplus part of their work is exported. Among nations to whom commerce and manufactures are little known, the sovereign, upon extraordinary occasions, can seldom draw any considerable aid from his subjects.[1] In modern war the great expense of fire arms gives an evident advantage to the nation which can best afford that expense; and, consequently, to an opulent and civilized over a poor and barbarous nation."

According to our author, some of these manufactures proceed from the original rude arts of the country cultivated and refined by the gradual progress of capital and of the division of labor; others are introduced from foreign states. This transfer takes place in the following manner. Trade first, by degrees, introduces a taste for the foreign manufacture; the demand for it increases with time and the opulence of the society. But when this trade has become so general as to occasion an extensive consumption, the merchants of the country, to save the expense attending the transport of the article from a foreign country, introduce the manufacture of it at home.

In some cases, then, the increase of capital, arising from the accumulation of individuals, and division of labour thence arising, is not, it would appear, sufficient alone to account for the progress of improvement, and consequent production of fresh funds out of which wealth may grow. For, in cases where the raw materials exist, and capital to divide labor and put it in motion also exists, these are sometimes confessedly dependent on the importation of new arts from other countries, for the means of being advantageously directed. These admitted facts are certainly not in accordance with our author's theory. Passing, however, the consideration of this at present, I should wish to direct the reader's attention to the application of his peculiar doctrines to events of this class; and, that I may do so, it is necessary to examine them with somewhat more attention.

[1] *Wealth of Nations*, B. IV. c. I.

When goods are transported from a distance, a great part of their price is made up of the expense, attending the transport. This arises not merely from the simple expense of carriage, but from the risk attending it, from the perils of land and water, and the carelessness or knavery of those who are entrusted with it; from the profits which the different capitalists, through whom they may be transferred, exact, and from the damage to which commodities are subject by being long kept on hand. The price of very many commodities transported from one country to another is doubled by the influence of these causes; not a few of them derive more than three fourths of their value from them.

Hence the transfer of the manufacture of such goods to the countries to which, when manufactured, they were before sent, is very highly advantageous to those countries. It is advantageous from the saving to the national income which it effects by doing away with the expense of transport; from furnishing, according to our author, a new and more profitable employment for capital; and from the general effects it produces on the national prosperity, as exemplified by him in the passages I have quoted. It must be allowed, moreover, that this introduction of such manufactures, by the violent operation, as he terms it, of the stocks of particular merchants and undertakers, who establish them in imitation of some foreign manufactures of the same kind, is a matter of great difficulty.

For, in the first place, the materials which the home supply affords, will, in all probability, be not altogether similar to those that are used for the same purpose in the foreign country. Some may be better, some worse adapted to the purpose, but they can scarcely be altogether alike. They must vary, too, in their price, some being cheaper, some dearer, than in the country from whence the manufacture is brought.

The greater part of manufactures are also influenced by the climate. The dryness or moisture of the atmosphere, the degrees of heat and cold, the brightness of the sky and consequent intensity of the light, are circumstances which all, more or less, affect many manufactures.

The proportion between the rates of wages and profits of stock is also very different in different countries, and it considerably influences the determination of what may be the most advantageous mode of conducting any process in any country.

When the discovery of that exact mode of procedure, which the relations and connexions that these new circumstances have to each other renders most expedient, has once been made, it may be found that they are on the whole more favorable and such as will produce a better article, at less cost, in the country to which the manufacture is transported, than in that in which it was originally exercised. To make the discovery, however, of this exact procedure is always a matter of difficulty, and implies almost necessarily the previous commission of many errors and mistakes, and the incurring of much needless expense and loss. A single individual, whatever intelligence and application he may possess, can scarce hope to arrive at it; it requires the efforts of many individuals, continued through a considerable course of time.

But these modifications, in the process of any manufacture, which its removal from one country to another demands, are far from being the only difficulty attending that removal. An accurate knowledge of the principles of the manufacture, and of the manner in which every part of it is carried on in the foreign country, must be obtained; the requisite machinery has to be provided, and workmen, possessing the skill and dexterity which each part of the process requires, must be procured. These are generally matters of great difficulty.

Very few individuals have a thorough knowledge of every different part of any complicated manufacture. In examining any large and successful manufacturing establishment, we commonly find that the various parts of it depend, for the perfection with which they are conducted, on the efforts of different individuals, who devote their whole attention to their own departments, and are not at all qualified to change places with each other; while the director of the whole has only such a general knowledge of each as enables him to say when it is properly conducted, not himself to point out the exact mode of best conducting it. It is his business to preserve the economy of the whole, and to search out the individuals best fitted for carrying on every part. Hence the undertaker of any such work, in a country where it has not been practised, has not only to engage one, but generally many individuals, in order that the different processes of the manufacture may be properly conducted. The difficulty of finding persons of sufficient intelligence and integrity for the purpose, who will remove to a distant country, without an extravagant reward, is very great, and the risk of being imposed on by engaging persons of insufficient skill, and consequently suffering considerable loss, is not small. The difficulty of transporting, or of constructing there, the necessary machinery, is often still greater; and when these are procured, workmen having the requisite skill and dexterity for performing the mere manual part are still wanting. These, if brought from a foreign country, as is often necessary, can only be induced to expatriate themselves by the receipt of exorbitant wages; and, even if the natives of the country where the new manufacture is to be established can be trained from the first to execute the necessary manual operations, besides the loss arising from their deficient dexterity, they will demand higher wages than those engaged in established employments. A man naturally prefers continuing in any sort of work which he understands, rather than displaying his awkwardness in attempting to perform an operation that is strange to him. Besides, he has, in general, reason to apprehend that, should the new manufacture fail, he will have difficulty in again finding employment in the trade he had forsaken. On these accounts it happens that "when a projector attempts to establish a new manufacture, he must at first entice his workmen from other employments by higher wages than they can either earn in their own trades, or than the nature of his work would otherwise require; and a considerable time must pass away before he can venture to reduce them to the common level."[1]

All these circumstances create so many obstacles to the efforts of private individuals, in their endeavors to carry a manufacture from a country in which it already prospers, to another in which it is unknown, that it is, I believe, very rarely they have succeeded in doing so, without the occurrence of some favorable conjuncture of events, to aid them in the project.

In point of fact it will be found, that the transfer of

[1] *Wealth of Nations*, B. I. c. X.

manufactures from one nation to another, or rather the general propagation, through all countries, of this most important source of the opulence of every one, has been chiefly owing to causes, which, at first sight, would seem little calculated to produce so beneficial effects. Wars and conquests, tyranny and persecution, the jealousy and hatred of rival states, have, strange to say, been the main agents in disseminating arts and industry over the globe, and thus ameliorating the social condition of the whole human race. Events, that, to those to whom they happened, brought nothing but calamity and suffering, have procured prosperity and opulence to the generations that have succeeded them,—convulsions, that disturb and derange the frame of civil society, like those which occasionally shake and desolate the globe, in the midst of present destruction and devastation, carrying often the elements of future fertility and abundance.

Manufactures have commonly been carried to a distance by the men who have exercised those manufactures. But no one willingly expatriates himself. They even, who would seem to have least to attach them to their native soil, the poor mechanic, and drudging laborer, cling to it with the greatest tenacity, and generally quit it not, unless forced from it by inevitable necessity or by the continued pressure of some heavy evil. In this way the ills that the tyranny of despots, or civil and religious factions, or war, or famine, bring upon communities, have often compelled great numbers of their most industrious citizens, to abandon their homes, and seek refuge in foreign countries. These emigrations have been powerfully instrumental in improving the arts of civilized life and diffusing a knowledge of them over the earth. Perhaps few arts would have much passed the narrow limits to which their first discovery confined them, had not communities been subject to be torn in pieces, and scattered abroad, by the violence of the events to which we allude, and which have been taking place in every age since the world began. Whenever such emigrations occur, they carry the knowledge and skill of the countries they leave, into those in which they settle, and diffuse them over them; by bringing together the different arts of different countries, they enable one to borrow from the other, and raise all nearer to perfection; and, by giving opportunity to them to unite with one another, from that union, they occasionally produce some that did not before exist. In all these modes, they have promoted very greatly the progress of human improvement. The influence of these causes, though more powerful in remote ages than in the present times, has not yet ceased. It is shown in events of very recent date or actual progress. To it we chiefly owe the origin of those flourishing states, which the European race have raised up in North America; and the rapid progress over the Western Hemisphere, of every improvement that art or science effects in the Eastern.

Besides the direct agency which these outbreakings of the violent passions of mankind, by disturbing and deranging the smooth and uniform course of human existence, have had in casting it into new and often improved forms, they have produced similar effects in a manner less conspicuous and evident. Commerce introduces a taste for the productions of the arts of one country into others, which are remote from it. These productions, at first regarded as mere superfluities or luxuries, pass, in time and from habit, into things essential to the comfort, almost to the existence, of those who have become accustomed to their use. War interrupts this commerce and thus cuts off the supply that it afforded of such articles. Excited by the rewards offered by the eagerness of a demand that cannot be supplied from abroad, the domestic industry of the country then exerts itself, first, to produce rude imitations of the foreign commodity, and at length, rival manufactures. This is a cause which has extensively operated in modern times, in spreading manufactures from country to country. It is to the wars springing out of the French revolution, and the interruption to European commerce that they occasioned, that the first rise of many manufactures in different parts of the old and new world, which are now in a very prosperous condition, is to be traced.

But besides the influence which the violent operation of foreign wars, and intestine commotions, has had in promoting the propagation of arts over the world, many of them unquestionably have been encouraged and enabled to extend themselves to, and take root in, countries remote from the seats where they originally flourished, by the direct efforts of the legislators of such countries, to draw them there, to cherish their first feeble advances, and to promote their subsequent growth and vigor. There are very few productions of modern art, that do not stand indebted to the legislators of the countries in which they are manufactured, for their advancement and perfection.

These three causes have, generally, more or less co-operated with each other in the extension and advancement of every branch of art. The cases where the efforts of private individuals, unaided by one or all of them, have been successful in transferring any manufacture to a distant country, are, as I have already observed, exceedingly rare.

In accordance with the doctrine which he supports throughout, it is here maintained by our author that the last of these causes operating in the production of new arts, or in their introduction into a country, viz., the interference of the legislator, is improper, because necessarily injurious; and that his agency, so directed, always, and from its very nature, instead of promoting the advancement of the general opulence and prosperity, operates in a manner prejudicial to both. Allowing that this introduction of new arts and manufactures from foreign states is, in itself, beneficial, in so much that he assigns it, as we have seen, as one of the causes of countries becoming wealthy and prosperous,—he maintains, that this particular mode of introducing them is necessarily injurious. We have then to inquire, if there are any other means by which, according to his principles, this acknowledged most beneficial result can be brought about.

The violent operation of foreign wars or domestic disturbances, will scarce, I think, be said to be more advantageous methods of effecting this purpose, than the restrictions and bounties of the legislator. At all events such causes are continually diminishing in their frequency and the vigor of their operations, and becoming more and more beyond the reach of our calculations. For spreading the useful arts from people to people, this element confessedly of very great importance in the advance of the general welfare of mankind, there remains then, according to these principles, but the unaided efforts of private individuals alone.

It must be kept in mind, that, by the efforts of individuals, are meant, according to our author, their endeavors to better their condition ; that is, as he defines it, to increase their fortunes. But, in order to add to his fortune, one must get more than he gives. No such efforts can ever lead any individual to embark in a project that will probably take more from him, than it will return to him. Now, to transfer a manufacture from one country to another, must always be a very tedious and expensive operation, for any individual to perform. The consideration of his own profit, the sole motive according to our author, which determines the owner of a capital to employ it in any undertaking, would never lead one, to engage in the enterprise of establishing a new manufacture in any country unless of such commodities as were of common consumption in it, and which he could therefore be sure to sell. Those commodities being of common consumption, and not produced within the country, must at the time be furnished by some foreign state, and, consequently, to procure their sale, he must be able to supply them, at as cheap a rate as that state. The effecting this, for reasons I have stated, would generally take more time and money, than any private individual can afford. But, granting that the funds of some private individuals could afford this requisite outlay, and that they should succeed in bringing the manufacture to such perfection as to enable them to sell the commodity on terms equal to those of the foreign merchant, or lower than his, the more difficult question is, how is this great outlay to be reimbursed ? A great part of an individual's capital has been expended. This expenditure can, evidently, be reimbursed to him only by his drawing proportionally larger profits, than he otherwise could, from what remains. To balance the extraordinary outlay, he must have extraordinary returns.

But profits far exceeding the usual rate of profit can scarcely ever be drawn, for any time, from any employment. " If, in the same neighborhood, there was any employment evidently more advantageous than the rest, so many people would crowd into it, that its advantages would soon return into the level of other employments."[1] It is no doubt true, that the proprietor of such new manufacture might, sometimes, not only succeed

[1] *Wealth of Nations*, B. I. c. X.

in establishing it, but in keeping secret the great profits he made from it, for a considerable period. This is a piece of good fortune, however, which, though it might sometimes befall an individual, he could never beforehand fairly calculate on. It is much more probable that his success would be blazoned abroad and exaggerated, that several projectors would establish themselves beside him, and, by bribing his workmen with somewhat higher wages, with comparative ease, succeed in depriving him of the profits he might otherwise have drawn from his extraordinary outlay of labor and capital.[1] It may, therefore, I think, be safely laid down as a principle, that, in all ordinary cases, a due regard to their own interests cannot be a motive sufficient to prompt individuals to such undertakings. It may no doubt happen, as capitalists are every now and then engaging in injudicious projects, and such as either injure or ruin them, that some one may be imprudent enough to enter on such a project as this, and may succeed in introducing a particular manufacture, though with the loss of part, or of the whole of his capital. But, even granting that such an occurrence as this may sometimes take place, it would be far from serving to help out the theory we are discussing. "Every injudicious and unsuccessful project in agriculture, mines, fisheries, trade, or manufactures, tends to diminish the funds destined for the maintenance of productive labor. In every such project, though the capital is consumed by productive hands only, yet, as by the injudicious manner they are employed, they do not produce the full value of their consumption, there must always be some diminution in what would otherwise have been the productive funds of the society."[2] This project then, being injudicious and unsuccessful, for it would have occasioned the loss of a portion of individual capital, must, by these principles, be injurious to the society.

If it be said by any supporter of these doctrines, that this

[1] This accounts for a remark of our author: "The undertaker of a great manufactory is sometimes alarmed if another work of the same kind is established within twenty miles of him. The Dutch undertaker of the woollen manufacture at Abbeville, stipulated, that no work of the same kind should be established within thirty leagues of that city."

[2] *Wealth of Nations*, B. II. c. III. p. 131.

is too strict and constrained an interpretation of them, and that the loss which the society sustains, by the destruction of the capital of the original introducer of the manufacture, must be allowed to be made up by the gain which it receives from the profits made by those who afterwards engage in it;[1] I reply, that I perfectly agree with him in his conclusions. I too think, that the small present expenditure of the funds of the society which the project may occasion, may be more than repaid, by the large future revenue that it will bring in. The only difference between us is, that the doctrines he advocates, teach us to wait, till the miscalculations of some unfortunate projector confer on us a public benefit, whereas, I hold, that it would be more just and judicious that the necessary first cost of the scheme should be borne by the whole community; more just, as thus the burden necessary to be borne to procure a common benefit will be divided amongst all, instead of being sustained by one; more judicious, as the society will not have to wait, for the attainment of a desirable object, on so doubtful a chance as the folly of projectors.

It may also happen, that an individual, by some rare concurrence of accidents, may become initiated into all the secrets of some foreign manufacture, and, by some equally rare and happy union of good fortune and ingenuity, may succeed in introducing it into his own country with profit to himself. To wait, however, for this, or any such like lucky chance, or singularly fortunate concurrence of circumstances, while better could be done, would be like waiting till the natural actions of the winds and tides should, by some strangely propitious concurrence of events, cast upon our shores a valuable plant or seed, that we might directly procure for the mere trouble and expense of sending for it.

There are, also, motives of another class, capable, no doubt, of leading even individuals into such undertakings, and of carrying them successfully through them. The love of country or fame, or the desire to gratify personal vanity,

---

[1] "The landlord can afford to try experiments and is generally disposed to do so. His unsuccessful experiments occasion only a moderate loss to himself. His successful ones contribute to the improvement and better cultivation of the whole country." B. V. c. II.

are powerful motives of human action, and may sometimes even be directed into such channels as this. But as the tendency of such motives to promote the growth of national wealth is opposed to the principles of our author, and is expressly denied by him, we need not here enter into any inquiry concerning them.

There is, however, one case, in which it cannot be denied, that the efforts of individuals to promote their own interests may be sufficient to introduce a new manufacture. If, in the progress of events, the requisites for a foreign manufacture come to be produced in so great abundance, and with so much facility, in any country, that a projector there finds that he can from the first afford to manufacture the commodity, and sell it at as low a rate as the foreign merchant, a due regard to self-interest will certainly direct a portion of the national capital into that employment. But, a case of the circumstances of a country being so peculiarly favorable to the practice of a foreign art, that, in the very first essays it makes in it, it can successfully compete with another, where that art has been long established, is assuredly very rare; and, if any such case occur, we may be satisfied that the manufacture might, with much advantage, have been previously introduced.

In a passage already quoted, it is observed, that, "when a taste for foreign manufactures becomes general, the merchants, in order to save the expense of carriage, naturally endeavor to establish some manufacture of the same kind in their own country." These expressions are somewhat too loose to coincide with our author's theory. It cannot be to save the expense of carriage, but to add to his own riches, that a merchant will endeavor to do any such thing. The consummation of such a measure, by saving a considerable expense to the community, might indeed add largely to the means of increasing their wealth in possession of all the merchants, or rather of all the members of the society; but "it is his own advantage, and not that of the society, which every member of it has in view;" and, in this system of perfect liberty and freedom from restraint, which is asserted to be the true plan of carrying the general prosperity of the community to the highest pitch, the difficulty is, to discover a method of inducing an individual to incur an unavoidable outlay, the returns from which, although very beneficial to the whole society, are no more so to him who lays out a great deal, than to others who lay out nothing. Union is said to give strength. But union cannot exist unless there be a bond to unite, and this bond must confine and restrain. The rods to make a bundle were *tied* together. Men are *tied* by law, a bond binding all to pursue the course supposed to conduce most to the general happiness. This bond, though restraining individual freedom of action, and preventing individuals from pursuing the course which they might find most conducive to their own private happiness, has not, on the whole, been esteemed to have slightly promoted the great end for which it exists, the general wellbeing of mankind. We seek to rectify its errors, not to abolish it. The peculiarity of this system, relating to this particular part of the field of human action, is, that it maintains that man cannot in it, as elsewhere, unite, so as to attain a common good. That, on the contrary, when they so unite, instead of attaining a common good, they necessarily burden themselves with a common evil. It aims, not to remedy any errors committed in adjusting the bond, but, to cut it asunder and cast it away. It is called a system of complete freedom from restraint and perfect liberty. These terms, when looked at nearly, will be found to mean a dissolution of all bonds and total isolation of interests. Hence, in this particular case, where an end is to be gained, the attainment of which it is admitted would be beneficial to all, it is yet maintained that it is impossible for all to bring it to pass without hurting instead of benefiting themselves.

It is impossible to shut the eyes to the fact, that the introduction of an art into any country, enabling the labor of its inhabitants at once to transmute the products, which nature, in conjunction with their own industry, procures for them, into the commodities their wants demand, instead of sending them to a distance to other people to effect that change, is a great good to all, were it only for the mere saving of transport thus effected; but it is maintained, that it is impossible for all the members of the community advantageously to unite in bringing about this common benefit. It is clearly seen, that a new channel might be opened from the exhaustless river of human power, springing from the mingled sources of nature and art; and that, if so, a plenteous stream would flow in on the community, drawing from which individuals might add largely to the general opulence. But some means must be employed to open it up. There is an obstruction in the way that must previously be overcome; a rock blocking it up that must be removed. No individual will open up the channel, because, were he so to do, he could derive no more benefit from the labor than others who had not labored. The whole society, or rather the legislator, the power acting for the whole society, might do so, and in similar cases has done so, and, to judge of the measure by the events consequent on it, with the happiest success. Why, then, should he not?

The arguments advanced by the author of the *Wealth of Nations*, to prove that the legislator ought never to lend his aid to effect such a purpose, are chiefly contained in the second chapter of the fourth book. They will be found to rest almost altogether on the assumption, that national and individual capital increase in precisely the same manner. This notion, I flatter myself I have shown, cannot, by any means, be taken as a self-evident principle, or one so firmly established as to serve as the basis of an important practical doctrine. But, even admitting that the two processes are similar, the [theoretical] arguments of Adam Smith would not altogether bear out his conclusions.

It is, he says, and the sentiment serves for a motto, and forms, indeed, the substance of two volumes that have contributed greatly to spread his doctrines over Europe, "It is the maxim of every prudent master of a family, never to attempt to make at home what it will cost him more to make than to buy. The tailor does not attempt to make his own shoes, but buys them of the shoemaker. The shoemaker does not attempt to make his own clothes, but employs a tailor. The farmer attempts to make neither the one nor the other, but employs those different artificers. All of them find it for their interest to employ their whole industry in a way in which they have some advantage over their neighbors, and to purchase with a part of its produce, or, what is the same thing, with the price of a part of it, whatever else they have occasion for. What is prudence in the conduct of every private family can scarce be folly in that of a great kingdom."

To make the fanciful parallel here assumed as complete, in any sense just, it would be necessary to place the tailor at a hundred miles distance from the shoemaker. Were he at this distance, and did he find that the expense of getting a pair of shoes carried so far was considerable, perhaps exceeding their first cost, he might find it good economy even to make them himself. To be sure, the procuring the requisite tools and the learning their use, would render the making of the first few pairs much more expensive than the purchasing of them would have been. But this necessary dearness of the first articles produced might be compensated by the cheapness of those produced subsequently. In the same way, though a farmer, if the tailor and shoemaker were near at hand, would do wisely to employ them, yet, if they were at a great distance, he might possibly with advantage dispense with their services, and set some of his family to make clothes and shoes for the rest. A farmer, indeed, would have peculiar inducements to practise some trades, those, namely, for which he supplied the raw materials, as by doing so he would be saved the carriage, both of the articles made, and of the stuff for making them. It is thus, that, in fact, in most countries where the population is scattered and the internal communications are bad, many trades are practised in the farmers' houses and by their own families. In this way it is that, in very many of the recently settled parts of North America, every operation that the wool undergoes, from the taking off the fleece to the cutting and making up the cloth, is performed in the farmer's house and by his own family. A similar state of things caused a similar practice to prevail in England a century ago, and, at present, keeps up many of those manufactures which are properly termed domestic, in many other parts of Europe. In Canada it is not uncommon for the farmer to have, not only the whole processes that wool undergoes till it come to be worn, carried on by the members of his own family, but also to get a great variety of other things made by them, which he could not procure otherwise unless by sending to an inconvenient distance. The mending of shoes, very generally, the making of them, not unfrequently, and sometimes even the manufacturing the leather, are in recent and remote settlements thus performed. The latter process, I may add, from various circumstances, but chiefly from the use of the bark of a sort of pine peculiar to the country and in general very common, and which, unlike that of the oak, is very thick and easily collected, is much less expensive in Canada than in Britain.

I knew two brothers whose farms or estates lay in one of the interior districts of that country, in the midst of its forests, and consequently at a considerable distance, perhaps twenty or thirty miles, from artificers of any description. Having each of them large families and productive farms, they had occasion for the services of various artificers, and had the means of paying them. Nevertheless, they very rarely employed them; almost every article they required was made by some one of the two families. As they were prudent and sagacious men, of which they produced the best evidence in the general success of their undertakings, and the prosperity of the settlement of which they were at the head, I think it likely, that in this also they had turned their means to the best account. In fact, as they who are familiar with the details of beginning settlements in North America will admit, by this plan they in a great measure obviated the two chief drawbacks on the prosperity of new and remote settlements, the excessive dearness of every article not produced there, from the great expense attending the transport of the raw produce and retransport of the manufactured goods, and the serious inconvenience arising from the difficulty, in such situations, of supplying, when necessary, unforeseen but pressing wants.

Among other things which they got made on their own farms, were boots, shoes, and leather. That they might get this done, they were at the pains and expense of sending one of the young men to some distance, to make himself sufficiently master of those trades for their purpose. They thought, however, that the cost they were thus put to was repaid, thrice over, by the saving of time and expense which it effected for them, in enabling them to make, out of leather which cost them very little, numerous articles that they must otherwise have been constantly sending for, to a great distance by roads that were almost impracticable a great part of the year. I do not know whether in this their conduct was judicious or otherwise, but, it is very certain, that however apparently prudent the measure may have been, and however great the saving effected by it might have been, it was completely contrary to our author's doctrines, and might easily be shown by them to have been necessarily and inevitably injurious.

We may suppose that, just at the time when these two legislators of this little community had come to the determination of taking means to dispense with the services of the distant tanner and shoemaker, they were addressed on this subject by a philosopher of this school. His reasonings would doubtless have been in the following strain. "You are assuredly wrong in the plan you are going to adopt, for it proceeds upon very erroneous and illiberal principles, as I can easily show you. You are in want, you say, of some pairs of shoes, surely then it is best for you to purchase them where you can get them cheapest. But, by the plan you are taking of going to a great expense to have them made at home, they will certainly cost you more when made there, than if bought at the place where you have hitherto purchased shoes. And, if that place can still supply you with this commodity cheaper than you yourself can make it, better buy it there with some part of the produce of your own industry. The general industry of your settlement must always be in proportion to the capital which employs it, and will not be diminished by being left to be employed in a way in which you have some advantage. By forcing it to produce an object which it can buy cheaper than it can make, it certainly is not employed to the greatest advantage. Let things therefore take their natural course, and shoes will be made at your doors when it is fit for them to be made there."

To these reasonings our legislators might possibly reply, "We confess that the first pairs of shoes that we get, will cost us much more, thus made at home, than they would do were we to buy them abroad. But then it will only be for the first articles manufactured that we shall pay so high, in the end they will come cheaper to us at home than from abroad; and it is to effect this desirable result, that we are going to undertake the project. We don't understand very well what you mean by the natural course of affairs, but we think the sooner we can get them to take a course, that will before long make things cheaper to us, the better." The answer to this in the words of our author would be: "I don't at all dispute, that, by means of this project, this particular manufacture may be acquired sooner than it could be otherwise, and after a certain time, may be made at home as cheap, or cheaper, than abroad. But, though the industry of your society may be thus carried with advantage into a particular channel sooner than it could have been otherwise, it will by no means follow that the sum total, either of its industry, or its revenue, can ever be augmented by any such project. The industry of your society can augment only in proportion as its capital augments, and its capital can augment only in proportion to what can be saved out of its revenue. But the immediate effect of this project of yours is to diminish its revenue; and what diminishes its revenue is certainly not very likely to augment its capital faster than it would augment, were you to leave capital and industry to find their natural employments."

Our legislators might still possibly answer. "As far as we can comprehend your arguments they reduce themselves to this. We have to give out what is a considerable sum to us, before we can carry this project into effect, and, for this outlay, you think we shall get no adequate return. Now in this our opinion differs from yours. We know indeed that we must expend something, but we think that in the long run we shall be better repaid for this expenditure, by this undertaking, than by any other in which we could employ our funds. We never yet got any thing without giving something for it, and, although we in this instance give money or money's worth, and get chiefly knowledge and skill in return, yet if you will take the trouble of examining the calculations we have been making of the saving which we shall in a few years effect, chiefly by means of this knowledge and skill, on what we annually pay for shoes and boots, we think you will agree with us that we shall gather in three times what we gave out."

"No, no," our philosopher would exclaim, "this is quite unnecessary, I see now how the case stands. I perceive you have got a theory as well as I have. But your theory is that of practical men who reason upon facts, whereas my theory is built upon general axioms. Now there is this great difference between two such theories, that when they are opposed to each other the latter, such as mine must always be right, the former such as yours, wrong. My main axiom on which is founded a great system is, that capital always augments by accumulation. This you perceive is a general axiom, and however it may be that there may be apparent exceptions to it, yet as it is a general axiom, it is a philosophical consequence that these exceptions can only be apparent. Your theory is opposed to this axiom of mine, for you pretend to say that capital may be augmented by other means than simple accumulation, and very strangely assert that, after giving it out of your hands, you will get it replaced to you, with large profit, out of the skill and knowledge which the outlay has procured you. But, as in proof of this you bring me only facts and figures, you will see of course that it is quite unnecessary for me to notice such arguments; for, however plainly it might from them appear that your scheme is practicable and must ultimately liberally repay your advances, yet, this conclusion being proved by reasoning, is a theory, and that theory having the disadvantage of not being drawn like mine from general axioms, and being merely a laborious deduction from particular observations, it must of necessity follow from indubitable philosophical principles, that it is wrong, and mine right. The case being so, you are, I hope, men of too good sense to dispute the matter farther. Should you however persevere I must take the liberty of telling you that you are too narrow-minded theorists, and that, by interfering, in the manner you are about to do, with the natural course of events, you will infallibly waste the resources of your infant community, and retard its prosperity."

I apprehend such philosophic arguments would not have had much success with them or other men of practice, and that, even should we take the procedure adopted by individuals, as a fit model for that of nations, we would not find that it altogether agreed with the rules which the doctrines of Adam Smith inculcate. The reason is, that individuals, as well as nations, acquire wealth from other sources than mere saving from revenue; that skill is as necessary, and consequently as valuable, a coöperator with the industry of both, as either capital or parsimony; and that therefore the expenditure which either may be called on to make to attain the requisite skill, is very well bestowed.

But, though skill is valuable both to nations and to individuals, there are many circumstances that render it more so to the former, than to the latter. In the first place, it is more durable. Whatever may be the perfection to which an individual may have brought his skill, dexterity, and judgment, in conducting any particular set of operations, that perfection perishes with him. Whatever expense it may have cost him to acquire this possession, and however valuable it may be to himself, he cannot transmit it to his heirs. But any addition which a society makes, to the skill, dexterity, and judgment, with which its members exercise any branch of industry, is not of this fleeting nature. Instead of the benefits derived from it, being bounded by the short space of time that the active life of an individual embraces, they are continuous with the national existence. If it be worth while paying a considerable apprentice-fee, for the acquisition of an art, which can probably only be exercised for twenty or thirty years, it must be better worth while to pay for one, the advantages derived from the possession of which, may be retained for hundreds or thousands of years.

Again, whatever an individual may expend in acquiring any degree of skill is, to a certain extent, lost to him; though he may draw a revenue, he cannot draw a capital from it. No portion of the future skilled labor of an individual can be sold, because it can only be sold with himself, and such bargains, sanctioned in ancient, are not so in modern times. Nowhere can one effectually make over his services for a certain time to any other person, because, nowhere can he give that person the power of enforcing their exertion. On the contrary, any portion of the future revenue, yielded by the skilled industry of a nation, may be sold, and, consequently an addition to the national skill gives a proportional addition to the command of national resources, to meet any sudden emergency. The produce of the general industry of Great Britain, stands mortgaged for a sum, which it would have appeared a century ago utterly impossible to conceive that industry could sustain, because, a century ago, it was impossible to conceive the vast increase which has since been made to the skill, dexterity, and judgment, with which it was then directed.

Besides these and other differences between the effects resulting from the acquisition of skill in the pursuits of industry by nations, and by individuals, there is one on which I have already enlarged. An increase of skill seems to be always a necessary concomitant of the increase of national wealth, whereas it is not always a concomitant of the increase of individual wealth. It is not therefore true, that nations and individuals increase their wealth in the same manner, nor, were it so, do the rules, which modern political economists lay down for the increase of national wealth, agree with those which individuals adopt in their endeavours to augment their private stocks.

The main arguments, however, which the author brings forward, are built on what he assumes to be general principles. The doctrine he maintains throughout his whole system, and more particularly in the chapter to which I have alluded, turns on the following passage.

"If a foreign country can supply us with a commodity cheaper than we ourselves can make it, better buy it of them with some part of the produce of our own industry, employed in a way in which we have some advantage. The general industry of the country being always in proportion to the capital which employs it, will not thereby be diminished, no more than the capital of an artificer is diminished who purchases an article from another practising a different art instead of making it himself. It will only be left to find out the way in which it can be employed with the greatest advantage. It is certainly not employed to the greatest advantage, when it is thus directed towards an object which it can buy cheaper than it can make. The value of its annual produce is certainly more or less diminished, when it is thus turned away from producing commodities evidently of more value than the commodity which it is directed to produce. According to the supposition, that commodity could be purchased from foreign countries cheaper than it can be made at home; it could therefore have been purchased with a part only of the commodities, or, what is the same thing, with a part only of the price of the commodities, which the industry employed by an equal capital would have produced at home, had it been left to follow its natural course. The industry of the country, therefore, is thus turned away from a more to a less advantageous employment; and the exchangable value of its annual produce, instead of being increased, according to the intention of the law-giver, must necessarily be diminished by every such regulation.

"By means of such regulations, indeed, a particular manufacture may sometimes be acquired sooner than it could have been otherwise, and after a certain time may be made at home as cheap, or cheaper, than in the foreign country. But though the industry of the society may be thus carried with advantage into a particular channel sooner than it could have been otherwise, it will by no means follow that the sum total either of its industry or of its revenue, can ever be augmented by any such regulation. The industry of the society can augment only in proportion as its capital augments, and its capital can augment only in proportion to what can be gradually saved out of its revenue. But the immediate effect of every such regulation is to diminish its revenue; and what diminishes its revenue is certainly not very likely to augment its capital faster than it would have augmented of its own accord, had both capital and industry been left to find out their natural employments.

"Though, for want of such regulations, the society should never acquire the proposed manufacture, it would not upon that account necessarily be the poorer in any one period of its duration. In every period of its duration its whole capital and industry might still have been employed, though upon different objects, in the manner that was most advantageous at the time. In every period its revenue might have been the greatest which its capital could afford, and both capital and revenue might have been augmented with the greatest possible rapidity.

"The natural advantages which one country has over another,

in producing particular commodities, are sometimes so great that it is acknowledged by all the world to be in vain to struggle with them. By means of glasses, hot-beds, and hot-walls, very good grapes can be raised in Scotland and very good wine, too, can be made of them, at about thirty times the expense for which at least equally good can be brought from foreign countries. Would it be a reasonable law to prohibit the importation of all foreign wines, merely to encourage the making of claret and burgundy in Scotland? But if there would be a manifest absurdity in turning towards any employment thirty times more of the capital and industry of the country than would be necessary to purchase from foreign countries an equal quantity of the commodities wanted, there must be an absurdity, though not altogether so glaring, yet exactly of the same kind, in turning towards any such employment a thirtieth, or even a three hundredth part of either. Whether the advantages which one country has over another be natural or acquired, is in this respect of no consequence. As long as the one country has those advantages and the other wants them, it will always be more advantageous for the latter rather to buy of the former than to make. It is an acquired advantage only, which one artificer has over his neighbor who exercises another trade; and yet they both find it more advantageous to buy of one another, than to make what does not belong to their particular trades."

I must be excused for running somewhat into repetition in observing, that the strength of this passage evidently lies in the axioms, "The industry of the society can augment only as its capital augments, and its capital can augment only in proportion to what can be gradually saved out of its revenue;" and that the proper answer to these axioms is, either, that they prove nothing, or, that they prove it by a begging of the question, by assuming that to be proved which is in process of proof. The expression, the industry of the society can augment only as its capital augments, may signify, either, that the augmentation of a society's capital, and an increase of its productive industry always accompany each other; or, that every augmentation of the productiveness of the general industry, is produced by an augmentation of capital, and can be produced by nothing else. In like manner, the expression, the capital of the society can augment only in proportion to what can be gradually saved out of its revenue, may signify, either, merely that the saving from revenue is a necessary part of the increase of the general capital, and measures its amount, or, that there are no other means of augmenting its capital but it. In the former of these two senses the axioms prove nothing; in the latter they prove all things desired, because they assume them as acknowledged truths. The double meaning of the assumptions contained in these axioms, and the fallacy into which they may, in consequence, be made to lead, may be easily perceived by an application of them to the transactions of an individual.

A person residing in England, owns an estate in the West Indies, which he proposes to visit. His motives to do so are, that he thinks, that, by his personal superintendence, he can give a better direction to the industry employed on it, and render the returns greater. In order to do so, it is necessary for him to procure and expend a certain sum to pay for the expense of the voyage, and the cost of the various articles which his private accommodation will require there; and he therefore takes measures to apply to this purpose a considerable part of one year's revenue of the estate. On account of this disbursement, some one objects to the project, and endeavors, in the following manner, to prove to him that it must be hurtful to his interests:

"The augmented productiveness of your estate, and the increased amount of capital at which it will be estimated, must go on together. But, to add to capital, it is necessary to save from revenue. Now the scheme you are about to embark in requires first a large expenditure of revenue. It must therefore tend to prevent your augmenting your capital, and consequently the productive industry of your estate, which two things always go on together." The answer to this reasoning would be: "It is chiefly because I am aware that the productiveness of my estate, and what it is worth, are inseparably conjoined, that I am about to be at this expense and trouble, for I believe they will enable me to put things in such a train that its productiveness will greatly increase, and, as its value I know depends on the revenue it yields, my capital will consequently be augmented by much more than the sum I am going to expend."

"I perceive I have not expressed my meaning properly," replies the adviser, "I should have said; an increased productiveness of your estate, can be produced by no other means than by an augmentation of the capital employed on it, and the amount of capital you can possess and can employ on it, can be augmented in no other way than by saving from your revenue. But this plan of yours causes an expenditure of your revenue, it must therefore prevent you from adding to your capital, and, consequently, from increasing the productiveness of the industry which is set in motion by it on your estate."

The West India proprietor might undoubtedly reply: "My dear Sir you are completely wrong. The productiveness of my estate depends, not only on the amount of the capital which sets the industry employed on it in motion, but on the sort of motion it gives it; and I hope so to improve this, by a more judicious regulation of it, that the same power will produce a far greater effect than it does at present, and thus to show you, that there are other means of augmenting capital than simple saving. For I take it, that if I add to my gains, without increasing my expenditure, the procedure may be just as effective to this end, as if I were to diminish my expenditure, and not add to my gains."

If we understand the axioms of our author in the former sense of the expressions, it is clear, that when applied to national capital, they prove nothing more than when applied to individual capital. For, if it be merely meant that the productiveness of national industry, and the augmentation of national capital advance together, the propriety of a proposed measure may as well be inferred from its tendency to render the industry of the community more productive, as its impropriety may be inferred from its requiring a small immediate expenditure of revenue. The question to be determined in every such case, would then be similar to that which an individual determines when deliberating on any scheme for the augmentation of his private capital, and would resolve itself into an inquiry, whether or not the probable returns from the proposed measure, be likely to be a sufficient remuneration for the expense of carrying it into effect. But, it is very clear, that this would be a constrained interpretation of the import of the passage; and that the inference the author wished his expressions to convey, is, that an increased productiveness of the industry of the society can be produced by no other means but by augmenting its capital, and that the only means entering into the process of augmenting its capital are saving from its revenue.

The proper answer to these axioms, so understood, is,—this is your theory no doubt, but it is a theory which is merely in process of proof, and not yet established. Surely, then, it is scarce logical to answer a very obvious objection to it, which the observation of human affairs presents, by assuming its truth; or, to deduce the impropriety of a practical measure, drawn from the phenomena which human affairs present, and apparently very beneficial, by showing that such measure is contrary to its principles.

The question hitherto stands thus. You pretend to account for the phenomena of the augmentation of national wealth by showing, that an increase of national capital tends to facilitate the division of labor; that this division of labor in itself greatly improves the productive powers of labor, and is the cause of all other improvements in them. That this increase of the productive powers of labor, being equivalent to an increase of the revenue of the society, adds to its power of accumulating fresh capital and giving farther extent to the division of labor, the great generator, according to your system, of all wealth. It is in this way that, according to you, the augmentation of the industry of the society is produced by an augmentation of its capital, and in no other manner, and its capital is augmented by saving from revenue and nothing else, and that, from the action and reaction of these principles on each other, the whole phenomena of the growth of national capital are deducible.

Now, admitting for the present that no fallacy can be detected in the principles themselves, they must still be admitted to be only possible or probable theoretical assumptions, to be proved by the observation of their coincidence with facts. Admitting then also that, as far as the facts which relate to what we may call the history of the internal progress of national wealth are concerned, they sufficiently accord with them, there is another class of facts admitted by you, which these principles do not explain, and to which, on the contrary, they seem to be opposed.

Arts and manufactures, the great sources of increase to the productive powers of labor, do, it is granted, pass from country to country. It would appear then, that the gradual increase which the accumulation of capital produces on the productive powers of any society, is not alone sufficient to call forth all the resources which that society possesses; but that it is often necessary to seek in other countries for the means, which give these resources full efficiency. In such cases, at least, therefore, the augmented wealth of the society cannot be said altogether to flow from the gradual increase of its capital by accumulation, the consequent division of labor, and the improvements thence resulting. Your theory is, therefore, so far most certainly defective, as it acknowledges the existence of a class of phenomena, the laws regulating which its principles by no means explain.

Instead, however, of attempting to answer the objections to your system, which this class of phenomena present, you pretend to say, that the practical rules directly, and in the simplest manner, deducible from them, are of necessity erroneous, because contrary to the principles of your system. It being acknowledged by every one, even by yourself, that the improvements of the productive powers of labor thus effected by the continued spread of the arts of civilized life from country to country, are among the chief causes of the progress of national wealth and prosperity, they who have had the management of national affairs, have in different cases come to the unavoidable conclusion, that they did well in even sacrificing a small portion of the national revenue, provided this outlay served to introduce acknowledged improvement in the national industry, and source of national wealth. They have acted in this as an individual would do in the management of his private affairs, they have endeavored to introduce an improvement into the management of the funds with which they were intrusted, and have considered the price to be paid for such improvement warranted by the increased productive powers it would give to the same capital, and consequent increase to the national revenue, and national funds, which it would tend to produce. Like individual schemes their projects seem sometimes to have succeeded, and sometimes to have failed. But though, when he acts, it is incident to man's imperfect nature occasionally to err, to sit down therefore in resolute inactivity would be the worst error he could commit.

The celebrated author admits, that a manufacture may be introduced by the operations of the legislator, sooner than it could otherwise be, and thus come to be made at home as cheap, or cheaper, than abroad. But then, he says, in spite of these apparent advantages of such a proceeding on his part, it must be wrong, because it is contrary to my system. And, before you can prove that it is justifiable, you must prove that the benefits resulting from it could not possibly have happened some other way. "Though, for want of such regulations, the society should never acquire the proposed manufacture, it would not upon that account necessarily be the poorer in any one period of its duration. In every period of its duration, its whole capital and industry might still have been employed, though upon different objects, in the manner that was most advantageous at the time. In every period its revenue might have been the greatest which its capital could afford, and both capital and revenue might have been augmented with the greatest possible rapidity."

Now, I conceive, that instead of calling on his opponents to prove, that all the advantages arising from any such scheme might possibly come to pass without it, he himself has to show, that they must come to pass without it. And, that he has to do so, not by assuming his theoretical principles as true, —for, if they are so, his axioms embrace and decide this and every case at once,—but by an examination of the course of human affairs, and a regular deduction from them, of the certainty of these apparent advantages, or others equivalent to them, flowing in from some other channel than that of which he would bar the opening.

A nation imports from a distance a manufactured commodity, which it is granted it could make as cheap, or cheaper, at home, were the manufacture introduced there. To introduce the manufacture is, however, too expensive a project to be carried into effect by any private individual. The whole society might do so, through the expenditure for a few years of a portion of its revenue, much less than what an equal number of years succeeding them will return to it in the diminished cost of the article. He, or they, who legislate for the society, embrace the apparent benefit, and, by means of a small expenditure, effect an increase of the productive powers of the community; that is, they give those powers the capability of producing the same quantity of an article with less expense, which certainly must be allowed to be an increase of them. In this the legislator acts in a manner that would be accounted prudence in a private person, who conducted any system of industry for his own emolument: in a planter, for instance, who owned and managed a West India estate. We should undoubtedly approve of such a person's being at considerable expense, in instructing his overseers and negroes, in any improved mode of conducting the business of the plantation, if this improvement more than proportionably augmented his revenue. Neither have the proceedings of legislators, in many cases parallel in principle to this, been ever objected to. It sometimes happens, for instance, that those engaged in cultivating the ground know that they can procure seeds of plants, or races of animals, at a distance, better fitted for their purposes than those they have at home. If the expense of procuring them is small, and such as will be remunerated to an individual by the gain, individuals send for such seeds and animals. If it is greater, they sometimes club in societies for the purpose. If it be too great for these societies, the legislator aids them in their scheme, or carries it into effect himself. In this way it was, that, it being thought that the culture of the bread fruit tree, a plant indigenous to the Pacific Ocean, could it be introduced into our West India Islands, would be of advantage to them, government were at the expense of sending more than one vessel, on that long voyage, in order to transport the plant there. No one did, or could object, to the outlay of a portion of the public revenue for a purpose so laudable. In this instance, it will be allowed by all, that it would have been as absurd to have waited in expectation that some individual should find, or should imagine he would find it for his own private advantage to undertake so expensive a scheme, as it would be to complain of the comparatively trifling expenditure of the common funds, which the accomplishment of this project conducive to the common good required. But the expenditure of a certain amount of national revenue, for the purpose of transporting an useful art from a distant country, bears, surely, a close analogy to a similar expenditure, for the purpose of transporting an useful plant.[1] If the one be praiseworthy, the other can scarce deserve the censure that has been heaped on it.

Our author further observes: "The natural advantages which one country has over another, in producing particular commodities are sometimes so great that it is acknowledged by all the world to be in vain to struggle with them." And, as an instance, he gives the project of raising grapes, for the purpose of making wine, in Scotland.

Extreme cases are useful, but, to be so, they should be correctly put. The main question in dispute is, whether or not it is proper to introduce a manufacture from abroad, by the aid of the legislator, which, when so introduced, will furnish a commodity for home consumption at as low, or at a lower price, than it can be bought for in the foreign country. The supposed case of a commodity which, if the manufacture of it be introduced at home, will cost thirty times more, or a thirtieth, or three hundredth part more there than abroad, can have nothing to do with the determination of such a question.

"Whether the advantages which one country has over another be natural or acquired, is in this respect of no consequence." On the contrary, in my opinion, it is of the greatest consequence, and, for this very reason, that it is only "as long as the one country has those advantages, and the other wants

---

[1] [In the case of the promotion of an industry by means of protective duties (in contrast to bounties), there is no "certain amount" of outlay of the resources of the people; there is no book-keeping possible; no one ever knows how much has been its cost.]

them, that it will more advantageous for the latter rather to buy of the former than to make." Now natural advantages cannot be procured by any expenditure of revenue or capital, but acquired advantages may often be got by means of a very small expenditure. One country cannot, at any purchase, acquire the soil, the climate, the commodiousness of situation for conducting trade, or any of the other natural advantages which another country possesses; were it so, the price would be very large that would not be willingly paid for them. But one country can often with ease, and at a trifling expense, acquire the practical skill and the knowledge of particular arts and manufactures which another possesses, and, by doing so, gain the advantage of procuring for itself the products of this skill and knowledge at home, instead of having to go abroad for them. In the passage quoted, natural advantages and acquired are reckoned equivalents, and so undoubtedly they are. They are both valuable on account of the products they yield to human labor. But they differ in this, that the latter can be transferred from one country to another, the former cannot. Could Scotland acquire the sunny skies and more genial climate of France, its hills might be covered with vineyards, instead of heather, and its inhabitants might procure many commodities at a fourth of the price which they now cost them. No one would object to a considerable expenditure to acquire so great an advantage. If then, the acquisition of natural advantages would be worth paying for, why object to a small expenditure to procure advantages which are allowed to be equivalent to those natural advantages?

As the author has given one supposed case, as he conceived illustrative of the question, I may be permitted to give another, also illustrative of it; not like his, however, springing from assumptions liable to be objected to, but, as will be seen, framed upon his very principles and admissions.

A certain country has the acquired advantage over another of possessing the knowledge of a particular art, which this other wants. The latter, therefore, imports from the former all the goods, the product of that art, which it has occasion for. As it has to pay for these goods, it luckily happens that it, on its side, has also acquired advantages in possessing the knowledge of another art, which the former wants, and the commodities produced by which it has occasion for. In this way, the one sort of goods pays for the other. The natural and acquired advantages of these two countries are either similar or equivalent. That is, their soil, climate, convenience of situation for trade, and their knowledge of other arts, though not exactly the same, are on the whole equally balanced, their population and capital are equal. In short, they as much resemble two neighbouring artificers, according to the comparison of our author, exercising different trades, as extensive communities inhabiting separate countries well can resemble single workmen whose dwellings are contiguous. The peculiar manufacture of the one nation is hats, of the other silk goods. The silk goods which the one annually consumes cost it £2,000,000; the hats which the other consumes, the same sum. Of these sums 25 per cent. is made up of transport, including in the term, not the mere freight, but the whole charges paid for internal transport, for warehousing, and for the profits of the different capitals, and wages of the various individuals concerned in collecting the commodities in the one country, carrying them to, and distributing them over the other. Thus the annual sum which these commodities cost each country, over and above the [prime] expense of producing them, is £400,000. In this situation things have long remained, and must continue to remain, unless altered by some change in the policy, or great revolution in the affairs of the two countries. "It being only for the sake of profit that any man employs a capital in the support of industry," and, from the acquired advantages which each country enjoys over the other in the production of its peculiar manufacture, it being impossible for any projector to manufacture hats, in the country where hats have not hitherto been made, or silks, in the country where silks have not hitherto been made, but at an outlay of more than 25 per cent. over what they cost in the country where these respective manufactures are established, no such project will be entered on. The legislators of the two countries, have hitherto agreed with our author, that, as it is the maxim of every prudent master of a family, never to make at home what it will cost him more to make than to buy; what is prudence in the conduct of every private family can scarce be folly in that of a great kingdom; and that, whether the advantages which one country has over another be natural or acquired, is of no consequence, it being an acquired advantage only, which one artificer has over his neighbor, who exercises another trade, though they both find it for their advantage, rather to buy of one another, than to make what does not belong to their peculiar trade Acting on these principles, they have thought it improper to make any alteration in the system.

About this time, however, a change takes place in their opinions, and they begin to think, that as, though it would not be very prudent in the tailor, that he might have his shoes made in his own workshop instead of his neighbor's, to set about making them himself, or the shoemaker, for the same reason, to set about making his own coat, yet, if there were a town in which there were no shoemakers, but more than enough of tailors, and another, a dozen miles off, in which there were no tailors, but more than enough of shoemakers, it would be a beneficial change for some of the tailors to remove to the one town, and some of the shoemakers to the other, that the inhabitants of both might have the articles fabricated by these different sorts of tradesmen, made at home, that is, within their respective towns,—so, two countries, of which the one made no hats, and the other no silk goods, might mutually benefit by the introduction of the manufacture in which each was deficient, the inhabitants of each in like manner as the inhabitants of each town, having that provided at home, which they must otherwise go abroad for, and thus being saved like them, the expense and inconvenience of transportation.

Though such a change, in either case, could not be brought about without expense, and though "its immediate effect would therefore be to diminish the revenue of the society," yet, as after a certain time, it would be likely that the new manufacture would be made at home in each case "as cheap or cheaper than abroad," its ultimate effect would be, more than proportionably, to increase the revenues of both towns and both countries.

Acting on these new views, the legislators of both countries, about the same time, commence encouraging the manufactures in which their respective countries are deficient; and, by means of a system of premiums, bounties, and duties, on the detail of which it is unnecessary to enter, succeed so far, in the course of years, that silk goods come actually to be fabricated in the country where no silk goods were manufactured, as cheaply as where they were exclusively manufactured, and hats to be made, where no hats were made, as cheaply as where hats were exclusively made. Part of the capital and industry which went in the one case to the manufacture of hats, goes to manufacture silk goods, and, in the other case, part of the capital and industry which went to manufacture silk goods, goes to manufacture hats. Both countries produce that at home, which they before imported from abroad, and are therefore saved the expense attending that importation.

Completely to effect this change requires an outlay, in both cases, of £1,000,000. Being effected however, it of course saves each country the expense of transport, which, at 25 per cent. on the imported goods, makes an annual saving of its expenditure, and increase therefore of its revenue, of £400,000; so that, in two or three years time, the sum expended is repaid, and each community supplied with a new fund to furnish additional comforts to its members, or to add to their capital. According to our author's tenets, this proceeding of both legislators, although admitted to be practicable, is yet held to be necessarily, and in its very nature, injurious.

Although it can seldom happen, that two countries are so circumstanced that both, according to our supposition, can benefit equally by the effecting of such a change, yet, if one effect such a change, as far as that country is concerned it would seem to be beneficial, on a simple calculation of expense and gain, provided the saving of revenue produced by it, is greater than the expenditure of revenue necessary for producing it. It is this end which the legislator generally aims at reaching by the regulations he imposes on the trade and industry of the society, and which, by these means, he often arrives at. Yet, even when in such cases successful, our author maintains, that his proceedings are necessarily, and essentially prejudicial to the interests of the society. That, even though they may cause a commodity to be produced at home, cheaper than abroad, they must diminish, instead of augmenting, the national revenue and riches. A conclusion so extraordinary, is arrived at by a process of reasoning as extraordinary. It is come to by setting out from it. Two general axioms, somewhat ambiguous and vague, are assumed as truths. As usually happens to all other axioms employed in general reasoning, and capable of conveying two senses, they are granted in the one sense, and applied in the other. We assent to the propositions, " the industry of the society can augment only in proportion as its capital augments, and its capital can augment only in proportion to what can be gradually saved out of its revenue," because we see, that the augmentation of industry and capital, the saving from revenue and increase of capital, are concomitants of each other; we perceive not, that in the application of these propositions, the sense in which we assented to them is abandoned, and that the augmentation of the capital of the society is assumed as the cause, and the sole cause of the increase of its industry, and the saving from revenue, as the cause, and the sole cause, of the augmentation of its capital. Whereas, from the observation of the increase of the productiveness of national industry, and of the amount of national capital, going on in general together, we may at least as justly infer that it is the industry which augments the capital, as the capital the industry, and rather come to the conclusion, that part of the national resources should be employed in giving perfection to the industry of the society than that they should be altogether devoted to attempts to increase its capital. In fact, as capital, according to Adam Smith himself, is only valuable for the addition it makes to the efficiency of the national industry, and, as that efficiency is also, according to him, mainly dependent on the skill, dexterity, and judgment, with which it is applied, an expenditure of capital or revenue, having the effect of increasing the national skill, dexterity, and judgment, would seem to be the most judicious possible, seeing it directly increases those sources of production, from the indirect addition that it makes to which, capital is said to derive its sole value.

It has been my endeavor to show, in the preceding examination of the system of Adam Smith, that the doctrine there maintained, of the expediency of the legislator's abstaining from any attempt to give increased efficiency to the industry of the society by encouraging the growth of domestic arts or the importation of foreign, founded on the supposition of the perfect identity of the means which add to the wealth of individuals and nations, is erroneous.

1. That the reasonings which make it assume the form of a self-evident principle, have their foundation in the ambiguities of language alone, and that, in reality, the presumption is against, not for it.

2. That viewed as a consequence of the theory of the accumulation of capital, the division of labor, and the improvements resulting from the action and reaction of these principles on each other, the judgment we form of it must be altogether determined by the probable accuracy of the principles on which that theory proceeds, and by its coincidence with facts; that granting, for the present, the apparent probability of the theoretical principles themselves, they nevertheless do not agree with the phenomena; that there is a class of admitted facts, which they not only do not explain, but to which they are in opposition; that the increase of the wealth of every community is acknowledged to be dependent, not only on the accumulation of capital and division of labor among its members, but also on the progress of arts in other communities, and their subsequent transfer to it; that to effect this transfer, a measure admitted to be all-important to the prosperity of the community, the efforts of individuals are insufficient; that, in his endeavors to prove that the legislator ought not here to interfere, Adam Smith runs into inconsistencies and contradictions, and that there hence arises a proof of the inapplicability of his doctrine to events of this order, and a strong presumption of the existence of some fundamental error in the general principles of his system.

[In the foregoing Rae successfully exposes some serious errors in the economic theory with which Adam Smith supported his doctrine of free trade. Especially is this true with respect to Smith's theory of saving.

But in the course of his own positive teaching on the subject of the benefits of an educational tariff, Rae does not himself avoid falling into errors in economics. The chief of these is his assumption that always, or nearly always, a new art introduced by measures of protection, will make improvements in its strange environment—will exhibit the working of the principle of invention—to such a degree, that its products will soon be furnished cheaper by the domestic manufacturer than before by the foreign importer. It is in the nature of things that there will be, with respect to such experiments, many cases of disappointment; and when this last takes place, it is inevitable that as a rule defeat will not be acknowledged and the project abandoned. But this brings us back again to politics.

It is especially worthy of note that Rae's argument for the adoption of measures of protection rests entirely upon indirect and collateral economic considerations. The direct and immediate effects of obstructing foreign trade in articles which are not luxuries are injurious—they retard the formation and exhaustion of instruments. The position taken in Chapter XI. is all that any free trader could desire. It is only the ulterior economic effects of protection (explained in the present Article) which may work beneficially, offsetting proximate effects.

It seems doubly strange, therefore, that Rae should have overlooked all the contingencies of a political nature respecting this subject. In all the rest of his writing he takes the high, comprehensive, sociological point of view, and is sagacious—scenting danger from afar. The chief evil of protectionism is that it leads inevitably to corruption—not merely corruption as ordinarily understood, but a general lowering of the tone of the national life. It is well known that in the United States to-day each interest and section prides itself on its superior finesse in securing tariff favors for itself—in getting money from fellow-citizens by indirection. The system as it actually works in practice has become primarily not a matter of national "creation," but a matter of individual and local "acquisition" of wealth, and it carries the spirit of graft into every corner of the land, and makes it respectable. What it means to a people to preserve its spiritual integrity—that it pays for a people to hold to ideals, even though arts perish—Rae very well knew. The following passage from his unpublished manuscript sets forth this important truth most eloquently :]

"Now though it is undoubtedly true in the general that with regard to external nature knowledge is the power which raises man in the scale of being and distinguishes him from the inferior animals, yet we by no means find that it is the degree in which they practically apply this knowledge that determines the relative position of particular races or communities. It is not the external and visible—what he eats, what he drinks, or wherewithal he is clothed—but his inner and secret life that makes the man, constitutes his joy and sorrow, shapes his course through this world and determines his fate for the next. So it is with nations. It is neither the form of their dwellings, the victuals that nourish them, nor the fashion of their dress; it is their interior life, the degree in which the perception of the true, the good, the beautiful permeates their being, the view which their social feelings and passions lead them to take of things external and the course of action they are thus prompted to pursue, that makes them what they are, which ultimately determines their relative positions and controls their destinies.

. . . .

"It is known that the northern portion of the island of Great Britain had at an early period made greater progress than the southern in the arts of peace. It could scarcely well have been otherwise. For, while for about two hundred years England was devastated by the cruel wars necessary for the subjugation of the Saxon to the Norman yoke, during all that time, Celt, Saxon, Norman, and Dane lived peacefully together in Scotland under a succession of native princes and were being blended into one common people. There is full evidence that the rude abundance of an agriculture successfully prosecuted was widely diffused among them; and facts are not wanting to testify that the more elaborate arts had there begun to flourish.

"But now the Norman having brought England completely under his rule sought to extend that rule over Scotland. His domination was hateful to the people and they determined never to submit to it. But how resist the united force of a kingdom so much more powerful than their own? They retreated to the fastnesses of their mountains, woods, and marshes, and, leaving the open country a prey to the enemy, they watched their opportunity, and only issued forth and gave battle when to conquer was possible. A warfare continued thus for many generations necessarily put to flight all but the most essential arts, rendering the country bare and barren, and the mode of life of the inhabitants the rudest possible. So their French auxiliaries describe them. They depict them as a poverty-stricken and barbarous race, among whom it was impossible to live. Here was, in many respects, a sensible retrogression—a retrogression to a state of semi-barbarism. The question is, was it altogether a retrogression? Had the Scot made a step backward, or was it in truth a step forward? In my opinion there can be no question that it was a step in advance. In thus throwing to the winds all the comforts of life, and counting as nothing what he sacrificed or suffered for his national liberties and national independence, the spirit of the Scot assumed a higher tone and his soul was trained greatly to dare and bravely to do, wherever great and worthy objects were to be achieved. Adversity was upon him,

> 'Stern rigid nurse, thy rugged lore
> With patience many a year he bore.'

"But he issued from her school a greater and nobler man than he ever otherwise could have become [and what he has accomplished in happier times all the world knows]."

AUTHOR'S NOTES.

NOTE A. *Referred to on page* 1.

"We derive from Dr. Smith no assistance in forming our opinions on this important subject; for he seems to have had no fixed ideas in relation to it. Indeed, there is no opinion that has been any where maintained on the subject of the sources of national wealth, which does not appear to have been adopted in different parts of the *Inquiry into the Wealth of Nations.*

1. "The annual labor of every nation is" at one time stated to be " the fund which originally supplies it with all the necessaries and conveniencies of life which it annually consumes, and which consists always either in the immediate produce of that labor, or in what is purchased with that produce from other nations."[1]

2. Lands, mines, and fisheries, elsewhere are regarded as replacing, "with a profit, not only the capitals employed in them, but all the other capitals employed in the community."[2] That, however, which replaces all the capital employed in the community, and is the source from whence they derive their profit, must be the sole source of wealth. Mankind are, therefore, here considered as deriving the whole of their wealth from land.[3]

3. Again, plain reason is stated to dictate that the real wealth of a country consists in the annual produce of its land

---

[1] *Wealth of Nations*, vol. I., p. 1, 4to. edit. This opinion is maintained by Mr. Hume. See his *Discourse of Commerce*, p. 12, edit. 1752.

[2] *Wealth of Nations*, vol. I., p. 338, 4to. edit.

[3] *Ibid.*, vol. I., p. 414.

and labor; and this opinion, which coincides with that of the Bishop of Cloyne,[1] and the learned author of the *Essay on Money and Coins*,[2] is most generally adhered to by Dr. Smith.

4. In another part of the work, however, we find it asserted, that "land and capital stock are the two original sources of all revenue, both private and public: capital stock pays the wages of productive labor, whether employed in agriculture, manufactures, or commerce."[3] Land and capital are, therefore, here deemed the sole sources of wealth; and labor is considered as deriving from them its wages, without adding to the opulence of the community.

5. Lastly, we are taught to consider land, labor, and capital, as being all three sources of wealth; for we are told that, "whoever derives his revenue from a fund that is his own, must draw it either from his labor, his stock, or his land. The revenue derived from labor is called wages; that from stock, profit; and from land, rent;"[4] an opinion which seems to have been hinted at by Sir William Petty,[5] when he stated it as an impediment to the wealth of England, that taxes were not levied upon lands, stock, and labor, but chiefly upon land alone, though land and labor are generally considered by that ingenious writer as the sole source of wealth.

In treating of political economy, the science which professes to display and to teach means of increasing the wealth of a state, it would seem that the first and most anxious object of inquiry ought to have been, what wealth is, and from what sources mankind derive it; for it appears impossible to discuss with precision the means of increasing any thing, without an accurate notion of its nature and of its origin." Lauderdale, [*Inquiry*, 2nd ed., pp. 112-116.]

To this catalogue of the various notions held out in the

---

[1] *Querist*, Quer. 4. "Whether the four elements, and man's labor therein, be not the true source of wealth."

[2] "Land and labor together are the sources of all wealth; without a competency of land, there would be no subsistence, and but a very poor and uncomfortable one without labor. So that *wealth* or *riches* consists either in a property in land, or in the products of land and labor."

[3] *Wealth of Nations*, Vol. II. p. 560.   [4] *Wealth of Nations*, Vol. II. p. 63.

[5] *Tracts*, edit. 1768, p. 268.

Wealth of Nations, concerning the nature of that wealth, Lord Lauderdale might have added another, showing some general resemblance to that exhibited in the present work. "Wealth," we are told, B. V. c. i., "always follows improvements of agriculture and manufactures, and is, in reality, no more than the accumulated produce of those improvements."

NOTE B. *Referred to on page* 3.

" Si l'on se demande en effet en quoi consiste la richesse, on n'est pas peu surpris de ne trouver dans les auteurs les plus estimés que des opinions différentes ou contraires.

" Les uns la font consister dans l'universalité des propriétés privées,[1] et d'autres dans l'abondance des denrées.[2]

" Ceux-là distinguent la richesse publique de la richesse particulière, donnent à la première *une valeur d'usage et non d'échange*, et à la seconde *une valeur d'échange et non d'usage*, et font consister cette dernière *dans la valeur vénale du produit net*.[3]

" Ceux-ci la composent de toutes les choses matérielles dont l'homme peut faire usage pour satisfaire un besoin ou une jouissance de sensualité, de fantaisie ou de vanité.[4]

" Un autre écrivain regarde la richesse comme la *possession d'une chose plus désirée par ceux qui ne l'ont pas que par ceux qui en jouissent.*[5]

" Un autre écrivain la définit *le superflu.*[6]

" Un autre écrivain la place dans l'accumulation du travail exigible.[7]

---

[1] Treatise of taxes, by Sir William Petty—Gregory King's Calculation, published by Davenant—Dr. Beeke, Observations on the produce of the income tax.

[2] Dîme royale du maréchal de Vauban.

[3] Physiocratie, p. 118—Philosophie rurale, p. 60.

[4] Essai sur la nature du commerce, par Cantillon.—Abrégé des principes d'économie politique, par M. le sénateur Germain Garnier, Paris, 1796. M. Malthus, Principes d'économie politique considérés par rapport à leurs applications practiques (page 23).

[5] Richezza è il possesso d'alcuna cosa che sia più desiderata dagli altri che dal possessore. Galiani, della Moneta.

[6] Il superfluo costituisce la ricchezza. Palmieri, pubblica Felicità, tome I. page 155.

[7] Princ. d'écon. polit., par M. Canard, Paris, 1801.

AUTHOR'S NOTES

"Adam-Smith dit tantôt qu'un homme est riche ou pauvre selon le plus ou moins de choses nécessaires, utiles ou agréables à la vie dont il peut se procurer la jouissance; tantôt qu'un homme est riche ou pauvre selon qu'il peut disposer de plus ou moins de travail; tantôt que la richesse réelle d'un pays consiste dans le produit annuel de ses terres et de son travail.[1]

"Un écrivain récent définit la richesse, tout ce que l'homme désire comme utile et agréable.[2]

"Les richesses, dit M. Say, se composent des choses qui ont une valeur.[3]

"M. Ricardo pense que la valeur diffère essentiellement de la richesse, et que les choses, une fois qu'elles sont reconnues utiles par elles-mêmes, tirent leur valeur échangeable de deux sources, de leur rareté, et de la quantité de travail nécessaire pour les acquérir.[4]

"M. Sismondi définit la richesse, le fruit du travail accumulé et non encore consommé.[5]

"Cette incertitude sur la nature de la richesse se reproduit dans l'examen des moyens qui peuvent contribuer à sa progression, à son accroissement et à sa grandeur.

"Ceux qui ont écrit les premiers sur cette matière importante, séduits par l'apparence des faits, ont attribué aux métaux précieux, obtenus en retour de l'exportation des produits du sol et de l'industrie de chaque pays, la cause de la richesse des peuples.[6]

---

[1] Rich. des nat., in 4to. vol. I. pag. 209 et 338.

[2] An inquiry into the nature and origin of public wealth, by the Earl of Lauderdale, chap. 2. pages 56 and 57.

[3] Traité d'écon. polit., page 1.

[4] Des principes de l'économie politique et de l'impôt, tome II. chap. 20.

[5] Nouveaux principes d'économie politique, tome I. page 60.

[6] En Angleterre, Raleigh, Essai sur le commerce, en 1595.—Edouard Misselden, Cercle du commerce, en 1623.—Louis Roberts, Trésor du trafic, en 1641.—Thomas Munn, Trésor de l'Angleterre pour le commerce étranger, en 1664.—Fortrey, Intérêts et améliorations de l'Angleterre, en 1664.—Davenant, dans son ouvrage relatif au commerce et au revenu de l'Angleterre, tome I. page 16, en 1696.—M. Martin, inspecteur-général des douanes, ou le Marchand anglais, en 1713.

En Hollande, Jean de Witt, Mémoires, en 1669.

En Italie, Serra, Breve tratto delle cose che possono far abondare li regni

" D'autres écrivains en ont placé la source dans la réduction de l'intérêt de l'argent.[1]

" Les économistes, entraînés par une théorie séduisante et captieuse, ont exalté le système agricole.[2]

" Adam-Smith lui a préféré le travail qui se perfectionne par sa division, et qui, après qu'il est fini, se fixe et se réalise dans un objet permanent.[3]

" Lord Lauderdale, dans l'ouvrage précité, ouvrage remarquable par la finesse de ses aperçus, fait dériver la richesse de l'art de simplifier et d'abréger le travail et d'améliorer ses produits, résultat nécessaire de l'accumulation et de la direction des capitaux.

" M. Say fait dériver la plus grande augmentation de la richesse, de l'emploi des capitaux dans l'agriculture.[4]

" De l'union des systèmes d'agriculture et de commerce, dit M. Malthus, dépend la plus grande prospérité nationale.[5]

" M. Ricardo est d'avis que la richesse d'un pays s'accroît de deux manières : par l'emploi d'une portion plus considérable du revenu à l'accroissement du travail productif, ou en rendant plus productive celle qui existe.[6]

" M. Sismondi ne voit l'accroissement des richesses que dans l'accroissement des jouissances nationales."[7]   Ganilh, *des Systèms*, tome I. p. 14.

d'oro, en 1613.—Genovesi, Lezioni di econom. civile, en 1764.—Muratori, Felicità pub., cap. 16, sul principio.—Corniani, Reflez. sulle monete.

En France, le cardinal de Richelieu et Colbert, Ordonnances et réglemens pendant leur administration.

[1] Thomas Culpeper's Useful remark on the mischief of an high national interest, en 1641.—Josias Child, Brief observations concerning trade and interest of money, en 1651.—Samuel Lamb, Banks and lumber houses, en 1657.—William Patterson, auteur du Projet de la banque de Londres, en 1694.—Barnard, dans ses Discours sur la réduction de l'intérêt de l'argent, en 1714.

[2] Physiocratie.

[3] Richesse des nations, liv. 11. chap. 3.—David Hume peut avoir donné à Adam-Smith l'idée de ce système. Il dit littéralement que les hommes ne peuvent acquérir que par le travail. (Essai sur le commerce, édit. d'Édimbourg, 1804, in 8vo, Vol. I. page 277.)

[4] *Ibid.*, tome II. page 231.

[5] Addition aux quatre premières éditions de l'Essai sur la population, chap. 11.

[6] *Ibid.*   [7] *Id.*, tome I. page 53.

NOTE C. *Referred to on page* 379.

At the time the reference to this note was made, it was my intention to have here inserted some extracts from the *North American Review*, and some other publications, for the purpose of showing the views entertained in this country concerning the system of Adam Smith, and some of his followers. As far as concerns this continent, however, these extracts would be superfluous, and I have, therefore, thought it better to omit them, until such time as the work appear in Great Britain.

NOTE D. *Referred to on page* 130.

Adam Smith here admits, to a certain extent, the correctness of the general notions concerning the nature and office of money, entertained by the school of political economists who preceded Hume. Had he done otherwise he would have acted very unfairly, for his own reasonings, on this subject, are sometimes little more than a repetition of theirs, as might be shown by an examination of parallel passages. Compare, for instance, the two following. "Although they who have their estates in money are said to be a great number, and to be worth £5,000 or £10,000 per annum, more or less, which amounts to many millions in all, yet are they not possessed thereof altogether at once, for it were vanity or against their profit to keep continually in their hands above £40 or £50 in a family to defray necessary charges. The rest must ever run from man to man in traffic for their benefit, whereby we may conceive that a little money (being made the measure of all our other means) doth rule and distribute great matters daily to all men in their just proportions."[1] "As the same guinea which pays the weekly pension of one man to day, may pay that of another tomorrow, and that of a third the day thereafter, the amount of the metal pieces which annually circulate in any country must always be of much less value than the whole money pensions annually paid with them."[2]

The more recent followers of Adam Smith have not always

[1] Mun, p. 42, 12mo edit., published in 1664.
[2] *Wealth of Nations*, B. II. c. II.

done the earlier writers equal justice. Thus Mr. M'Culloch, in his *Principles of Political Economy,* asserts that the mercantile system, of which he esteems Mun one of the earliest and ablest defenders, reckoned money the only wealth, and remarks, that "the simple consideration, that all buying and selling is in reality nothing more than the bartering of one commodity for another,—of a certain quantity of corn or wool, for example, for a certain quantity of gold or silver, and *vice versa,* was entirely overlooked." Now instead of considering money as the only wealth, Mun, on the contrary, says, "they that have wares cannot want money;—neither is it that money is the life of trade as if it could not subsist without the same; for we know that there was great trading by way of commutation or barter, when there was little money stirring in the world."[1] That the true use of money is its affording a fixed standard for the price of other things, is a doctrine, indeed, laid down by Bodin a century earlier than Mun. "Car si la monoye, qui doit regler le prix de toutes choses est muable et incertaine, il n'y a personne qui puisse fair estat au vray de ce qu'il a; les contracts seront incertains, les changes, taxes, gages, etc., incertaines," etc.[2] The real error of those writers was their transferring to national wealth the rules which apply to individual wealth; it was I apprehend, therefore, the same in kind as I have hinted in the text, as that of Adam Smith himself, though different from it in degree.

NOTE F. *Referred to on page* 90.

"Memorial dans lequel on propose à l'Empereur un moyen de secourir le peuple dans les années stériles." (*Lettres Edifiantes,* Tom. XI. p. 427.)

Lieou-que-y, (the Mandarin who memorializes,) after narrating the miseries suffered from famine in the province Chansi, from which he dates, and stating the insufficiency of the ancient provisions of the empire, which suppose a quantity of rice to be stored up in the imperial magazines, sufficient for all emergencies, but which are neglected by the superior Mandarines, from the multiplicity of the affairs they have to

---

[1] *Wealth of Nations,* p. 24. [2] *De la Republique,* liv. VI.

manage, or abused by their dependents, and which are, in fact, regarded as obsolete; proceeds to state his own scheme for obviating, in future, similar calamities.

"Ne seroit-il donc pas à propos de profiter de ce temps d'abondance pour remplir de grains les greniers publics, en les payant de l'argent tiré du trésor de votre majesté? Par exemple, supposons que pendant cinq ans on y prit chaque année quatre cent mille francs, destinées à ces provisions pour soulager le peuple dans les besoins pressans. On emploira d'abord cent mille francs pour réparer les anciens magazins de Tay-quen, capital de la province, pour en bâtir de nouveaux, et pour amasser du riz, afin d'assister dans le temps de stérilité le territoire de cette ville, de Fuen-tchou et autres lieux qui n'en sont fort éloignés. Du côté du midi est la ville de Ping-yang, de King-tcheou, et autres endroits circonvoisins. La grande ville de Laugan est située vers l'occident; en y faisant la même dépense, on sera en état de distribuer du riz à Ke-tcheau, à Leao-tcheau, et autres villes subalternes de sa dépendance. Enfin de semblables magasins qu'on établira dans la ville de Tai-tong, qui est au nord, pourront aider à la subsistence des petites villes de Long-pin Kingvou, et autres semblables. Ce sont-là les quatres principales villes de la province, où seront placés les magasins généraux, et d'où les grains se repandront dans les lieux qui en auront besoin."

He next mentions the precautions he conceives necessary to guard against malversation. "Or après des précautions si nécessaires, supposons que, de la libéralité de votre majesté, il soit donné cette année à chacun de ces villes cent mille francs pour capital: si l'année est abondante, on peut, de ces cent mille francs, acheter au moins trente mille grandes mesures de riz, lesquelles multipliées par quatre, feront, dans les quatre villes, cent vingt mille mesures. Depuis la récolte jusqu'à la fin de l'année le prix du riz est médiocre; ce n'est que dans le printemps que le prix commence à augmenter, alors on ouvrira les magasins, et on vendra ce riz. De cette vente on aura deux avantages; l'un est qu'en mettant l'abondance, on empêchera que le prix du riz ne croisse trop: l'autre, que le vendant alors un peu plus cher qu'il n'a été acheté dans le temps de la récolte, on sera en état, au moyen de ce profit, d'acheter après la nouvelle moisson au moins dix mille mesures de riz dans chaque endroit, de plus qu'on n'en avait l'année précédente. Par-là, l'ancien riz sort des greniers, et le nouveau le remplace. Il sort à un prix plus cher et rentre à bon marché. N'est-ce pas un excellent moyen de multiplier ce riz, en soulageant même le peuple ? car on ne prétend pas s'enrichir aux depens du public. Ce riz tiré des magasins sera vendu au cours et à un prix raisonnable, quoique plus cher qu'il n'était huit mois auparavant. Rien de plus juste et de plus utile dans les années abondantes. Par cette conduite, le riz chaque année se multiplie dans le magasin ; et si pendant cinq années il se fait une abondante récolte, la provision d'un endroit, qui n'étoit d'abord que de trente mille mesures, peut se trouver à la cinquième année de plus de quatre cent mille mesures de riz. En cas de nécessité, n'est ce pas déjà un excellent moyen de soulager toute une province ? . . . dans les disettes ordinaires, le rix sera vendu à une juste prix. Dans celles qui passeront un peu l'ordinaire, on en prêtera au peuple, et dans les grands nécessités on le distribuera par aumône." *Tirée de la Gazette Publique* par le R. Père Contancin.

The inhabitants of the island of Trong-ming often enter into voluntary associations, which have for their object the relief of some individual whose affairs have become deranged. They give him the means of reestablishing himself in a way which they conceive burdens them a little, though not very much. The association consists of seven individuals, including the person for whose relief it is formed. The principle of it will be understood from the following table.

First year.		*Second year.*	
The first, that is, the person for whose benefit the company is formed, receives	60 pistoles	The first gives	15
		second receives	60
		third gives	13
The second gives	15	fourth	11
third	13	fifth	9
fourth	11	sixth	7
fifth	9	seventh	5
sixth	7		
seventh	5		

Third year.
The first gives	15
second	13
third receives	60
fourth gives	11
fifth	9
sixth	7
seventh	5

Fourth year.
The first gives	15
second	13
third	11
fourth receives	60
fifth gives	9
sixth	11
seventh	5

Fifth year.
The first gives	15
second	13
third	11
fourth	9
fifth receives	60
sixth gives	7
seventh	5

Sixth year.
The first gives	15
second	13
third	11
fourth	9
fifth	7
sixth receives	60
seventh gives	5

Seventh year.
The first gives	15
second	13
third	11
fourth	9

Seventh year.
fifth gives	7
sixth	5
seventh receives	60

Although the sum paid by each of the associates is unequal, and that the first disburse more each year than the last, yet the Chinese think that the conditions of the contract are much more favorable for the former than for the latter, because they sooner receive the sum of sixty pistoles, and the great profits they derive from commerce, well indemnifies them for the advances they have to make. Letter of Father Jacquemin. *Lettres Edifiantes*, Tom. X. p. 127.

I subjoin a few extracts from different authors, indicative of the strength of the accumulative principle in China, of the orders at which instruments remain there, and of some other circumstances in the condition of that empire, which I have referred to in the text.

"The spirit of gain by working on an extensive plan, and by new methods, for supplying multitudes with particular articles, is not prevalent among the Chinese, unless in large or maritime towns. Some there are, however, in almost every village, who seek to accumulate wealth by taking advantage of the wants of the people around them. Shops for lending money on pledges are common everywhere. Very high interest upon loans is allowed by law. The practice of such loans implies, certainly, great improvidence in the multitude, or great uncertainty in the success of their pursuits. The facility of culture, and the abundance of crops, when no calamity intervenes, enables them in many places to bear such burdens, though often in a very impoverished condition." *Staunton*, Vol. II. p. 44.

"Pawn-brokers shops are as numerous in Chinese cities as in London." *Ellis' Embassy*, p. 120.

"L'usure qui règne parmi les Chinois est un autre obstacle bien difficile à vaincre. Lorsqu'on leur dit qu'avant que de recevoir le baptême, ils doivent restituer des biens acquis par ces voies illicites, et aussi ruiner en un jour toute leur famille, vous m'avouerez qu'il faut un grand miracle de la grâce pour les y déterminer." *Lettres Edifiantes*, Tom. X. p. 379.

"La deuxième cause de la disette n'est pas seulement, comme on se persuade, la multitude du peuple Chinois; j'avoue qu'elle y contribue beaucoup; cependant je crois que la Chine fournit des grains suffisamment pour la subsistence de tous ces habitans: mais c'est qu'on ne ménage pas assez les grains, et qu'on en fait une consommation étonnante pour fabriquer du riz et de l'eau-de-vie ou de la raque. . . . c'est surtout le soir avant que de se coucher qu'ils en font usage, principalement les marchands, les artisans et les soldats. Ils ont chacun dans la chambre où ils couchent un fourneau à charbon de pierre où ils font cuire le riz, le thé, et chauffer cette sort de boisson; ils la prennent en mangeant des herbes salées, et s'enivrent à peu de frais. Si par mégarde, ou étant à moitié ivres, ils laissent tomber de cette raque dans le feu, la flamme s'élève bientôt jusqu'au plancher, qui n'est fait que de nattes d'osier ou de châssis de papier, et dont la hauteur n'est faite que de trois ou quatre pieds au dessus de la tête d'un homme. Alors dans un instant, toute la chambre est en feu; et parce que les boutiques où couchent les marchands et la plupart des maisons du peuple, ne sont pas séparées de leur voisins par des maîtresses murailles, et que souvent les charpentes sont liés ensemble. le feu s'étend avec rapidité et fait de grands ravages avant qu'on ait pu l'éteindre.

"Ajoutez à cela que l'usage trop fréquent de cette boisson fait mourir quantité de menu peuple d'une maladie qu'on nomme yeche à la quelle on n'a pu trouver aucun remède.

"Si la disette n'éclaircissoit pas de temps en temps ce grande nombre d'habitants qui contient la Chine, il seroit difficile qu'elle pût subsister en paix. Il n'y a point de guerre comme en Europe, ni de pertes ni de maladies populaires; à peine en voit-on dans un siècle." *Lettres Edifiantes*, Vol. XII. p. 200.

Many circumstances might be adduced, to show that it is not so much the want of power to accumulate, as the want of a desire to accumulate sufficiently strong to prompt to effective action, which prevents individuals in the lower classes in China, from rising to opulence. Of these I might mention the number of eating-houses, and the goodness of their fare, and the occasional richness of the attire of the common people, as described by recent travellers. I prefer, however, citing an anecdote from the *Lettres Edifiantes*, as these are probably less known to the reader.

" Un vieillard vient le trouver " (le missionnaire) " pour lui représenter l'extrême désir qu'il avoit que l'on construisît une église dans son village. Votre zèle est louable, lui dit le missionnaire, mais je n'ai pas maintenant de quoi fournir à une pareille dépense. Je prétends bien la faire moi-même, repartit le villageois. Le missionnaire, accoutumé à le voir depuis plusieurs années mener une vie très-pauvre, le crut hors d'état d'accomplir ce qu'il promettoit; il loua de nouveau ses bonnes intentions, en lui représentant que son village étant très-considérable, il y falloit bâtir une église aussi grande que celle qui était dans la ville voisine; que dans la suite il pourrait y contribuer selon ses forces; mais que seul il ne pourrait suffire à de si grands frais. Excusez moi, reprit le paysan, je me crois en situation de faire ce que je propose. Mais savez vous, répliqua le père, que pour une pareille entreprise, il faut au moins deux mille écus? Je les ai tout prêts, répondit le vieillard, et si je ne les avait pas, je n'aurois garde de vous importuner par une semblable demande. Le père fut charmé d'apprendre que ce bon homme, qu'il avoit cru fort pauvre, se trouvât néanmoins avoir tant d'argent comptant, et qu'il voulût l'employer si utilement. Mais il fut bien plus surpris, lorsqu' ayant eu la curiosité de demander à ce villageois comment il avoit pu se procurer cette somme, il répondit ingénument que depuis quarante ans qu'il avait conçu ce dessein, il retranchait de sa nourriture et de son vêtement tout ce qui n'étoit pas absolument nécessaire, afin d'avoir la consolation avant de mourir de laisser dans son village une église élevée à l'honneur du vrai Dieu. Vol. XII. p. 363.

To these extracts I am induced to add the two following, as strikingly illustrative of the strange contrasts which the morality of the Chinese exhibits.

"This dominion is tempered," (that of husbands over their wives) "indeed, by the maxims of mild conduct in the different relations of life, inculcated from early childhood, amongst the lowest as well as the highest classes of society. The old persons of a family live generally with the young. The former serve to moderate any occasional impetuosity, violence, or passion of the latter. The influence of age over youth is supported by the sentiments of nature, by the habit of obedience, by the precepts of morality engrafted in the law of the land, and by the unremitted policy and honest arts of parents to that effect. They who are past labor, deal out the rules which they have learned, and the wisdom which experience taught them, to those who are rising to manhood, or to those lately arrived at it. Plain sentences of morals are written up in the common hall, where the male branches of the family assemble. Some one, at least, is capable of reading them to the rest. In almost every house is hung up a tablet of the ancestors of the persons then residing in it. References are often made, in conversation, to their actions. Their example, as far as it was good, serves as an incitement to travel in the same path. The descendants from a common stock visit the tombs of their forefathers together, at stated times. This joint care, and indeed other occasions, collect and unite the most remote relations. They cannot lose sight of each other; and seldom become indifferent to their respective concerns. The child is bound to labor and to provide for his parents' maintenance and comfort, and the brother for the brother and sister that are in extreme want, the failure of which duty would be followed by such detestation that it is not necessary to enforce it by positive law. Even the most distant kinsman, reduced to misery by accident or ill health, has a claim on his kindred for relief. Manners, stronger far than laws, and, indeed, inclination, produced and nurtured by intercourse and intimacy, secure assistance for him." *Staunton's China*, Vol. II., p. 21.

"The frail females in the boats had not embraced this double occupation, after having quitted their parents, or on being abandoned by them on account of their misconduct; but the parents themselves, taking no other interest in the chastity of their daughters, than as it might contribute to an advantageous disposal of them to wealthy husbands, feel little reluctance, when no such prospect offers, to devote them to one employment," (that of conveying passengers in boats) "with a view to the profits of another." (of prostitution.) *Ibid.* p. 328.

NOTE J. *Referred to on page* 267.

A gentleman of my acquaintance, who had been long among the Indians, and ranked among them as a brother warrior, once travelled a great distance in the far interior to visit a chief. His friend received him in the spirit of hospitality natural to the red man. In proof of it, he declared he would feast him, as he had seen white men feasting their friends,— for he too had been a traveller. Accordingly, his "womankind" not being adequate to the task, he set about cooking and serving dinner himself, and, considering all things, succeeded wonderfully. As imitators, however, will often copy rather defects than merits, so the relish of the repast would have been somewhat improved, by his memory having been a little less tenacious of a few, of what doubtless seemed to him the strange ceremonies of the white men. For example; he had seen at the houses of some of his white friends, their young men employed rubbing the dishes, off of which the guests ate, with a small square piece of cloth. Now, the only piece of cloth, like this, which he happened to have, formed an article of dress in use among the Indians, but unknown, and undescribable by modern Europeans. It seems, notwithstanding, to have been in use among their ancestors, being, if I mistake not, that very garment, of which Ulysses threatened to strip the unhappy Thersytes, the day he made him feel that he did not bear the sceptre in vain.

$$\tau \acute{\alpha}\ \tau \alpha \iota \delta \hat{\omega}\ \dot{\alpha}\mu\phi\iota\kappa\alpha\lambda \acute{\upsilon}\pi\tau\epsilon\iota.$$

To divest himself of it, was no doubt an inconvenience, but this was not to be reckoned in the service of a guest. Accordingly, hanging it over his arm, he rubbed his visitor's platter with it very carefully, at every change. My friend had nothing for it but to honor the care of his host by eating gravely and abundantly. Had he done otherwise, the chief, who was himself the most polite of men, would have regarded it as an unpardonable *grossièreté*.

Note L. *Referred to on page* 149.

[As to the ulterior effects of wars, revolutions, persecutions, and the like, there is of course more to be said than Rae sets forth in the text. Some excerpts from his *Essay on Education* (1843), mentioned in the biographical sketch, may be here given to advantage. It will be noticed that his main idea is in full accord with that of Bagehot in *Physics and Politics*.]

"The whole earth is strewn with the ruins of empires. Civilization seems, at distant intervals, to have assumed form, and gathered strength in various points, and from each of these in succession, to have spread itself and the races that were the possessors of it, over large regions of the globe. Now it is very clear that each of these civilizations must have had a period of advance, a period when they were collecting that amount of knowledge of science and arts, and of civil rights and laws, which they possessed at the acme of their progress, and which gave them their superiority over the other races of their times. Like us, each of them must have witnessed a period when the social condition was ameliorating from age to age; like us, they must have looked forward to still succeeding improvement. Yet each of these civilizations nursed within it some disease that, coming to activity, nipped the germ of prosperity and life, and brought on decay and death.

. . . .

"With the exception of Greece, whose contracted territory unfits it for a parallel, other antecedent civilizations are known to history only in their concluding stages when the hand of death was on them. We cannot tell, we can only conjecture, what their condition was in the previous and more vigorous periods of their existence. But with regard to all of them, so far as we can glean anything of them from history, or trace them in their monuments, the remarkable fact is brought before us that the stage of their being immediately preceding their decay, and of course the form of existence with which the ruins of them that remain are impressed, was that of fixity and immobility. A period of torpid repose preceded their decay and dissolution. There is also another remarkable fact which we gather by carefully scrutinizing the faint traces, that in several of them the ages anterior to the concluding period of repose and immobility have left behind them. Preceding this period, an era of great strife and contention between the principles of which the particular civilization was made up, comes pretty distinctly before us. The result of the contest seems to have been, the preponderance of one of those main elements, and its crushing, subduing, and altogether preventing any farther expansion of the others, and, by the cramped position in which it placed them, occasioning their decay and death.

. . . .

"It well then becomes all men, having power to exert effective action in this our era, to see if we can gather any lessons of instruction from bygone ages, if there be any circumstances of the times having a tendency to produce a similar conflict of the existing elements of our civilization, possibly resulting in the domination of some of them, with like fatal influence."

NOTE M. *Referred to on page* 296.

[The following from Rae's unpublished manuscript is not without interest in connection with the subject of the elision through taxation of the costs of luxury to a society. The special taxtion of the rent of land, if feasible, would cut off a large part of luxury at the source.]

"The revenue of every society of men, or nation, is derived from three sources,—labor, capital, and land. I have endeavored elsewhere to show that capital consists altogether of instruments by means of which man is enabled to draw forth for his own use, by the powers which nature has given to the bodies within his reach, such articles of necessity, comfort, or convenience as his wants urge him to procure. I have also endeavored to trace the laws which regulate the increase or diminution of this general stock or capital. It is a somewhat difficult task to determine the laws regulating the distribution of the annual revenue among the powers producing it. I believe it is a general truth which, though to some it may appear paradoxical, is nevertheless capable of demonstration from the constitution of man and of external nature, that the larger the share falling to labor the more rapid will be the increase of capital, and the more prosperous the condition of the society. It is certain, however, that the portion remaining after labor and capital have divided their shares, naturally falls to land.

"To get an accurate idea of what the real return of the land, or what is called rent, actually is we must separate from what are the natural powers of the soil those additions which art may have made to it. Thus much land owes a great part of its fertility to some system of drainage which has been employed to carry off its superfluous waters. This clearly belongs to capital and any return it makes is to be considered interest or profit. What may be the real powers of different soils in their natural state is a problem not perhaps as yet capable of being accurately resolved, but which modern chemistry promises ere long to give us the means of determining with precision. These native powers [and advantages of situation] would seem to be the things for which a rent comes in the course of time to be paid. Now in examining how this rent is to be appropriated at some future time in some particular society, we cannot with propriety take as our standard the mode in which it is now appropriated in any existing society of men. For society is continually changing its phase over the earth, and what we may assume now as the best condition of affairs, may at some future day appear quite defective. It may be allowable therefore to assume that in the society in question it comes at the future period, to which we have reference, to be so appropriated as may most conduce to the wellbeing of the whole community. Considered thus theoretically, I think we may assume that it should be given to those purposes which are for the general good. I may name education in its largest sense; rewards to men whose genius, talents, or industry have added to the stock of human happiness in general or of the one particular society; the supplying the funds necessary for the prosecution of experiments tending to enlarge the boundaries of human knowledge and power: and also a provision for those whom accident has deprived of the means of supporting themselves. I may say in general, in relieving the community from what is now called taxation, but a taxation required for other purposes than those upon which it is at present expended."

RESIDUA.

PASSAGES OMITTED IN SOME PART OF THE TEXT AND NOT ELSEWHERE REPRODUCED.

Number 1. *From page* 1.

Twenty or thirty years ago, according to the prevailing political system, every circumstance in the condition of the empire was at variance with what should give prosperity to a state. To meet the enormous annual expenditure occasioned by the most wasteful of all preceding wars, a revenue as enormous was drawn by taxation from the people, while, instead of their industry enjoying the boasted advantages of perfect freedom, at home it was restrained by regulations of old established, and abroad its products were legally shut out from every continental port, and could only any where force an entrance with much hazard, and at heavy expense.

True; making its power felt through the element that had ever been most propitious to it, it had subjugated almost every spot on the globe, colonized by Europeans, and by this means, in defiance of its enemies, maintained an extended commerce with all parts of the world. But this vast extent of empire, preserved by force of arms, and at great expense, according to the dicta of modern politicians, was an evil of the greatest magnitude, and one which, though the burden attending it is now reduced to comparative insignificance, they are continually assuring us we ought, as quickly as possible, to get rid of.

Notwithstanding all these disadvantages, however, there

is no period in its history in which the condition of Great Britain was apparently more flourishing. The exertions of the laborer were liberally rewarded, the expenditure of the capitalist richly repaid. Everything gave token of rapidly increasing wealth and abundance.

The triumph of that cause, in aid of which war had been embraced, gave peace to the empire and to Europe. The annual expenditure was diminished by one half, and the nation was no longer restrained, but in comparatively a very trifling degree, from participating in all those advantages, which, in every instance, one country, according to prevailing notions, is supposed to gain by free intercourse with another. But, though markets for the manufacture, and channels for the commerce of the kingdom were largely multiplied, its resources, instead of augmenting, seemed diminishing. The whole fabric of society seemed ready to sink under the pressure of some new burden,—ruin began to threaten, often to overwhelm the man of capital,—want to look industry in the face. In vain were taxes to a large amount repealed, in vain were endeavors made to trace the depression of the times to mere revolutions in the channels of trade, and to other temporary causes, and hopes held out that they would speedily pass away. The evil proved to be not partial and temporary, but pervading and permanent. Far from confidence in the modern science being shaken by a result contrary to all its principles, it was resolved to seek a remedy for the acknowledged distress, by adopting largely the policy which this science inculcates.

It cannot be denied that the results of the experiment, as far as it has hitherto been carried, have been in the whole, unhappy. The events which have followed, not to say flowed from recent enactments, regulating the internal and external commerce of the nation, have been at least unfortunate. The operations of the banking system, and the extension of general confidence and security in all transactions, which that system is calculated to afford, seem clogged and restrained. The returns which industry and capital receive, have been still farther diminished. Wealth is barren. Labor, plied with all the skill, and more than all the assiduity to which human nature is long adequate, does not always keep famine at a distance.

. . . .

Number 2. From page 5.

By entering on such an investigation immediately, however, the subject will be brought before the reader under an aspect so different from that in which it is viewed in the *Wealth of Nations*, and subsequent works following in the same train of thought, that I should not have an opportunity of directly meeting some of the arguments there advanced. For this reason I shall first endeavor to show, that even proceeding on similar principles to those adopted in the *Wealth of Nations* itself, there exist great and insuperable objections to the doctrines in question. This forms the subject of the First Book. In the Second, I enter on the analysis of the nature of wealth and the laws governing its increase and diminution.[1] The Third is devoted to a practical application to the doctrines in question, of the principles established.

Number 3. From page 204.

There are then, it would appear from the preceding chapters, two great classes into which commodities may be divided; luxuries, and articles of consumption which are not luxuries, but, were the term permitted, might be named *utilities*. When the events in which instruments issue are of the latter class, then instruments may properly be said to be exhausted; when of the former, they are on the contrary dissipated.

Number 4.

The investigations in which we have been engaged in the preceding chapters seem to indicate several great causes as determining the nature and production of stock. They may be divided into three classes.

I. Regarding things material.

---

[1] [Is it an inadvertence that Rae here speaks of his second " Book " as dealing with " wealth," when the formal title made it deal with " stock " ?]

1. The nature of the material world, producing a series of events succeeding each other in regular order.

2. The nature of man, as a being in part material, acted on, therefore, by matter, and whose existence and pleasures are, consequently, dependent on events taking place among material objects.

3. Also the nature of man, as a being in part material, and whose corporeal powers—his labor, enable him to change the positions of the matters around him.

II. Regarding things not material.

1. The intellectual faculties of man, reaching not to an absolute knowledge of the material world, but to a perception of the order in which events succeed each other in it, and to a discovery of the means of producing events necessary, or desirable to him, by applying his corporeal powers to change the positions of the materials within his reach.

2. The moral nature of man,—the motives by which he acts, determining the degree in which he will be excited to apply himself to the discovery of the order in which events succeed each other, and to changing the positions of materials, and so constructing instruments producing events ministering to future necessities or pleasures.

Concerning these two last causes, the general conclusions at which we arrived were; that the more the intellectual faculties are expanded, the greater the power to extend the knowledge of the succession of events, and to form materials into instruments; and that the greater the strength of the moral powers—the social and benevolent affections—the greater the desire to discover the order of the succession of events, and to apply such discoveries to the formation of materials into instruments. And conversely; that the feebler the intellectual faculties and moral powers, the less both the ability to discover, and the inclination to apply discoveries to the formation of instruments, and the greater the tendency to dissipate the capacity of the instruments formed in luxury, and to waste it through deceit and violence.

III. Causes derived partly from the nature of the material world, and partly from the nature of man.

1. Change; arising from revolutions of all sorts, by which

men and arts are moved from region to region. This places man and matter in new positions, and discloses to him new connexions and relations, in the natures of the bodies within reach of his operations.

2. Servile imitation; the antagonist of the former, by which men are led to operate by rule, and not of knowledge, and the progress of invention and improvement are retarded.

Strength of intellect and moral feeling gives *continuity* of existence to the society, and leading the men composing it to take an interest in distant events, extends the operations of their powers to the intelligence, and application to useful purposes, of a wide circle of events. Their weakness, and the prevalence of the opposing causes, folly and pure selfishness, *isolates* each member of society, contracts the operations of the powers of the whole to the consideration and application of a narrow circle of events, and dissipates and wastes them, in efforts made by each to raise himself superior to others, and by force or fraud to take from them what they possess.

There are thus two great principles, the inventive, and accumulative, generating stock and adding to it, and they are both excited and moved, and enfeebled and restrained, by similar powers.

I. The inventive principle.

Its strength extending the power of man, augments stock, by carrying the instruments composing it to orders of quicker return. It is accompanied by economy, by fidelity to engagements, by a diminished inclination to luxury and waste.

Its weakness, by contracting the power of man, prevents the augmentation of stock. It is accompanied by extravagance, by infidelity to engagements, by a propensity to luxury and waste.

II. The accumulative principle.

Its strength leading men to embrace in their operations a wide circle of events, accumulates stock, by giving additional capacity to instruments already formed, or by working up new materials. It carries instruments to orders of slower return, and is accompanied also by economy, by fidelity to engagements, by a diminished inclination to luxury and waste.

RESIDUA 471

Its weakness, contracting the compass of events on which there is an inclination to operate, diminishes stock, by allowing materials to escape from it, and lie idle, which, formed into instruments, would yield abundant, though distant returns. Under it instruments can only exist at the more quickly returning orders. It is accompanied, also, by extravagance, by infidelity to engagements, by a propensity to luxury and waste.

The consideration of the mode of operation of these two principles suggests the following remark.

. . . .

Upon these two principles, the third set of causes referred to operate somewhat differently. Change excites the principle of invention, but often directly restrains that of accumulation. Imitation restrains invention, but does not directly retard accumulation.

The several causes referred to, rank among the chief agents in the production of the phenomena which the progress of society exhibits. We have considered them separately, but they never appear so, always acting in combination. This circumstance would not of itself affect any conclusions concerning them, for it applies to phenomena of all sorts, the causes influencing every one being compound.

. . . .

Number 5. From page 276.

SECTION 1. Narcotics, in so far as their effects are not measured by the quantity consumed, may be classed with luxuries.

SECTION 2. A question concerning the effects resulting from their cheapness considered.

SECTION I.

In the preceding part of this chapter we have considered the loss occasioned to the stock of societies, from part of the products that would otherwise be yielded by the industry of their members, applied to the formation of instruments, being dissipated through the operation of an affection of the mind. We are now to consider a similar loss, occasioned by a peculiarity in the combined corporeal and mental constitution of man.

There are various matters that physiologists have attempted to comprehend under the general term of narcotics, of which the primary operation is directed to the nervous system. What their ultimate effects may be on man, considered not in the individual, but in the species, this is not the fit place to discuss. There are, however, some general laws that belong to them, which it concerns the present inquiry to notice.

1. A gradual increase in the quantity consumed does not produce a correspondent increase in the effects first experienced. One commencing with twenty drops of laudanum, if he make a habit of consuming that drug, and attempt to continue the effects first experienced, must double, quadruple, or further increase the quantity. A few glasses of wine will at first cause a degree of exhilaration equal to what it will take a bottle or two finally to produce. Unlike things consumed to satisfy hunger, thirst, or warmth, their effects are by no means determined by the quantity consumed. We may reckon that a slice of bread, or a glass of water, will one year hence supply the wants for which any individual consumes them, as well as now, however great his consumption of these articles may be in the interim. But if a person now daily drinks a glass of brandy, there is no saying how many glasses, ten years hence, he may find himself obliged to take to produce the same effects. This is a property common to all narcotics, though not in an equal degree. The effects of tea and coffee on the nervous system diminish through use, as well as those of brandy and tobacco, though not in an equal degree, and the quantity taken may be gradually very greatly augmented.

2. The temporary exhilaration produced by the consumption of these substances is followed by a temporary depression. They produce evil as well as good. Whether, when taken in small quantities, the former overbalance the latter, or the latter the former, is a point undetermined; but it is well known that as the quantity is increased, the evil effects predominate, until at last both the bodily and mental energies sink under their operation. Hence what is called the abuse,

to which the consumption of all this class of commodities is apt to lead. The labor bestowed on them is very often not only useless, but absolutely prejudicial to the society.

3. Their consumption is regulated, in a great degree, by the influence of the imitative propensity. We may form a near guess whether a person is in the custom of drinking wine, or tea, or coffee, or smoking tobacco, from knowing the habits of his associates.

4. Their consumption is also greatly regulated by the passion of vanity. This is especially the case, as I have already remarked, in vinous liquors. These liquors derive their narcotic properties from containing a portion of the fluid termed alcohol. In addition to its power over the nervous system, this substance has that of preventing, or retarding, the changes that naturally go on in vegetable juices. Liquors, therefore, impregnated with it, long retain their peculiar flavor and other properties, and may thus be consumed in times and at places remote from those in which they were produced. This serves to render them matters on which vanity can easily lay hold and convert into luxuries. Besides serving as marks to this passion, the vegetable juices and salts contained in these liquors have probably other effects. They afford a certain degree of nourishment, and present the spirit in a diluted form. Hence a part of their medicinal effects, and hence, also, their greater safety as narcotics. The stomach gets loaded with them sooner than with diluted alcohol, which might be absorbed with less immediate inconvenience to the digestive powers, though its permanent effects may be more pernicious. In this respect there is a real cause for the preference given them, although, in this view also, beer is the best, because the safest of all liquors.

The fermented liquors, produced from the juice of the grape, are most esteemed in Europe. It is, however, at least problematical whether they have, or have not, any great, or indeed any real superiority. Their chemical analysis does not show much grounds for the preference, and we would not, *a priori*, conceive that the substances, which by the art of the chemist may be made into a compound not to be distinguished from them, would produce a liquid peculiarly beneficial to the constitution, or agreeable to the palate.[1] If we inquire into the tastes of other nations, we find, by the testimony of travellers, that over the greater part of the world, they are rather disrelished. Captain Basil Hall, in his voyage to Loo Choo, says he has found cherry brandy the most generally esteemed liquor among all nations, and we may see a reason for the preference given to such a beverage. The sensation, with which even diluted alcohol at first affects the organ of taste, is unpleasant. Most people take some plan to subdue or correct its harshness. The mixture of matters themselves pleasant in flavor or taste, as in that sort of cordial, one would suppose the most effectual and agreeable means of doing so. The Chinese have grapes, but make no use of them for the formation of fermented liquors. Our European travellers tax them in consequence with want of taste and ingenuity. They, in turn, are surprised at our folly in manufacturing what seems to them a more harsh, and unpleasant, and generally far more expensive beverage than theirs. Which has most reason on his side, the European or the Chinese, is difficult to determine; for, when the passion of vanity joins with the imitative propensity, the two have a singular power in producing obstinately opposing opinions, especially when they have an organ to work on so pliant in the reception of impressions as the palate. The fashionable drink of the Prussians of old was fermented mare's milk; while the nobles drank this, the common people were content with mead. This, at least, can be said in favor of the choice, that the latter liquor must have been easily got in the country of wild honey, and would therefore be vulgar; the former could only be procured by the wealthy, and would therefore indicate rank.

[1] Many thousand pipes of spoiled cider are annually brought to London from the country, for the purpose of being converted into port wine. One, probably, of the least noxious of the methods of producing the change, is to add to the cider beet root juice, alcohol, logwood, and Rhatany root. The interior of the cask is then crusted with supertartrite of potash, colored with Brazil wood, that the merchant, after bottling off the wine, may impose on his customers by taking to pieces the cask, and exhibiting the beautiful dark coloured and fine crystalline crust, as an indubitable proof of the age of the wine; a practice by no means uncommon, to flatter the vanity of those who pride themselves in their acute discrimination of wines. See Accum on *Adulterations*.

On the whole, as it must be allowed that vanity has a very great influence in determining the preference which is given to one sort of alcoholic liquor over another, so it is very difficult to determine the point where its operation ceases. This, perhaps, can only be done in cases where the degree in which some agreeable flavor or relish is possessed is in question, or where some positively disagreeable flavor or taste, or injurious quality, is communicated in the process of preparation.

It is also to be observed, with regard to these liquors, that, with the exception, perhaps, of the negro, whose physical constitution is so different from that of the white that no conclusion can be drawn from the one to the other, the propensity to their consumption is stronger among people living at a distance from the equator, than among those who inhabit regions lying near it. Were it necessary to assign reasons for a fact generally observed, we might find them in the grosser feeding of the inhabitants of cold climates, and in their diminished susceptibility to the impressions of the sexual desires.

SECTION 2.

I have discussed the subject of these liquors at a length which I fear may appear tedious. Some reasons for having done so will show themselves afterwards. There is one that has immediately to appear.

A very important question concerning their consumption arises, which, it seems to me, has been too hastily determined, and that determination rashly acted on, in a manner that has produced very injurious effects.[1] As far as we have presently

---

[1] [Light is thrown upon at least one of the occurrences to which Rae here alludes, by the following passage in a communication to the Hawaiian Government respecting excise legislation :—]

"My attention was first called to this subject about the year 1819. At that time the propriety of greatly reducing the duties on ardent spirits was a question much agitated in Scotland, my native land ; and while my position led me to listen to the discussion going on, my prospects were then such as to make that and all other questions connected with the well-being of the people a matter of considerable interest to me. The Highlands of Scotland were then, and had long been, famous for the manufacture of a sort of whiskey which, partly perhaps from its being made in small stills, was thought of superior flavour, and was greatly esteemed. The traffic was altogether illicit, and

to consider the doctrine and practice, they may, in a great measure, be traced to the following passage in the *Wealth of Nations*.

"Though individuals may sometimes ruin their fortunes by an excessive consumption of fermented liquors, there seems to be no risk that a nation should do so. Though in every country there are many people who spend upon such liquors more than they can afford, there are always many more who spend less. It deserves to be remarked, too, that if we consult experience, the cheapness of wine seems to be a cause, not of drunkenness, but of sobriety. The inhabitants of the wine countries are, in general, the soberest people of Europe; witness the Spaniards, the Italians, and the inhabitants of the southern provinces of France. People are seldom guilty of excess in what is their daily fare. Nobody affects the character of liberality and good fellowship by being profuse of a liquor which is as cheap as small beer. On the contrary, in the countries which, either from excessive heat or cold, produce no grapes, and where wine consequently is dear and a rarity, drunkenness is a common vice, as among the northern nations, and all those who live between the tropics, the negroes, for example, on the coast of Guinea. When a French regiment comes from some of the northern provinces of France,

---

there was a constant struggle between the smugglers and the revenue officers, the one striving to carry through their objects by stratagem or force, the other endeavouring to baffle them; so that the magistracy and the courts of justice had constantly cases coming before them which were generally settled by fine or imprisonment, and not infrequently by transportation. It was proposed to put an end to this state of things by greatly reducing the duty on legally manufactured whiskey, and by authorizing its manufacture in stills of a small size. Almost everyone thought that great good would result from such a change of system, and laughed at the fears which some few entertained of its bad effects on the general morals of the people. The authority of Adam Smith was cited as decisive of the question, and the measure was carried through amid a general acclaim of approbation. I own that I was among the doubters, and that knowing the habits of my countrymen I feared that the immediate and obvious good resulting would be counterbalanced by more remote but greater evils. It was in vain for me, however, to open my mouth against the general voice, and when I attempted it my impertinence in opposing my elders and betters was only excused as one of the eccentricities of a strange youth. Time has now shown that I was not far wrong."

where wine is somewhat dear, to be quartered in the southern, where it is very cheap, the soldiers, I have frequently heard it observed, are at first debauched by the cheapness and novelty of good wine; but after a few months' residence, the greater part of them become as sober as the rest of the inhabitants. Were the duties upon foreign wines, and the excises upon malt, beer, and ale, to be taken away all at once, it might, in the same manner, occasion in Great Britain a pretty general and temporary drunkenness among the middling and inferior ranks of people, which would probably be soon followed by a permanent and almost universal sobriety. At present drunkenness is by no means the vice of people of fashion, or of those who can easily afford the most expensive liquors. A gentleman drunk with ale has scarce ever been seen amongst us."[1]

The general question that may here be said to be proposed is, whether, or not, in any particular country, the cheapness or the dearness of intoxicating liquors will most excite to their intemperate use?

The excessive cheapness of any of these liquors renders it incapable of affording any gratification to vanity, and an equal cheapness in them all would universally produce the same effect. That passion would, therefore, in such a case have to turn itself to other objects, and these liquors ceasing to be luxuries, one main cause of their consumption would be done away with. To excite to their abuse, there would remain only the pleasure arising from their intoxicating qualities, joined to the facility with which it might be indulged. Whether, or not, the ease with which this propensity might be gratified would lead to long enduring excess, or the vulgarity of the enjoyment to speedy and general temperance, would probably depend on various circumstances.—On the climate, whether near the equator, or at a distance from it.—On the sort of liquor, whether purely alcoholic or mixed with much of foreign matter.—On the strength of the effective desire of accumulation, for that desire, when strong, leads to a restricted consumption of things of which the immediate benefit is problematical, and the dangers to futurity, from excess in them, very great. If, then, the principle is naturally weak, or

[1] *Wealth of Nations*, B. IV. c. III.

at the moment its action be clogged by the stock of instruments in the society being wrought fully up to the orders correspondent to it, or having passed these, then there will be a great probability of injurious and long continued national excesses.

Unless, then, we have the means of knowing perfectly the condition in which all these circumstances, and perhaps some others, exist in any society, it is impossible to ascertain, with any precision, what may be the effect of reducing very greatly the price of alcoholic liquors. The national drunkenness that Adam Smith speaks of may be short or long, or, for ought that we can say, perpetual. Over the greater part of the United States of America whiskey has long sold at about a shilling sterling per gallon, so that one day's wages of a common laborer will purchase a dozen bottles of that spirit. It is therefore put out of the class of luxuries as completely as any intoxicating liquor can well be. The consumption of it has, notwithstanding, been very great, and in few countries have instances of injurious excess been more frequent. It is true that the evil, now exposed to view stripped of every disguise, is seen in all its hideousness, and is in a fair way of being corrected. After having endured for more than one generation, what Adam Smith terms the period of general drunkenness, is probably passing away. If the cure be thus effected, it may fairly be reckoned radical. Is it in all cases advisable to go through a similar course, even with the probability of a similar result ?—to induce a season of national drunkenness, even with the prospect of the public feeling being effectually roused to put down the vice forever ? To me it seems, that the remedy is so violent, that in many cases there might be a risk of the patient's sinking under its operation. A general drunkenness among the middle and inferior classes, however temporary, is a thing surely not to be lightly discussed in any speculations that lead to practice. Compared with it, the temporary subjugation of a country by a foreign enemy would, in its immediate effects, be a small practical evil. If an experiment fit to be tried, it should certainly only be so under the most favorable circumstances; to peril it when the vital powers are in an enfeebled condition, would be the height of rashness.

The analogy which Adam Smith, in the passage quoted, draws between the French soldier transported from a part of France where wine is scarce, to another where it abounds, and a nation suddenly overflowed with an abundance of these liquors, will not hold; for, the imitative propensity, in the one case, tends as powerfully to check, as in the other it operates to excite to the abuse in question. If a man be brought among sober people, he has every chance to remain, or to become sober; if, on the contrary, he get among drunkards, it requires all his resolution to avoid becoming one. A nation having a taste for these pleasures, and suddenly obtaining the means of indulging in them, may be compared to a company inclined to be jovial assembled round an abundant table, where each excites the other to excess; a band of soldiers living and mixing with the inhabitants of a country where, even though cheap, these liquors are temperately consumed, may, on the contrary, be compared to an individual partaking of his solitary bottle in the midst of those who despise the pleasure, and view him with contempt for indulging in it.

It is, however, particularly to be remarked, that the author refers to fermented, not to purely alcoholic liquors, and the former are certainly much less apt to lead to excess, than the latter. I apprehend, however, that his reasonings in the preceding, and one or two other passages, have been generally received as applicable to both.

To return to the subject of narcotics in general, all excess in their consumption, whether it be regarded as an application of labor to a useless purpose, or to one partially hurtful; whether it proceed from vanity or pernicious habits, may not improperly be termed dissipation, as the articles so consumed may be termed luxuries. It is not necessary that we should pretend to determine what this loss may in any case amount to; it is sufficient to mark its existence, as a quantity to be taken into account in a consideration of the causes, influencing the increase or decrease of the national stock.

Number 6. From page 352.

The doctrine, as it has been maintained, has the advantage or disadvantage of being somewhat paradoxical; but omitting the consideration of this circumstance, it is worth while to examine whether or not, when applied to practice, it has brought about the anticipated results. Of the many instances that might be produced of events of this class turning out contrary to the predictions of the votaries of the science, I select one from the *Cours d'Economie Politique* (Vol. IV., p. 266) of Mr. Storch, a work which, according to Mr. M'Culloch, stands at the head of all those on Political Economy ever imported from the continent into England.

That author brings forward Ireland as an example of great prosperity, and very rapid progress in wealth, in consequence of that nation following the rules of the system. " The sudden and prodigious increase," he observes, " which took place in the consumption of spirituous liquors, sugar and tea, soon after the union, is the more remarkable, from its having occurred at a time when these commodities were charged with additional duties, that in any other country would have been equivalent to an absolute prohibition.

"To date from the union, the consumption of wine has augmented by half; and yet the consumers, to buy half more than they formerly did, are obliged to pay three times the price. As for rum, and other foreign spirits, although the duties have been doubled, the consumption has increased eightfold.

"The importation of tea has risen, since the union, from 2,260,600 pounds to 3,706,771. The amount of sugar purchased has risen from 211,209 hundred weight to 447,404, so that Ireland consumes more of that nourishing, agreeable, and healthy commodity, than both Russia and France conjoined. In short, an examination of the table of importations of Ireland shows that, with the exception of a small number of articles, the additional consumption of those commodities, the production of other countries, of which the increasing demand most marks the growing riches of a people, has equalled, or rather surpassed the whole consumption before the union. The facts which we have thus analyzed," he continues, " present a statistical picture altogether singular, and such as the most flourishing colonies have never furnished. It is true that, by this prodigious increase of importations, the purchases of the people of Ireland have increased in a greater ratio than their sales; but this circumstance, which would spread alarm among most other nations, is regarded in Great Britain as a symptom of prosperity. I know nothing more calculated to show how much those continental governments are deceived, who see only objects of alarm in observing the increase of importations. 'They send the money out of the country, they favor foreign industry at the prejudice of domestic, and ruin the inhabitants by exciting them to expenses beyond their incomes.' Such is the cry of these alarmists. Perhaps I return too frequently to a consideration of such errors; but they are so common, and, at the same time, so injurious, that I think it my duty to neglect no opportunity to prove their fallacy, whether by arguments or by examples; *and what more striking example could I oppose to this doctrine than that of the prosperity of the Irish?"*

Speaking of the probability of a rise in the price of colonial productions, he observes farther, "that it may possibly diminish their consumption, but that it is much more likely that the Irish, who have acquired a taste for such enjoyments, will work still harder, and produce still more linen, hemp, and oats, *that they may have plenty of sugar and rum.* With a people so ingenious, all that is requisite is to give them wants, and excite them to labor."

Science is said to be prophetic; does this then sound like her voice.

Number 7. From page 364.

But an investigation of all these particulars would extend far beyond the bounds which I have prescribed myself. I purpose, therefore, to confine myself to two of them, and to limit the subject of this book to show that the legislator may operate with advantage to the community, 1st, in the transfer of foreign arts to his own country; 2d, in applying to useful purposes funds which would otherwise be dissipated in luxury.

Number 8. From page 375.

It is only necessary for me here, then, to state very shortly the objections, and the answers to them.

It is said capital can only augment by accumulation, and, as the interference of the legislator takes something from individual revenue, it must also take from the power to accumulate, and, consequently, instead of augmenting, must tend to diminish the sum of the capitals of all the individuals in the society, that is, the national capital or stock. This objection proceeds on two assumptions, the first, that the nature of national capital, or stock, about which the whole discussion turns, which it is the object of the inquiry to investigate, and concerning which scarce two authors of note agree in opinion, is known previously to any investigation, and is precisely identical with the notion suggested by the same term applied to individual wealth. The second, that what is generally true concerning individual capital, is universally true concerning national capital, and that, as the former commonly augments by accumulation, the latter can do so in no other manner.

The answer to this objection is, that the proceedings of the legislator may increase the absolute capital and stock of the society, the provision, that is, for future wants, embodied in the stock of instruments possessed by it, though they may not increase, and may even a little diminish its relative capital, or the sum which would be brought out by measuring those instruments with one another. That it is the amount of the absolute capital of the society, which is the proper measure of the wealth of the whole, and of each individual, and that whatever augments it not only directly, and of itself, advances national wealth, but ultimately, also, does so indirectly, through the stimulus given to the accumulative principle, and the addition thence arising to relative capital.

This objection and the answer to it apply to utilities. The second objection, now to be considered, refers to the proceedings of the legislator concerning commodities wholly or in part luxuries.

Number 9. From page 296.

If the legislator, by an arbitrary and secret act, could impose a duty on the share of any commodity consumed by an individual, the rest of the community going free, that individual would undoubtedly be exactly so much a loser. It would be to him a matter of indifference what the commodity in question were. If the circumstances of his condition obliged his wife to wear jewels, or him to have a supply of claret on his table, an arbitrary impost of the sort on the claret he consumed, or the jewels his wife wore, would probably be to him equivalent, to a like exaction on coals or bread. In the same way, a secret remission to a single individual of the duty levied on any article, would be just so much gain to him.

The fundamental error on this subject of Adam Smith, and the present prevailing school of political economists in England, lies, in their assuming, that what is true concerning an individual, is true, also, concerning a community, and maintaining, consequently, that every impost is so much absolute loss to the society, and every diminution of it, so much gain. Before this assumption can be made good, with regard to any particular impost, it is necessary that the three following questions concerning it should be determined.

1st. Will the duty so levied, by directly or indirectly effecting an improvement in the arts, increase the absolute capital of the society?

2d. Will it prevent future waste, by the transfer of an art producing useful commodities, the supply of which is liable to sudden interruptions?

3d. Does it fall partly or altogether on luxuries, and is its real effect, consequently, not to diminish, by so much, the annual revenue of the society, but only to apply a part of it, which would otherwise have been dissipated by vanity, to supply funds for the necessary expenditure of the legislator?

Unless these questions can be all answered in the negative, the assumed parallel between the effects of an impost on an individual, and on a community, does not hold, and the whole reasoning founded on it falls to the ground.

READER'S GUIDE.

Original Volume.	Present Reprint.	
	Pages Pages	
Preface, - - - -	iii.-vii. = xlv.-l.	Author's Preface.
,, - - - -	vii.-viii. = 466-468	App., Residua, No. 1.
,, - - - -	viii.-x. = l.-lii.	Author's Preface.
Table of Contents, - -	xi.-xvi. = v.-xiii.	Table of Contents.
Introduction, - - -	1- 5 = 1- 5	Introduction.
,, - - -	5- 6 = 468	App., Residua, No. 2.
Book I.		
Introduction, - - -	7- 8 = 377-379	App., Art. VIII., Part I.
Chap. I., - - -	9- 17 = 379-388	,, ,, ,, ,,
,, ,, - - -	17- 19 = 130-131	Chap. VIII., Suffix. ,,
,, ,, - - -	19- 24 = 151-157	Chap. X., Prefix.
,, ,, - - -	24- 31 = 388-396	App., Art. VIII., Part. I.
Chap. II., - - -	32- 77 = 396-444	,, ,, ,, Part II.
Book II.		
Introduction, - - -	78- 79 = 5- 6	Introduction, Suffix.
Chaps. I.-VII., - -	80-163 = 7-101	Chaps. I.-VII.
Chap. VIII., - - -	164-184 = 102-125	Chap. VIII.
,, ,, - -	185-193 = 297-306	App., Art. IV., Part I.
,, ,, - -	193-197 = 125-130	Chap. VIII.
Chap. IX., - - -	198-207 = 218-228	Chap. XIII., 1st Half.
Chap. X., - - -	208-223 = 132-149	Chap. IX.
,, ,, - - -	223-264 = 158-203	Chap. X.
Chap. XI., Part I., -	265-292 = 245-276	App., Art. I.
,, ,, Part II., -	292-299 = 471-479	App., Residua, No. 5.
Chap. XII. 1 Paragraph, -	300 = 468	App., Residua, No. 3.
,, ,, - - -	300-305 = 204-210	Chap. XI., 1st Part.
,, ,, - - -	305-312 = 277-285	App., Art. II.
Chap. XIII., - - -	313-315 = 213-216	Chap. XII., 1st Part.
,, ,, - - -	315-317 = 210-212	Chap. XI., 2nd Part.
,, ,, 1 Paragraph,	317-318 = 282	App., Art. II., Interpol.
,, ,, - - -	318-319 = 216-217	Chap. XII., 2nd Part.
Chap. XIV., - - -	320-323 = 468-471	App., Residua, No. 4.
,, ,, 1 Paragraph,	322 = 202	Chap. X., Interpolation.
,, ,, 3 Paragraphs,	323 = 357-358	App., Art. VI., Ending.
,, ,, - - -	323-327 = 229-233	Chap. XIII., 2nd Half.
Chap. XV., - - -	328-349 = 329-352	App., Art. V.
,, ,, - - -	349-350 = 479-481	App., Residua, No. 6.
,, ,, - - -	350-351 = 352-353	App., Art. V.
Appendix, - - -	352-357 = 237-242	Chap. XIV.

READER'S GUIDE

ORIGINAL VOLUME.		PRESENT REPRINT.
Book III.	Pages Pages	
Introduction, - -	358-362 = 359-364	App., Art. VII., 1st Part.
„ 1 Paragraph,	362 = 481	App., Residua, No. 7.
Chap. I., - - - -	363-368 = 364-370	App., Art. VII., 2nd Part.
Chap. II., - - -	369-376 = 286-294	App., Art. III., 1st Part.
Chap. III., - - -	377-381 = 370-375	App., Art. VII., 3rd Part.
„ „ - - -	381-382 = 481-482	App., Residua, No. 8.
„ „ - - -	382-383 = 294-296	App., Art. III., 2nd Part.
„ „ - - -	384-385 = 482-483	App., Residua, No. 9.
NOTES.		
A (reference page 1), -	387-388 = 448-450	App., Author's Notes, A.
B („ „ 4), -	388-390 = 450-452	App., „ „ B.
C („ „ 8), -	390 = 453	App., „ „ C.
D („ „ 18), -	391 = 453-454	App., „ „ D
E („ „ 87), -	392 = 15	Chap. 1., footnote.
F („ „ 153), -	392-397 = 454-461	App., Author's Notes, F.
G („ „ 193), -	397-412 = 306-328	App., Art. IV., Part II.
H („ „ 249), -	412 = 185	Chap. X., footnote.
I („ „ 276), -	412-413 = 257-258	App., Art. I., footnote.
J („ „ 285), -	413 = 461-462	App., Author's Notes, J.
K („ „ 345), -	413-414 = 347	App., Art. V., footnote.

Milton Keynes UK
Ingram Content Group UK Ltd.
UKHW040049180324
439604UK00006B/1094